LEGAL REASONING
AND LEGAL WRITING

LEGAL REASONING AND LEGAL WRITING

Structure, Strategy, and Style

SECOND EDITION

Richard K. Neumann, Jr.
Professor of Law
Hofstra University

Little, Brown and Company
Boston   New York   Toronto   London

Library of Congress Catalog Card No. 93-80973
ISBN 0-316-60390-2

Second Printing

ICP

Published simultaneously in Canada
by Little, Brown & Company (Canada) Limited

Printed in the United States of America

for

Richard K. Neumann, Sr. and
Marjorie Batter Neumann,

who taught everything
on which this book is based

The power of clear statement is the great power at the bar.

—*Daniel Webster*
(also attributed to
Rufus Choate,
Judah P. Benjamin,
and perhaps others)

Summary
of Contents

Table of Contents

11. Working with Precedent 119

12. Working with Statutes 137

13. Working with Facts 161

14. Paragraphing 173

V
THE SHIFT TO PERSUASION   235

Preface

This is a text both for first-year legal writing and moot court programs and for second-year appellate advocacy courses and competitions. Most students are so challenged by the writing and reasoning problems in these settings that they benefit from a unified treatment through progressively more difficult stages of instruction on closely related skills. A teacher in a first-year program can use a large number of the book's features to teach legal writing and the reasoning that goes into it. In a second-year appellate advocacy course or competition, the text shows students how to carry that instruction to a much more sophisticated level. The text has been designed so that it can be used in the first year alone, in the first and second years together, or in the second year alone.

It has become a commonplace that writing is better learned when combined with at least some instruction in legal reasoning. But it is also true that legal reasoning is learned more thoroughly when combined with legal writing. Because the act of writing forces the writer to test thought in order to express it fully and precisely, complex analysis cannot be said to be complete until it becomes written and written well.

The text focuses on constructing proof of a conclusion of law and teaches format, style, and grammar collaterally. The goal is to help students learn how to make the kind of writing decisions that center on the need to prove analysis. Most students have substantial difficulties learning how to construct proof. If format and style receive primary emphasis, the problem is compounded because the student is invited to mimic the customary appearance of a document, rather than to think through its content and inner logic. Moreover, format comes easier to students who have already learned the dynamics of proof, and legal writing's heightened requirements of style and grammar may be easier to accept when they are explained as ways of clarifying proof. And as a skill, style is much more valuable when rewriting second and third drafts than in producing a first draft.

Part I of the text introduces students to the court and litigation systems, the structure and operation of rules of law, judicial opinions, and methods of briefing them. Legal writing in general is introduced in Part II. Part III explains how to write an office memorandum; organize proof of a conclusion of law; use authority; analyze facts; and use paragraphing, style, and citations. Part IV helps students with their first law school examinations. Part V introduces the advocacy skills of theory development, argumentation, and accurate handling of procedural postures. Writing a persuasive motion memorandum is covered in Part VI; appellate briefs in Part VII; and oral argument in Part VIII.

On the inside covers of the book is a list of questions that students should ask themselves while working through successive drafts of a document. Each question represents a recurring problem in student writing—the sort that a teacher marks over and over again on student papers. Students can use these questions to make sure they have attended to likely problems. And teachers can use them to ease the burden of writing so many comments on student papers. Rather than write the same or a similar comment repetitiously, a teacher can circle the problem passage on the student's paper and write the question number ("8-A," which would be in Chapter 8, for example) in the margin. In the corresponding section in the chapter, the student will find a complete explanation of the problem, what causes it, and how to fix it.

Richard K. Neumann, Jr.

March 1994

Acknowledgments

I am grateful to many people who generously contributed their thoughts to the development of this book in its first or second edition or in both. Among them are Burton Agata, Lisa Aisner, Aaron Balasny, Kathleen Beckett, Sara Bennett, Susan Brody, Susan Bryant, Mark Carroll, Kimberly Klein Cauthorn, Robin Charlow, Barbara Child, Alice Duecker, Deborah Ezbitski, Peter Falkenstein, Neal Feigenson, Eric M. Freedman, William Ginsburg, John DeWitt Gregory, Marc Grinker, Donna Hill, Joseph Holmes, Steven Jamar, Ellen James, Lawrence Kessler, Martha Krisel, Eric Lane, Lisa Eggert Litvin, Ed McDougal, Juliet Neisser, Stuart Rabinowitz, John Regan, Kathryn Sampson, Carole Shapiro, Suzanne Spector, Aaron Twerski, Ursula Weigold, Mary White, and Mark Wojcik, as well as the anonymous reviewers who examined the first edition manuscript for Little, Brown and those who responded to the questionnaire distributed by Little, Brown in preparation for the second edition. I am also grateful for research assistance by Ellen Leibowitz, Christine Lombardi, Fusae Nara, Karen Nielsen, Dan Wallach, and Carolyn Weissbach, supplemented by Darmin Bachu, Ann Carrozza, Nicole Gamble, Rori Goldman, Bill Kalten, Beth Rogoff, Victoria Saunders, and Corey Wishner, together with administrative assistance by Angela Wooden. Elliott Milstein and Joseph Harbaugh had much influence on the pedagogy that has shaped this book. Richard Heuser, Carol McGeehan, Betsy Kenny, Richard Audet, Nick Niemeyer, Cate Rickard, Lisa Wehrle, Kurt Hughes, and their colleagues at Little, Brown have enormous insight into the qualities that make a text useful; their perceptiveness and creativity ultimately caused this book to become a different and far better text than it otherwise would have been. And Deborah Ezbitski inspired in countless ways.

Copyright Acknowledgments

LEGAL REASONING
AND LEGAL WRITING

I
INTRODUCTION TO LAW AND ITS STUDY

1 An Introduction to American Law

§1.1 The Origin of Common Law

At Pevensey, on the south coast of England, a man named William, Duke of Normandy, came ashore, together with ten thousand soldiers and knights, on a morning in late September 1066. Finding the town unsatisfactory for his purpose, he destroyed it and moved his people nine miles east to a coastal village called Hastings. A few days later, the English king, Harold, arrived with an army of roughly the same size. The English had always fought on foot, rather than on horseback, and in a day-long battle they were cut down by the Norman knights. According to legend, Harold was at first disabled by a random arrow shot through his eye and then killed by William himself, who marched his army north, burning villages on the way and terrorizing London into submission.

Although in December he had himself crowned king of England, William controlled only a small part of the country, and in the following years he had to embark on what modern governments would call campaigns to pacify the countryside. In 1069, for example, his army marched to York, executed every English male of any age found along the way, flattened the town, and then marched on to Durham, burning every farm and killing every English-speaking person to be found — all with the result that seventeen years later the survey recorded in Domesday Book revealed almost no population in Yorkshire. In the five years after William landed at Pevensey, one-fifth of the population of England was killed by the Norman army of occupation or died of starvation after the Normans burned the food supply. To atone for all this, William later built a monastery at Hastings. For nine centuries, it has been known as Battle Abbey, and its altar sits on the spot where Harold is said to have died.

The picturesque Norman castles throughout England were built not to defend the island from further invasion, but to subjugate and imprison the English themselves while William expropriated nearly all the land in the country and gave it to Normans, who became a new aristocracy. With the exception of a few collaborators, everyone whose native language was English became — regardless of earlier social station — landless and impoverished. Normans quickly occupied even the most local positions of power, and suddenly the average English person knew no one in authority who understood English customs, English law, or even much of the language. William himself never learned to speak it.

Pollock and Maitland call the Norman Conquest "a catastrophe which determines the whole future history of English law."[1] Although the Conquest's influences on English law were many, for the moment let us focus only on two.

The first concerns the language of law and lawyers. Norman French was the tongue of the new rulers, and eventually it became the language of the courts as well. The sub-language called Norman Law French could still be heard in courtrooms many centuries later,[2] even after the everyday version of Norman French had merged with Middle English to produce Modern English, a language rich in nuance because it thus inherited two entire vocabularies. As late as 1731, Parliament was compelled to enact a statute providing that all court documents "shall be in the English tongue only, and not in Latin or French."[3]

Law is filled with terms of art that express technical and specialized meanings, and a large proportion of these terms survive from Norman Law French. Some of the more familiar examples include *appeal, arrest, assault, attorney, contract, counsel, court, crime, defendant, evidence, judge, jury, plaintiff, suit,* and *verdict.* In the next few pages, you will also encounter *allegation, cause of action, demurrer, indictment, party,* and *plead.* And in the next few months you will come across *battery, damages, devise, easement, estoppel, felony, larceny, lien, livery of seisin, misdemeanor, replevin, slander, tenant,* and *tort.*[4] Even the bailiff's cry that still opens many American court sessions — "Oyez, oyez, oyez!" — is the Norman French equivalent of "Listen up!"

Some words entered the English language directly from the events of the Conquest itself. In the course on property, you will soon become familiar with various types of *fees: fee simple absolute, fee simple conditional, fee simple defeasible, fee tail.* These are not money paid for services. They are forms of property rights, and they are descended directly from the feudal enfeoffments that William introduced into England in order to distribute the

---

§1.1   1. Frederick Pollock & Frederick William Maitland, *The History of English Law Before the Time of Edward I* 79 (2d ed. 1899).

2. Blackstone called Norman Law French a "badge of slavery." 4 William Blackstone, *Commentaries* *416. Before the Conquest, courts were conducted in English, and law was written in English or Latin.

3. Records in English Act, 1731, 4 Geo. II ch. 26.

4. Begin now the habit of looking up every unfamiliar term of art in a law dictionary, which you should keep close at hand while studying for each of your courses.

country's land among his followers. Even today, these terms appear in the French word order (noun first, modifiers afterward).

The second, and more important, influence concerns the way law is created. It is a comparatively modern invention for a legislature to "pass a law." (Lawyers say "enact a statute.") The embryonic medieval parliaments of England and Scandinavia instead made more specific decisions, such as when to plunder Visby or whether to banish Hrothgar. Although in some countries law might come from royal decree, in England before the Conquest it arose more often from the custom of each locality, as known to and enforced by the local courts. What was legal in one village or shire might be illegal (because it offended local custom) in the next. "This crazyquilt of decentralized judicial administration was doomed after 1066. From the time of the Norman Conquest, . . . the steady development in England was one of increasing dominance of the royal courts of justice over the local, customary-law courts."[5] The reason was that the newly created Norman aristocracy, which now operated the local courts, got into conflict with the Norman monarch over the spoils of power, while the English, defeated in their own country, began to find more justice in the king's courts than in their local lords' capricious enforcement of what had once been reliable custom.

Because communication and travel were so primitive, the "crazyquilt" pattern of customary law had not before troubled the English. Instead, it had given them an agreeable opportunity to develop, through local habit, rules that suited each region and village relatively well. For two reasons, however, the king's courts would not enforce customary law. The practical reason was that a judge of a national court cannot know the customary law of each locality. The political reason was that the monarchy's goal was to centralize power in itself and its institutions. Out of this grew a uniform set of rules, common to every place in the country and eventually known as the common law of England. Centuries later, British colonists in North America were governed according to that common law, and, upon declaring their independence, adopted it as each state's original body of law. Although a fair proportion of the common law has since been changed through statute or judicial decision, it remains the foundation of our legal system, and common law methods of reasoning dominate the practice and study of law.

In a medieval England without a "law-passing" legislature and with a king far too busy to create a body of law by decree, where did this common law come from? The somewhat oversimplified answer is that the judges figured it out for themselves. They started from the few rules that plainly could not be missing from medieval society, and over centuries — faced with new conditions and reasoning by analogy — they discovered other rules of common law, as though each rule had been there from the beginning, but hidden. The central tool in this process has been a rule called *stare decisis*, Latin for "let stand that which has been decided," or, more loosely, "follow the rules courts have followed in the past." A lay person might assume that the law is made only in legislatures and that the only value to reading judicial

---

5. Harry W. Jones, *Our Uncommon Common Law*, 42 Tenn. L. Rev. 443, 450 (1975).

decisions would be to see illustrations of how the law is applied. But judicial opinions[6] in common law countries[7] are not mere illustrations of law at work. In a common law country, decisions — or *precedent* — are one of the two main sources of law. Statutes and statute-like enactments are the other.

Before you can begin to learn about precedent (in Chapters 3 and 4), you will need some background in how courts are structured (§1.2), how they operate (§§1.3-1.5), and how rules of law are used (Chapter 2).

§1.2 How American Courts Are Organized

Because the United States has a federal system of government, it has two different kinds of court systems. Each state has its own courts, enforcing that state's law, and in addition the federal government has courts throughout the country, enforcing federal law.[1] The Constitution allocates certain responsibilities to the federal government and reserves the rest to the states. State court systems tend to be organized as variations, from state to state, on similar themes, while the federal courts operate rather differently.

§1.2.1 State Courts

A very simple state court system might include one trial court in each county seat, together with an appellate court in the state capital to hear appeals arising out of the work of the trial courts. Although that was once the system in most states, so simple an organization would be unrealistic under modern conditions. Virtually every state now has several different kinds of trial court, and most now have more than one appellate court.

The usual pattern goes something like this: A trial court of *general jurisdiction* — called the Circuit Court, the Superior Court, the Court of Common Pleas, or something similar — will try all cases except those that fall within the *limited jurisdiction* of some specialized trial court. Specialized courts might include a Court of Claims to hear suits against the state government, a Probate Court to adjudicate questions involving wills and inheritances, a Family Court to settle matters of support and child custody, a Juvenile Court to determine whether minors have committed crimes or are otherwise in need of special supervision, a Small Claims Court to decide (perhaps without lawyers) disputes where the value at stake is not large, a Magistrate's Court or the like to try some misdemeanors and other offenses,

---

6. Lawyers call judicial opinions "cases," even though the opinions represent only a small part of what happens in litigation. A lawsuit may have begun years before — and may sometimes continue for years after — a particular opinion is written.

7. The doctrine of stare decisis is generally observed only in countries whose law is descended in one way or another from English law. For the most part, stare decisis is *not* observed in continental Europe or in Latin America.

§1.2 1. As you will learn in the course on civil procedure, federal courts on occasion will enforce a state's law, and vice versa.

and a Housing Court to resolve litigation between landlords and tenants. Often these functions are merged. A Family Court, for instance, might have jurisdiction not only over support and custody, but also over matters that, in another state, would be adjudicated by a Juvenile Court. A Small Claims Court might not be a separate court, but instead a Small Claims Division of the court of general jurisdiction.

About two-thirds of the states have intermediate courts of appeal, which sit organizationally between the trial courts and the final appellate court. In some states, such as Pennsylvania and Maryland, the intermediate court of appeals hears appeals from every part of the state, while in others, such as California, New York, and Florida, the intermediate appellate court is divided geographically into districts, departments, or the equivalent, which function as coordinate courts of equal rank. In any event, a party dissatisfied with the result in an intermediate court of appeals can attempt to appeal —within certain limitations — to the highest court in the state.

The names of these courts are not consistent from state to state. In California and many other states, the Superior Court is the trial court of general jurisdiction, but in Pennsylvania the Superior Court is the intermediate court of appeal. In Maryland and New York, the Court of Appeals is the highest court in the state, but in many other states the intermediate appellate court has that name or a similar one. In New York, the trial court of general jurisdiction is called the Supreme Court, but in most states that is the name of the highest court in the state.

§1.2.2 Federal Courts

The federal court system is organized around a general trial court (the United States District Court); a few specialized courts (such as the United States Tax Court); an intermediate appellate court (the United States Court of Appeals); and the final appellate court (the United States Supreme Court).

The United States District Courts are organized into approximately one hundred districts. Where a state has only one district, the court is referred to, for example, as the United States District Court for the District of Montana. Some states have more than one district court. California, for instance, has four: the United States District Court for the Northern District of California (at San Francisco), the Eastern District of California (at Sacramento), the Central District of California (at Los Angeles), and the Southern District of California (at San Diego).

The United States Courts of Appeals are organized into thirteen circuits. Eleven of the circuits include various combinations of states: the Fifth Circuit, for example, hears appeals from the district courts in Louisiana, Mississippi, and Texas. There is also a United States Court of Appeals for the District of Columbia and another for the Federal Circuit, which hears appeals from certain specialized lower tribunals.

The United States Supreme Court hears selected appeals from the United States Courts of Appeals and from the highest state courts where the state court's decision has been based on federal law. The United States Supreme Court does not decide questions of state law.

§1.3 An Overview of the Litigation Process

A client brings a problem to a lawyer, who concludes that the most productive solution would be to sue someone. This is not started by calling up the courthouse to schedule a date with a jury. The lawsuit will be more complicated than that. It will grow and evolve through some or all of the following phases (1) *service of process, pleadings,* and *motions* challenging the pleadings; (2) fact *discovery,* negotiation, and additional motions; (3) trial in a lower court; (4) post-trial motions challenging aspects of the trial; (5) *appeal* to one or more appellate courts; and (6) in the event of *reversal* on appeal, post-appeal proceedings in the trial court (such as a new trial). For one reason or another, the vast majority of suits do not complete the full cycle, most often because the attorneys negotiate a compromise.

Once litigation begins, the person who has consulted the attorney is transformed into a *plaintiff* (or, in some cases, a *petitioner* or *claimant*), and the person who is sued becomes a *defendant* (or, in some cases, a *respondent*). Collectively, they are the *parties.*

§1.3.1 Phase 1: Pleadings and Service of Process

Service of process is the delivery (either literally or *constructively*) to the defendant of a *summons* accompanied by a *complaint.* The summons performs the dual functions of (1) notifying the defendant that a lawsuit (also called an *action*) has been started, and (2) bringing the defendant under the power of the court in which the case is to be tried. The power of a court to adjudicate is called its *jurisdiction,* a subtle and complex concept that you will study in much detail in the first-year course in civil procedure.

The complaint is the first *pleading* in a lawsuit. Pleadings are documents filed by the parties to outline the most critical facts that they intend to prove at trial. In that way, pleadings define the controversy between the parties. In the complaint, the plaintiff must allege facts that, taken together, constitute a *cause of action.* The defendant can respond to the summons and complaint with either or both of two steps:

The defendant's first option is to move to dismiss. Such a *motion*[1] can be made on any of a number of grounds. In law school casebooks, the ground

---

§1.3 1. A motion is a request, by a party, for a court order. In moving to dismiss a complaint, the defendant asks the court to order that the complaint be deemed a nullity. If the motion is granted, the court clerk will *not* tear up the complaint and throw it away. Instead, both the complaint and the order are placed in the court's file on the case. Even years later, both documents can be read by anyone who inspects the file, but the order destroys the legal effect of the complaint.

you will most often encounter is the failure to state a cause of action.[2] Here, the defendant argues that the complaint should be dismissed because it does not allege facts that — even if proved later — would constitute a wrong that the law will remedy. The idea is that the plaintiff should not be permitted to tie up the court system with a trial that the plaintiff cannot win even if able to prove everything claimed in the complaint. The purpose of a trial is to determine the facts, and a trial is a waste of effort if the plaintiff's claims — even if true — are less than a cause of action. Depending on the state whose courts are involved, a motion to dismiss on this basis is called a *motion to dismiss for failure to state a cause of action,* a *motion to dismiss for failure to state a claim,* or a *demurrer.* (In federal courts, it is called a *motion to dismiss for failure to state a claim upon which relief can be granted.*) If the defendant wins such a motion, the complaint is stricken and the plaintiff loses the suit unless he or she is able to serve and file an amended complaint that would survive a similar motion.[3]

DEMURRER

FAILURE TO STATE A CLAIM (CAUSE OF ACTION)

The defendant's other alternative is to serve an *answer.* In fact, a defendant must serve an answer if he or she does not move to dismiss or makes such a motion and loses it. In other words, a motion to dismiss is optional, but an answer is required unless the motion is both made and granted. The answer must admit or deny each of the allegations in the complaint and may also pose one or more affirmative defenses by alleging additional facts. In the answer, the defendant might also plead a *counterclaim,* in which the roles are reversed and the defendant seeks relief from the plaintiff for an alleged cause of action. If the defendant pleads a counterclaim, the plaintiff must serve a *reply,* which admits or denies the allegations in the counterclaim.

Although a motion attacking the sufficiency of the complaint calls for a ruling from the trial court, an answer, which is intended to outline the defendant's side of the case, does not. If the defendant has served and filed only an answer, the case proceeds in the general direction of trial. The reason for this distinction is that, while an answer merely responds to the allegations in the complaint so that it becomes clear which allegations are disputed, a motion challenging the sufficiency of the complaint asks the court to do something (dismiss the complaint).

§1.3.2 Phase 2: Between Pleadings and Trial

If the action has not been dismissed in the pleading phase, the attorneys will conduct *discovery.* They might also negotiate, and they might make motions for *summary judgment.*

---

2. Depending on the procedural rules governing the court in which the suit has been brought, a defendant might also choose to make such a motion on the grounds that the court lacks jurisdiction over the defendant; that the court lacks jurisdiction over the subject matter of the litigation; that venue is improper; that the issues between the parties have already been resolved in another action; and so on.

3. A plaintiff gets another chance to plead because, in dismissing a complaint, a court decides only that the complaint does not *state* a cause of action. The plaintiff might actually *have* a cause of action but, for one reason or another, might have failed to articulate it properly in the complaint.

Discovery is a collection of formal and informal procedures in which each party obtains information and evidence from the other. The most frequently used discovery devices are *interrogatories* and *depositions*. Interrogatories are written questions that one party poses to the other; the answers must be in writing and under oath. A deposition, on the other hand, is an oral examination: either attorney can subpoena a witness or an opposing party, who must appear before a court reporter, take an oath, and answer questions posed by the attorney. If the parties negotiate, their attorneys will explore the possibility of resolving the case through an agreement between themselves, rather than asking a judge and perhaps a jury to decide. In the course on civil procedure, you will learn more about the tools of discovery, and later in clinical and simulated practice courses you will have an opportunity to learn about negotiation and trial preparation.

When a court grants a summary judgment, it decides the case without a trial because the case lacks *issues of fact*. If the evidence does not conflict about what happened between the parties before the suit was filed — in other words, if only one story is supported by evidence — then there is no issue of fact and no need for a trial (because the purpose of a trial is to determine the facts). There would still be *issues of law* if the parties disagree about what the relevant law is or about how it treats that one story. And a judge can decide issues of law without a trial and without a jury, and on that basis grant summary judgment.

§1.3.3   Phase 3: Trial

At trial, the lawsuit undergoes a radical transformation. While the pretrial phase is prolonged and often preoccupied with the written word, trial is a confrontation within a concentrated period of time, dominated by *testimony* from witnesses and by oral objections and argument from the attorneys.

At trial, the plaintiff must present evidence to prove facts that substantiate each element of the cause of action. If the plaintiff does not do so — and thus does not make out a *prima facie case* — the plaintiff will lose. On the other hand, if the plaintiff succeeds in proving a prima facie case, the defendant will lose unless he or she presents evidence that negates the plaintiff's proof or proves additional facts constituting an affirmative defense (which is explained in Chapter 2).

In a trial with a jury, the jury's role is to decide — in the form of a *verdict* — issues of fact, while the role of the judge is to decide issues of law, including questions of procedure and the admissibility of evidence. In a bench trial (where there is no jury), the judge decides both kinds of issues by making *findings of fact* and *conclusions of law,* which are set out in a written or oral opinion. In a jury trial, the jury is the *trier of fact*; in a bench trial, the trier of fact is the judge.

Aside from selection of the jury (if there is one), the first event in a trial is an *opening statement,* in which the plaintiff's attorney outlines the case he or she hopes to prove. The defendant's attorney follows with a similar

10

statement. Then, during the evidence-taking phase of the trial, the plaintiff presents his or her case in the form of witnesses and exhibits, and, after the plaintiff *rests,* the defendant follows by doing the same thing. After the evidence-taking phase is complete, the attorneys make oral *summations* of their cases to the jury (or to the judge if there is no jury). In the *charge,* the judge instructs the jury how to apply the law to whatever facts the jury might find. Because the jury may resolve only issues of fact, these *jury instructions* correspond to the judge's holdings of law in a trial to the bench. The judge's holdings (in a bench trial) or his instructions (in a jury trial) are his interpretations of the applicable substantive law. In accordance with the verdict in a jury trial, or with the findings of fact in a bench trial, the judge signs a *judgment* which, depending on who has won, either provides or denies the remedy asked for by the plaintiff (and, if the answer includes a counterclaim, likewise for the defendant).

At trial, lawyers can make a motion that tests the sufficiency of an opponent's evidence and that, if granted, results directly in judgment for the party making the motion. In jury trials, this is most often called a *motion for a directed verdict.* Generally, a party can make such a motion after the opponent has rested. These motions can be made more than once, but they will be granted only if the judge concludes that on the evidence a jury could not reasonably return a verdict against the party making the motion. In bench trials, the corresponding motion is most commonly called a *motion for judgment.*

The fourth and fifth phases in the lawsuit's life cycle revert to emphasis on the written word.

§1.3.4 Phase 4: Post-Trial Motions

The most important post-trial motions are the *motion to set aside the verdict and grant a new trial* and the *motion for judgment notwithstanding the verdict.* Both are made to the trial court, and both challenge the sufficiency of the evidence on which the verdict is based.

Depending on local procedural rules, a motion to set aside the verdict and grant a new trial can be granted where the judge erred in a ruling that prejudiced the verdict, where new evidence that would have changed the verdict has been discovered, or where the verdict was at least in part the result of misconduct by a witness, an attorney, a juror, the judge, or a court employee.

The motion for judgment notwithstanding the verdict is commonly referred to as a "motion for judgment n.o.v.," from the Latin expression *non obstante veredicto* ("notwithstanding the verdict"). It can be granted only where the judge denied but, in hindsight, ought to have granted an earlier motion for a directed verdict. Because courts generally prefer to give a jury at least a chance to come to an appropriate verdict, a trial judge might deny a motion for directed verdict but subsequently grant a motion for judgment n.o.v. made on the same ground, even though both motions are to be decided according to the same reasoning.

§1.3.5   Phase 5: Appeal

An *appeal* is a request by the losing party for a higher court to reverse or alter one or more *rulings* by the trial court. The party taking the appeal becomes the *appellant* (or, in some instances, the *petitioner*), while the other party becomes the *appellee* (or the *respondent*). The appellate court does not retry the case. Instead, it examines the trial court's *record,* which might include the pleadings, the motions, the trial transcript, the verdict, the judgment, and so forth. If the appellate court agrees that the complained-of rulings were in error, it reverses the judgment below and *remands* the case to the trial court with instructions to cure the error, perhaps by entering judgment for the appellant or by holding a new trial. On the other hand, if the appellate court finds no error, it *affirms* the judgment.

Jury verdicts are not usually reviewed on appeal, and findings of fact are reviewed infrequently. Rather, the appellant's attorney points to specific rulings on the law by the trial judge and argues that those rulings were incorrect and *materially* led to the adverse judgment.

In the opinions you will read in law school casebooks, you will repeatedly see appeals from orders dismissing complaints, summary judgments, directed verdicts, jury instructions, orders granting new trials, and judgments n.o.v. In order to understand what the court has done in these opinions, you must be able to understand the case's *procedural posture,* which encompasses the type of motion involved, the party who made it, and the context in which it was made. As you will learn, the logic used by the court to make a decision varies according to the procedural posture.

§1.3.6   Phase 6: Post-Appeal Proceedings

If an appellate court reverses and remands, the trial court has more work to do. That work might be much, such as holding a new trial, or it might be little, such as modifying the judgment or order appealed from so that it conforms with the decision of the appellate court. Sometimes, one of the parties concludes that the trial court has committed additional error after the remand, and yet another appeal ensues.

§1.3.7   Criminal Cases

The phases of a criminal case are roughly analogous to those of civil litigation, but the procedures and terminology can be quite different.

In a criminal case, a *prosecuting attorney* represents the government, which alone can start the litigation. The initial allegations are in an *indictment* or *information,* which a criminal defendant might move to dismiss just as a civil defendant might move to dismiss a complaint. There are no interrogatories or depositions in a criminal case, but there may be a *preliminary hearing.* If at trial the defendant is *convicted,* the remedy will be a *sentence,* such as imprisonment, probation, or a fine. In the course on criminal procedure, you will learn about *suppression motions, grand juries,* and other matters peculiar to criminal litigation.

A case is not criminal merely because a government is a party. Governments often can sue and be sued in civil actions as well. A relatively simple example occurs where a private car collides with a truck owned by a government: generally, the government and the owner of the car can sue each other in civil proceedings to determine who pays the cost of repairs. If the police believe either driver violated the traffic laws, that driver might be prosecuted in a separate criminal or quasi-criminal proceeding.

§1.4   *The Importance of Understanding Procedure*

At this point, you are probably at least somewhat puzzled about procedure. But in law school courses, you will not be able to understand the material or explain your analysis precisely unless you understand the procedure governing the issue at hand. To gain that knowledge, do the following:

1. Read §1.3 again — and again — until the fog begins to clear away and at least the main features of the terrain become apparent.

2. Diagram the chronological sequence of procedural events described in §1.3. It matters little what kind of diagram you make, so long as the result is complete and accurate. The act of diagramming will help you absorb the details, and you can use the diagram later to help orient yourself if you do not understand how a particular procedural event fits into the whole.

3. Throughout the year, in this course and in others, whenever you read a court's opinion, look for the procedural event that led to the decision. Refer back to §1.3 and to your legal dictionary if you have not yet learned how that procedural event operates and what its ramifications are. Courts decide different kinds of motions differently, and, unless you understand the differences, you will not be able to figure out what the court is up to.

§1.5   *The Adversary System*

Although the legislative and executive branches of government take the initiative themselves in making decisions and solving problems, one of the distinguishing features of the judicial branch is its passivity. Judges are permitted to solve only those problems that have been presented by parties to a lawsuit and only those problems that have been presented in the proper procedural formats — largely in the motions and appeals about which you have just read. Litigation is thus "*party-initiated* and *party-controlled.* The case is organized and the issues defined by exchanges between the parties. . . . The trial judge is a neutral arbiter of their interactions who decides questions of law only if they are put in issue by an appropriate move of a party."[1]

Judicial passivity is a product of the *adversary system,* which is peculiar to those countries whose legal institutions are descended from the English common law. Ramifications of the adversary system permeate every aspect of the American legal profession, determining the lawyer's role, skills, and ethical responsibilities. The adversary system survives partly because of the distrust of authority that permeates English and American history. In countries with a traditionally greater deference to government, courts operate differently. In the European inquisitorial system, for example, the judge is a far more active player. In most European countries, the judge identifies the issues, investigates the facts, selects the witnesses and questions them, and takes most of the procedural initiatives, while the attorneys sit by, interjecting now and then. In the adversary system, on the other hand, the attorneys — through their disagreements — frame the issues and dominate the litigation, and the judge acts only when the attorneys ask for a ruling.

The common law trial judge is not charged with the European trial judge's active responsibility to find the truth. Instead, the theory of the adversary system is a theory of debate, if not combat: from the clash of two active advocates committed to differing viewpoints, the passive decision-maker should be able to separate the persuasive from the unpersuasive. The inquisitorial theory, on the other hand, is one of semi-scientific experiment: the judge is investigator evaluating data that has not been manipulated by advocates.

Paradoxically, the common law appellate judge is considered by European legal scholars to be a figure of awesome power. What common law trial judges lack in authority to guide the progress of an individual lawsuit is more than made up for by the common law appellate judges' power to guide, through precedent, the growth of the law itself. (Most European courts do not make law through stare decisis.) But common law judges cannot make law on any subject they please: with few exceptions, precedent occurs only when a court rules on issues framed by the parties. Karl Llewellyn put it this way:

> The court can decide *only* the particular dispute which is before it. When it speaks to that question, it speaks ex cathedra, with authority, . . . with an almost magical power. When it speaks to the question before it, it announces *law,* and if what it announces is new, . . . it *makes* the law. But when it speaks to any other question at all, it says mere words, which no man needs to follow. Are such words worthless? They are not. We know them as judicial *dicta;* when they are wholly off the point at issue we call them *obiter dicta* — words dropped along the road, wayside remarks. Yet even wayside remarks shed light on the remarker. They may be very useful in the future to him, or to us. But he will not feel bound to them, as to his ex cathedra utterance.[2]

---

§1.5   1. Abram Chayes, *The Role of the Judge in Public Law Litigation,* 89 Harv. L. Rev. 1281, 1283 (1976) (emphasis in original).
   2. Karl N. Llewellyn, The Bramble Bush 42 (1960) (emphasis in original).

2 Rule-Based Reasoning[1]

§2.1   The Inner Structure of a Rule

> At this moment the King, who had for some time been busily writing in his notebook, called out "Silence!" and read from his book, "Rule Forty-two. *All persons more than a mile high to leave the court.*"
>
> Everyone looked at Alice.
>
> "*I'm* not a mile high," said Alice.
>
> "You are," said the King.
>
> "Nearly *two* miles high," added the Queen.
>
> — *Lewis Carroll,*
> Alice in Wonderland

A rule is a formula for making a decision.

Some rules are *mandatory* ("any person who pays a fee of a thousand rubles shall be entitled to a beach permit"), while others are *prohibitory* ("no person shall transfer more than two million pesos to another country without a license from the Ministry of Finance") or *discretionary* ("the curator of the Louvre may permit flash photographs to be taken when, in his or her judgment, no damage to art will result"). Some appear to be one kind of rule, but on examination turn out to be something else. For example, the following seems mandatory: "a person in charge of a dog that fouls the footway shall be fined ten pounds." But it would actually be discretionary if some other rule were to empower the judge to suspend sentence.

Every rule has three separate components: (1) a set of elements, collec-

---

1. This term was suggested by Steven Jamar.

15

(1) (2) = ELEMENTS

RULE: (1) ALL [PERSON] [MORE THAN A MILE HIGH] (2) TO [LEAVE] THE COURT] (3)

(3) = RESULT CAUSAL TERM HERE IS MANDATORY

tively called a *test;* (2) a result that occurs when all the elements are present (and the test is thus satisfied); and (3) what, for lack of a better expression, could be called a causal term that determines whether the result is mandatory, prohibitory, or discretionary. (As the examples below illustrate, the result and the causal term are usually integrated into the same phrase or clause.) Additionally, many rules have (4) one or more exceptions that, if present, would defeat the result, even if all the elements are present.

Consider Alice's situation. She was confronted with a test of two elements. The first was the status of being a person, which mattered because at the time she was in the company of a lot of animals — including one with the head and wings of an eagle and the body of a lion — all of whom seem to have been exempt from any requirement to leave. The second element went to height — specifically a height of more than a mile. The result would have been departure from the court, and the causal term was mandatory ("*All* persons . . . *to* leave . . ."). No exceptions were provided for. Alice has denied the second element (her height), impliedly conceding the first (her personhood). The Queen has offered to prove a height of two miles. What would happen if the Queen were not able to make good on her promise and instead produced evidence showing only a height of 1.241 miles? (Read the rule.) What if the Queen were to produce no evidence and if Alice were to prove that her height was only 0.984 miles?

A causal component is always mandatory (such as "shall"), or prohibitory ("shall not"), or discretionary or permissive ("may"). The following excerpts from the Freedom of Information Act illustrate each type of causal term. (At first, these look impenetrable, but we will see in a moment how you can get inside the meaning of a rule by figuring out its structure.[1])

> Except with respect to the records made available under paragraphs (1) and (2) of this subsection, each agency, upon any request for records which (A) reasonably describes such records and (B) is made in accordance with published rules stating the time, place, fees (if any), and procedures to be followed, *shall* make the records promptly available to any person.[2]

> The Court *may* assess against the United States reasonable attorneys' fees and other litigation costs reasonably incurred in any case under this section in which the complainant has substantially prevailed.[3]

EXCEPTION (1)

> (Except to the extent that a person has actual and timely notice of the terms thereof,) a person *may not* in any manner be required to resort to, or be adversely affected by, a matter required to be published in the Federal Register and not so published.[4]

To make sense out of rules like these, you might diagram them out on scratch paper. The third example above could be diagrammed as shown on the next page. The diagrammed rule has two elements and two results, each of which is prohibitory ("may not").

---

§2.1   1. In other courses, you will soon be studying equally complex rules in the Federal Rules of Civil Procedure and the Uniform Commercial Code.
   2. 5 U.S.C. § 552(a)(3) (1988) (emphasis added).
   3. 5 U.S.C. § 552(a)(4)(E) (1988) (emphasis added).
   4. 5 U.S.C. § 552(a)(1) (1988) (emphasis added).

A RULE

EXCEPTIONS WOULD DEFEAT THE RESULT EVEN IF ALL ELEMENTS ARE PRESENT

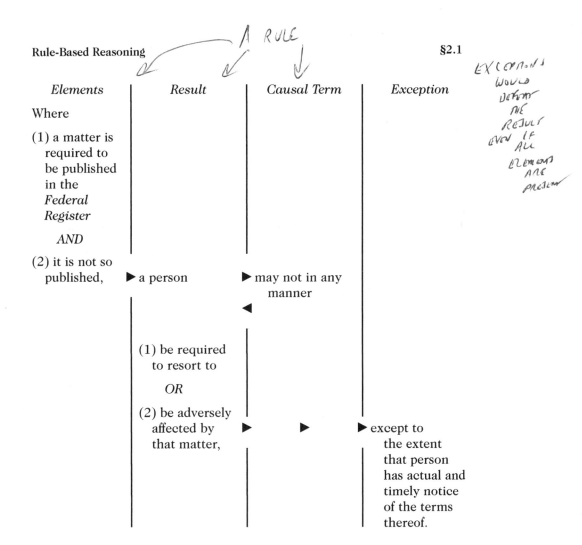

Elements	Result	Causal Term	Exception
Where			
(1) a matter is required to be published in the *Federal Register*			
AND			
(2) it is not so published,	▶ a person	▶ may not in any manner ◀	
(1) be required to resort to *OR* (2) be adversely affected by that matter,	▶	▶	▶ except to the extent that person has actual and timely notice of the terms thereof.

The conjunctions *and* and *or* reveal some of the rule's structure. In the rule diagrammed above, "and" means that the elements are cumulative: they both must be substantiated in the facts, or the rule will not operate. If "and" were to be replaced with "or," the elements would instead become *alternatives:* either of them alone — even in the absence of the other — would cause the result.

Diagramming the rule not only breaks it down so that it can be understood, but it also permits putting the rule back together so that it is easier to apply. This comes straight out of the diagram:

> Where a matter is required to be published in the *Federal Register* and is not so published, a person may not in any manner be required to resort to or be adversely affected by that matter, except to the extent that the person has actual and timely notice of the terms thereof.

When the rule is reorganized this way, we can more easily see the questions we would have to ask when applying it. Suppose that our client says that the federal government is trying to penalize her for violating a regulation she knew nothing about. The reorganized rule tells us what to ask: Was the regulation required to be published in the *Federal Register*? Was it in fact published there? Even if it was not, did the client know about the regulation through some other source before she violated it? If the answers to those questions are, respectively, "yes," "no," and "no," then our client cannot be punished.

In the reorganized example above, the elements are best listed first because there are only two of them and because this particular rule can be more concisely expressed in that way. (Try stating it coherently with the elements listed last.) A rule with a simple result but a complex set of elements might be better expressed with the elements at the end:

> A person is guilty of common law burglary when he or she breaks and enters the dwelling of another in the nighttime with intent to commit a felony therein.[5]

How do you determine how many elements are in a rule? Think of each element as an integral fact, the absence of which in any group of facts would prevent the rule's operation, and then explore the logic behind the rule's words. If you can think of a reasonably predictable scenario in which only part of what you believe to be one element could be true, then you have inadvertently combined two or more elements. For example, is "the dwelling of another" one element or two? A person might be guilty of another crime, but he is not guilty of common law burglary where he breaks and enters the restaurant of another, even in the nighttime and with intent to commit a felony therein. The same is true where he breaks and enters his own dwelling. In each instance, part of the element is present and part missing. "The dwelling of another" thus includes two factual integers — the nature of the building and the identity of its resident — and therefore two elements.

Often you cannot know the number of elements in a rule until you have consulted the precedents interpreting it. Is "breaking and entering" one element or two? The precedents define "breaking" in this sense as the creation of a gap in a building's protective enclosure, such as by opening a door, even where the door was left unlocked and the building is thus not damaged. The cases further define "entering" for this purpose as placing inside the dwelling any part of oneself or any object under one's control, such as a crowbar.[6] Can a person "break" without "entering"? A would-be burglar would seem

---

5. This was the crime at common law. Because of the way its elements are broken out, it does a good job of illustrating several different things about rule structure. But the definition of burglary in a modern criminal code will differ. A statute might break the crime up into gradations (burglary in the first degree, burglary in the second degree, and so on). A typical modern statute would not require that the crime happen in the nighttime, and at least the lower gradations would not require that the building be a dwelling.

6. This sentence contains an example of what might be thought of as a definitional rule — a rule that defines an element of another rule, in this instance the element of an "entering." (The preceding sentence does the same thing for the "breaking" element.) You might think of these definitions as sub-rules, since their purpose is to assist analysis based on the rule for common law burglary.

to have done so where she has opened a window by pushing it up from the outside, and where, before proceeding further, she has been apprehended by an alert police officer — literally a moment too soon. "Breaking" and "entering" are therefore two elements, but one could not know for sure without discovering precisely how the courts have defined the terms used.

Where the elements are complex or ambiguous, an enumeration may add clarity to the list:

> A person is guilty of common law burglary when he or she (1) breaks and (2) enters (3) the dwelling (4) of another (5) in the nighttime (6) with intent to commit a felony therein.

Instead of elements, some rules have criteria or guidelines. These tend to be rules that empower a court or other authority to make discretionary decisions, and the criteria define the scope of the decision-maker's discretion. For example, under a typical modern divorce statute,[7] marital property is distributed as follows:

> Marital property shall be distributed equitably between the parties, considering the circumstances of the case and of the respective parties.
>
> In determining an equitable disposition of property . . . , the court shall consider:
>
> (1) the income and property of each party at the time of marriage, and at the time of the commencement of the action;
>
> (2) the duration of the marriage and the age and health of both parties;
>
> (3) the need of a custodial parent to occupy or own the marital residence and to use or own its household effects;
>
> (4) the loss of inheritance and pension rights upon dissolution of the marriage as of the date of dissolution;
>
> (5) any award of maintenance;
>
> (6) any equitable claim to, interest in, or direct or indirect contribution made to the acquisition of such marital property by the party not having title, including joint efforts of expenditures and contributions and services as a spouse, parent, wage earner and homemaker, and to the career or career potential of the other party;
>
> (7) the liquid or non-liquid character of all marital property;
>
> (8) the probable future financial circumstances of each party;
>
> (9) the impossibility or difficulty of evaluating any component asset or any interest in a business, corporation, or profession, and the economic desirability of retaining such asset or interest intact and free from any claim or interference by the other party;
>
> (10) the tax consequences to each party;
>
> (11) the wasteful disposition of assets by either spouse;
>
> (12) any transfer or encumbrance made in contemplation of a [divorce] action without fair consideration;
>
> (13) any other factor which the court shall expressly find to be just and proper.

7. N.Y. Dom. Rel. Law § 236, Part B(5)(c) & (d) (McKinney 1986).

Only seldom would all of these criteria tip in the same direction. With a rule like this, a judge does something of a balancing test, deciding according to the tilt of the criteria as a whole, together with the angle of the tilt. If the criteria favor a party only slightly, he or she may get most of the marital property, but less than if the party had been favored overwhelmingly.

You will meet only a few of these criteria rules in the first year of law school. They are a relatively new development in the law and grow out of a recent tendency to define more precisely the discretion of judges and other officials. You will see criteria rules more often in the second and third years of law school, where the focus is on parts of the law dominated by the innovations of modern statutes. The first year, however, is largely devoted to subjects closer to the common law: property, contracts, torts, and criminal law. In those fields, and in the law as a whole, the prevalent rule structure is that of a set of elements, the presence of which leads to a particular result in the absence of an exception.

§2.2   Organizing the Application of a Rule

Welty and Lutz are students who have rented apartments on the same floor of the same building. At midnight, Welty is studying, while Lutz is listening to a Stone Temple Pilots album with his new four-foot speakers. Welty has put up with this for two or three hours, and finally she pounds on Lutz's door. Lutz opens the door about six inches, and, when he realizes that he cannot hear what Welty is saying, he steps back into the room a few feet to turn the volume down, without opening the door further. Continuing to express outrage, Welty pushes the door completely open and strides into the room. Lutz turns on Welty and orders her to leave. Welty finds this to be too much and punches Lutz so hard that he suffers substantial injury. In this jurisdiction, the punch is a felonious assault. Is Welty also guilty of common law burglary?

You probably say "no," and your reasoning probably goes something like this: "That's not burglary. Burglary happens when somebody gets into the house when you're not around and steals all the valuables. Maybe this will turn out to be some kind of trespass." But in law school a satisfactory answer is never merely "yes" or "no." An answer necessarily includes a sound *reason,* and, regardless of whether Welty is guilty of burglary, this answer is wrong because the reasoning is wrong. The answer can be determined only by applying a rule like the definition of burglary found on page 18. *Anything else is a guess.*

Where do you start? Remember that a rule is a structured idea: the presence of all the elements causes the result, and the absence of any of them causes the rule not to operate. Assume that in our jurisdiction the elements of burglary are what they were at common law:[1]

1. a breaking
2. and an entry
3. of the dwelling
4. of another
5. in the nighttime
6. with intent to commit a felony therein.

To discover whether each element is present in the facts, simply annotate the list:

1. *a breaking:* If a breaking can be the enlarging of an opening between the door and the jam without permission, and if Lutz's actions do not imply permission, there was a breaking.
2. *and an entry:* Welty "entered," for the purposes of the rule on burglary, by walking into the room, unless Lutz's actions implied permission to enter.
3. *of the dwelling:* Lutz's apartment was a dwelling.
4. *of another:* And it was not Welty's dwelling: she lives down the hall.
5. *in the nighttime:* Midnight is in the nighttime.
6. *with intent to commit a felony therein:* Did Welty intend to assault Lutz when she strode through the door? If not, this element is missing.

You can see how much the first answer ("it doesn't sound like burglary") was a guess. By examining each element separately, you find that elements 3, 4, and 5 are present, but that you are not sure about the others without some hard thinking about the facts and without consulting the precedents in this jurisdiction that have interpreted elements 1, 2, and 6.

The case law might turn up a variety of results. Suppose that, although local precedent defines Welty's actions as a breaking and an entry, the cases on the sixth element strictly require corroborative evidence that a defendant had a fully formed felonious intent when entering the dwelling. That kind of evidence might be present, for example, where an accused was in possession of safecracking tools when he broke and entered, or where, before breaking and entering, the accused had confided to another that he intended to murder the occupant. Against that background, the answer here might be something like the following: "Welty is not guilty of burglary because, although she broke and entered the dwelling of another in the nighttime, there is no evidence that she had a felonious intent when entering the dwelling."

Suppose, on the other hand, that under local case law Welty's actions again are a breaking and an entry; that the local cases do not require cor-

§2.2   1. See page 18, note 5.

roborative evidence of a felonious intent; and that local precedent defines a felonious intent for the purposes of burglary to be one that the defendant could have been forming — even if not yet consciously — when entering the dwelling. Under those sub-rules, if you believe that Welty had the requisite felonious intent, your answer would be something like this: "Welty is guilty of burglary because she broke and entered the dwelling of another in the nighttime with intent to commit a felony therein, thus meeting all the elements of common law burglary." These are real answers to the question of whether Welty is guilty of burglary: they state not only the result, but the reason why.

§2.3 Some Things to Be Careful About with Rules

Rules must be expressed in terms of categories of actions, things, conditions, and people, and you have already had a taste of how slippery those kinds of definitions can be. Some of the slipperiness is there because precision takes constant effort, like weeding a garden. But some of it is there to give law the flexibility needed for sound decision-making. The language "in which law is necessarily expressed . . . is not an instrument of mathematical precision but possesses . . . an 'open texture.'"[1] That is because a rule's quality is measured not by its logical elegance — few rules of law have that — but by how well the rule guides a court into making sound decisions. A rule that causes poor decisions begs to be changed.

In addition, a given rule might be expressed in any of a number of ways. Where law is made through precedent — as much of our law is — different judges, writing in varying circumstances, may enunciate what seems like the same rule in a variety of distinct phrasings. At times, it can be hard to tell whether the judges have spoken of the same rule in different voices or instead have spoken of slightly different rules. In either situation, it can be harder still to discover — because of the variety — exactly what the rule is or what the rules are. All this may at first seem bewildering, but in fact it opens up one of the most fertile opportunities for a lawyer's creativity because in litigation each side is free to argue a favorable interpretation of the mosaic of rule statements found in the precedents, and courts are free to mutate the law through their own interpretation of the same mosaic.

And even where the rule is expressed in one voice, ambiguity and vagueness can obscure intended meaning unless the person stating the rule is extraordinarily careful in using and defining language. The classic example asks whether a person riding a bicycle through a park violates a rule prohibiting the use there of "vehicles." (What had the rule-maker intended? How could the intention have been made more clear?) Even where the rule-maker is careful with language, the structure of a rule does not always easily

§2.3   1. Dennis Lloyd & M. D. A. Freeman, *Lloyd's Introduction to Jurisprudence* 1139 (5th ed. 1985).

accommodate an expression of the rule's purpose — or, as lawyers say, the policy underlying the rule — even though the rule's policy or purpose is the key to unravelling ambiguities within the rule. (Is a self-propelled lawn mower a prohibited "vehicle"? To answer that question, try to imagine the problem the rule-makers were trying to solve.) Not only is it difficult to frame a rule so that it controls all the rule-maker wishes to control, but after a rule is framed, situations inevitably crop up that the rule-maker did not contemplate or could not have been expected to contemplate. (Is a baby carriage powered by solar batteries a "vehicle"?)

Finally, the parts of a rule may be so many and their interrelationships so complex that it may be hard to pin down exactly what the rule is and how it works. And this is compounded by interaction between and among rules. A word or phrase in a rule may be defined, for example, by another rule. Or the application of one rule may be governed by yet another rule — or even a whole body of rules.

More than any others, two skills will help you become agile in the lawyerly use of rules. The first is language mastery, including an "ability to spot ambiguities, to recognize vagueness, to identify the emotive pull of a word . . . and to analyze and elucidate class words and abstractions."[2] The second is the capacity to think structurally. A rule is, after all, an idea with structure to it, and, even though the words inside a rule might lack mathematical precision, the rule's structure is more like an algebraic formula than a value judgment. You need to be able to figure out the structure of an idea, break it down into sub-ideas, organize the sub-ideas usefully and accurately, and apply the organized idea to facts.

§2.4 Causes of Action and Affirmative Defenses

The law cannot remedy every wrong, and many problems are more effectively resolved through other means, such as the political process, mediation, bargaining, and economic and social pressure. Unless the legal system focuses its resources on resolving those problems it handles best, it would collapse under the sheer weight of an unmanageable workload and would thus be prevented from attempting even the problem-solving it does well. Thus, a threshold task in law is the definition of wrongs for which courts will provide a remedy.

A harm the law will remedy is called a *cause of action* (or, in some courts, a *claim* or a *claim for relief*). If a plaintiff proves a cause of action, a court will order a remedy unless the defendant proves an *affirmative defense*. If the defendant proves an affirmative defense, the plaintiff will get no remedy, even if that plaintiff has proved a cause of action. Causes of action and affirmative defenses (like other legal rules) are formulated as tests with elements and the other components explained in §2.1.

---

2. William L. Twining & David Miers, *How to Do Things with Rules* 120 (1976).

For example, where a plaintiff proves that a defendant intentionally confined him and that the defendant was not a law enforcement officer acting within the scope of an authority to arrest, the plaintiff has proved a cause of action called *false imprisonment.* The test is expressed as a list of elements: "False imprisonment consists of (1) a confinement (2) of the plaintiff (3) by the defendant (4) intentionally (5) where the defendant is not a sworn law enforcement officer acting within his or her authority." Proof of false imprisonment would customarily result in a court's awarding a remedy called *damages,* which obliges the defendant to compensate the plaintiff in money for the latter's injuries.

But that is not always so: if the defendant can prove that she caught the plaintiff shoplifting in her store and restrained him only until the police arrived, she might have an affirmative defense that is sometimes called a *shopkeeper's privilege.* Where a defendant proves a shopkeeper's privilege, a court will not award the plaintiff damages, even if he has proved false imprisonment. Again, the test is expressed as a list of elements: "A shopkeeper's privilege exists where (1) a shopkeeper or shopkeeper's employee (2) has reasonable cause to believe that (3) the plaintiff (4) has shoplifted (5) in the shopkeeper's place of business and (6) the confinement occurs in a reasonable manner, for a reasonable time, and no more than needed to detain the plaintiff for law enforcement purposes."

Notice that some elements encompass physical activity ("a confinement"), while others specify states of mind ("intentionally") or address status or condition ("a shopkeeper or shopkeeper's employee") or require abstract qualities ("in a reasonable manner, for a reasonable time, and no more than needed to detain the plaintiff for law enforcement purposes"). State-of-mind and abstract-quality elements will probably puzzle you more than others will. The plaintiff, for example, might be able to prove a confinement through a witness who saw a door being locked. And if the shopkeeper's own testimony is not good enough to prove her status, she can probably produce a license to do business at the place where the plaintiff says he was confined, or some other evidence tending to show that one operates a store. These elements are straightforward because they are tangible.

But how will the plaintiff be able to prove that the defendant acted "intentionally," and how will the defendant be able to show that she confined the plaintiff "in a reasonable manner, for a reasonable time, and no more than needed to detain the plaintiff for law enforcement purposes"? Because thoughts and abstractions cannot be witnessed, the law is left to judge an abstraction or a party's state of mind from the actions and other events surrounding it. If, for example, the plaintiff can prove that the defendant took him by the arm, pulled him into a room, and then locked the door herself, he may be able to carry his burden of showing that she acted "intentionally." And the defendant may be able to carry her burden of proving the confinement to have been reasonably carried out if she can show that when she took the defendant by the arm, he had been trying to run from the store; that she called the police immediately; and that she turned the defendant over to the police as soon as they arrived.

Because each state can devise its own rules of law — within limits explored in the course on constitutional law — the elements of a given test may differ from state to state. Even though virtually all states condition a shopkeeper's privilege on proof of the shopkeeper's "reasonable cause to believe" (or similar words to the same effect), a state could require much more (such as "belief held to a moral certainty") or even much less (perhaps "mere suspicion, regardless of its basis").

3 An Introduction to Judicial Opinions

§3.1 The Anatomy of Opinions

In an opinion announcing a court's decision, one might find nine different kinds of pronouncement:

1. a recitation of procedural events
2. a recitation of pleaded or evidentiary events
3. a statement of the issue or issues to be decided by the court
4. a summary of the arguments made by each side
5. the court's holding on each issue
6. the rule or rules of law the court enforces through each holding
7. the court's reasoning
8. dicta
9. a statement of the relief granted or denied

Only infrequently, however, do all nine occur in the same opinion.

Opinions often begin with (1) a recitation of *procedural events* inside the litigation that have raised the issue decided by the court. Examples are motions, hearings, trial, judgment, and appeal. Although the court's description of these events may — because of unfamiliar terminology — seem at first confusing, you must be able to understand procedural histories because the manner in which an issue is raised determines the method a court will use to decide it. A court decides a motion for a directed verdict, for example, very differently from the way it rules on a request for a jury instruction, even though both might require the court to consider the same point of law. The procedural events add up to the case's procedural posture at the time the decision was made.

27

Frequently, the court will next describe (2) the *pleaded events* or the *evidentiary events* on which the ruling is based. In litigation, parties plead facts and then prove them. The court has no other way of knowing what transpired between the parties before the lawsuit began. If the procedural posture involved a motion to dismiss a pleading[1] — before any evidence could be submitted — the decision will be based on the allegations in the challenged pleading (usually a complaint). Otherwise, the court's knowledge of the facts will come from evidentiary events such as testimony and exhibits at trial or at a hearing, or perhaps affidavits and exhibits submitted in connection with a motion.

A court might also set out (3) a statement of the *issue or issues* before the court for decision and (4) a *summary of the arguments* made by each side, although either or both are often only implied. A court will further state (or at least imply) (5) the *holding* on each of the issues and (6) the *rule or rules* of law the court enforces in making each holding, together with (7) the *reasoning behind* — often called the *rationale for* — its decision. Somewhere in the opinion, the court might place some (8) *dicta.* (You will learn more about dicta in the next few months, but for the moment think of it as discussion unnecessary to support a holding and therefore lacking binding precedential authority.)

An opinion usually ends with (9) *a statement of the relief granted or denied.* If the opinion represents the decision of an appellate court, the relief may be an affirmance, a reversal, or a reversal combined with a direction to the trial court to proceed in a specified manner. If the opinion is from a trial court, the relief is most commonly the granting or denial of a motion.

Exercise I.   *Dissecting the Text of* Meints v. Huntington

Read *Meints v. Huntington* and determine where (if anywhere) each of these types of pronouncement occurs. Mark up the text generously and be prepared to discuss your analysis in class. Look up in a legal dictionary every unfamiliar word and every familiar word that is used in an unfamiliar way.

MEINTS v. HUNTINGTON
276 F. 245 (8th Cir. 1921)

LEWIS, District Judge. John Meints, a resident and citizen of South Dakota, brought this action against O. P. Huntington and others, residents and citizens of Rock County, Minnesota, to recover damages, on the charge that they deported him from Minnesota to South Dakota on the night of August 19, 1918, and maltreated him on the way. After a lengthy trial, exhibited here by 1100 pages of testimony, the greater part of which relates to the loyalty of the defendants and the disloyalty of plaintiff during the late World War, there was verdict and judgment for defendants.

---

§3.1   1. See pages 8-9.

The plaintiff was born in Illinois, went to Rock County, Minnesota, and resided there in the town of Luverne for sixteen or seventeen years prior to the summer of 1918. In the spring of that year he was suspected of being interested in or of having contributed to the support of a Non-Partisan League newspaper printed and published in that town; on account of that, and also because it was claimed that he was disloyal, a large body of men, including some of the defendants, went to his house about midnight of June 19th, woke him up, compelled him to dress and come out, and some of them in automobiles took him across the State line into Iowa, a distance of about fifteen miles, told him not to return and left him there. He then went to St. Paul and reported the occurrence to a U.S. Government agent in the Department of Justice. That agent sent two men to Rock County to make an investigation, and on their report, Mr. Campbell of that Department advised plaintiff to return to Rock County but to go to the home of his two sons, some twelve miles out from Luverne, and remain there. He did return the latter part of July and went to his sons' home. On the night of August 3rd, men in eight or nine automobiles went out to the sons' house. Among them were the defendants Huntington, Connell, Ihlan, Miner, Turnbull and Kimmerling. They tried to enter the house by unlocking the doors with keys which they had, but were not able to do so, and finally obtained entrance by going through the cellar. They were hunting for plaintiff, but could not find him. In the late afternoon of August 19th some seventy-five to eighty men in about twenty-five automobiles, most of them from Luverne, met at a church about four miles from the sons' house, and proceeded from there in a body, arriving at the sons' house about dusk. The plaintiff and his sons saw them coming, went into the house and fastened the screen door on the inner side. The married son's wife and children were also in the house and shortly became greatly excited and alarmed, as their outcries demonstrated. Huntington and others went to the door and demanded to know where the plaintiff was, and that they be permitted to enter. The son who stood inside the door refused to open it and declined to admit them. The defendant Long at once forced the door open and a number of men immediately entered, including Long and Huntington. The son testified that he was assaulted by them and thrown out of the house. They denied that, and testified that his bloody face was caused by his own struggles while they held him to prevent violence on his part. The plaintiff stood at the head of the stairway with a gun and a fork handle. At first he refused to come down or to permit anyone to come up. The other son was induced by some of the defendants, or others with them, to go up and tell his father that they did not intend violence. The plaintiff sent back word by his son that the defendant Long might come up and he would talk with him. He then came down with Long and was taken in Huntington's automobile to Luverne. Huntington drove, and some of the other defendants were in the car with him and the plaintiff. Most of the crowd went with them, but a few turned west toward the South Dakota line before Luverne was reached. Plaintiff was held at Luverne until about eleven o'clock, and while there was refused permission to see his wife or to talk with her over the telephone. About that hour he was again put in Huntington's car. Defendants Huntington, Long, Michaelson and Smith also got in, and they started for the South Dakota line, some fifteen miles away, accompanied by another auto in which were defendants Turnbull, Connell, Kimmerling and McDermott. They reached the State line about midnight, and were stopped there by armed men whose faces were masked. They took Meints from Huntington's car, assaulted him, whipped him, threatened to shoot him, besmeared his body with tar and feathers, and told him to cross the line into South Dakota, and that if he ever returned to Minnesota he would be hanged. . . .

On the foregoing facts, . . . there can be no doubt that from the time the crowd reached the sons' house and on up to the time Meints crossed the State line, he was coerced and compelled by a show of force to submit himself to the will of others, that he was unlawfully restrained of his liberty, falsely imprisoned for the time being, . . . and that this was done . . . to drive him from the State of Minnesota. And so we say at once that the trial court erred in refusing to instruct a verdict for the plaintiff and against all defendants who took part; for it cannot be maintained that because Meints may have been, in their opinion, disloyal, and was interested in and gave support to the Non-Partisan League Newspaper, that that would put him at the mercy of defendants and invest them with the right and power to adjudge and inflict punishment, nor would the fact that the defendants were loyal men . . . have the slightest tendency to excuse or justify in the eyes of the law the acts charged against them. . . . Mr. Cooley, in his work on Torts, says [that] ". . . any restraint put by fear or force upon the actions of another is unlawful and constitutes a false imprisonment, unless a showing of justification makes it a true or legal imprisonment." . . .

The court yielded to the contention of the defendants that the plaintiff could not recover for anything that was done prior to the assaults made upon him, when the State line was reached, on the claim that he had consented to everything that had happened before that, and so instructed the jury over the objection of the plaintiff. This was prejudicial error. Can it be seriously thought that it was the wish of plaintiff to leave Rock County? His home was in Luverne, his wife was there, he had lived there for many years, all of his family and all of his interests were in Rock County; he had, to the knowledge of some, if not all, of the defendants but recently returned to remain there. He evidently knew the purpose of these men when he saw them coming, some of them had been hunting for him in the nighttime a few days before. He armed himself to resist them, but they came in such numbers and invaded the home in such a ruthless and high-handed manner that resistance was obviously futile. He knew, and every rational thought convinces, that if he had not submitted he would have been more severely treated. Who would have the temerity to argue that they would have permitted him to remain, or after starting, to have alighted from Huntington's auto and return? While they held him for two or three hours in Luverne he was refused permission to see his wife or to talk with her over the 'phone. He was in a large room with a crowd about him who jeered him and asked him questions so thickly that there was no opportunity to attempt to answer, and an attempt, if it had been made, would have been without avail. No argument can blot out the fact, which stands predominant throughout the record, that he was a prisoner from the time these men reached his sons' house until he passed over the State line into South Dakota, and everyone who reads the record must know that resistance on his part to their will would not have been tolerated. In *Comer v. Knowles,* 17 Kan. 436, it is said:

> False imprisonment is necessarily a wrongful interference with the personal liberty of an individual. The wrong may be committed by words alone, or by acts alone, or by both, and by merely operating on the will of the individual, or by personal violence, or by both. It is not necessary that the individual be confined within a prison, or within walls; or that he be assaulted, or even touched. It is not necessary that there should be any injury done to the individual's person, or to his character, or reputation. Nor is it necessary that the wrongful act be committed with malice, or ill will, or even with the slightest wrongful intention. Nor is it necessary that the act be under color of any legal or judicial proceeding. All that is necessary is, that the individual be restrained of his liberty without any sufficient legal cause therefor, and by words or acts which he fears to disregard.

In *Pike v. Hanson,* 9 N.H. 491, the plaintiff did not intend to pay a tax, and the collector was so informed. He, in demanding the tax, declared to the plaintiff that he arrested her, and she paid the money under that restraint. It was held that the facts were sufficient to sustain her action for assault and false imprisonment. The court summarized the doctrine announced by Starkie on *Evidence,* thus:

> That in ordinary practice words are sufficient to constitute an imprisonment, if they impose a restraint upon the person and the plaintiff is accordingly restrained, for he is not obliged to incur risk of personal violence and insult by resisting until actual violence be used.

. . . The court, acting on its conclusion of fact that plaintiff had consented to everything before the State line was reached, instructed the jury over plaintiff's objection and exception that he could recover only against those who maltreated him at the South Dakota line, and that if the evidence was not sufficient in the judgment of the jury to satisfy them as to the identity of those men they would return a verdict for the defendants, there being no liability on the part of any of the defendants except those, if any, who assaulted him there. This we think was also error. As already said, those who took the plaintiff from the sons' home, those who participated to any extent in so doing, those who aided in his deportation on the way, and those who abused him at the State line and warned him that if he ever returned to Minnesota he would be hanged, were all actively engaged in the execution of one purpose, and the transaction throughout . . . was for the accomplishment of that purpose. . . .

It is also claimed by the defendants that what was done by them was done to protect the plaintiff against others who might injure him because of his disloyalty, or his reputation for disloyalty. This presents a new doctrine unknown to us, and no authority has been cited to support it. We cannot believe that the law will ever sanction the claim, either in defense or miti-

gation, that the rights of one may be violated for the purpose of preventing others from doing the same thing. . . .

The judgment is reversed and the cause remanded for a new trial.

A decision's *citation* is made up of the case's name, references to the reporter or reporters in which the decision was printed, the name of the court where the decision was made, and the year of the decision. For *Meints,* all this information appears in the heading on page 28.

The case name is composed by separating the last names of the parties with a "v." If the opinion was written by a trial court, the name of the plaintiff appears first. In some appellate courts, the name of the appellant comes first, but in others the parties are listed as they were in the trial court. In a case with multiple plaintiffs or defendants, the name of only the first listed per side appears in the case name.

Reporters are publications that print opinions, mostly from appellate courts. There are two kinds: official reporters published under the control of courts and unofficial ones published by private companies. Most opinions appear both in an official reporter and in at least one unofficial reporter. Some courts, however, publish their decisions in only one reporter, which has an official status but an unofficial format. *Meints v. Huntington* was decided by the Eighth Circuit of the United States Court of Appeals. Decisions of the United States Courts of Appeals appear only in the Federal Reporter (abbreviated "F."). The decision you have just read begins on page 245 of volume 276.

Thus, *Meints* is cited to in the following form: *Meints v. Huntington,* 276 F. 245 (8th Cir. 1921).[2]

§3.2   The Interdependence Among Facts, Issues, and Rules

Many facts are mentioned in an opinion merely to provide background, continuity, or what journalists call "human interest" to what would otherwise be a tedious and disjointed recitation. Of the remaining facts, some are merely related to the court's thinking, while others *caused* the court to come to its decision. This last group could be called the *determinative facts* or the *essential facts*. They are essential to the court's decision because they determined it: if they had been different, the decision would have been different. The determinative facts lead to the rule of the case — the rule of law for which the case stands as precedent — and the discovery of that rule is the most important goal of case analysis. (Of course, where several issues are raised together in a case, the court must make several rulings and an opinion may thus stand for several different rules.)

---

2. In Chapter 16, you will learn more about constructing legal citations.

DETERMINATIVE FACTS

The determinative facts can be identified by asking the following question: *if a particular fact had not happened, or if it had happened differently, would the court have made a different decision?* If so, that fact is one of the determinative facts. This can be illustrated through a nonjudicial decision of a sort with which you might recently have had some experience. Assume that a rental agent has just shown you an apartment and that the following are true:

A. The apartment is located half a mile from the law school.
B. It is a studio apartment (one room plus a kitchenette and bathroom)
C. The building appears to be well-maintained and safe.
D. The apartment is at the corner of the building, and windows on two sides provide ample light and ventilation.
E. It is on the third floor, away from the street, and the neighbors do not appear to be disagreeable.
F. The rent is $400 per month, furnished.
G. The landlord will require a year's lease, and if you do not stay in the apartment for the full year, subleasing it to someone else would be difficult.
H. You have a widowed aunt, with whom you get along well and who lives alone in a house 45 minutes by bus from the law school, and she has offered to let you use the second floor of her house during the school year. The house and neighborhood are safe and quiet, and the living arrangements would be satisfactory to you.
I. You have made a commitment to work next summer in El Paso.
J. You have taken out substantial loans to go to law school.
K. You neither own nor have access to a car.
L. Reliable local people have told you that you are unlikely to find an apartment that is better, cheaper, or more convenient than the one you have just inspected.

Which facts are essential to your decision? If the apartment had been two miles from the law school (rather than a half-mile), would your decision be different? If not, the first listed fact could not be determinative. It might be part of the factual mosaic and might explain why you looked at the apartment in the first place, but you would not base your decision on it. (Go through the listed facts and mark in the margin whether each would determine your decision.)

Facts recited specifically in an opinion can sometimes be reformulated generically. In the hypothetical above, for example, a generic restatement of fact *H* might be the following: "you have a rent-free alternative to the apartment, but the alternative would require 45 minutes of travel each way plus the expense of public transportation." That formulation is generic because it includes other specific possibilities that in the end have the same relevant characteristics and effect. It would include, for example, the following, seemingly different, facts: "you are a member of the clergy in a religion that has given you a leave of absence to attend law school; you may continue to live rent-free in the satisfactory quarters your religion has provided, but to get to the law school, you will have to walk 15 minutes and then ride a subway for 30 minutes more, at the same cost as a bus."

A rule of law is, in essence, a principle that governs how a particular type of decision is to be made — or, put another way, how certain types of facts are to be treated by the official (such as a judge) who must make a decision. Where a court does not state a rule of the case, or where it ambiguously states a rule, you might arrive at an arguably supportable formulation of the rule by considering the determinative facts to have caused the result. There is room for interpretive maneuver where one could reasonably interpret the determinative facts narrowly (specifically) or broadly (generically).

Notice how different formulations of a rule can be extracted from the apartment example. A narrow formulation might be the following:

> A law student who has a choice between renting an apartment and living in the second floor of an aunt's house should choose the latter where the student has had to borrow money to go to law school; where the apartment's rent is $400 per month but the aunt's second floor is free except for bus fares; where the student must work in El Paso during the summer; and where it is difficult locally to sublease an apartment.

Because this formulation is limited to the specific facts given in the hypothetical, it could directly govern only an extremely small number of future decision-makers. It would not, for example, directly govern the member of the clergy described above, even if she must spend next summer doing relief work in Eritrea.

Although a decision-maker in a future situation might be able to reason by analogy from the narrow rule set out above, a broader, more widely applicable formulation, stated generically, would directly govern both situations:

> A student on a tight budget should not sign a year's lease where the student cannot live in the leased property during the summer and where a nearly free alternative is available.

An even more general formulation would govern an even wider circle of applications:

> A person with limited funds should not lease property that that person cannot fully use where there is a nearly free alternative.

The following, however, is so broad as to be meaningless:

> A person should not spend money in a way that would later lead to problems.

The interpretation of opinions is not easy. "Cases do not unfold their principles for the asking," wrote Cardozo. "They yield up their kernel slowly and painfully."[1] Courts often do not explicitly state the issue, the holding, or the rule for which the case is to stand as precedent, and the determinative facts are not usually labelled as such. Whenever a court gives less than a full explanation, you must use what is explicitly stated to pin down what is only implied.

Fortunately, the determinative facts, the issue, the holding, and the rule are all dependent on each other. In the apartment hypothetical, for example, if the issue were different — say, "How shall I respond to an offer to join the American Automobile Association?" — the selection of determinative facts would also change. (In fact, the only determinative one would be fact K: "You neither own nor have access to a car.") You will often find yourself using what the court tells you about the issue or the holding to fill in what the court has not told you about the determinative facts — and vice versa.

For example, if the court states the issue but does not identify the rule or specify which facts are determinative, you might discover the rule and the determinative facts by answering the following questions:

1. Who is suing whom over what series of events and to get what relief?
2. What issue does the court say it intends to decide?
3. How does the court decide that issue?
4. On what facts does the court rely in making that decision?
5. What rule does the court enforce?[2]

One of the cardinal rules of intellectual detective work — whether done by a scientist in the laboratory, by an historian with freshly discovered but ambiguous documents, or by V. I. Warshawski with the murder evidence — is this: design the sequence of inquiry so that you begin with what you already know and can progress through what you do not know in a manner that helps you build on each thing you discover along the way.

Cases are hard not because judges like to make puzzles, but for more practical reasons. Even the most prescient judges cannot foresee every ramification of every decision or all of the future factual contexts to which a precedent might be applied. Sometimes, an inadvertently imprecise phrase in an opinion creates room for interpretation. And, invariably, it is not humanly possible for a court to explain all its reasoning: the effort would be so immense that many fewer cases could be decided. In any event, one of the most important skills of effective lawyering is the ability to find room for interpretive maneuver and to exploit it to advantage. The lawyer's art is in part to see meaning that is both favorable to the client and at the same time credible and persuasive to a court. Fact interpretation is a very large part of that skill.

§3.2 1. Benjamin Nathan Cardozo, *The Nature of the Judicial Process* 29 (1921).
2. In answering this question, use the same kind of reasoning we applied to the apartment hypothetical; develop several different phrasings of the rule (broad, narrow, middling); and identify the one the court is most likely to have had in mind.

Exercise II.   Analyzing the Meaning of Meints v. Huntington

What was the issue on appeal in *Meints*? What rule did the appellate court enforce? What were the determinative facts? Be prepared to state and argue your conclusions in class.

4 Briefing Cases

§4.1 Introduction

In law school, the word *brief* can mean either of two things. Within a few months, you will learn how to write an *appellate brief,* which — despite its name — is a large and complex document, written to persuade a court to rule in favor of one's client.

Another kind of brief is a short analytical outline of a court's opinion. Students make these outlines to prepare for class, and you are about to write one now. (In law students' vernacular, you are about to *brief a case.*) The purpose of briefing is to figure out the logic through which the case was decided.

§4.2 How to Brief a Case

Just as no two lawyers share exactly the same thinking and working methods, no two law students brief in precisely the same way. Moreover, you will brief individual cases differently depending on the case's complexity and the course for which you are reading it.

Think of the briefing method set out below as a starting point. Adapt it as needed to the different sorts of opinions you study, and, as you go along, modify it also to suit the work habits you find most effective in the different classes for which you must prepare.

A brief might include, in outline form, the following items:

1. the title of the case, its date, the name of the court, and the place where the opinion can be found
2. the identities of the parties
3. the procedural history
4. the facts
5. the issue or issues
6. a summary of the arguments made by each side
7. the holding and the rule for which the case stands
8. the court's reasoning
9. the order or judgment the court made as a result of its decision
10. any comments of your own that may be useful but that are not covered by any other category

Each of these categories bears explanation.

1. Title, date, court, location of opinion.

This is the easiest part. For *Meints*, a brief might begin as follows:

Case: *Meints v. Huntington*
                                (8th Cir. 1921)
                                    page 28

If you were briefing a case in the library, however, you would use the citation (276 F. 245) in place of a page number in the text. The point is to note the place where the opinion can be found.

2. Identities of parties.

This requires some thought: how do the identities of the parties frame the controversy? In *Meints*, for example, you might write:

Parties: P = dissenter in WWI
                                Ds = residents of Rock Co., Minn.

Should you add that the plaintiff was a resident of South Dakota, and that he also had been a resident of Rock County before the events sued over? In the second paragraph of the opinion the court goes to considerable effort to describe a prior incident — not a part of this lawsuit — in which the plaintiff had been forcibly taken from his home into Iowa and was "told . . . not to return." In the first paragraph of the opinion, the court uses the word *deported* to describe the events that caused the plaintiff to end up in South Dakota. What does all this tell you about whether the plaintiff's prior and current residences are determinative facts? If you believe they are mere background facts, then you would include them in your brief only if they are needed to make sense out of the story. On the other hand, if you believe that the court's reasoning is based on the view that the law cannot permit private citizens to "deport" to other states people who hold unpopular opinions, then you should make sure that your brief records where the plaintiff lived at the time of the litigation and at the time of the events complained of. (Because this is a matter of identity as well as an arguably determinative fact, it really does not matter much whether you add it under "Parties" or under "Facts.")

3. Procedural history. Here list the litigation events that are essential to the decision the court must make. Most published opinions are from appellate courts, and an appellate procedural history includes the trial court rulings appealed from. In *Meints,* for example:

> **Proc. Hist.:** P sued for false imprisonment and assault. (Assault holding deleted from op.) Verdict for Ds. P appealed from trial judge's instructions to jury that P could not recover for events before he was assaulted at South Dakota state line.

4. Facts. Here write a short narrative limited to the determinative facts and whatever other details are necessary to make sense out of the story. Omit facts that neither are determinative nor are needed to make the story coherent.

5. The issue. *Define* the dispute before the court. The following are inadequate attempts to state the issue in *Meints*:

Were Ds liable for false imprisonment?

Had P consented to be transported to South Dakota?

Did the trial court correctly instruct the jury?

Did the trial court correctly instruct the jury on the law of consent in false imprisonment?

The first example is wrong because the appellate court was not asked to decide whether the defendants were liable. The plaintiff-appellant argued instead that the trial judge had made an error when he instructed the jury. The question of liability would have been decided by the jury. And jury verdicts, you will recall, are not in themselves appealable — although the actions of the trial judge are. The second example is wrong for the same reason as the first, although the second example specifies the question of consent and thus gets closer to the analytical problem posed by the case. The third example is at least premised on an understanding that the appellate court is confined to reviewing the jury instructions. But the third example is faulty because it merely *describes* — and does not *define* — the dispute on appeal: the third example does not set out what the claimed error in the instructions might have been. The fourth example is better, in that it alludes to the part of the law involved, but it is still not a definition of the question before the court.

There are many adequate ways to phrase the issue in *Meints,* one of which would be the following:

Issue: Did the trial court err in instructing the jury that P could not recover for false imprisonment because he had consented to be taken to another state and left there?

This is a definition of the issue and not a mere description of it: it is exactly the question that the *Meints* court answered. Frame your issues with care and keep the following in mind:

First, your statement of the issue must be phrased in terms of the procedural events that have created a need for a decision. In *Meints,* those procedural events are the specified jury instructions and an appeal based on them. In law school classes, the appeal is such a routine event that it can be implied in your brief.

Second, refer to the governing rule and specify the element that is in controversy. The example on this page mentions a cause of action (a kind of rule) for false imprisonment, as well as an element of that cause of action (the plaintiff's lack of consent to the restraint).

Third, allude to enough of the determinative facts to make the issue concrete. The example on this page refers to the trip to South Dakota, which is the form of restraint claimed by the plaintiff. That is probably enough here. Do not pack into the issue every one of a long list of determinative facts. Include only the most central ones.

Finally, an issue can often be more profitably stated as a question about a rule of law: "Has a false imprisonment plaintiff been restrained without his consent where he does not object to being taken away after . . . ?" In each course, you will be able to get some indication, from the professor's evaluation of student discussion in class, of whether a rule-oriented statement of the issue is more appropriate to the material.

6. A summary of the arguments made by each side.   Do not go overboard. Record the *essential* points of each side's argument.

7. The holding and the rule.   Strictly speaking, the holding and the rule are two different things.

The holding answers the question posed by the issue. In *Meints,* the holding is that the trial court did err by instructing the jury that the plaintiff had consented to be taken to South Dakota.

The rule for which the case stands is a principle that can be applied to decide other controversies in the future. Just as we formulated broad and narrow principles from the apartment hypothetical in §3.2, a case's rule can be stated narrowly or broadly, depending on how you conceptualize the determinative facts:

narrow: A person does not consent to be restrained where he submits only after a large number of men break into his sons' house, throw one son out of the building [and so on, with a list of every fact that deprived this plaintiff of freedom of movement].

broad: A person does not consent to be restrained where he submits only because of "words or acts which he fears to disregard."

As with the apartment, the narrow rule would directly govern only an exceedingly small number of future controversies, while the broader formulation will have a wider utility. Broad formulations should not, however, be taken too far. The following does not accurately represent the rule enforced in *Meints*:

> A person does not consent to be restrained where he refrains from doing what he wants out of fear that otherwise he might suffer.

Part of a lawyer's creativity is discovering deeper meaning in an opinion by devising several alternative formulations of a rule. The art is to phrase the rule broadly enough that it has a reasonably general applicability, but not so broadly that it exceeds the principle that the court thought it was following. Within these limits, most opinions will afford several different but arguable ways to phrase a particular rule.

Sometimes a court provides a succinct statement of the rule. At other times, the court merely sets out the facts and issue and then, without saying much more, decides for one party or the other. In the first kind of opinion, the court's words provide one — sometimes the only — phrasing of the rule. In the latter, you must construct the rule yourself out of the determinative facts. *Meints* is somewhere in between. The court does not state a rule in a single sentence, but it does provide wording (some of which appears in the "broad" example above) that can be used to state generically the determinative facts. Even where the court provides a succinct statement of the rule, it is often possible to arrive at a different but arguable formulation of the rule by examining what the court did with the determinative facts.

Although there is a difference between the rule (which is stated so as to govern future controversies) and the holding (which decides questions like whether the trial court erred in the current case), the distinction tends to blur because lawyers often casually use "holding" to refer to the rule. That is understandable: after all, we read these cases to learn about that rule and for little else.

A law school professor who asks you the "holding" of a case might want to know the holding (in the narrow sense), or the rule, or both. An efficient way of briefing is to record both:

Issue: Did the trial court err in instructing the jury that P could not recover for false imprisonment because he had consented to be taken to another state and left there?

Holding: Yes.

Rule: A person does not consent to be restrained where he submits only because of "words or acts which he fears to disregard."

8. The court's reasoning.   Here summarize the court's thinking, noting both the steps of logic the court went through and the public policies the court thought it was advancing through its decision.

9. Judgment or order.   What did the court do as a result of its holding? Usually, it will be enough for you to write "reversed," "affirmed," "motion denied," or whatever order or judgment the court made.

10. Comments.   Did the court write any instructive dicta? Do you agree or disagree with the decision? Why? Does the briefed case give you a deeper understanding of other cases you have already studied in the same course? Does material in a concurring or dissenting opinion add to your understanding?

═══════════════

If an opinion resolves several issues, you will need to go through items 5 through 8 separately for each issue. For example, the middle of a brief of a two-issue decision might look something like this:

Issue #1: . . .   arguments: . . .
                           holding: . . .
                           rule: . . .
                           reasoning: . . .

Issue #2: . . .   arguments: . . .
                           holding: . . .
                           rule: . . .
                           reasoning: . . .

Read the entire opinion at least once before beginning to brief. You might work efficiently by making some temporary notes as you read, but you will waste effort if you start structuring your understanding — which is what briefing does — before you are able to see the decision *as a whole.*

A long-winded brief filled with the court's own words is far less useful than a short one in which you have boiled the opinion down to its essence. In the sample excerpts from a brief that appear on the preceding pages, you might have noticed that the court is quoted only once, but that those quoted words are perhaps the most important ones in the opinion. Briefs are a means, not an end: for you the hard work will be to understand what happened in the case and why, and the brief is only a repository for your analysis. You will waste effort if you spend too much time in writing and too little in thinking. In fact, if you do little more than edit the court's words into a brief, you have probably not understood the case. A better practice is to quote only those words that are absolutely essential to the case's meaning.

Exercise. Briefing Eilers v. Coy

Using the techniques described above, write out a brief of *Eilers v. Coy.*

EILERS v. COY
582 F. Supp. 1093 (D. Minn. 1984)

MacLaughlin, District Judge. The plaintiff in this case, William Eilers, has moved [for] a directed verdict against the defendants on his claims that the defendants falsely imprisoned him. . . .

. . . The plaintiff [was] abducted . . . in Winona, Minnesota in the early afternoon of Monday, August 16, 1982, by [his] parents . . . and by the defendant deprogrammers who had been hired by the parents. . . . The plaintiff was 24 years old at the time. . . .

At the time of the abduction, [the plaintiff was a member] of the religious group Disciples of the Lord Jesus Christ. There is ample evidence that this group is an authoritarian religious fellowship directed with an iron hand by Brother Rama Behera. There is also evidence that Bill Eilers' personality, and to some extent his appearance, changed substantially after he became a member of the group. These changes were clearly of great concern to members of the plaintiff's family. However, other than as they may have affected the intent of the parents . . . in the actions they took . . . , the beliefs and practices of the Disciples of the Lord Jesus Christ should not be, and are not, on trial in this case.

[In] Winona . . . on August 16, 1982, the plaintiff, who was on crutches at the time due to an earlier fall, was grabbed from behind by two or more security men, forced into a waiting van, and driven to the Tau Center in Winona, Minnesota. Forcibly resisting, he was carried by four men to a room on the top floor of the dormitory-style building. The windows of this room were boarded over with plywood, as were the windows in his bathroom and in the hallway of the floor. The telephone in the hallway had been dismantled.

The plaintiff was held at the Tau Center for five and one-half days and subjected to the defendants' attempts to deprogram him. Shortly after his arrival at the Tau Center, and after a violent struggle with his captors, the plaintiff was handcuffed to a bed. He remained handcuffed to the bed for at least the first two days of his confinement. During this initial period, he was allowed out of the room only to use the bathroom, and was heavily guarded during those times. On one occasion, the plaintiff dashed down the hall in an attempt to escape, but was forcibly restrained and taken back to the room. . . .

On the evening of Saturday, August 21, 1982, as the plaintiff was leaving the Tau Center to be transported to Iowa City, Iowa for further deprogramming, he took advantage of his first opportunity to escape and jumped from the car in which he was riding. . . .

. . . [W]ithin three weeks before the abduction occurred, the plaintiff's relatives had contacted authorities in Trempealeau County, Wisconsin [where he was living at the time] in an attempt to have the plaintiff civilly committed. Family members have testified that they believed the plaintiff was suicidal because of a letter he had written to his grandmother before joining the Disciples of the Lord Jesus Christ in which he wrote that demons were attacking his mind and telling him to kill himself rather than go to the Lord. . . . Joyce Peterson, a psychiatric social worker, interviewed the plaintiff in person on July 26, 1982. After interviewing the plaintiff and consulting with the Trempealeau County Attorney, Peterson informed the plaintiff's relatives that no legal grounds existed in Wisconsin for confining the plaintiff because he showed no signs of being a danger to himself or to others. The defendants in this case were aware of that information at the time they abducted and held the plaintiff. . . .

. . . [G]iven that the defendants falsely imprisoned the plaintiff, were their actions legally justified so as to preclude liability for false imprisonment? As justification for their actions, the defendants rely on the defense of necessity. They claim that the confinement and attempted deprogramming of the plaintiff [were] necessary to prevent him from committing suicide or from otherwise harming himself or others. . . .

The defense of necessity has three elements. The first element is that the defendants must have acted under the reasonable belief that there was a danger of imminent physical injury to the plaintiff or to others. [Citations omitted.]

It is not clear that such a danger existed on August 16, 1982. The alleged threats of suicide made by the plaintiff were contained in a letter dated June 14, 1982, and that letter recounted impressions the plaintiff had had some time earlier. Moreover, Joyce Peterson, the psychiatric social worker who personally interviewed the plaintiff on July 26, 1982, concluded in her report, and reported to the plaintiff's relatives, that the plaintiff was not dangerous to himself or to others. Nevertheless, viewing the evidence in the light most favorable to the defendants, the Court will assume for purposes of this motion that the plaintiff was in imminent danger of causing physical injury to himself or to others.

The second and third elements of the necessity defense are intertwined. The second element is that the right to confine a person in order to prevent harm to that person lasts only as long as is necessary to get the person to the proper lawful authorities. . . . The third element is that the actor must use the least restrictive means of preventing the apprehended harm. [Citations omitted.]

In this case, the defendants' conduct wholly fails to satisfy either of these elements of the necessity defense. Once having gained control of the plaintiff, the defendants had several legal options available to them. They could have:

(1) turned the plaintiff over to the police;

(2) sought to initiate civil commitment proceedings against the plaintiff pursuant to Minn. Stat. § 253B.07 (1982);

(3) sought professional psychiatric or psychological help for the plaintiff

with the possibility of emergency hospitalization if necessary pursuant to Minn. Stat. § 253B.05 (1982).

At no time did the defendants attempt, or even consider attempting, any of these lawful alternatives during the five and one-half days they held the plaintiff, the first five of which were business days. Instead, they took the plaintiff to a secluded location with boarded-up windows, held him incommunicado, and proceeded to inflict their own crude methods of "therapy" upon him — methods which even the defendants' own expert witness has condemned. Well aware that the police were searching for the plaintiff, the defendants deliberately concealed the plaintiff's location from the police.

. . . [T]he Minnesota Legislature has prescribed specific procedures that must be followed before a person can be deprived of his or her liberty on the basis of mental illness. Minn. Stat. § 253B.07 et seq. (1982). . . . Those procedures include examination of the proposed patient by qualified professionals, Minn. Stat. § 253B.07, subd. 1 (1982), and a judicial determination that the proposed patient is dangerous and in need of treatment, *id.*, subd. 6. Manifold procedural protections, including the right to counsel, Minn. Stat. § 253B.03, subd. 9 (1982), are afforded the proposed patient at all stages of this civil commitment proceeding. Obviously, none of these protections were afforded the plaintiff in this case.

Minnesota law also provides that, in situations where there is not time to obtain a court order, a person may be admitted or held for emergency care and treatment in a hospital, without a court order, upon a written statement by a licensed physician or psychologist that the person is mentally ill and is in imminent danger of causing injury to himself or to others. Minn. Stat. § 253B.05, subd. 1 (1982). The defendants in this case — unlicensed and untrained individuals — made no effort to obtain any such statements from a licensed physician or psychologist.

The defendants' failure to even attempt to use the lawful alternatives available to them is fatal to their assertion of the necessity defense. Where the Legislature has prescribed specific procedures that must be followed before a person can be deprived of his or her liberty on the ground of mental illness, not even parents or their agents acting under the best of motives are entitled to disregard those procedures entirely.

The Court has assumed for the purpose of this motion that the defendants were justified in initially restraining the plaintiff based upon their belief that he was in imminent danger of harming himself or others. But even under those circumstances, the defense of necessity eventually dissipates as a matter of law. No specific time limit can be set, because the period during which an actor is acting out of necessity will vary depending on the circumstances of each case. In this particular case, however, where the defendants held the plaintiff, a 24-year-old adult, for five and one-half days with no attempt to resort to lawful alternatives available to them, the Court could not sustain a jury verdict in the defendants' favor on the issue of false imprisonment. Accordingly, the Court rules as a matter of law that the plaintiff was falsely imprisoned without justification. The issue of what amount of damages, if any, the plaintiff suffered from this false imprisonment is a question for the jury. . . .

> *Based on the foregoing, . . . the plaintiff's motion for a directed verdict is granted as to his claim for false imprisonment. . . .*

========================

After briefing a decision, ask yourself how it fits into the subject you are learning. Why did the editor of the casebook include the decision you briefed? What lesson does it teach you about the law? If the preceding decision or decisions involve similar issues, how does the one you have just briefed expand on what you learned from the others? What, for example, did you learn about false imprisonment from *Meints,* and how does *Eilers* add to that? In other words, step back far enough to see the larger picture.

II

INTRODUCTION TO LEGAL WRITING

5 The Art of Legal Writing

§5.1 The Language as a Professional Tool

Contrary to the aphorism, a lawyer's stock-in-trade is neither time nor advice. It is words: writing them, speaking them, and interpreting them. That is true not only because legal work involves so much reading and writing, but — more importantly — because words are the most fundamental tool lawyers use to gain advantage for their clients. The constant question for a lawyer is how to use words to cause a result, whether in court, in negotiation, in drafting a contract or a will, or in writing an appellate brief.

Lawyers are fond of comparing words to surgeons' tools: "Words are the principal tools of lawyers and judges, whether we like it or not. They are to us what the scalpel and insulin are to the doctor."[1] Law is "one of the principal literary professions. One might hazard the supposition that the average lawyer in the course of a lifetime does more writing than a novelist. . . . He must use that double-edged tool, the English language, with all the precision of any surgeon handling a scalpel."[2] "Language is the lawyer's scalpel. If he cannot use it skillfully, he is apt to butcher his suffering client's case."[3]

Because litigation is not done in secret, a large number of a lawyer's writings become public records, available in courthouses for anyone who is interested. Every law library holds thousands of volumes of opinions in which courts quote and interpret the written words of lawyers, both great and or-

§5.1 1. Zachariah Chafee, Jr., *The Disorderly Conduct of Words,* 41 Colum. L. Rev. 381, 382 (1941).

2. William L. Prosser, *English As She Is Wrote,* 7 J. Leg. Ed. 155, 156 (1954).

3. Irving R. Kaufman, *Appellate Advocacy in the Federal Courts,* 79 F.R.D. 165, 170 (1978).

dinary. And much of this writing is done according to standards that are not consistent with the way students are taught to write before they come to law school.

As a professional tool, the English language is remarkably adaptable. Less rigid than many other languages, English often provides dozens of different methods of expressing roughly the same idea, each one conveying a nuance slightly different from the others. That is possible because English allows sentences and clauses to be constructed in a multitude of ways and because English has a huge vocabulary, having inherited from Norman French and Old English and having borrowed heavily from Latin and Greek. But that very flexibility creates risks each time you try to write precisely. Although a careful writer can find a way to express a difficult idea through all of English's options in structure, vocabulary, and nuance, a careless writer of English is easily tempted — because of those options — into writing mush.

In few fields is that as true as it is in law. If obscurity and other faults in your writing distract the reader's attention, you and your client will suffer for several reasons.

First, the typical reader begins to resist and may not finish reading because lawyers and judges are busy people who do not have time to wade through poor writing. Simply put, "[b]ad writing is not read."[4] Those readers will expect you to express difficult ideas so that they are quickly and fully understood. Second, mediocre writing implies mediocrity in general as a lawyer. In law, readers are quick to draw that inference and will dismiss a bad writer as an unreliable professional. Third, the busy reader may misunderstand what you are trying to say. (You might underestimate that danger because most students have not had much experience making important decisions based on the rapid reading of complex documents.) Legal writing should give the viewer a quick and clear view, without distractions, of the idea behind it. Legal writing works well only if it transmits thoughts with the clarity of Orwell's pane of glass.[5]

In law and in law school, what counts is what *works*. Legal writing is put to practical tests in a real world. Office memoranda must provide everything needed to advise a client or plan litigation. Motion memoranda and appellate briefs must persuade judges to decide in the client's favor. And contracts, wills, opinions, statutes, and regulations must create or define legal rights and obligations. If these documents are to do their jobs, they must be able to withstand attack from what has been called the "reader in bad faith" — the opposing attorney who would like to distort an ambiguous phrase into something the writer never meant, the unsympathetic judge looking for a misstatement on which to base an adverse ruling, "and all the others who will want to twist the meaning of words for their own ends."[6] In law, good writing is power. If other lawyers are better at it than you are, you will be at their mercy.

You are, of course, at somewhat of a disadvantage in the beginning because you have no firsthand experience with the type of reader you are

4. Donald N. McCloskey, *The Writing of Economics* 3 (1987).
5. "Good prose is like a windowpane." George Orwell, *Why I Write* (1947), in *The Orwell Reader* 390, 395 (1956).
6. Henry Weihofen, *Legal Writing Style* 8 (2d ed. 1980).

writing for. Whether judge or supervisor, however, the typical reader of your future work is marked by five characteristics. First, the reader must make a decision and wants from you exactly the material needed for the decision — not less and not more. Second, the reader is a busy person, must read quickly, and cannot afford to read twice. Third, the reader is aggressively skeptical and — with the predatory instincts of a shark — will search for any gap or weakness in your analysis. (That is not because lawyers are particularly nasty people: skepticism simply causes better decisions.) Fourth, the reader will be disgusted by sloppiness, imprecision, inaccuracy, or anything that impedes the reader's decision-making process or hints that you might be unreliable. And fifth, the reader will be conservative about matters of grammar, style, citation form, and document format.

No one will try to straightjacket you into a single style of writing. There are many different ways of doing any legal writing chore effectively, and many more of doing it badly. But there are objective standards that can be used to separate writing that *works* from writing that does not. Although reasonable lawyers, teachers, and judges might disagree about a few small points, you will find among them a surprising amount of agreement about professional standards of writing. That should hardly be surprising, since all these people must use writing for similar practical purposes, and since all of them are familiar with the consequences of mediocre writing.

An ability to write well is often essential to a young lawyer looking for a job. When asked which skills are most important to the practice of law, lawyers list oral and written communication ahead of anything else. And when law firms are asked which skills they expect applicants to have learned before starting work, they most often name oral and written communication and library research. Employers routinely require applicants to submit writing samples. And when you scan employment announcements looking for your first job, you will see phrases like the following over and over: "seeks attorney with proven writing ability," "excellent research and writing skills required," "recruiting for associate with superb writing skills." It has been said that "good writing pays well and bad writing pays badly."[7]

The demands of lawyerly writing come as a shock to many law students. Not only are there new writing skills to be learned in law school, but if you have had trouble with your writing in the past, now is the time to learn to do it right. In fact, this is probably your *last* opportunity before your writing begins to affect your career.

Your goal now is to learn the essence of professional writing: how to write *to make things happen.*

§5.2 Predictive Writing and Persuasive Writing

Lawyers are regularly asked to predict what a court will do. For example, a newspaper might ask its attorneys whether, if it publishes a particular

7. Donald N. McCloskey, *The Writing of Economics* 2 (1987).

article, it will have to pay damages for defamation or invasion of privacy to some of the people mentioned in the article. If the answer is yes, the newspaper will want to know what changes in the article would prevent that. Clients also ask lawyers to investigate the value of litigating. After the article is published, a person mentioned in it might ask a lawyer whether a lawsuit against the newspaper is likely to succeed. In each of these situations, a client will make a decision relying on an attorney's prediction of how the courts will rule. If the newspaper is sued, lawyers on both sides will make further predictions in order to plan their litigation strategies.

For two reasons, lawyers record, in writing, their predictions and the reasoning behind them. The first is preservation for the future. Predictions tend to be used more than once. The same prediction (and the reasoning supporting it) might be used in deciding whether to sue, in drafting the complaint, in responding to motions to dismiss or for summary judgment, in conducting discovery, in negotiating with opposing counsel, in planning the trial, and in pursuing an appeal — all of which may stretch over a period of years. In addition, two or more lawyers might work for the same client, and the lawyer who makes the initial prediction will need to record it in detail for supervisors and colleagues.

The second reason for reducing predictions to writing is that the act of writing improves the quality of the prediction. *The writing process and the thinking process are inseparable:* when an idea is spoken about, it might be half-formed, but if it is written about with care, it will have to become fully developed. The number of variables to be considered can make predictive judgments so complex that an attorney is lost unless thoughts can be worked out on paper. It is not unusual for an attorney to start writing on the basis of a tentative prediction already made, only to find, after much writing — and rewriting — that the prediction "won't write" and must be changed.

Predictive writing is sometimes called objective writing, but objectivity only partly defines the genre. Any writing that makes a disinterested report of what the law is can be classified as objective. Predictive writing does more than that: it foretells how the law will resolve a particular controversy.

Suppose the newspaper publishes the article and is sued. Whenever in this litigation a court is asked to make an important decision, each party will submit documents intended to persuade the court to rule in that party's favor. This, not surprisingly, is called persuasive writing. The documents' intended audience is the judge (in the trial court) or the judges (on appeal) who will rule on the controversy, together with the law clerks or research attorneys who assist them. Persuasive writing contains *argument,* rather than prediction.

Persuasive writing and predictive writing have some things in common. For both, the typical reader is skeptical, busy, and cautious, and, in both situations, that person reads for the purpose of making a decision and expects the document to be useful.

But persuasive writing and predictive writing also differ in fundamental ways. The goal of predictive writing is to foretell what will really happen, whether pleasant or unpleasant. If the newspaper will become liable for damages, it might do things before publication to limit its exposure if the editors are warned beforehand. And if a person mentioned in the article is not likely to be awarded damages, he will want to know that before deciding whether to sue. In persuasive writing, on the other hand, the goal is to influence the court to make a favorable decision. Persuasive writing requires all the skills needed for predictive writing, but it requires others as well: strategic thinking, for example, and the ability to make compelling arguments.

§5.3   The Art Forms of Legal Writing

Predictive writing is done in *office memoranda*. Persuasive writing appears in two kinds of documents: *motion memoranda* submitted to trial courts and *appellate briefs*[1] submitted to appellate courts. Motion memoranda and appellate briefs become public records, kept in the court clerk's files. But an office memorandum is a confidential document not normally distributed outside the lawyer's office.

Chapters 7-16 explain how to write an office memorandum. Chapters 18-20 introduce essential concepts of persuasive writing. Chapters 21-24 explain how to write motion memoranda. And Chapters 25-27 do the same for appellate briefs.

Think of memoranda and briefs as manuals to guide the reader's decision-making. Generally, memoranda and briefs, like manuals, are read intermittently and piecemeal. Unlike essays, they are not read from beginning to end. The reader may open up a particular memorandum or brief on several different occasions, and the reader's purpose at any given time determines the portions of the document that will be read and the order in which they will be read. In that way, these documents are very much like an owner's manual for an appliance or for an automobile. The reader's need at the moment may be limited, and it must be satisfied without having to read the entire document.

Lawyers write a wide range of other things too: contracts, wills, trusts, pleadings, motions, interrogatories, affidavits, stipulations, judicial opinions, orders, judgments, opinion letters for clients, statutes, administrative regulations, and more. But with the possible exception of opinion letters and judicial opinions — which have some things in common with the Discussion portion of an office memorandum — instruction in these other forms of legal writing must wait until after you have learned much more about law and procedure and are able to enroll in upper-class drafting courses, clinics, and simulation courses.

---

§5.3   1. This is *not* the type of brief explained in Chapter 4.

6 The Process of Writing

§6.1 Writing in Four Stages

Writing happens in four stages: (1) analyzing the issues and the raw materials that can be used to resolve the issues and raw materials; (2) organizing them so that they can be written about; (3) producing a first draft; and (4) rewriting through several further drafts until the final product is achieved. To some extent, these stages overlap. You will, for example, continue to analyze while organizing, writing the first draft, and rewriting, although most of the analytical work comes at the beginning.

This chapter explores the four stages (in §§6.2-6.5) and concludes with some general advice about writing (in §6.6).

§6.2 Analyzing

The writing process and the thinking process are inseparable. Or, as Donald McCloskey has put it, "writing is thinking."[1]

A supervising attorney gives you an assignment to write a memorandum or a brief. You read the statutes and cases, and you look at the facts carefully. What are the issues? How can the authorities be interpreted? What infer-

---

§6.2 1. Donald N. McCloskey, *The Writing of Economics* 3 (1987).

ences can be drawn from the facts? What interpretations and inferences are most likely to persuade a court?

Chapters 10-13 explain how to answer questions like these. And §9.4 illustrates how to integrate them into the writing process. Later, when you do persuasive writing, you will also learn strategic analysis in Chapters 18-19.

In the meantime, consider this: effective analysis depends on a willingness to peel away assumptions and appearances while opening up several different ways of looking at things. This is what Robert Heidt calls "recasting":[2]

Mr. Projectionist, roll the film please:

Fade In.

Five people walk into an open and uncrowded public park in the afternoon. One sets a stepstool on a pathway, ascends the stepstool, and begins to criticize U.S. foreign policy and to urge listeners to resist that policy. A small crowd gathers. Shouts hostile to the person on the stepstool emerge from the crowd. Shouts hostile to those shouts emerge from others in the crowd. A policeman on the scene arrests the person on the stepstool, directs her to a police car, and drives her away.

Dissolve.

What did we just see? How do we describe what the person on the stepstool did?

To her attorney, she merely exercised her constitutionally protected right to free speech. All she did was talk. She didn't hit, touch, or threaten. . . . If any crimes or civil violations occurred, they were the illegal arrest committed by the police who should have protected, rather than arrested her, and the assaults and emotional distress torts committed by anyone in the crowd who threatened or outrageously insulted her.

To the prosecutors, she breached the peace, incited to riot, and engaged in disorderly conduct. . . . She may also have obstructed a public right of way, committed a public nuisance, and participated in an unlawful assembly. Because she came in a group, she probably also violated the separate laws against conspiring to commit these offenses. . . .

A passerby accidentally injured when the crowd dispersed, or when the crowd's presence blocked the pathway, would describe what she did differently. To the passerby, she negligently caused physical injury. After all, by foreseeably gathering the crowd, she increased the risk that the passerby would suffer the injury he did. Likewise, a listener intentionally injured by a member of the crowd might describe her conduct as negligent use of language which foreseeably angered the one who struck him. . . . A listener indirectly referred to and criticized by her remarks might describe her behavior as slander or, failing that, intentional infliction of emotional distress.

These examples barely scratch the surface of the possible descriptions of what the woman in the park did. If she was profane, she may be guilty of obscenity. If she called for a strike, she may have committed an unfair labor

2. Robert Heidt, *Recasting Behavior: An Essay for Beginning Law Students,* 49 U. Pitt. L. Rev. 1065 (1988).

practice. If she called for a boycott, she may have conspired to restrain trade. If she spoke loudly, she may have violated a noise ordinance. If she or her friends handed out leaflets, we may describe what she did as littering. . . . Had this not been a largely unregulated public park, she might also have violated a host of permit laws as well as other laws regulating the time, place and manner of such expression.

[The goal for the moment] is not to discuss whether these various claims would necessarily succeed but to awaken you to the many different ways a lawyer can recast, that is, describe, phenomena. Our language and our law are wonderfully rich for this purpose. As an aspiring lawyer, you want to cultivate your capacity to recast phenomena in as many different ways as possible. You cannot rely on your client for this. It is part of your job. The client may bring you the phenomena. The client may, in effect, show you the film excerpt we've just seen. But it is up to you, the lawyer, to conceive the different recastings, the different descriptions of phenomena, the different stories that can be told. . . .[3]

The biggest impediment to this kind of thinking is "the false assumption that . . . facts are facts, and that they can be, or ought to be, described in just a couple of ways."[4] That assumption will lock you into the first credible idea that comes into your mind, and it will blind you to all the other possibilities.

§6.3 Organizing

Good organization is crucial in legal writing. There are two reasons.

First, legal writing is a highly *structured* form of expression. As you learned in Chapter 2, rules of law are by nature structured ideas. And any effective discussion of them is also unavoidably structured and requires a well-organized presentation.

Second, legal writing is judged entirely by how well it educates and convinces the reader that your reasoning is correct. The final product must be designed so that it can be easily digested by the reader, and that cannot happen without good organization. In college, teachers criticize organization infrequently. But the reader of lawyerly writing is different from the reader for whom college essays are written. To the law-trained reader, unplanned writing resembles an irritating and inaccessible stream-of-consciousness, rather than something useful.

Students are told to outline but often resist doing it. Outlining seems like an arbitrary and useless requirement. If you dislike outlining, the problem may be that you were taught an outlining method that is unnecessarily rigid. Rigid methods of outlining demand that you draw an outline tree with ro-

3. *Id.* at 1065-67.
4. *Id.* at 1067-68.

man numerals, capital letters, arabic numerals, lower-case letters, and italic numerals. That stifles creativity, and it is *not* the way effective writers write.

A fluid outlining method is simpler and *helps* you write. A fluid outline is a flexible collection of lists. Your raw materials (cases, facts, hypotheses, and so on) flow through it and into your first draft.

Chapter 9 explains the most effective methods of organizing analytical legal writing, and §9.4 explains how to make a fluid outline.

§6.4   *The First Draft*

Many students treat the first draft as the most important part of writing. But that is wrong: the first draft is actually the *least* important part. Analysis, organizing, and rewriting all do much more to cause an effective final product.

Your only goal during the first draft is get things down on the page so that you can start rewriting. The first draft has no other value. Regardless of how many faults it has, the first draft accomplishes its entire purpose merely by coming into existence.

The main problem in first drafts is the occasional experience of feeling blocked. Sometimes, you sit down to write, and nothing happens. You stare at the page or the computer screen, and it seems to stare right back at you. This does not mean that you are an inadequate writer. It happens regularly to everyone. Try working on another part of the document. If, for example, you are blocked when you attempt to write on your first issue, turn to the third one instead.

If that does not work, do something unrelated for a while. Prepare for class, do the dishes, or jog. While you are doing that, your unconscious will continue to work on the first draft. (This is called incubation.) After a while, ideas will come into your head, unexpectedly, and you will need to sit down and start writing again. (But be careful: in law, you are usually writing against a deadline, and an intermission to do something else cannot go on too long.)

If you are chronically blocked when you try to do first drafts, it might be because you expect yourself to produce, in one draft, a polished final version. That is expecting too much. Even the most talented writers cannot do it. "We tend to freeze when we write because once we put words down on the page they seem *permanent*. But permanence is an illusion."[1] Remember that the first draft is the least important part of writing. You can afford to write horribly in the first draft because during *re*writing you will change it all "again and again until you get it to say what you mean it to say."[2]

---

§6.4   1. Michael H. Cohen, *Creative Writing for Lawyers* 25 (1991) (emphasis in original).
2. *Id.*

§6.5 Rewriting

There is no such thing as good writing. There is only good rewriting.

— *Justice Louis Brandeis*

A clear sentence is no accident. Very few sentences come out right the first time, or the third.

— *William Zinsser*

In college, you might have completed assignments "by turning in what were basically first drafts, lightly edited to fix glaring errors."[1] As you will see in a moment, that will not work when you are creating a professional product.

A first draft is for the writer: you write to put your thoughts on the page. But in subsequent drafts, the focus shifts to the reader. Will he or she become convinced that you are right? Will the reader understand what you say without having to read twice?

To answer these questions, impersonate — while you read your work — the reader for whom you are writing. Will this skeptical person see issues that you have not addressed? Will this busy person become impatient at having to wade through material of marginal value that somehow got into your first draft? Will this careful person be satisfied that you have written accurately and precisely?

You will do a better job of impersonating the reader if, between drafts, you stop writing for a day or two, clear your mind by working on something else, and come back to do the next draft both "cold" and "fresh." Obviously, that cannot happen if you put off starting the project and later have to put it together frantically at the last minute. To make sure that you have time to rewrite, start on an assignment as soon as you get it, and then pace yourself, working at regular intervals within the time allotted.

(There is another benefit to starting early and working steadily: it is the most effective method of reducing anxiety. Many students procrastinate because they worry about writing. But procrastination just increases tension because it prevents you from bringing the task under control — which you can do only by working on it.)

Do not be afraid to ax material from your first draft. The fact that you have written something does not mean that you have to keep it.

And do not be afraid to change your mind about your analysis of the law and the facts. Most writers have experienced the abandonment of an idea that felt valuable when thought about, sounded valuable when spoken, but nevertheless proved faulty when — in the end — it "wouldn't write." Most writers have experienced the obverse as well: sitting down to write with a single idea and finding that the act of writing draws the idea out, fertilizes it, causes it to sprout limbs and roots, to germinate, and to spread into a

---

§6.5 1. Steven V. Armstrong & Timothy P. Terrell, *Thinking Like a Writer* 9-18 (1992).

forest of ideas. The amount of understanding reflected in a good final draft is many times the amount that surfaced in the first draft because the writing process and the thinking process are inseparable, each stimulating and advancing the other. ("You do not learn the details of an argument until writing it in detail, and in writing the details you uncover flaws in the fundamentals."[2])

A writer produces a first draft by putting down on paper ideas so fragmentary that one might be ashamed of them. They might not even be quarter-baked — much less half-baked — but on paper they will at least be out in the open. At that point, a writer who is *satisfied* is engaged in self-delusion. But an undeluded writer will rewrite, and rewrite, and rewrite — and rewrite again. After a while, the product becomes moderately lucid and perhaps only then does the writer even begin to understand the ideas being written about.

While rewriting, use the lettered checklists on the inside front and back covers of this book to test your writing for good organization, paragraphing, style, and use of quotations. (If you are writing an office memorandum, a checklist on the inside back cover will also help you test your writing for predictiveness.) Use Appendix A (and a legal dictionary) to make sure that you are using legal terminology properly. Use Appendix B to check your writing for punctuation errors. And use the Bluebook to make sure that your citations are in proper form.[3]

And step back and consider your tone: does it make you sound like a responsible and prudent person — the kind of person the reader can rely upon?

Eventually, you will notice, after putting the writing through several drafts, that after a certain point the problems you are finding are mostly typographical errors and small matters of grammar, style, and citation. When that happens, you are working on the natural final draft, and the job is nearly finished. But do not rush this. Now that your attention is focused on details, make sure that they are right. In professional work, harsh consequences can grow out of small faults (such as misplaced commas and decimal points that turn ten thousand dollars into ten million dollars).

§6.6 Some General Advice about Writing

> Writing is easy. You just sit at a typewriter until blood appears on your forehead.
>
> — *Red Smith*

It is not *that* hard. But at times it can *feel* that way. If you know the sensation Red Smith describes, that does not mean that you are a bad writ-

---

2. Donald N. McCloskey, *The Writing of Economics* 4 (1987).
3. The Bluebook is the standard manual of legal citation. Chapter 16 explains how to use it.

er. Red Smith was the leading sports journalist of his time. Every day, millions of people opened their newspapers to read what he had written the night before. Obviously, he was not a bad writer — and still he knew that feeling. (So has nearly everybody else whose writing you have ever enjoyed reading.)

Learning how to write like a lawyer is the beginning of learning how to make professional decisions. Professional work differs from other methods of earning a living partly because a professional must constantly decide — in very unclear situations — how to proceed. (We pay professionals like doctors and lawyers because they know how to figure that out.) There is no easy, simple, cookbook-like formula for writing well. When you write — and in every other part of the practice of law — you will be confronted continually with a range of choices about what to do. And your success as a lawyer will depend on your ability to understand the choices available and to select wisely among them. Now is a good time to start learning how.

As you write and rewrite, avoid the temptation to imitate unquestioningly whatever you happen to find in judicial opinions that appear in your casebooks. Those opinions are in casebooks for what they tell you about the law — not for what they tell you about how to write. In the last decade or so, there has been a revolution in the way lawyers and judges look at writing. Verbosity, obscurity, arcaneness, and disorganization that were tolerated a generation ago are now viewed as flatly unacceptable because they make the reader's job harder and sometimes impossible. That means that before you adopt a practice or device that you have seen in an opinion, you should ask yourself *whether you are tempted to do so because it will actually accomplish your purpose or because you feel safer doing what a judge has done.* The latter is not a sound basis for a professional decision. To get an idea of how things have changed since many of the opinions in your casebooks were written, read the opening paragraphs below of two decisions on the same issue.[1] One opinion is written in a style that was once common, while the other has the clarity and forthrightness that supervisors and judges will expect of you:

UNITED STATES v. ASKEY	UNITED STATES v. PALMER
108 F. Supp. 408	*864 F.2d 524*
(S.D. Tex. 1952)	*(7th Cir. 1988)*

ALLRED, District Judge. Counts 1 and 2 of the indictment charged defendant with violating 18 U.S.C. § 1708. Counts 3 and 4 charged violation of 18 U.S.C. § 495. The court sustained a motion to dismiss

EASTERBROOK, Circuit Judge. About a month after settling into a house, Mildred Palmer found in her mailbox three envelopes addressed to Clifton Powell, Jr., the former occupant. Instead of returning the

---

§6.6 1. The issue is whether a person who steals mail after it has been delivered by the post office has violated 18 U.S.C. § 1708 (1988), which penalizes stealing "from or out of any mail, post office, or station thereof, letter box, mail receptacle, or any mail route or other authorized depository for mail matter, or from a letter or mail carrier."

Count 2 and submitted the remaining counts to a jury which found defendant guilty as charged. The court had carried defendant's motion for judgment of acquittal on Count 1 along with the case. After receiving the verdict, the court announced that the verdict would be set aside as to Count 1. Defendant was sentenced on Counts 3 and 4. The purpose of this memorandum is to reflect the basis of the court's ruling on Counts 1 and 2. . . .

Omitting formal parts, Count 2 charges that defendant unlawfully abstracted and removed "from a letter addressed to Annice Beatrice Brown . . . the contents of such letter" — a described Treasury check. There is no allegation that the letter, from which defendant abstracted the Treasury check, was a *mailed* letter or one which had been removed from some office, station, letter box, receptacle or authorized depository. The language . . . from the statute prohibits the abstracting or removing from "such letter," clearly referring back to the first part of the statute, dealing with letters *in the mails,* or taken from some post office, receptacle or depository. In other words, it would be no offense to remove the contents of a letter never deposited for mailing or transmitted through the mails; yet, that is all that is charged in Count 2. It charges no offense.

Count 1 sufficiently charges the taking of a described letter from an authorized depository for mail. The motion for verdict of acquittal goes to the sufficiency of the evidence as to whether the place from which defendant removed the letter was an authorized depository for mail matter.

envelopes to the Postal Service, Palmer opened them. She found three checks (technically, warrants on Illinois's treasury) — no surprise, for the envelopes in which Illinois mails checks are distinctive. The district court described what happened next:

> Richard Morrison was present when Palmer brought the mail into the house and knew she had received the state warrants. Palmer and Morrison discussed negotiating the warrants and getting the proceeds. Someone endorsed Clifton Powell, Jr.'s name without his authority on the reverse side of each warrant. The warrants were then delivered by Morrison to a man named Lawrence Armour, Sr. Armour had something which neither Palmer nor Morrison had: a bank account. For a fee Armour negotiated the three state warrants through his bank account and returned the balance of the proceeds to Morrison who shared them with Palmer.

The United States charged Palmer and Morrison with possession of checks stolen from the mails, in violation of 18 U.S.C. § 1708. The jury found them guilty. . . . We must decide whether converting the contents of an envelope violates § 1708 when the envelope was delivered to an outdated address. . . . The prosecutor believes that the three envelopes were stolen from the "mail" because they had not been delivered to Powell. The defendants emphasize that the envelopes had been delivered to the address they bore and that when Palmer took the envelopes out of the mail box, she did not intend to steal them — for she reasonably believed that everything in the mailbox was hers.

The letter in question, containing a Treasury check, was addressed to Annice Beatrice Brown, 1608 Chipito Street, Corpus Christi, Texas. It was delivered by a city carrier, at the address given, by dropping it through a small letter slot in the wall at the left of the door. It simply dropped on the floor, as did all other mail at this address. No receptacle or box or container was provided.

Annice Beatrice Brown formerly received her mail at this address but had removed from Corpus Christi. Defendant lived with two other men at the Chipito Street address but received his mail at 2310 Nueces Street. He picked up the letter in question. . . .

When Palmer discovered that the envelopes were not, she purloined their contents, but by then the envelopes were no longer part of the mail. If the checks had been addressed to Palmer and had been stolen from her on the way to the bank, the theft would not have violated § 1708; no more does her larceny, she insists.

Palmer and Morrison were not charged with stealing out of a "letter box [or] mail receptacle," which would make Palmer's intent at the time of the withdrawal pertinent. They were charged with stealing out of the "mail." . . .

Which opinion would you rather finish reading? Has one of these judges simply written out the material without seeming to think much about your needs as a reader? If so, what in the opinion prevents you from easily understanding what the judge is trying to say? If you understand the issue better from the other opinion, what did that judge do to make it easier for you? By the way, are you more curious about the outcome of one of these cases than you are about the other?

III

OFFICE MEMORANDA

7 Office Memoranda

§7.1 Office Memorandum Format

Form follows function.

> — *motto of the Bauhaus school of architecture*

This chapter describes the format of an office memorandum and the process of writing one. Chapters 8-13 explain the skills needed to analyze and organize the Discussion part of the memorandum: using rules to predict, organization, selecting and analyzing authority, and analyzing facts. Chapters 14-16 explain three skills — paragraphing, style, and using citations and quotations — that are most important during the rewriting process, as the memorandum evolves into a final draft.

An office memorandum might be read many times over a period of months or years by several different attorneys, including the writer, who may use it as a resource long after it is drafted. A memorandum might be written, for example, after a client has asked whether a lawsuit would be worth commencing. It would be used most immediately for advice to the client. If the result is a suit, some parts of the memorandum might be read again when the complaint is drafted. The memorandum might be consulted a third time when the attorney responds to a motion to dismiss; a fourth time while drafting interrogatories; a fifth time before making a motion for summary judgment; a sixth time before trial; and a seventh time in preparing an appeal.

Although the details of format may vary from law office to law office and from case to case, a thorough office memorandum usually includes the following:

1. a memorandum heading
2. the Issue or Issues = *question prosam*
3. a Brief Answer
4. the Facts
5. a Discussion
6. a Conclusion
7. the author's signature

(The rest of this chapter is easier to follow if you look to the memorandum in Appendix C for illustration as you read the description below of each of these components.)

The *memorandum heading* simply identifies the writer, the immediately intended reader (who is often the writer's supervisor), the date on which the memorandum was completed, and the subject matter.

Question(s) ← The *Issue* (or Issues) states the question (or questions) that the memo-
problem randum resolves. The Issue also itemizes the few facts that you predict to be crucial to the answer. You can phrase the Issue either as a question about how the law treats the problem or about how the courts would rule. A fact-sensitive Issue will include a specific — but short — list of determinative facts. This one asks about how the courts will rule in a case that is especially fact-sensitive:

> Will a constructive trust in favor of Eli Goslin be imposed on the title to his home and only asset, which he deeded over to his nephew after the latter promised to make the remaining three years of payments to prevent foreclosure, where Goslin made no statement at the time that would reveal his reasons for giving the deed, and where the nephew has since then threatened to throw Goslin out of the home?

The following Issue asks how the law treats a matter that is less fact-sensitive:

> Under the Freedom of Information Act, must the FBI release its file on the song *Louie, Louie*?

The *Brief Answer* states the writer's prediction and summarizes concisely why it is likely to happen. This usually involves at least an allusion to the determinative facts and rules, together with some expression of how the facts and rules come together to cause the predicted result. (The complete analysis occurs in the Discussion.)

For the reader in a hurry, the Brief Answer should set out the bottom-line response in the most accessible way. Compare two Brief Answers, both of which respond to the following Issue:

ISSUE

Did the District Attorney act unethically in announcing an indictment at a press conference where the defendant's criminal record was recited, an alleged tape-recorded confession was played, ballistics tests on an alleged murder weapon were described, and the defendant was produced for photographers without the knowledge of her attorney?

BRIEF ANSWER

Under DR 7-107(B) of the Code of Professional Responsibility, it is unethical for a prosecutor before trial to publicize, among other things, any criminal record the defendant might have, any confession she might allegedly have made, or the results of any tests the government might have undertaken. Under DR 1-102(A)(5), it is also unethical to engage in conduct "prejudicial to the administration of justice." That has occurred here if the press conference — and particularly the presentation of the defendant for photographers — created so much pretrial publicity that the jury pool has been prejudiced. Therefore, the District Attorney violated DR 7-107(B) and may have violated DR 1-102(A)(5).

BRIEF ANSWER

Yes. Except for the production of the defendant for photographers, all the actions listed in the Question Presented are specifically prohibited by DR 7-107(B) of the Code of Professional Responsibility. In addition, if producing the defendant for photographers tainted the jury pool, it was unethical under DR 1-102(A)(5), which prohibits conduct "prejudicial to the administration of justice."

The first example is closer to the way you might think through the Brief Answer. But to make it useful to the reader you would have to rewrite it into something like the second example, which can be more quickly read and understood.

The *Facts* set out the facts on which the prediction is based. This part of the memorandum is usually a narrative of what has happened to the client. It should include all facts you consider determinative, together with any explanatory facts needed to help the story make sense.[1] Include dates only if they are determinative[2] or needed to avoid confusion.

§7.1   1. See §13.2.
2. A date could be determinative if the issue is based on time (such as a statute of limitations).

The *Discussion* is the largest and most complex part of the memorandum. It proves the conclusion set out in the Brief Answer. If the discussion is highly detailed or analyzes several issues, it can be broken up with subheadings to help the reader locate the portions that might be needed at any given time. When writing a Discussion, you will use rules to predict what a court will do; organize proof of your conclusion; select authority to back up your conclusion; work with precedent, statutes, and facts; and use citations and quotations. Chapters 8-13 and 16 explain how.

The *Conclusion* summarizes the discussion in a bit more detail than the Brief Answer does. The Brief Answer is designed to inform the reader who needs to know the bottom line but has no time to read more. The Conclusion is for the reader who needs and has time for more detail, but not as much as the Discussion offers. The Conclusion or Brief Answer can also provide an overview for the reader about to plunge into the discussion. Although the Brief Answer is limited to answering the Question Presented, the Conclusion is an appropriate place to suggest alternatives or to recommend among the various options under consideration. If the Conclusion or Brief Answer is conditioned on a fact not yet known, specify the condition ("if producing the defendant for photographers tainted the jury pool").

The *signature* appears under the typed words "Respectfully submitted."

§7.2 Writing an Office Memorandum

Some lawyers tend to write the Discussion before writing anything else; their reason is that the other components of the memorandum will be shaped in part by insights gained while putting the Discussion together. Other lawyers start by writing the Facts because they seem easier to describe. (Lawyers who write the Discussion first would say that they cannot start by writing the Facts because, until they have worked out the Discussion, they do not know which facts are determinative.) Another group of lawyers are flexible. They start with whatever component begins to "jell" first, and they often draft two or more components simultaneously.

As you put the memorandum through its final drafts, you will need to pay particular attention to paragraphing (see Chapter 14), style (Chapter 15), and citations and quotations (Chapter 16). Ask yourself the questions in the checklists in each of these chapters.

8 Predictive Writing

§8.1 How to Predict

The prophecies of what the courts will do in fact, and nothing more pretentious, are what I mean by the law.

— *Oliver Wendell Holmes*

The difference between predictive writing and persuasive writing is explained in §5.2.

What kind of reasoning creates a prediction about how a court will rule? Before beginning to write — for this is an example of the analytical process mentioned in §6.2 — develop arguments for *each* side on every issue. Think of the reasons why your client should win. And think of the reasons why the opposing party should win. (You are predicting which arguments will persuade a court, and you can do that only if you know the arguments both sides will make.) Then, evaluate each argument to see whether it is likely to persuade a judge. Bearing your evaluations in mind, how would a court rule on each issue? Then step back and consider the case as a whole. In light of your predictions on the individual issues, how will the court decide the entire controversy?

For example, assume that, in the jurisdiction in question, the crime of common law burglary has been reduced to statute in the following form (and renamed burglary in the first degree):

> *Criminal Code § 102:* A person commits burglary in the first degree by breaking and entering the dwelling of another in the nighttime with intent to commit a felony therein.

71

And assume that the elements of burglary in the first degree have been statutorily defined as follows:

> *Criminal Code § 101(c):* A "breaking" is the making of an opening, or the enlarging of an opening, so as to permit entry into a building, or a closed off portion thereof, provided that neither owner nor occupant has consented thereto.

> *Criminal Code § 101(g):* An "entering" or an "entry" is the placing, by the defendant, of any part of his body or anything under his control within a building, or a closed off portion thereof, provided that neither owner nor occupant has consented thereto.

> *Criminal Code § 101(e):* A "closed off portion" of a building is one divided from the remainder of the building by walls, partitions, or the like so that it can be secured against entry.

> *Criminal Code § 101(f):* A "dwelling" is any building, or any closed off portion thereof, in which one or more persons habitually sleep.

> *Criminal Code § 101(n):* A dwelling is "of another" if the defendant does not by right habitually sleep there.

> *Criminal Code § 101(m):* "Nighttime" is the period between sunset and sunrise.

> *Criminal Code § 101(k):* "Intent to commit a felony therein" is the design or purpose of committing, within a building or closed off portion thereof, a crime classified in this Code as a felony, provided that the defendant had such design or purpose at the time both of a breaking and of an entering.

Assume further that the legislature has also enacted the following:

> *Criminal Code § 10:* No person shall be convicted of a crime except on evidence proving guilt beyond a reasonable doubt.

> *Criminal Code § 403:* An assault causing substantial injury is a felony.

Finally, assume — for the sake of simplicity — that none of these sections have yet been interpreted by the courts, and that you are therefore limited to the statute itself. (That is an unusual situation. More often, you will also be working with judicial decisions that have interpreted the statute.)

Let us take up Welty's facts from §2.2. A lawyer making a prediction might *think* about it in the following way:

> If we want to know whether Welty will be convicted of first-degree burglary, the controlling rule would be the test for first-degree burglary, which is set out in Criminal Code § 102. It has six elements and no exceptions. [See §2.1.] And in section 101, the legislature has conveniently defined the elements. She is guilty only if each element is

proved beyond a reasonable doubt (section 11). I'll make a list of the elements and annotate it by listing next to each element the facts relevant to it. [Lawyer does that.]

The argument for a breaking is that when she pushed the door back, she enlarged an opening without Lutz's consent, and Lutz's apartment is a closed off portion of a building. The best argument against a breaking is that there is no proof beyond a reasonable doubt that she did not have permission from the owner, if Lutz is only a tenant. But that loses. There's no evidence that an owner knew anything of this, which makes it a speculative doubt and not a reasonable one.

The argument that she entered is that she walked in. There is no contrary argument: she was in the apartment, and there's no evidence that she was pushed in by somebody else. Similarly, his apartment is plainly the dwelling of another, and this was at night.

What she did next is a felony under section 403, but under section 101(k), she is not guilty of first degree burglary unless — at the time she pushed the door open and walked in — she already had the intent to hit him. The argument that she did is that she was already furious and walked right over and punched him, without hesitation. The contrary argument is that something else intervened after the breaking and entering and before the punch: Lutz turned on her and ordered her to leave, and she will testify that she "found this to be too much." That creates reasonable doubt that she had the intent to strike him at the time of the breaking and entering. She may have been angry when she pushed the door open and walked in, but anger does not necessarily include an intent to hit somebody.

Okay, stepping back and looking at the overall picture, the prosecution will be able to prove every element but the last one. And since they will be missing an element, she will be acquitted.

If the lawyer were asked to record that prediction in the Discussion portion of an office memorandum, the lawyer might write something like the following. (Notice the organization.)

Welty will not be convicted of burglary in the first degree because the evidence does not show beyond a reasonable doubt that she had formed the intent to commit a felony when she broke and entered Lutz's apartment. Under section 102 of the Criminal Code, a person is guilty of burglary if he or she (1) breaks and (2) enters (3) the dwelling (4) of another (5) in the nighttime (6) "with intent to commit a felony therein." Under section 11, a defendant can be convicted only "on evidence proving guilt beyond a reasonable doubt."

The first sentence expresses the ultimate conclusion that the entire Discussion is intended to support.

The basic rule governing the controversy.

In a longer Discussion, tell the reader the order in which you will address the issues; here some of that is implied.

A rule of application that permeates the Discussion.

[Handwritten margin notes: INDIVIDUAL COMPONENTS OF ACTION DISCUSSION ITEMS]

Although (as shown below) Welty broke and entered Lutz's dwelling in the night-time, and although the assault she committed there is classified as a felony by section 403, the evidence does not prove beyond a reasonable doubt that she had formed the intent to assault Lutz when she broke and entered. *[Handwritten margin note: RULE = DEFINITION OF INTENT]* Section 101(k) defines "intent to commit a felony therein" as "the design or purpose of committing, within a building or closed off portion thereof, a . . . felony, provided that the defendant had such design or purpose at the time both of a breaking and of an entering." *[Handwritten margin note: APPLICATION]* When Lutz turned around and ordered her to leave while she was protesting his noise, she found this to be "too much" and punched him. A reasonable explanation for her intent is that it was formed after she was already in the room, and no words or action on her part show that she had the intent to punch Lutz before she actually did so. Although, in her rage, she might have contemplated an assault before or when she broke and entered, there is a difference between considering an act and having the "design or purpose of committing" it, and her actions before she struck Lutz show no more than an intent to complain.

Welty's pushing open Lutz's apartment door was, however, a breaking, which section 101(c) defines as "the making of an opening, or the enlarging of an opening, so as to permit entry into a building, or a closed off portion thereof, provided that neither owner nor occupant has consented thereto." Lutz's apartment is a "closed off portion" of a building, which is defined by section 101(e) as "one divided from the remainder of the building by walls, partitions, or the like so that it can be secured against entry." Although Lutz's apartment is not described, it would be difficult to imagine an apartment that is not thus divided from the building in which it is located. During the incident in question, Lutz opened his front door about six inches after Welty knocked on it to complain of noise, and,

The determinative issue is considered first. Why consider first an element that the statute lists last? If one element is unprovable, it becomes the most important element because Welty can be convicted only if all the elements are proven. Why, then, bother to consider the other elements at all? You might be wrong about the element you think is dispositive, and, for reasons explained in Chapter 9, the reader is entitled to a full accounting.

A counter-analysis. (See §9.1.)

Notice how this paragraph begins with the writer's conclusion on the breaking issue, followed by the rule defining a breaking, an application of the rule to the facts, and more than one counter-analysis.

when she walked into his apartment moments later, he immediately ordered her out. The initial opening of six inches would not have been enough to admit Welty, and Lutz's prompt order to leave shows beyond a reasonable doubt that he had not consented to her opening the door farther. And nothing suggests that Welty had consent from an owner of the apartment, who conceivably might have been someone other than Lutz.

Welty's walking into Lutz's apartment was an entry, which section 101(g) defines as "the placing, by the defendant, of any part of his body or anything under his control within a building, or a closed off portion thereof, provided that neither owner nor occupant has consented thereto." Welty walked into Lutz's apartment, and the circumstances do not show consent to an entry for the same reasons that they do not show consent to a breaking.

The other elements are all substantiated beyond a reasonable doubt. First, Lutz's apartment is a dwelling. Section 101(f) defines a dwelling as "any building, or closed off portion thereof, in which one or more persons habitually sleep," and nothing suggests that Lutz does not habitually sleep in his own apartment. Additionally, that apartment is, to Welty, the dwelling of another, as defined by section 101(n), because nothing suggests that she herself habitually sleeps there. Finally, all these events transpired between sunset and sunrise, and therefore within section 101(m)'s definition of nighttime.

> This paragraph is structured like the preceding one, except that for economy it incorporates by reference the parallel analysis set out earlier.

> On these facts, it is not easy to determine whether Welty broke or entered Lutz's apartment, or whether she intended, while doing so, to commit a felony inside. Above, a paragraph has justifiably been devoted to each of those issues. But the other elements are easier: a reader can quickly agree that Lutz's apartment is the dwelling of another and that the incident happened in the nighttime. Although the reader must be told enough about these elements to create confidence in the ultimate conclusion, the analysis can be compressed.

This is only one of many effective ways to organize an explanation of this material. When you write, resist the temptation to copy uncritically the style of this example. It might not be appropriate to your assignment, and another approach might be more appropriate to your analysis. In Chapter 9, you will learn how to expand this type of organization into a paradigm that can be varied in many ways to structure almost any kind of practical discussion involving the application of law to facts.

The issues here are not difficult, and the facts given were few. *Even the earliest writing you do in law school will require both more extensive dis-*

cussion and deeper analysis, using the skills of interpreting authority and analyzing facts that are explained in Chapters 10-13.

§8.2   How to Test Your Writing for Predictiveness

After you have written a first draft — and before you start on later drafts — ask yourself the following questions.[1]

8-A **Have you concentrated on solving a problem, rather than on writing a college essay?** A college essay is a forum for academic analysis — analysis to satisfy curiosity — rather than practical problem-solving. In a college essay, you can reason in any logical manner toward any sensible goal you select, even at whim. But legal writing is practical work, and, although curiosity is an extremely valuable asset in problem-solving, it is not an end in itself. Rather, *your Discussion must be directed toward resolving specific questions.* Words not helpful in resolving those questions should be cut.

8-B **Have you edited out waffling?** Law exists to resolve disputes, and it does not have the leisure that other disciplines do to play indefinitely with gray areas of analysis. (Historians have spent half a century trying to figure out whether it was necessary to drop a nuclear bomb on Hiroshima, and they will probably continue arguing about it forever. But if the issue were tried in court, the jury would have to decide the issue *now.*) Because of the law's need to decide, your thinking will be useful only if you take a position and prove it. Vague and mushy waffling represented by words like "seems to," "appears," and their synonyms makes a lawyer's advice less useful to clients and supervising attorneys. When a lawyer is disagreed with, lightning does not strike the lawyer down on the spot. To the contrary, supervisors and judges are grateful for forthrightness and impatient with hedging. (But it is not waffling to say that "the plaintiff *probably* will win an appeal" or "*is likely to* win an appeal." No prediction can be a certainty.)

8-C **Have you told the reader whether your prediction is qualified in any way?** For precision, a prediction should at least imply the degree of accuracy ascribed to it by the writer. Is the underlying rule a matter of "settled law" and are the facts clear-cut? If the law is not settled, is that because different courts have interpreted it differently or because the authority is scanty? Is the prediction "iffy" or confident? Overt qualifications of accuracy are usually not necessary, since the prediction can be stated in a way that implies your degree of confidence in it. The implication

---

§8.2   1. When writing comments on your work, your teacher might refer to these questions by using the number-letter codes that appear next to each question here.

comes not from "weasel words" like "seems to" or "perhaps" (see item 8-B), but instead from a precise statement of the variables on which the prediction is based ("The defendant should prevail unless . . .").

Have you accounted for gaps in *the law*? Occasionally, the law has gaps — holes that have not yet been filled in by legislation or **8-D** by precedent. Max Weber wrote that, unlike some of the legal structures of continental Europe, the English system of common law has never made a pretense of being a "gapless system of rules."[2] He might have added that one of the glories of the common law is the way it routinely fills in gaps by analogizing from precedent and by synthesizing different holdings into a new rule.[3] To an effective lawyer, gaps present creative opportunities to make new law while obtaining what a client wants. If the lawyer can persuade a court to rule for the client in a case of first impression in the lawyer's jurisdiction, the new precedent thus set fills part or all of a gap, and new law is thus made. Few things are more professionally satisfying to a litigator. On the other hand, students tend to want more certainty in the law and to view these gaps with terror because they make prediction difficult. One of the signs of growing self-confidence and maturity in a young lawyer is an increasing ability to feel comfortable with gaps in the law and to make reliable predictions in spite of them. For that to happen, each gap must be defined and explained, rather than glossed over.

Have you accounted for gaps in *the facts*? You will also encounter gaps in facts. What can you do when a critical or apparently critical **8-E** fact cannot be learned before analysis must be committed to paper? Often you can figure out that the unknown fact is limited to a short list of possibilities, and you can analyze each of these possibilities in writing. For example, if the client is a defendant charged with burglary, he might not know whether the structure involved was used as a dwelling at the time of the alleged breaking and entry: the structure may be in a secluded location, and the owner may refuse to discuss the matter with anyone representing the client. Under local law, although breaking and entering a non-dwelling is undoubtedly criminal, it may be a lower degree of crime — with a less severe punishment — than burglarizing a dwelling. If a memorandum must be written now, you can explore *both* possibilities, and, when the fact is ultimately learned, the answer will already have been analyzed in writing. When this happens, the conclusion can be expressed either alternatively ("If the building turns out to be a dwelling, . . . But if not, . . .") or conditionally ("Unless the building turns out not to be a dwelling, . . ."). The factual gap and the possibilities that might fill it must be clearly identified. (Sometimes, the process of analyzing each possibility will lead you to discover that the unknown fact actually cannot affect the result because all the possibilities lead to the same answer.)

2. Max Weber, *On Law in Economy and Society* 62 (Edward Shils & Max Rheinstein trans. 1954).
3. These techniques are explained in Chapter 11.

8-F **Have you refused to hide from bad news?** Good predictive writing squarely faces two sources of unhappiness. One is weaknesses in the client's case, and the other is arguments that might challenge your conclusion. No one is helped where a prediction turns out to be inaccurate because unpleasant possibilities have been avoided, and these kinds of avoidances are easily spotted by the typical reader, who has learned through experience that few legal conclusions are immune from attack, that every client's case has weaknesses, and that the client is always best protected when the *complete* situation is known from the beginning. That kind of reader is worried by writing that too easily reaches the conclusion that the client is in the right, as well as by writing that does not fully consider arguments that could challenge your conclusion. A writer shows maturity and dependability by exploring in depth both ideas that might put the client in the wrong and ideas that could show the writer to be incorrect. Predictive writing is frank and disinterested *diagnosis.* Advocacy has another time and place.

8-G **Have you ignored red herrings?** A student might feel obligated to discuss every fact, rule, case, and statute available so that the teacher does not think the student has done an incomplete job. "Why is that fact there if you didn't want us to talk about it?" a student might ask a teacher. Sometimes, it is there to test your ability to distinguish between that which is relevant and that which does not matter. Or it might be there merely to duplicate the mosaic of real life, in which the relevant and the irrelevant mingle freely. Because a lawyer is responsible for separating one from the other, you should be able, if asked, to explain how you differentiated between the relevant and the irrelevant. In your writing, address every true issue, but do not waste valuable time and space discussing things that will not affect how the controversy will be resolved.

Exercise I. Nansen and Byrd

1. With the aid of sections 16 and 221(a) of the Criminal Code (below), break down the rule in section 220 into a list of elements and exceptions. Annotate the list by adding definitions for the elements (and for any exceptions you might come across). (Under each element you list, leave lots of white space. When you do the second part of this exercise, you will need room to write more.)

> *Criminal Code § 16:* When a term describing a kind of intent or knowledge appears in a statute defining a crime, that term applies to every element of the crime unless the definition of the crime clearly indicates that the term is meant to apply only to certain elements and not to others.

> *Criminal Code § 220:* A person is guilty of criminal sale of a controlled substance when he knowingly sells any quantity of a controlled substance.

> *Criminal Code § 221(a):* As used in section 220 of this code, "sell" means to exchange for goods or money, to give, or to offer or agree to do the same, except where the seller is a licensed physician dispensing the con-

trolled substance pursuant to a permit issued by the Drug Enforcement Commission or where the seller is a licensed pharmacist dispensing the controlled substance as directed by a prescription issued by a licensed physician pursuant to a permit issued by the Drug Enforcement Commission.

2. You have interviewed Nansen, who lives with Byrd. Neither is a licensed physician nor a licensed pharmacist. At about noon on July 15, both were arrested and charged with criminal sale of a controlled substance. Nansen has told you the following:

> "Byrd keeps a supply of cocaine in our apartment. He had been out of town for a month, and I had used up his stash while he was gone. I knew that was going to bend Byrd completely out of shape, but I thought I was going to get away with it. I had replaced it all with plaster. When you grind plaster down real fine, it looks like coke. For other reasons, I had decided to go to Alaska on an afternoon flight on July 15 and not come back. Byrd was supposed to get back into town on July 16, and by the time he figured out what had happened, I would be in the Tongass Forest.
>
> "But on the morning of the 15th, Byrd opened the door of the apartment and walked in, saying he had decided to come back a day early. I hadn't started packing, yet — I wouldn't have much to pack anyway — but I didn't know how I was going to pack with Byrd standing around because of all the explaining I'd have to do. I also didn't want Byrd hanging around the apartment and working up an urge for some cocaine that wasn't there. So I said, 'Let's go hang out on the street.'
>
> "We had been on the sidewalk about ten or fifteen minutes when a guy came up to us and started talking. He was dressed a little too well to be a regular street person, but he looked kind of desperate. I figured he was looking to buy some drugs. Then I realized that that was the solution to at least some of my problem. I took Byrd aside and said, 'This guy looks like he's ready to buy big. What do you think he'd pay for your stash?' Byrd looked reluctant, so I turned to the guy and said, 'We can sell you about three ounces of coke, but we have to have a thousand for it.' When the guy said, 'Yeah,' Byrd said, 'Wait here' and ran inside the apartment building. A thousand was far more than the stuff was worth.
>
> "Byrd walked out onto the stoop with the whole stash in his hand in the zip-lock bag he kept it in, and while he was walking down the steps, about ten feet away from me and the guy who wanted to buy, two uniforms appeared out of nowhere and arrested Byrd and me."

The "guy" turned out to be Officer D'Asconni, an undercover policeman who will testify to the conversation Nansen has described. The police laboratory reports that the bag contained 2.8 ounces of plaster and 0.007 ounces of cocaine. When you told Nansen about the laboratory report, he said the following:

> "I didn't think there was any coke in that bag. What they found must have been residue. I had used up every last bit of Byrd's stuff. I clearly remember looking at that empty bag after I had used it all and wondering

how much plaster to put in it so that it would at least look like the coke Byrd had left behind. I certainly didn't see any point in scrubbing the bag with cleanser before I put the plaster in it."

With the aid of Criminal Code § 221 (below), finish annotating your list of elements by writing, under each element, the facts that are relevant to that element.

> *Criminal Code § 221:* As used in section 220, "controlled substance" includes any of the following: . . . cocaine. . . .

3. You have been asked to determine whether Nansen or Byrd is likely to be convicted of criminal sale of a controlled substance. The question is not whether Nansen or Byrd criminally sold a controlled substance, but whether either of them is likely to be convicted of doing that. To make that prediction, take into account section 10(a) of the Criminal Code.

> *Criminal Code § 10:* No person shall be convicted of a crime except on evidence proving guilt beyond a reasonable doubt.

Using your annotated outline of elements, decide whether each element can be proved beyond a reasonable doubt, and whether any exceptions are satisfied. Then make your prediction. Finally, decide the order in which the elements would best be explored in the Discussion section of an office memorandum.

Exercise II.   The Hartleys and Debenture

1. Break down the rule in Contracts Code § 206 into a list of elements and exceptions. With the aid of section 210, do the same with the rule in section 209. Annotate the list by adding definitions for the elements (and for any exceptions you might come across). (Under each element you list, leave lots of white space. When you do the second part of this exercise, you will need room to write more.)

> *Contracts Code § 206:* A contract made by an intoxicated person is voidable by that person if, at the time the contract was made, the other party to the contract had reason to know that the intoxicated party, because of the intoxication, was unable to understand the nature and consequences of the transaction.

> *Contracts Code § 209:* A person who makes a contract because of duress can void the contract.

> *Contracts Code § 210:* Duress occurs where a person makes a contract only because of an improper threat by the other party that causes the threatened person reasonably to believe that he or she has no reasonable alternative to the contract. In judging whether the threat caused such a belief and whether the belief was reasonable, all attendant circumstances shall be considered.

2. Your client is Irma Hartley. She married Myron Hartley six years ago. They have two children, twins born four years ago and named Ariel and Jason. Myron is employed as an investment banker. Irma has a part-time job as a salesperson in an art gallery. Both have college degrees in liberal arts. Irma, who has never retained a lawyer before, has just hired you and wants to know her rights concerning the following situation:

Irma has explained to you that she and Myron have had marital difficulties. For the past two years, they have bickered often, and she cannot stand it when the bickering turns into shouting. On three occasions during those two years, Myron struck her, once on each occasion, in the face, at the end of a shouting match. The tension in this situation has caused Irma to drink, on average, a scotch or two a day. Myron does not drink.

When the Hartleys got married, Myron owned a German shepard and Irma owned an Akita. Because the two dogs did not get along, Irma gave the Akita to her brother. The shepard (whose name is Debenture) remained and has been a good watchdog. Although Debenture has never, to Irma's knowledge, bitten anyone, he bares his teeth and growls when Myron shouts, and this makes Irma nervous.

During the evening last Sunday, after a weekend of bitter arguing, Myron announced that he had had enough and was leaving. He quickly packed a bag and left.

Myron returned Monday evening and told Irma that he had consulted a lawyer, and that the lawyer had drafted a separation agreement. The agreement provided that Myron and Irma would live apart, beginning immediately, that they would have joint custody of the children, and that a divorce would be obtained as soon as possible. It provided that there would be no alimony, and in elaborate detail it divided up the couple's property. The agreement provided that it would become effective when signed by both parties. Myron had already signed it.

The art gallery where Irma works laid off half its staff on Monday morning. Irma was able to keep her job, but when she came home from work at six o'clock, she was depressed and worried about whether the gallery would close, throwing her out of work. She had one drink when she got home and another when Myron arrived a little more than an hour later. At 7:30, she was drinking a third scotch when Myron put the agreement on the table and angrily demanded that she sign it. Debenture was sitting in the corner, and Irma could see him perk up and become more attentive as Myron's voice became louder.

Myron told Irma that if she did not sign the agreement, he would tell the court that her "artsy friends do drugs in front of Ariel and Jason." Myron added that no one would believe her if she were to deny these accusations because it would be her word against his and he would make a much better witness than she would. Angrily and in a very loud voice, Myron said that the court would therefore take the children away from her and give her none of their property. At this point, Myron was pounding the coffee table and Debenture was on his feet, staring at her very attentively.

Irma signed the agreement and asked Myron to leave immediately and to take Debenture with him. Myron left ten minutes later, taking his camcorder and laptop computer and Debenture. Irma made herself another scotch and phoned a friend. She asked the friend to come over and spend a few hours with her because she felt very worried.

Irma's friends do not "do drugs." She knows nothing about divorce law, and before consulting you, she had no idea whether Myron's predictions about divorce and the courts were accurate. (You believe that, in the absence of a separation agreement, a court would probably award Irma custody of the children, child support, and three to five years of alimony. You also believe that, in the absence of a separation agreement, a court would probably divide the property in a way that is more fair to Irma.)

Irma has a clear memory of what she saw and heard Monday night.

With the aid of Contracts Code § 201 and Domestic Relations Act § 401 (below), finish annotating your list of elements by writing, under each element, the facts that are relevant to that element.

> *Contracts Code § 201*: If a contract is voidable by one of the parties, that party need not obey the contract.

> *Domestic Relations Act § 401*: A separation agreement is a contract.

3. You have been asked to determine whether Irma can void the separation agreement. Using your annotated list of elements, decide whether each element is satisfied and whether any exceptions are satisfied. Then make your prediction. Finally, decide the order in which the elements would best be explored in the Discussion section of an office memorandum.

9 How to Organize Proof of a Conclusion of Law

§9.1 A Paradigm for Structuring Proof

When a supervising lawyer reads a predictive Discussion in an office memorandum, he or she is preparing to make a decision. So is a judge who reads persuasive writing in a motion memorandum or appellate brief. They will make different kinds of decisions. (The lawyer will decide what to advise the client or how to handle the client's case. The judge will decide how to rule on a motion or appeal.) But both look for a tightly constructed analysis that makes your conclusion seem inevitable.

The reader making a decision needs to know first what your conclusion is; then the rule on which your conclusion is primarily based; next, proof that the rule has been stated accurately; and, finally, application of the rules to the facts.

Thus, to the reader who must make a decision, analysis is most easily understood if it is organized into the paradigm at the top of the next page (or into some variation of it), the steps of which are the components of a proof of a conclusion of law.

What do these terms mean?

Your conclusion is the decision you have reached on a given issue. In an office memorandum, it is expressed either as your prediction of how a court would rule — "MacPherson probably will be convicted of insider trading" — or as how the law treats the facts involved — "Schmitt does not have a cause of action for slander of title." (In persuasive writing — which you will do later in a motion memorandum or appellate brief — your conclusion will be the one you want the court to adopt, such as "the defendant should be enjoined from using the plaintiff's name in commerce.")

---

1. statement of your conclusion;

2. a statement of the rule that supports the conclusion;

3. proof of the rule through citation to authority, through explanations of how the authority stands for the rule, through analyses of policy, and through counter-analyses; and

4. application of the rule's elements to the facts with the aid of supporting authority, policy considerations, and counter-analyses, thus completing proof of the conclusion.

The rule is the principal rule on which you rely in reaching your conclusion. Other rules might also be involved, but this is the main one on which your analysis rests. For the three conclusions quoted in the preceding paragraph, the main rules would be the rule defining inside trading, the rule defining slander of title, and the rule setting out the test for a preliminary injunction.

Proof of the rule (or *rule proof*) is a demonstration that the rule on which you rely really is law in the jurisdiction involved. The reader needs to know for certain that the rule exists in the jurisdiction, and that you have expressed it accurately. Both can be done through citations to authority, such as statutes and precedent, together with explanations of how that authority stands for the rule as you have stated it. (This chapter and Chapters 10-12 explain how to do that.)

Application of the rule (or *rule application*) is a demonstration that the rule + the facts = your conclusion. Explain your logic, and use authority to show that your result is what the law has in mind. (This chapter and Chapters 10-13 explain how.) Sometimes, authority that you use in rule proof might reappear in rule application, but for a different purpose. For example, suppose that *Alger v. Rittenhouse* held that a boat crew that caught a shark became its owner to the exclusion of the fisherman who hooked but lost the shark an hour before. (In your case, ranchers trapped in their corral a wild mustang that immediately jumped over the fence and ran onto your client's land, where it was captured by your client.) In rule proof, you can use *Alger* to prove that your jurisdiction has adopted the rule that wild animals become the property of the first person to reduce them to possession. In rule application, you can use *Alger* again — this time to show that your client satisfies that rule because her position is analogous to that of the boat crew.

A rule's *policy* is the rule's reason for being. The law does not create rules at random. Each rule is designed to accomplish something (usually, preventing a particular type of harm). When courts are unsure of what a rule means or how to apply it, they interpret the rule in the way that would be most consistent with the policy behind it. Thus, policy can be used to show what the rule is (in rule proof) and how to apply it (in rule application).

A *counter-analysis*[1] evaluates the arguments that could reasonably[2] be made against your conclusion. In predictive writing, the counter-analysis is an objective evaluation of each contrary argument with an honest report of its strengths and weaknesses. You must decide whether your conclusion can withstand attack. And you must consider the possibility that other analyses might be better than the one you have selected. Like authority and policy, counter-analyses can appear both in rule proof and in rule application — but for different purposes. (In persuasive writing in a motion memorandum or appellate brief, a counter-analysis is called a counter-argument. It does not objectively consider contrary points of view. It argues against them, stressing their weaknesses and showing their strengths to be unconvincing.)

If you think of the paradigm as a tool to *help* you organize, you will find it flexible. It can be varied in many ways, although you should do so only for a good and articulable reason (§9.3 shows how). This chapter explains why readers prefer that you organize your analysis this way (see §9.2); how to start using the paradigm (§9.4); and how to check your writing to see whether it is organized effectively (§9.5).[3]

§9.2 Why Readers Prefer This Type of Organization

All of your readers will share three characteristics. Remember that all of your readers will be practical. They will read your memorandum or brief because they must make a decision. And they will be skeptics about everything.

State your conclusion first because a practical and busy reader needs to know why you say things before you start to say them. If your conclusion is mentioned for the first time after the analysis that supports it (or in the middle of that analysis), some or all your reasoning seems pointless to the reader who does not yet know what your reasoning is supposed to prove. Effective writers usually state their conclusions boldly at the beginning of a Discussion or Argument ("The plaintiff does not have a cause of action because . . ."). This may take some getting used to. It is contrary to the way writing is often done in college. And most of us have been socialized since childhood to state a conclusion only after a proof — even in the most informal situations — to avoid appearing opinionated, arrogant, or confrontational. Far from being offended, however, the reader who has to make a decision is grateful not to be kept in suspense. That kind of reader becomes frustrated and annoyed while struggling through passages the relevance of which cannot be understood because the writer has delayed announcing the proposition the passages are intended to prove.

State the rule next because, after reading a conclusion of law, the skep-

---

§9.1   1. This is a term used by law teachers, but not by many practicing lawyers.

2. Do not waste the reader's time by considering marginal or far-fetched arguments.

3. The paradigm explained here is designed for practical writing in memoranda and appellate briefs. Do not use it in this form when you take law school examinations. Instead, use the organization explained in Chapter 17.

tical law-trained mind instinctively wants to know what principles of law require that conclusion instead of others. After all, the whole idea of law is that things are to be done according to the rules.

Then prove the rule because the reader will refuse to follow you further until you have established the validity of the rule on which you rely. The skeptical law-trained mind will not accept a rule statement as genuine unless it has been proved with authority. And you cannot apply a rule that the reader has not yet accepted.

Apply the rule last because it is the only thing left. When you apply the rule to the facts, you complete the proof of a conclusion of law.

Counter-analyze opposing arguments because the skeptical law-trained mind will be able to think up many of those arguments and will want them evaluated. Almost *every* train of reasoning can be challenged with reasonable arguments. If you do not account for them, the reader will doubt you because it will look as though you are avoiding problems, rather than solving them.

§9.3 How to Vary the Paradigm to Suit Your Needs

This paradigm can be varied in three ways.

First, you can vary the sequence in which the components appear. (See §9.3.1 for how.)

Second, in rule proof and in rule application, you can vary the depth of your explanation to suit the amount of skepticism you expect from the reader. (See §9.3.2.)

Third, you can combine separately paradigmed analyses into a unified explanation of several issues and sub-issues. (See §9.3.3.)

§9.3.1 Variations of Sequence

In some situations, you might vary the sequence of the paradigm components — for example, by stating the rule first and the conclusion second — although the order should not be illogical or confusing. Think long and hard before deciding to vary the sequence given in §9.1, and, if you do vary it, you should be able, if asked, to give a good reason for doing so. In particular, *rule proof should generally be completed before rule application begins.* Variations in sequence usually do not work well in office memoranda. They are more likely to be useful in persuasive writing in motion memoranda and appellate briefs. The reasons are explained in Chapter 19.[1]

---

§9.3 1. See pages 258-59.

§9.3.2 Variations in Depth

Variations in depth go to rule proof, to rule application, or to both. In one situation, rule proof might need only a sentence, while rule application would require three pages. In another situation, the reverse could happen. Each can be explained in a way that is *conclusory, substantiating,* or *comprehensive.*

A *conclusory explanation* does no more than allude to some basis for the deduction made by the writer:

> Gaedel has no cause of action for false imprisonment because he did not learn of the restraint until it had ended. A person has not been confined, and therefore has not been falsely imprisoned, unless he knew of the restraint at the time it happened. *Herring v. Boyle,* 1 Cr. M. & R. 377, 149 Eng. Rep. 1126 (Ex. 1834).[2] *[CITATION TO CASE THAT CONTAINS RULE]*

Here the rule (the second paradigm component) is clearly set out, but the only proof of it (the third component) is a citation to a decision, without any explanation of the court's reasoning or of the facts there adjudicated. The conclusion (the first component) is also plainly stated, but the only explanation for the way the conclusion is derived from the rule (the fourth component) is an allusion to a single fact: Gaedel did not contemporaneously know that he had been restrained. In addition, there are no counteranalyses and no discussion of policy.

A conclusory explanation is appropriate only where the reader will easily agree with you, or where the point is peripheral to your analysis. In those situations, a more detailed analysis would seem tedious to the reader. Elsewhere, however, a conclusory explanation would deprive the reader of information essential to the decision the reader must make. For example, a judge who has been asked to grant summary judgment against Gaedel could hardly, from the passage above, have the kind of confidence needed for such a decision. At the very least, the judge would need to know the reasoning relied on by the *Herring* court and how the facts of *Herring* are analogous to Gaedel's, together with some policy analysis, and any useful counteranalyses. In predictive writing, the same information would be needed by a lawyer who must decide whether to advise Gaedel to sue.

A *substantiating explanation* goes more deeply into the writer's reasoning, but still does not state the analysis completely: *[→ MAYBE FACT DOESN'T FIT EXACTLY — NEED TO CLARIFY — DISCUSS AN EXAMPLE]* *[VERY SIMPLE]*

> Gaedel does not have a cause of action for false imprisonment. A person has not been confined — and therefore has not been falsely imprisoned — unless he knew at the time of the restraint that he would not be able to move about freely. In *Herring v. Boyle,* 1 Cr. M. & R. 377, 149 Eng. Rep. 1126 (Ex. 1834), a plaintiff was held not to have proved confinement where there was no evidence that he knew

---

2. Assume that *Herring* is the only relevant appellate case in the jurisdiction where these events take place.

of the restraint at the time it allegedly occurred. He "may have been willing to stay," *id.* at 381 (Bolland, B.), and "[t]here was no evidence [of] compulsion upon" him, *id.* at 382 (Gurney, B.). Similarly, in the present case, Gaedel, out of his own free will, entered Lopez's office and remained there, unaware until after he had left that the door had been locked from the outside.

This passage provides more rule proof and more rule application. Although we are still not told the facts of *Herring,* we learn a little about the court's reasoning. And although the passage lacks a policy discussion and a counter-analysis, it includes at least some statement about how *Herring* should govern the writer's facts.

A substantiating explanation is appropriate where the reader needs more than a conclusory explanation, but where the point being made is not central to the analysis. It would not be appropriate where the reader's skepticism is likely to be aggressive. The substantiating passage above would not, for example, satisfy the lawyer who must decide whether to recommend a lawsuit to Gaedel or the judge who has been asked to grant summary judgment against Gaedel. These are difficult decisions, and each of these people would need more information.

A comprehensive explanation includes whatever analyses are necessary to satisfy an aggressive skepticism. Rule proof and rule application can be augmented with further detail about the law and the facts, with added or expanded counter-analyses, and with policy discussions sufficient to give the skeptical reader confidence that the law's goals would be achieved through your conclusion:

[handwritten margin note: THIS IS A FULL BLOWN PROOF]

Gaedel does not have a cause of action for false imprisonment because he did not know when it happened that he was being restrained.	The writer's conclusion.
A person has not been confined — and therefore has not been falsely imprisoned — unless he knew at the time of the restraint that he would not be able to move about freely. *Herring v. Boyle,* 1 Cr. M. & R. 377, 149 Eng. Rep. 1126 (Ex. 1834). In *Herring,* a ten-year-old boy attended the defendant's boarding school. When his mother sought to take him home for the Christmas holidays, the defendant refused even to let her see her son unless the tuition bill was paid. This continued for seventeen days and ended only after the mother sued for a writ of habeas corpus. There was, however, no evidence that the child knew of his mother's attempts to take him home, or that he wished to leave or felt	The rule on which the conclusion is based. Rule proof begins with an explanation of the controlling case. *[handwritten: DETAIL STARTS HERE]* If you had to make a decision based on this writer's analysis, would the explanation of *Herring* convince you — or would you want to know more about the court's reasoning?

[handwritten margin note: WHICH FACTS IS PROVING SOMETHING IS FALSE IMPRISONMENT]

himself restrained. "[T]he boy may have been willing to stay. . . ." *Id.* at 381 (Bolland, B.). "There was no evidence . . . which showed that there was any compulsion upon the boy." *Id.* at 382 (Gurney, B.).

Although the Restatement (Second) of Torts, § 42, would provide liability wherever the plaintiff is harmed by a restraint, even if not contemporaneously aware of it, the Restatement's position had not been adopted in this jurisdiction, *Herring* being the only case on point. And *Herring* represents the sounder view. False imprisonment law protects both physical freedom of movement and the emotion of freedom. A person unaware of any restraint has been deprived of neither. If a plaintiff is truly prevented from moving about as much as he wants, he will learn of that when he reaches the boundaries of the restraint. And if a person is restrained but does not know of it at the time, he has not suffered the emotion of imprisonment. While it might seem attractive to compensate a plaintiff who was tricked, for example, into contemporaneous ignorance of the restraint, the unpleasantness that person might suffer on later learning the truth is both too slender and too intangible to quantify into damages.

Here Gaedel did not learn of the restraint until a week after it happened. He was summoned by Lopez, his employer, into her office for questioning about thefts from the workplace. Lopez, unknown to Gaedel, had ordered her security guard to keep the office door locked from the outside throughout the interrogation. Although Gaedel might have been shocked and suffered unhappiness when he eventually learned of this restraint, his ignorance of it while it was happening deprives him of a cause of action.

Even if *Herring* were to be repudiated and the Restatement view adopted, Gaedel's loss was not the type of harm contemplated by the Restatement. The Restatement illustrates the required harm with three hypotheticals: a six-day-old baby who suffers

[handwritten margin notes: "RESTATEMENT OF TORTS IS PERSUASIVE AUTHORITY"; "CONFLICT"]

A counter-analysis of an argument that could challenge the writer's rule proof. *Herring,* the controlling case, is old enough that it might be infirm, and the Restatement's position suggests that the common law elsewhere has evolved away from *Herring*. The writer says that *Herring* represents the sounder policy. Does this explanation satisfy you? Would you want to know whether these theories about policy have been adopted by courts in this jurisdiction or in others?

[handwritten: "RULE PROOF RESOLVED CONFLICT 2 BETWEEN DIFFERENT RULES"]

Rule application begins with a sentence that points to the most determinative fact.

[handwritten: "STATE FACTS HERE"]

[handwritten: "USUALLY INVOLVED MAKING A SPECIFIC COMPARISON"]

A counter-analysis of an argument that could challenge the writer's rule application. What will happen if the prediction in the writer's rule proof turns out to be wrong? In other words, what will happen if the local courts adopt the Restatement's rule? The writer shows that the result would be the same under either rule.

[handwritten: "IS THERE A VIABLE ARGUMENT AGAINST?"]

medically while locked for two days in a bank vault; a "wealthy idiot" kidnapped for ransom and deprived of his family's care; and a diabetic in insulin shock who is jailed mistakenly as a drunkard and suffers both medically and emotionally. Restatement (Second) of Torts § 42 (1965) comment *a*. Gaedel's only injury is the humiliation he felt when he later learned that he had been locked inside Lopez's office. Gaedel suffered no physical injury, and, because he would have been in Lopez's office anyway, he was not cut off from his family or friends or anything he would have wanted or needed to do. Although he is unhappy about knowing that he was locked in an office by a security guard, that event is not comparable to the jailing of a diabetic in insulin shock. The stigma of the jailing is much greater, and the diabetic suffered medically, as well as emotionally.

Here, only one element of the test for false imprisonment is at issue. For situations where more than one element is at issue, see §9.3.3.

Beginning students sometimes write explanations so *cryptic* as to be less than conclusory. The writer of a passage like the following has tried to put too much into a small bottle:

> Gaedel, who did not know he was restrained, does not have a cause of action for false imprisonment. *Herring v. Boyle,* 1 Cr. M. & R. 377, 149 Eng. Rep. 1126 (Ex. 1834).

A cryptic explanation is never enough — even in a situation where a conclusory explanation would suffice — because a cryptic explanation omits any statement of the rule on which the conclusion is to be based. Compare this cryptic passage to the conclusory one on page 87. The reader of the conclusory passage might agree with it if she is willing (1) to believe, without further explanation, that *Herring* stands for the rule stated, and (2) to assume that the only determinative fact in the present case is Gaedel's contemporaneous ignorance of the restraint. But even if willing to make those assumptions, a reader cannot agree without knowing what the controlling rule is — but that is exactly what the cryptic passage asks the reader to do.[3]

---

3. In addition, the citation in the cryptic passage cannot possibly prove the literal truthfulness of the sentence that precedes it. Rule 1.2(a) in *The Bluebook* permits citation without a signal (such as "E.g.," "Cf.," etc.) only where the authority "states the proposition" that precedes the citation, or is the source of a quotation, or is named in text and cited to in a footnote. The second and third possibilities are not relevant here. *Herring* does not

How can you tell how much depth is needed? Ask yourself three questions.

First, how much explanation will convince the reader that the conclusion is correct? That depends on the reader's level of skepticism, which in turn depends on how important the issue is to the decision the reader must make, and on how many possibilities for error the reader would predictably see in the conclusion. Sometimes, a full explanation of your reasoning is neither needed nor wanted, especially when you write about preliminary and ancillary matters with which the reader can agree without much hesitation.

Second, how much explanation will prevent the reader from studying independently the authorities you rely on? The second question poses what might be called the need-to-read test: you have not explained enough if your reader would find it hard to agree with you without actually studying the authorities you have cited. A reader's need to go to the books is predicated on the context. A reader is more likely to feel that need with a critical, difficult, or obscure point than with a simple, peripheral, or routine one. A reader's need to know more is particularly great for authority that is the only support or the central basis for your conclusion.

Third, how much explanation would tell the reader those things needed to make an informed decision? Put another way, if the reader were to go to the books, would the reader be startled to find the things you have left out? Part of your job *is* to leave things out. The reader is counting on you to cut out the things that do not matter. But do not leave out so much that the reader is deprived of information on which a decision would have to be based.

Do not explore an issue in more depth than a reader would need. Remember that the reader is a busy person, almost as intolerant of too much explanation as of too little. Where you include much detail about peripheral, routine, or easily accepted propositions, the writer gets bogged down in tedium.

But most students underestimate the skepticism of readers. Therefore, if you have no idea how much to explain, err on the side of making a more complete explanation until you have gained a better sense of what must be fully proven and where proof can be at least partially implied.

§9.3.3 Combinations of Separately Structured Explanations

If you reach several conclusions or sub-conclusions, the reader will expect a separately structured proof for each one. The third type of paradigm variation does that by combining separately structured proofs into a unified presentation. This is needed in three situations: where more than one element of a rule is in dispute; where you must resolve separate but related

---

"state the proposition" that Gaedel—whom the *Herring* court had never heard of — has no cause of action. When a citation "states the proposition," it proves the literal truthfulness of the words that precede it.

issues; and where a conclusion can be justified through two or more independent theories, which you propound in the alternative.

More than one element at issue: In all the passages quoted in §9.3.2, only one of the elements of false imprisonment was at issue. But if you must resolve every element, you will have an ultimate conclusion for the rule as a whole, together with a sub-conclusion for each element:

[handwritten margin note: UNLAWFUL RESTRAINT of A PERSON]

Ultimate Conclusion on the Ultimate Issue:	"Lopez is not liable for false imprisonment."
Sub-Conclusions on Sub-Issues:	Element #1: "Gaedel *was restrained within fixed boundaries*."
	Element #2: "Gaedel was restrained within fixed boundaries *by Lopez or at her direction*."
	Element #3: "Lopez *acted with the intent to confine*."
	Element #4: "But Gaedel *was not contemporaneously aware of the restraint*."
	Element #5: "Lopez *did not act within the scope of a lawful authority to arrest*."

If this analysis were to be written out, the opening paragraph would state the conclusion ("Lopez is not liable for false imprisonment") and the essence of the reason ("because Gaedel was not contemporaneously aware of the restraint"). The opening paragraph would also recite the rule on which it is based (here, the elements of false imprisonment). If the rule is settled law, it might be proved in the opening paragraph with little more than a citation to authority. Otherwise, rule proof would require one or more additional paragraphs.

Then each element, as a sub-conclusion on a sub-issue, would have to be proved separately through an independent but paradigm-structured discussion. Each element would have to be defined (through a definitional rule); the definition would have to be proved through authority (rule proof); and the facts would have to be analyzed in light of the definition (rule application).

The opening paragraph of such a Discussion — or paragraphs, if the underlying rule is hard to prove — would at first seem to be an incomplete paradigm structure because it lacks rule application and definitions of the elements. But the opening paragraph or paragraphs would actually function as an "umbrella" paradigm structure that covers, organizes, and incorporates the subordinate, structured proofs of the elements. (For an illustration, see the Discussion in the office memorandum in Appendix C.)

The most dispositive issues or sub-issues usually — but not always — should be addressed first. Here, because the fourth element of false imprisonment is the dispositive one, its analysis could wisely precede that of the others. (Because it is missing, there is no cause of action.) If you believe, however, that all the elements can be proven, you could instead analyze them in the order in which they appear in the rule. That might be easier for the reader to follow if no element takes vastly more space than another to explain. But the situation might be different if one element were to consume, for example, three-quarters of the Discussion. There, the reader might be able to follow the analysis more easily if you were to dispose of the other elements first to set up the context.

You might be tempted to focus on one element, conclude that it is not satisfied in the facts, and then ignore the other elements as moot on the theory that the one you have analyzed disposes of the whole controversy. That will not work because it might turn out that you are wrong about the element you believe to be dispositive. Here, for example, you cannot ignore the other elements of false imprisonment merely because you believe that the fourth element (contemporaneous awareness) is unsatisfied. The reader of predictive writing is entitled to know what will happen if you turn out to be wrong.

Separate issues: Your supervising attorney wants to know whether the client will be awarded damages in a tort case. You need to figure out whether the client has a cause of action (first issue). And you anticipate that the defendant will raise the affirmative defenses of comparative negligence (second issue) and sovereign immunity (third issue). Although this is a more complex situation than the one where several elements of a single rule are in dispute, it is handled in the same way. An umbrella paradigm-structure is constructed, and underneath it the sub-conclusions are proved through separate, subordinate paradigm-structured analyses. Here, the ultimate conclusion might be that the client will not be awarded damages because, although she has a cause of action (first sub-conclusion) and was not comparatively negligent (second sub-conclusion), the claim falls within the defendant's sovereign immunity (third sub-conclusion).

Alternative theories proving a single conclusion: In the first year of law school, this typically occurs in a moot court assignment where the jurisdiction has no rule on point, where it could choose between or among competing rules, and where one can argue that either of two or more competing rules will — independently of one another — justify the conclusion. It, too, is handled through the umbrella paradigm structure.

§9.4 How to Start Working with the Paradigm

Think of the paradigm as a tool to *help* you organize and to keep your material from getting out of control.

This section describes one method of starting to work with the paradigm. It is only a suggestion for the first time you write. If you develop a different procedure that works well for you, use that instead.

Begin by figuring out how many issues and sub-issues you have. Each one will be analyzed through a separate paradigm structure.

For each issue or sub-issue, identify the rule that is central to and governs the answer. (You might also use other rules, but for the moment focus on the rule that — more than any other — compels your answer.)

Now, inventory your raw materials. *For each issue or sub-issue,* sort everything you have into two categories: rule proof and rule application. Some methods of sorting seem to work better than others. Dividing your notes into two piles, for example, does *not* seem to work very well.

A better method is to go through your notes and write "RP" in the margin next to everything that you might use to prove that your rule really is the law and "RA" next to everything that might help the reader understand how to apply the rule. Some ideas or authorities might do both and get a notation of "RP/RA." If you have several issues or sub-issues, you can work out a method of marking them separately, such as "#3RP" for "rule proof on issue 3" or "#1RA" for "rule application on issue 1." If you have photocopied cases, write these notations next to each part of the case that you will use. Go through your facts, too, marking the ones that are important enough to talk about during rule application. If you have been thinking about ideas that are not in your notes, write them down and note where they go.

Now, think about how all these things add up. If you have not yet drawn a conclusion, do it now. If you decided previously on a conclusion, check it against your raw materials to see whether it still seems like the best conclusion.

Ask yourself whether a reasonable argument could be made against any part of your analysis. If so, make a note of it and of where it goes. Decide whether the argument is so attractive that it would probably persuade a judge. And decide exactly *why* a judge would — or would not — be persuaded. If you decide that the argument is likely to persuade, modify your analysis accordingly. (If you cannot find any arguments at all that might work against your analysis, you may be avoiding problems that other people will later see.)

You have now completed most of the analytical process described in §6.2. And your notes are now complete enough to be organized into an outline based on some variation of the paradigm. You have labelled everything so that you know where it goes.

To make the fluid outline described in §6.3, just assemble everything. *For each issue or sub-issue,* take a piece of paper and write four abbreviated headings on it (for example: "concl" or "sub-concl," "rule," "RP," and "RA"). Under "concl" or "sub-concl," write your conclusion or sub-conclusion for that issue in whatever shorthand will remind you later of what your thinking is (for example: "no diversity — Wharton/citizen of Maine"). Under "rule," do something similar. Under "RP," list your raw materials for rule proof. For each item listed, do not write a lot — just enough so that you can see at a glance everything you have. If you are listing something found in a case you have photocopied, a catch-phrase and a reference to a page in the case might be enough (for example: "intent to return — *Wiggins* p.352"). Under "RA," do the same for rule application. Make sure that everything you have on that issue is listed in an appropriate place on that page.

Assume that for a certain issue you have listed six items for rule proof. You have not yet decided the order in which you will discuss them when you prove the rule. In most situations, the decision will be easier and more apt if you do not make it while outlining. The best time to decide is just before you write that issue's rule proof in your first draft. (*You do not need to know exactly where everything will go before you start the first draft.*) When you decide, just write a number next to each item ("1" next to the first one you will discuss, and so on).

When you write the first draft (§6.4), you probably will not use everything that you previously marked into one category or another. Inevitably, some material will not seem as useful while you are writing as it did when you were sorting, and you will discard it.

You can keep track of what you are doing by checking off each item in the outline as you put it into the first draft. When everything has been checked off, you have completed the first draft of your Discussion in an office memorandum (or Argument if you are writing a motion memorandum or appellate brief).

So far, you have concentrated on making sure that all worthwhile raw materials get into your first draft. During rewriting, your focus will change. While you rewrite (§6.5), look to see where things are. If you find conclusions at the end of analysis, for example, move them to the beginning. While rewriting, ask yourself the questions in §9.5.

§9.5 How to Test Your Writing for Effective Organization

A well-organized presentation of analysis is immediately recognizable. Issues and sub-issues are handled separately, and each issue is clearly resolved before the next is taken up. Inside each issue and each sub-issue, the material is organized around the elements of the controlling rule or rules, and not around individual court decisions. Rule proof is always completed before rule application begins. Each issue and each sub-issue is explored through a well-chosen variation of the paradigm explained in this chapter. The reader is given neither too little nor too much explanation, but instead is able to read quickly and finish confident that the writer's conclusion is correct. Authority is discussed in the order of its logical importance, not necessarily in the chronological order in which it developed. Finally, the writer's organization is apparent throughout: the reader always knows where he is and how everything fits together. These things all come from sound *architecture:* from a wisely chosen building plan that the writer can explain and justify if asked to do so.

To figure out whether you have accomplished these things, ask yourself the following questions after you have written a first draft.[1]

---

§9.5 1. When marking up your work, your teacher might refer to these questions by using the number-letter codes that appear next to each question here.

9-A For each issue, have you stated your *conclusion*? If so, where? State it precisely, succinctly, and in such a way that the reader knows from the very beginning what you intend to demonstrate. Some lawyers express a prediction openly ("Kolchak will not be convicted of robbery"), while others imply the prediction by stating the conclusion on which it is based ("The evidence does not establish beyond a reasonable doubt that Kolchak is guilty of robbery").

9-B For each issue, have you stated the *rule* or rules on which your conclusion is based? If so, where? If the cases on which you rely have not formulated an explicit statement of the rule, you might be tempted just to describe the cases and let the reader decide what rule they stand for. If you feel that temptation, you probably have not yet figured out yourself exactly what the rule is. And if you have not done it, the reader will not do it for you. Formulate a credible rule, and prove it by analyzing the authority at hand.

9-C For each issue, have you *proved* the rule? If so, where? And do you explain the rule proof in an appropriate amount of depth? Is your rule proof conclusory, substantiating, or comprehensive? How did you decide how much depth to use? If you were in the decision-maker's position, would you need more rule proof? Less? Is policy accounted for? (If the rule seems arbitrary, the reader will resist agreeing that it is the correct one to use. The reader will more easily agree if you at least allude to the policy behind the rule and the social benefits the rule causes.) Have you counter-analyzed attractive arguments that might challenge your choice or formulation of the rule?

9-D For each issue, have you *applied* the rule to the facts? If so, where? And do you explain the rule application in an appropriate amount of depth? Is your rule application conclusory, substantiating, or comprehensive? How did you decide how much depth to use? If you were in the decision-maker's position, would you need more rule application? Less? Is policy accounted for? Have you counter-analyzed attractive arguments that might challenge your application of the rule?

9-E Have you completed rule proof before starting rule application? If you let the material get out of control, the result may be a little rule proof, followed by a little rule application, followed by a little more rule proof, followed by a little more rule application — and so on, back and forth and back and forth. Finish proving the rule before you start applying it. If you start to apply a rule before you have finished proving it, the reader will refuse to agree with what you are doing.

9-F Have you varied the sequence of the paradigm only where truly necessary? If you have varied the sequence of the components of

[handwritten margin note: IN Comprehensive Proof, Rule Proof = Heart of Legal Analysis]

the paradigm, why? Was your goal more valuable than any clarity you might have sacrificed by varying the sequence?

Have you organized a multi-issue presentation so that the reader understands how everything fits together? If you have combined | **9-G** |
separately structured explanations, did you identify separate sub-conclusions? Are the combined paradigms covered by an umbrella paradigm? Is the result crystal-clear to the reader? If not, how could it be made so? (If you are writing a persuasive motion memorandum or appellate brief, see §20.3.)

Have you organized around tests and elements, rather than around cases? Your goal is not to dump before the reader the | **9-H** |
cases you found in the library. The law is, after all, the rules themselves, and a case merely proves a rule's existence and accuracy. The cases are raw materials, and your job is not complete until you have built them into a coherent discussion organized around the applicable tests and their elements. A mere list of relevant cases, with discussion of each, is not helpful to a decision-maker, who needs to understand how the rules affect the facts. This fault is easy to spot in a student's paper: the reader sees an unconnected series of paragraphs, each of which is devoted to discussion of a single case. The impression made is sometimes called "show-and-tell" because the writer seems to be doing nothing more than holding up newly found possessions. A student not making this mistake might use five cases to analyze the first element of a test, one case — if it is dispositive — to analyze the second, three for the third, and so on, deploying cases where they will do what is needed.

how do cases illustrate a particular rule??

Have you avoided presenting authority in chronological order un- | **9-I** |
less you have a special need to do so? The reader wants to know what the current law is and how it governs the facts at hand. Although a little history might be useful somewhere in the discussion, you will waste the reader's time if you begin with the kind of historical background typical of a college essay. Unless there is some special need to do otherwise, present authority in the order of its logical importance, not the order in which it came to be.

Have you collected closely related ideas, rather than scattering | **9-J** |
them? If there are three reasons why the defendant will not be convicted, list them and then explain each in turn. The reader looking for the big picture cannot follow you if you introduce the first reason on page 1; mention the second for the first time on page 4; and surprise the reader with the third on page 6. If you have more than one item or idea, listing them at the beginning helps the reader keep things in perspective. It also forces you to organize and evaluate your thoughts. Sometimes, in the act of

listing, you may find that there are really fewer or more reasons — or whatever else you are listing — than you had originally thought.

Exercise I.   Teddy Washburn's Gun (Analyzing and Organizing)

This exercise is designed to help you organize raw materials — rules, facts, cases, and so on — into an outline that tracks the components of the paradigm.

In his prime, Gorilla Morrell was often on the bill at Friday Night Wrestling. Now he is reduced to hanging around Washburn's Weights Room & Gym, which is next door to Washburn's Bar & Grill. Gorilla is good for Teddy Washburn's business because customers in the Weights Room try to take Gorilla on. When this happens, customers from the Bar wander into the Weights Room to watch. There they order more drinks, which Washburn passes through a hole he has cut through the wall. Afterward, Gorilla, his adversary, and the spectators tend to adjourn back to the Bar, where the spirit of conviviality usually leads to games of billiards accompanied by further orders of food and drink.

Washburn has let Gorilla build up a bill of $183.62, dating back over several weeks. Last night, they had words over the matter. Gorilla took a swing at Washburn, who came out from behind the bar and chased Gorilla out into the street. There Gorilla took another swing at Washburn, and Washburn, demanding his money, pulled out a gun (which he bought and for which he has a license).

Gorilla grabbed for the gun, but it fell out of Washburn's hand, sliding five or six feet along the sidewalk and coming to rest at the feet of Snare Drum Bennett, a mechanic who was returning from work. Bennett happened onto this scene only in time to hear Washburn demand money and to see him pull out the gun and have it knocked from his hand.

Bennett, Washburn, and Gorilla looked at the gun, then at each other, and then at the gun again. Finally, Bennett crouched down, picked up the gun, checked to make sure the safety was on, and put it in her coat pocket. "Washburn," she said, "you haven't paid *me* yet for the front end work I did on your car."

"I will," said Washburn.

"It's $275," said Bennett, "and it's been three weeks. I think you should go back inside. You ought to pay your own debts before you accuse other people of welshing out on you."

"How can I pay you," exclaimed Washburn, "if he won't pay me?"

"That's your problem," said Bennett, "I'm holding on to the gun. You can't seem to handle it right now, and I want my money."

At that point, Gorilla clobbered Washburn in the face and sent him staggering. Bennett turned around, walked a half-dozen steps, and began to turn into a dark alley. Washburn started to get up, called out "Hey, you!" and took a step in Bennett's direction. Bennett took the gun from her coat, pointed it at Washburn, smiled, and said, "Back off, bucko."

Washburn froze, and Bennett walked into the alley. As soon as she was out of sight, she dropped the gun into an open but full trash dumpster. The dumpster belongs to a grocery store and is about five feet inside the alley, which in turn is about twenty feet from the front door of Washburn's bar.

An hour or so later, the police came to Bennett's home and arrested her for robbing Washburn of his gun. Bennett told them where she had dropped it. The police went straight to the dumpster but found nothing inside, not even the trash that had muffled the gun's fall.

You have been asked to determine whether Bennett is likely to be convicted of robbing Washburn of his gun. This exercise takes you through the ground work needed to make that prediction.

Read the two statutes and three cases that follow. Then, make a list of the issues that you must resolve. *For each issue,* take a separate piece of paper and, using the process described in §9.4, answer the following questions: (1) What rule from the cases below disposes of the issue? (If you cannot find a rule that would dispose of the issue, say so. If that is true, it means that additional authority is needed from the library.) (2) What passages from these authorities prove the rule? (3) What facts in Bennett's story would be determinative for the issue? (4) What passages from these authorities would guide you in applying the rule to those determinative facts? (If you find none for a given issue, say so. Again, if you are right, more authority is needed.)

When you are finished, you will have the beginnings of an outline from which to write. There might be holes in the outline, but they should be so obvious that you will know what has to be filled in.

> *Criminal Code § 10:* No person shall be convicted of a crime except on evidence proving guilt beyond a reasonable doubt.
>
> *Criminal Code § 302:* A person is guilty of robbery when he or she takes, with the intent to steal, the property of another, from the other's person or in the other's presence, and through violence or intimidation.

BUTTS v. STATE

The defendant had worked for the Royal Guano company for two and a half days when he was fired. He demanded his wages but was told that he would have to wait until Saturday, which was payday. He was ordered off the premises and left. After a few hours, he returned with a gun, found the shift foreman, and demanded his wages again. The foreman told him to come back on Saturday. (The company agrees that it owed the defendant wages, but insists that he wait until payday to receive them.) When the foreman refused, the defendant showed the gun and demanded again. The foreman then paid the amount the defendant requested.

An intent to steal is an intent to deprive the owner permanently of his property. There is no intent to steal if the defendant in good faith believes that the property taken is his or her own property and not the property of somebody else.

The defendant could reasonably have supposed that he was entitled to his pay when his connection with the company was severed. He was wrong because the money was the property of the company until the company paid it to him. But he acted in good faith and therefore did not have the intent to steal (although he may be guilty of crimes other than robbery).

GREEN v. STATE

We reverse the defendant's conviction for robbing Mrs. Lillie Priddy.

Although there was evidence that the defendant assaulted Mrs. Priddy, that alone does not prove robbery. Mrs. Priddy testified as follows: She was walking along a road and came upon the defendant, who struck her so that she lost consciousness. After a minute or two, her mind cleared, and she saw the defendant standing in the road and her purse on the ground about five feet from each of them. The contents of the purse were spilled out on the ground. She kicked him and ran, never seeing her purse again.

The issue is whether there was a "taking" sufficient to support a charge of robbery. A taking is the securing dominion over or absolute control of the property. Absolute control must exist at some time, even if only for a moment.

If Mrs. Priddy was unconscious, she could not know whether the defendant ever had control of her purse, or whether it simply fell to the ground and was later taken away by someone else. None of its contents were found in the defendant's home. The testimony showed a very violent assault and battery upon her by the defendant, but does not establish a robbery.

STATE v. SMITH & JORDAN

The defendants overpowered and disarmed the complainant of his knife. He had surprised them after they broke into his gas station. With the complainant's knife (but not the complainant), they got into their car and drove off. Later, the police found the defendants standing by their wrecked car. The complainant's knife was on the ground nearby. The defendants were convicted of robbery.

To convict for robbery, the defendant must have intended permanently to deprive the complainant of the taken property. If a defendant takes another's property for the taker's immediate and temporary use with no intent permanently to deprive the owner of his property, he is not guilty of robbery.

It would be unreasonable to assume that the defendants, fleeing from arrest for the crime of breaking into the gas station, had any expectation of returning the knife. They would have been captured if they had tried. For the purpose of decision here, we assume that defendant took the knife "for temporary use" and that after it had served the purpose of escape, they intended to abandon it at the first opportunity lest it lead to their detection. That, however, would leave the complainant's recovery of his knife to mere chance and thus constitute a reckless exposure to loss that is consistent with an intent permanently to deprive the owner of his property. In abandoning it, the defendants put it beyond their power to return the knife. When, in order to serve a temporary purpose of one's own, one takes property (1) with the specific intent wholly and permanently to deprive the owner of it, or (2) under circumstances which render it unlikely that the owner will ever recover his property and which disclose the taker's total indifference to his rights, one takes with the intent to steal.

Exercise II.   Griggs and the Anti-Bandit (Checking Organization During Rewriting)

This exercise is designed to help you spot organizational problems in your own writing so that you can fix them during the rewriting process.

Griggs has been charged in Maryland with receipt of stolen goods,[2] specifically a BMW floor mat and an Anti-Bandit automobile tape deck. He told Officer Ochs that he had driven onto the shoulder of a rural road after realizing that he was lost, and that he had attempted to turn around by backing his van up a few feet into the woods, where it became stuck in the mud. According to Griggs, he got out, tried to rock the van out of the mud, and noticed the mat and the Anti-Bandit lying on the ground. The Anti-Bandit comes with a handle and is designed to be removed from the car and carried away at the owner's convenience. Griggs says that he did not notice, twenty feet further into the woods, a BMW stripped of tires, battery, and the like. (The police have found nothing else taken from the BMW.) Griggs says that he worked the mat under one of his rear wheels to gain traction, and that, when his baby woke up in the front seat and started screaming, he slid the Anti-Bandit into his dashboard (from which his own had been stolen some weeks before) and started playing the Everly Brothers' "Bye Bye Love," which his daughter finds soothing. Appearing just as Griggs was about to drive his van away with the mat and the Anti-Bandit inside, Officer Ochs believed none of this and placed Griggs under arrest.

Using the questions outlined in §9.5, scrutinize the Discussion below for organizational effectiveness. You might find this easier if you mark it up, dividing it into the components of the paradigm. Does the writer's analysis allay your skepticism? If yes, what convinces you? If not, what causes doubt? If you need to know more in order to be convinced, what should the writer have told you? What effect does the writer's organization have on you and your skepticism? How would you reorganize this passage? Be prepared to discuss your thinking in class.

In Maryland, a person is guilty of receiving stolen property when he (1) receives from another person (2) property that at the time of receipt had been stolen (3) knowing that it has been stolen and (4) with a fraudulent intent in receiving it. *Carroll v. State*, 6 Md. App. 647, 252 A.2d 496 (1969).

At about 1 A.M. Officer Ochs found Griggs in possession of the floor mat and the Anti-Bandit. Both were later shown to have come from a BMW that was stolen between 9 and 10 o'clock the previous evening. Griggs admitted that the radio and floor mat were not his. Hence, Griggs was in exclusive possession of a stolen radio and a stolen floor mat, and, since they were recently stolen, the receipt element is satisfied. Where a defendant is found in unexplained and exclusive possession of recently stolen property, a receipt from another person will be inferred. *Mills v. State*, 3 Md. App. 693, 241 A.2d 166 (1968).

In *Carroll*, the defendant met an acquaintance on a deserted back road and purchased a car engine from him at substantially below market value.

---

2. Normally, a modern criminal law issue centers on a statute, such as one defining a crime. But that will not be true here because the state involved follows the unusual practice of defining this crime (and a few others) through the common law and not by statute.

While driving off with the engine in his truck, the defendant was arrested and subsequently convicted of receiving stolen goods. On appeal, he argued that because he had no direct knowledge that the property was stolen, he could not be convicted of receiving stolen goods. The Court of Special Appeals rejected this argument and held that a defendant's knowledge of property's stolen character can be proved by evidence showing that under the circumstances the defendant "knew or could reasonably have suspected that the property in his possession was stolen." *Carroll*, 6 Md. App. at 650, 252 A.2d at 498. The court further held that mere possession itself can be significant circumstantial evidence of guilty knowledge, although it is not alone dispositive. *Id.* Because of the prosecution's obligation to prove guilt beyond a reasonable doubt, a conviction can be based solely on circumstantial evidence only where "the circumstances, taken together . . . exclude every reasonable hypothesis or theory of innocence." *Mills*, 3 Md. App. at 697, 241 A.2d at 168. Therefore, Griggs knew or could reasonably have suspected that the BMW floor mat and the Banzai Anti-Bandit radio were stolen property.

For intent to be fraudulent it "need not be *lucri causa* [for the sake of gain], but . . . merely hostile to the title of the true owner." *Carroll*, 6 Md. App. at 650-51, 252 A.2d at 498. In *Carroll*, the defendant's possession of the engine was fraudulent because he planned on installing it in his own car, which was certainly hostile to the title of the true owner. Here Griggs's actions show a similar intent. First, he had the radio and floor mat in his van. Second, he had used the Anti-Bandit to quiet his baby and the floor mat to free his van from the mud. Third, although Griggs told Officer Ochs that he "hadn't had a chance" to decide what he intended to do with these items eventually, he had started the van's engine and was beginning to drive off. Therefore, Griggs had a fraudulent intent when he received the Anti-Bandit floor mat. Although a defendant is presumed innocent and the prosecution must prove guilt beyond a reasonable doubt, "the trier of facts in a criminal case . . . is not commanded to be naive and to believe without scrutiny every glib suggestion or farfetched fairy tale." *Berry v. State*, 202 Md. 62, 67, 95 A.2d 319, 321 (1952).

Therefore, Griggs will be convicted of receiving stolen goods.

10 Selecting Authority

§10.1 Introduction

You need authority both in rule proof — to show that your formulation of the rule accurately states the law — and in rule application — to show that your resolution of the facts conforms to what the law intends. This chapter explains how to select the best available authority. Chapters 11 and 12 explain how to use the two most important kinds of authority: case law and statutes.

Courts use a complicated set of preferences to determine which authority they will follow. A hierarchy (explained in §10.2) ranks authorities so that, in the event of conflict, one can be chosen over another. There are special problems with dicta (§10.3), with precedent from other jurisdictions (§§10.4-10.5), and with the selection of nonmandatory precedent (§10.6). Finally, §10.7 explains how to integrate work in the library with the task of writing.

A special problem — addressed at several points in this chapter — involves filling gaps in the law. A gap exists where the jurisdiction whose law governs a particular case does not have all of the legal rules needed to decide the case. (See question 8-D on page 77.) For example, suppose — hypothetically — that the courts in four states have decided through precedent to adopt a newly invented cause of action. Suppose further that the courts of ten other states have held that in those states no such cause of action exists. The remaining 36 states have large gaps in their law on this subject because in each of them there is no local authority on point. If, in any of those 36 states, you bring a suit based on this new cause of action, the courts will have to fill the gap by deciding whether to recognize it locally.

Gaps routinely occur in every jurisdiction's law because law-makers cannot foresee every type of controversy that the law could be called upon to resolve. When a currently litigated case is affected by a gap, the lawyers involved propose methods of deciding the case that might, through precedent, fill the gap at the same time. (Section 10.5 explains how.) In fact, gaps are also routinely filled as the law continually reshapes itself through precedent.

§10.2   The Hierarchy of Authority

There are two kinds of authority. *Primary authority* includes decisions, statutes, and statute-like materials such as constitutions, court rules, and administrative regulations. (For brevity, we can refer to statutes and statute-like materials collectively as "enactments.") Treatises, law review articles, and other commentaries on the law are *secondary authority.* Primary authority is produced by a legislature, a court, or some other governmental entity acting within an official capacity to make or determine law. Secondary authority, on the other hand, is only a description of what a private person or a private group believes the law to be; the author of secondary authority may be knowledgeable, but he or she lacks the power to create law.

Primary authority is in turn subdivided into two varieties. *Mandatory authority* — which must be obeyed — includes enactments of the sovereignty whose law governs the question to be resolved, as well as the decisions of the appellate courts to which an appeal could be taken from the trial court where the issue is being or could be litigated.[1] *Persuasive primary authority* — which need not be obeyed — has been produced by an entity empowered to make law, but not by the entity whose law controls the matter at issue.

Within a single sovereignty, some mandatory authority outranks other mandatory authority. A constitution prevails over an inconsistent statute, and either a constitution or a statute trumps an inconsistent regulation promulgated by an administrative agency. That is basic civics: a constitution is the fundamental law creating a government in the first place; a legislature can enact only those kinds of statutes allowed by a constitution; and an administrative agency is still more subservient and is allowed to regulate only to the extent permitted by statute. Moreover, later enactments prevail over earlier ones of the same rank. A later statute, for example, prevails over an earlier one, but not over an earlier constitutional provision. In addition, a constitution or a statute will prevail over an inconsistent common law precedent. And case law made by higher courts prevails over inconsistent

---

§10.2   1. Before reading the rest of this chapter, you might want to review §1.2 on how courts are organized.

case law made by lower courts. Finally, later decisions prevail over inconsistent earlier ones from the same court.

Persuasive primary authority occurs in four forms: (1) decisions by the courts of sovereignties whose law does not govern the particular dispute in question (for example, a decision from another state); (2) decisions by coordinate appellate courts, to which an appeal could not be taken from the trial court where the issue would be or is being litigated (an example is given in the next paragraph); (3) decisions made by trial courts, regardless of the sovereignty; and (4) dicta in any decision.

A precedent is not mandatory merely because it was made by an appellate court in the jurisdiction where a present controversy is being or would be litigated. To be mandatory, a decision must have been made by an appellate court to which the matter at hand could be or already has been appealed. For example, the United States Court of Appeals for the Sixth Circuit hears appeals from federal trial courts in Kentucky, Michigan, Ohio, and Tennessee, while the coordinate court for the Third Circuit decides appeals from federal trial courts in Delaware, New Jersey, and Pennsylvania. An opinion by the Sixth Circuit is mandatory authority to a United States District Court in Cleveland, because the Sixth Circuit can reverse, on appeal, a decision of that trial court. The same opinion is mandatory to the Sixth Circuit itself, which is bound by its own prior decisions. But that opinion is only persuasive authority to a United States District Court in Pittsburgh, because the Third Circuit — not the Sixth — hears appeals from federal trial courts in Pennsylvania. And that opinion is only persuasive authority in the Court of Appeals for the Third Circuit (a coordinate court to the Sixth Circuit) and in the Supreme Court of the United States (which is superior to all the circuits).

Decisions by the United States Supreme Court, on the other hand, are mandatory in every federal court because the Supreme Court has the power ultimately to reverse a decision by any federal court.[2] But decisions of the United States Supreme Court are mandatory authority in a state court only on issues of federal law because the United States Supreme Court has no jurisdiction to decide matters of state law.

In contrast to primary authority, which may be either mandatory or persuasive, secondary authority is always persuasive and never mandatory. The most significant forms of secondary authority are (1) restatements, which are formulations of the common law drafted by scholars commissioned by the American Law Institute; (2) treatises written by scholars; and

---

2. The Supreme Court's refusal to grant a writ of certiorari in a particular case is not precedent. A petition for certiorari is a request for permission to appeal to the Supreme Court. The overwhelming majority of these petitions are denied simply because the Supreme Court cannot possibly decide the thousands of cases annually that various parties want to appeal to the nation's highest court. The Court itself has held that "the denial of a writ of certiorari imports no expression of opinion upon the merits of the case." *United States v. Carver,* 260 U.S. 482, 490 (1922). On the other hand, if you cite to a decision below from which the Supreme Court has "denied cert.," rule 10.7 in *The Bluebook* requires that you incorporate the denial into the citation as part of the case's "subsequent history." See §16.2.1.

(3) articles and similar material published in law reviews. If secondary authority is both on point and needed to fill a gap in the law, a court is most likely to be influenced by a restatement. On an issue not considered by the restatements, the most influential secondary authority will usually be a treatise or article written by a renowned scholar.

Since 1923, the American Law Institute has commissioned restatements in contracts, property, torts, and several other fields in an attempt to express some consensus about the common law as it has developed in the 50 states. When a restatement is no longer up-to-date, it is superseded by a second version. Thus, the Restatement (Second) of Torts has replaced the Restatement of Torts. A restatement consists of a series of black-letter law rules organized into sections, to which commentary is appended. Although some states' courts are relatively unimpressed by restatements, other states give special respect to one or another of the restatements. You can find out whether a state's courts defer to a particular restatement by checking the manner and frequency with which the restatement is cited in the state's decisions.

The authoritativeness of a treatise depends on the reputation of its author and on whether the treatise has been kept up-to-date. Some of the outstanding treatises have been written by Wigmore (evidence), Corbin (contracts), Williston (contracts), Prosser and Keeton (torts), and Davis (administrative law). Some of the renowned but older treatises have not been — and could not possibly be — revised to reflect current law. These include the commentaries written in the nineteenth century by Story and by Kent, those written in the eighteenth century by Blackstone, Coke's seventeenth-century *Institutes,* and Littleton's *Tenures,* written in the fifteenth century. Some treatises are multivolume works; some are in a single volume; some double as hornbooks; some are hardbound with pocket parts or other annual supplements; and some are in looseleaf binders for easier updating.

Law reviews print two kinds of material: articles (written by scholars, judges, and practitioners) and comments and notes (written by students). If an article is thorough, insightful, or authored by a respected scholar, it may influence a court and may therefore be worth citing. Most articles, however, do not fit that description, and an article's publication should not be taken to mean that it will be influential.[3] Only in the most unusual of circumstances does a student comment or note influence a court. But even where law review material will not be influential (and therefore would not be worth citing), it might nevertheless stimulate your thinking, and its footnotes can help you find cases, statutes, and other authority.

Legal encyclopedias, legal dictionaries, digests, and *American Law Reports* are not authority. They are not written by scholars, and their only function is to collect cases and to summarize parts of them. The definitions

---

3. A respected appellate judge writes, "My experience teaches . . . that too few law review articles prove helpful in appellate decision making. They tend to be too talky, too unselective in separating the relevant from the irrelevant, too exhaustive, too exhausting, too hedged, too cautious about reaching a definite conclusion. When they do, they strive too hard for innovation or shock effect at the expense of feasibility or practicality." Patricia M. Wald, *Teaching the Trade: An Appellate Judge's View of Practice-Oriented Legal Education,* 36 J. Leg. Ed. 35, 42 (1986).

in legal dictionaries are taken from opinions, often verbatim. Not only is the true authority the decision itself, but the dictionary rarely uses a case from the jurisdiction where your issue arises. Legal encyclopedias discuss more complex material but suffer from the same fault. Although digests and *American Law Reports* are more exhaustive, the true authority is still the cases they cite.[4]

§10.3 How Courts Use Dicta

As you already know, a dictum is not a holding and thus cannot be controlling authority, no matter what court it comes from. Once, after hearing an argument based on dictum from *Marbury v. Madison* — the single most important decision in American constitutional law — the Supreme Court held that

> general expressions [that] go beyond the case . . . may be respected, but ought not to control the judgment in a subsequent suit. . . . The reason . . . is obvious. The question actually before the Court is investigated with care, and considered in its full extent. Other principles which may serve to illustrate it, are considered in their relation to the case decided, but their possible bearing on [future] cases is seldom completely investigated.[1]

If that is so, why do courts write dicta in the first place?

Sometimes it adds clarity to an opinion. A court may want, for example, to make clear what the case is *not* ("if the plaintiff had presented evidence of injury to his reputation, he might be entitled to damages"). Or the court may wish to illustrate the possible ramifications of its decision ("when a minor is at the controls of a power boat — or for that matter an automobile or an airplane — she is held to the standard of care expected of a reasonable adult"). Occasionally, a court will add dicta to justify an apparently harsh decision ("although these facts constitute a cause of action for defamation — which the plaintiff did not bring — they do not substantiate the invasion of privacy cause of action asserted in the complaint") or to make a suggestion to a lower court on remand ("although the parties have not appealed on the question of appropriate damages, that issue will inevitably arise in the new trial we order, and we believe it necessary to point out . . .").

Sometimes a dictum is inadvertent. A judge might get a bit carried away or might formulate the issue or the rule or the determinative facts so that it is not clear whether a particular comment is really within the scope of the decision. Even when a judge is careful in defining the issue, rule, and deter-

4. Years ago, lawyers and judges were in the habit of citing to legal encyclopedias and dictionaries, even though they were not authority, and you will see that done occasionally in opinions printed in your casebooks. That practice is no longer considered acceptable. Today lawyers and judges seek real authority, and if you cite to a legal dictionary or encyclopedia, the reader will doubt you, and you risk creating an impression of sloppiness.

§10.3 1. *Cohens v. Virginia*, 19 U.S. (6 Wheat.) 264, 399-400 (1821).

minative facts, readers might reasonably disagree about whether a particular comment is necessary to the resolution of the issue at hand.[2]

In any event, a dictum can never be mandatory authority. But if the court
that wrote the dictum can reverse the court in which the current matter is
now being litigated, the dictum, though still not mandatory, becomes especially influential.[3] That is particularly so where the court that produced the
dictum went out of its way to express it in a deliberative fashion:

> While we can agree that what Mr. Justice Marshall volunteered in Part III of
> his opinion is dictum, it does not at all follow that we can cavalierly disregard
> it. There is authority for the proposition that a distinction should be drawn
> between "obiter dictum," which constitutes an aside or an unnecessary exten-
> sion of comments, and considered or "judicial dictum" where the Court, as in
> this case, is providing a construction of a statute to guide the future conduct
> of inferior courts. While such dictum is not binding upon us, it must be given
> considerable weight and cannot be ignored in the resolution of the close ques-
> tion we have to decide.[4]

Thus, it is not wrong to use a dictum, but it is wrong to use it inappropriately. Although a dictum can be used to supplement reliance on unclear
or incomplete holdings, it can never take the place of a holding, and it
is inappropriate to treat it as though it could. And where a dictum is used,
it must be identified as such or the result can be viewed as an attempted
deception.

§10.4   How Courts React to Foreign Precedent

Lawyers and judges use the term "foreign law" usually to mean law from
another state (not law from another country). In addition, it may help here
to use four phrases not common among lawyers and judges. For brevity, we
can call the court that authored a precedent the "precedential court," and
we can use the expression "decisional court" for the court that has been or
could be asked to adjudicate a current controversy in which the precedent
might be used.[1] Where the courts are in different states, we can refer to one
as the "precedential state" and the other as the "decisional state."

Cases from other jurisdictions are consulted only for guidance and only

---

2. If a court decides an issue on two independent grounds, either of which would alone
have been sufficient, neither is dictum. Both were the basis of the decision, even if only one
would have been needed.

3. "[A] federal district court is required to give great weight to the pronouncements of
its Court of Appeals, even though those pronouncements appear by way of dictum. 'While
not excused from making an independent examination of the precise issue presented, we
cannot assume that our Court of Appeals writes merely for intellectual exercise.'" *Max M.
v. Thompson,* 585 F. Supp. 317, 324 (N.D. Ill. 1984) (citation omitted).

4. *United States v. Bell,* 524 F.2d 202, 206 (2d Cir. 1975).

§10.4   1. These terms come from James Hardisty, *Reflections on Stare Decisis,* 55 Ind.
L.J. 41, 45 (1979).

where a gap appears in local law.[2] Although some courts prefer to fill a gap by analogizing to existing local law,[3] most courts are curious about foreign precedent when local law is not dispositive.[4] Even then, a decisional court will not be influenced by foreign holdings that are inconsistent with policies embedded in the decisional court's own local law.[5]

A decisional court will not be persuaded merely because a court in another state has taken a particular position.[6] Although a court might be impressed because a doctrine is the rule of a majority of states that have ruled on the matter, or because there is a trend among recent decisions toward or away from a rule, a court will nevertheless reject a rule it believes unwise. In determining the majority and minority rules and any recent trend, a court considers the number of states that have taken a particular position, not the number of courts or the number of decisions.[7] A precedential state's law becomes settled only when so held by that state's highest court.[8] Until a precedential state's highest court has ruled, the opinion of a lower court, while significant, is only a tentative expression of that state's law on the point.

Precedent interpreting statutes in other jurisdictions is treated somewhat differently from precedent interpreting the common law. That is because decisions interpreting statutes are not free-floating authority for what the law is in some generalized sense: they are authority for the meaning of specific words found in specific statutes, and they have no life independent of the words interpreted. If, for example, a statute were to be repealed, the cases interpreting it would no longer represent current law.

Opinions interpreting statutes in another state can be persuasive authority, but only if the statutory provisions are similar.[9] Foreign precedent in-

2. "Absent any Florida case directly in point, we may look elsewhere for persuasive authority." *Tonkovich v. South Florida Citrus Indus., Inc.,* 185 So. 2d 710, 715 (Fla. Ct. App. 1966).

3. "In cases of first impression in Alabama we believe it our duty to draw upon well established principles that have been long adhered to by our Supreme Court, if they provide a solution to the problem, before going to the law of other states for guidance." *Lammers v. State Farm Mutual Automobile Ins. Co.,* 48 Ala. App. 36, 40, 261 So. 2d 757, 761 (Civ. App.), *cert. denied,* 288 Ala. 745, 261 So. 2d 766 (1972).

4. "Comparable court decisions of other jurisdictions, while not determinative of issues before an Illinois court, are persuasive authority and entitled to respect." *In re Marriage of Raski,* 64 Ill. App. 3d 629, 633, 381 N.E.2d 744, 748 (App. Ct. 1978).

5. "[D]ecisions setting forth the public policies of other jurisdictions will not be followed if not harmonious with the judicially declared public policy of Illinois." *Galler v. Galler,* 32 Ill. 2d 16, 26, 203 N.E.2d 577, 583 (1964).

6. "Decisions of courts of other jurisdictions, even if based upon identical facts, are no more than persuasive, and they are persuasive only to the extent that their reasoning is regarded as logical." *Mauzy v. Legislative Redistricting Bd.,* 471 S.W.2d 570, 573 (Tex. 1971).

7. "Like witnesses, foreign authorities should be weighed and not counted." *Michigan Mutual Liability Co. v. Stallings,* 523 S.W.2d 539, 545 (Mo. Ct. App. 1975).

8. "The decision of a court not of last resort in other jurisdictions, while entitled to respect, is not determinative of the law of the state in which the decision is rendered." *Van Wagenberg v. Van Wagenberg,* 241 Md. 154, 215 A.2d 812, 821 (1966).

9. "[W]e remain unpersuaded. . . . [A]ppellants cite no direct Arizona authority for their concept. They cite instead a number of cases from other jurisdictions which may or may not have use tax exemptions similar to our A.R.S. § 42-1409(B)(2). No direct comparison is made [in appellants' brief] between the statutes. . . ." *State Tax Comm'n v. Anderson Dev. Corp.,* 117 Ariz. 555, 557, 574 P.2d 43, 45 (Ct. App. 1977).

terpreting a statute has an especially strong impact where the local statute is derived from the foreign one, especially where the foreign decision predates enactment of the derivative statute in the decisional state.[10] Less weight is given to foreign precedent that interprets the original statute after the derivative version was enacted in the decisional state.[11] Where the source of the local statute is a model or uniform draft, such as the Uniform Commercial Code, a local court can be persuaded not only by the interpretations of the same statute in other states, but also by the commentaries written by the drafters and published with the model statute.[12]

Be careful: different states have formulated different principles on the reception of foreign precedent, and only the case law of the decisional state will explain the terms on which it is willing to receive foreign precedent. The comments and quotations here merely illustrate the intellectual process; they do not define the approach a particular state will take.

§10.5   How to Use Foreign Precedent and Other Nonmandatory Authority to Fill a Gap in Local Law

There are two steps. First, lay a foundation for reliance on nonmandatory authority (§10.5.1). Then use it to fill the gap (§10.5.2).

§10.5.1   Laying the Foundation

Because foreign law is used only to help fill gaps in local law, you can use it *only after laying a foundation* for it. A foundation is laid when you define the gap and specify how local law does not dispose of the controversy.

A particularly deep gap occurs where the issue is one of "first impression" in the decisional state, which means that the appellate courts there have never before had occasion to resolve it. If some local courts have ruled, the issue is no longer one of first impression, but a gap would still exist if the rulings are all from nonmandatory courts. (The law is still not settled.) If those courts have ruled infrequently or are in disagreement, the gap is deep,

---

10. "[W]hen Arizona adopts a statute from another state, it will be presumed to have been adopted with the construction previously placed on it by the courts of that state." *England v. Ally Ong Hing*, 105 Ariz. 65, 68, 459 P.2d 498, 501 (1969).

11. "Appellants correctly point out that our statutes of limitations were adopted from Texas, and that a Texas court has held that the statute of limitations for libel did not apply to an action for damages to business caused by false statements. . . . Since that case was decided after the statute was adopted by Arizona, however, its holding, although persuasive, is not controlling." *Gee v. Pima County*, 126 Ariz. 116, 117, 612 P.2d 1079, 1080 (Ct. App. 1980).

12. "While we are not bound by the interpretation of the Commissioners on Uniform State Laws in their prefatory note to the draft of 1939 of the Uniform Acknowledgment Act, it is highly persuasive and should be adopted unless it is erroneous or contrary to the settled policy of this State." *Valley Nat'l Bank v. Avco Dev. Co.*, 14 Ariz. App. 56, 60, 480 P.2d 671, 675 (1971).

and foreign precedent may have a significant role in resolving it. If, however, the lower courts have ruled often and agree with each other, the gap is shallower, and the role of foreign precedent is limited to providing context for a discussion of whether the jurisdiction's highest court will or should overrule the lower courts despite the consensus below. (Wherever a gap is shallow, an evaluation of foreign authority is only a sideline to a main discussion of local cases.)

Another possibility is that local cases, even from the highest court in the jurisdiction, may be so infirm from age or poor reasoning that foreign precedent can again provide context for a discussion of whether the decisional jurisdiction will or should change course. But be careful: a precedent is not infirm just because it is old or just because you or your client do not like its reasoning. Age weakens a precedent when society has so changed that the precedent no longer represents public policy on the matter in question. And a precedent can be damaged by its own reasoning if doubted by a significant body of thought among judges and scholars.

Still another possibility is that local cases might have come very close to the issue but without directly resolving it. Because analogies to and syntheses[1] of local authority are often capable of disposing of the issue, this kind of gap is probably not deep, and the role of foreign precedent is limited to noting whether the resulting analogy or synthesis is consistent with what has happened elsewhere.

To lay the foundation, do three things: (1) state the issue precisely; (2) describe the topography of local law; and (3) show exactly how local law does not resolve the dispute. The following is the first of three examples that lay a foundation very concisely:

> No appellate court in this state has decided whether the sale of a newly built home implies a warranty of habitability, and the legislature has enacted no statute that would resolve the issue. However, a common law warranty of habitability has been recognized in. . . .

Here, the gap is total: there are no statutes and no case law. But it is usually not this easy. For example, there might be cases that have nibbled around the edges of the issue; or cases to which analogies can be made; or cases setting out public policy; or even a case that gives the false impression of having resolved the question. If so, the foundation is not complete until you have explained — in as much detail as the reader would need to agree with you — why the issue is still open.

> No reported decision has determined whether a violation of § 432 [a state statute] is negligence per se. But Colorado and Arizona [neighboring states with similar conditions] have enacted similar statutes. [*Here, add an explanation of the statutes sufficient to convince the reader that they really are similar.*] Courts in those states have held. . . .

§10.5   1. Analogy and synthesis are explained in Chapter 11.

Now, there is a statute, but the courts have not yet decided a certain aspect of its meaning (whether a violation is negligence per se). The foundation would not be complete until the similarity of the Colorado and Arizona statutes has been demonstrated.

> The Second District Court of Appeal has permitted this type of jury instruction, but the Fourth District considers it so confusing to the jury that it is reversible error unless clarified by other instructions. [*Here, add explanations of the Second and Fourth District cases.*] It is also reversible error in the federal courts and in most of the states that have considered the issue. . . .

In this example, there are in-state cases, but they disagree with each other. To complete this foundation — and before discussing the out-of-state authority — the Second and Fourth District cases would have to be explained.

This is *not* a foundation:

> Kansas [the decisional state] has not addressed this issue.

We are not told what the issue is. Nor are we told what Kansas has done. Are there no analogous precedents? Is there nothing in Kansas law that would set out local public policy on the question? (Unless shown otherwise, the reader will suspect that there are analogous cases and expressions of public policy, but that the writer either did not find them or is not willing to talk about them.)

Do not lecture the reader on basic principles of the hierarchy of authority ("since there are no reported decisions in this state on this issue, it is necessary to look to the law of other jurisdictions"). The reader long ago learned that that is the standard way of filling local gaps.

§10.5.2 Filling the Gap

A gap in the decisional state's common law can be filled by relying on precedent from other jurisdictions and on the views of scholarly commentators. If the gap centers on the meaning of an unclear statute, the gap can be filled only by relying on foreign precedent that interprets similar statutes elsewhere and on scholarly commentators who discuss the same or similar statutes. (If other states have statutes on the question and the decisional state has none, that is not necessarily a gap in the law. The decisional state's courts might hold that when the legislature refused to enact such a statute, it decided to exclude from the decisional state's law the provisions adopted elsewhere.)

Once the foundation has been laid, describe precisely the topography of foreign precedent. Synthesize it into a pattern where possible, and analogize where necessary.[2] It is not enough to cite to some scattered out-of-state

2. Synthesis and analogy are discussed in Chapter 11.

cases with analogous facts. The decisional court is free to ignore nonmandatory authority, and it will do so unless you can show that the foreign precedents fit nicely into the gap in local law. *The snuggest fit occurs where the policy behind the foreign cases coincides with established public policy in the decisional state.* The focus usually should be on the case law. The views of commentators generally play a secondary role.

If a large number of jurisdictions have ruled on the question, the reader will need to know which is the majority or plurality rule and which rule is favored by the recent trend of decisions. This can be supported only by a precise statement of the score: the number of jurisdictions that have adopted the majority or plurality rule; the number of jurisdictions that have adopted other rules; and the number of jurisdictions that have switched since a date that you have selected in order to define the trend.

If the issue is crucial to your analysis, the score should in turn be supported by a citation for each jurisdiction.[3] It may be powerful to say that 31 states have adopted the position you believe to be correct, but there are three inherent risks in trying to back up that kind of claim by citing to a law review article or judicial opinion that collects the citations on which you rely. First, the law review article or opinion may be a few years old, and in the interim the list of states may have shrunk or grown. Second, readers depend on you to report what *you* have found, rather than secondhand information that you have not yourself verified. Third, the reader who wants to check your authority will want to know directly from your writing where to find it, and that reader will not want to trace your research through second and third sources.[4]

But in an office memo, if the matter is peripheral to your analysis, you may be able to prove the score through a citation to a *recent* precedent or article or an annotation in *American Law Reports* (using the up-date in the pocket part), if either of them tabulates the scores and cites cases. (As readers, judges are less flexible. In a memo or brief submitted to a court, the score always must be proved the long way, by a citation for each jurisdiction.)

§10.6   How to Select Nonmandatory Precedent

So many opinions have been published that they occupy millions of pages in thousands of volumes of reporters, filling shelf after shelf in law libraries. The mass is so large that computers are increasingly used to keep track of it. After you have isolated those opinions that touch on the subject to be

---

3. If the gap is a matter of unsettled federal law, you may need to show the reader how each of the federal circuits has ruled.

4. This is one of the very few situations where a string citation, a footnote, or both are acceptable in a memorandum or brief. (A string citation lists many cites. For an example, see the first block quotation in rule 1.3 of the Bluebook (page 24 in the 15th edition).) In a string cite, one case per jurisdiction is usually sufficient.

written about, how do you choose, first, the opinions to rely on and, second, those to emphasize?

If you have found mandatory authority, it will have to dominate your analysis. If local but not mandatory precedent is to be considered, or if you need to refer to foreign precedent, you must make some difficult choices unless the available precedent is so sparse that the only option is to discuss it all. Since your goal is to predict a court's action (or, in a motion memo or appellate brief, to persuade a court to act), your criteria for selecting non-mandatory precedent will have to be the same criteria the courts use.

The task would be easier if courts were to adopt uniform and well-defined rules on the selection of nonmandatory precedent on which to rely, but any such rules would deprive judges of some of the flexibility and creativity so valuable to judicial decision-making. Instead, without having made any overt rules on the subject, most courts, in most cases, apply a relatively uniform set of criteria. Generally, courts are impressed as follows, in approximately this order of priority:

First: whether a precedent is on point with the issue before the decisional court, or, if not on point, whether a sound analogy or synthesis makes it useful anyway. If the opinion is easily distinguished, or if a synthesis would be logically faulty, the decisional court will not be influenced.

Second: the quality of the precedent's reasoning. Is the logic of the holding sound? Is it based on a reasonable interpretation of other authority? Is it based on public policy agreeable to the decisional court? Even long-standing precedent will not persuade if it does not make good sense. "It is revolting," Justice Holmes once wrote, "to have no better reason for a rule of law than that so it was laid down in the time of Henry IV. It is still more revolting if the grounds upon which it was laid down have vanished long since, and the rule simply persists from blind imitation of the past."[1]

Third: the identity of the precedential court. Is it the highest court in its jurisdiction? Is it a court with recognized expertise or leadership in the field (such as the New Jersey and California supreme courts in negligence law)? Is it a court that has in the past influenced the courts of the decisional state? Is it in a state where the relevant conditions are similar to those prevailing in the decisional state? Is it a court philosophically compatible with the decisional court? (California negligence decisions, for example, are not influential in New York.)

Fourth: the treatment of the precedent (or the rule it stands for) in other reported opinions.[2] Is the precedent or rule discussed with approval or with skepticism? Is it part of a general trend or widely accepted body of law? Or is it a lonely straggler that the rest of the law seems to be leaving behind? Do courts seem to be looking for excuses not to enforce the rule the precedent stands for? (If in its own state the precedent has been overruled —

---

§10.6   1. O.W. Holmes, *The Path of the Law*, 10 Harv. L. Rev. 457, 469 (1897).

2. Scholarly commentary on an opinion may be persuasive in court, but not as frequently as students sometimes believe, except where the scholarly opinion is sharp and insightful, widely shared, or the product of a well-known scholar in the field.

even if only impliedly[3] — this criterion becomes, of course, the most portant.)

Fifth: the clarity with which the holding is expressed. If the rationale for the holding is unstated or vaguely stated, the opinion is, to that extent, less probative of what the law is.

Sixth: when the precedent was decided. Judges are predisposed to treat newer opinions as more authoritative than substantially older ones, simply because changing social conditions can make a rule inapt. On the other hand, a holding so new as not to have been tested through experience may be treated a little warily at first. A rule adopted only by a minority of states may be especially persuasive if the recent case law shows a trend toward it, making it the "emerging trend."

Seventh: positions taken by judges in the precedential court. Was the decision unanimous? If not, was the dissent well reasoned and eloquent or written by a respected judge? For that matter, was the majority opinion written by an influential judge?[4]

§10.7   *How to Work Effectively in the Library*

Prepare yourself for the library. You will not work efficiently if you research like a vacuum cleaner. Instead, look carefully at the facts you have been given and define, as precisely as you can, the issue or issues you have been asked to resolve. While in the library, focus exclusively on what you are looking for, and ignore extraneous material, no matter how interesting it may be. Remember that your goal is to discover authority *against* — as well as for — your conclusion because you cannot predict without counter-analyzing that authority, and you cannot persuade a court without arguing against it.

How should you store all the things you find in the library? Some lawyers use large index cards or pages in a binder, usually putting only one case on a card or page. The advantage of cards is that they can be shuffled easily while researching and writing. The advantage of pages is that more can be written on them.

Another storage medium is the photocopying of critical or quotable authority. Brief all cases, whether you photocopy them or not, because briefing makes you analyze the case. For the same reason, outline statutes, even if you also photocopy them. The advantage of photocopying the most critical

---

3. A court does not usually list each prior decision it overrules when the law alters course. So many cases would have to be listed that it would be impractical. And sometimes the law is changed more than the opinion suggests, either because the court chooses not to emphasize its modification or rejection of prior law or because the logical or practical ramifications of the decision are not immediately apparent even to the court itself.

4. Like scholarly comment on precedent, the answers to these questions are often overrated by students. The other criteria are harder to apply than this one, but they also have much more effect.

authority is that you can return to it again and again at home when you realize that you have not fully understood the authority's possibilities. The advantage of photocopying pages from which you might quote is that your quotations are more likely to be accurate if taken directly from the photocopy.

Photocopying, however, is much overrated by students, many of whom try to reduce anxiety by spending time and effort at the library's photocopy machines. Although photocopied cases look impressive, the student who copies dozens of barely read cases only defers thinking about them until later. (When the student finally does read the cases, a surprisingly high percentage of them will turn out to have little or no value.) The wiser student is the one who photocopies only what is truly needed and who does much of the analysis while reading authority in the original sources at a library table.

While making notes in the library, write down *accurately* what you need — both the substance of the authority and its full citation. (For the latter, keep a copy of *The Bluebook* close at hand so that you can write out the citation in complete form while you are using the books in the library.[1]) Be sure that your notes are complete enough to include all the citation information you will need when you start to write.

Read several authorities before you start taking detailed notes. You will not know what is really important until you have strolled around a bit in the landscape of authority that you must eventually explain to the reader. But even if you defer briefing until you know some of the lay of the land, you will still find that your earliest briefs are the least well done. Near the end of the research, go back to some of the important authorities you read first: you may be surprised at what you missed. If, when you return to them, you find that your first notes seem a little naive, do not be discouraged: that happens even to experienced lawyers when they research a field that is new to them.

Start writing *before* you have finished the research. As you work, gradually spend an increasing proportion of your time writing and a progressively smaller proportion researching. Early in your research, snatches of what you will write — a paragraph or two, perhaps — will come to you while you are working in the library. They are worth writing down, although you will certainly change them substantially later. Eventually, you will be writing so much that you will visit the library only to verify something in your notes or to fill a small gap in your research that you had not noticed before.

You will do a better job overall if you resist the anxious urge to put off writing until you are fully "protected" with authority ("I can't write — I don't have enough"). If you try to do "all" the research before beginning to write, you will waste large amounts of time in the library because you will not be able to know when you have already found everything you need. (Writing tells you when you have enough because writing determines what you need.) And you may find yourself putting off writing until you no longer

---

§10.7   1. Chapter 16 explains Bluebook rules on citation and quotation.

have time to do a good job. Research, thinking, and writing are not really separable activities. They are all part of a single process of creation.

Start organizing the entire Discussion — or Argument if you are working on a motion memorandum or appellate brief — as soon as your research has begun to show you the contours of what you will say. The outline (see §6.3) will give you strong clues about what still must be found in the library.

Exercise.   The Hierarchy of Authority

You are working on a case that is now being litigated in the United States District Court for the District of Nevada. You have been asked to find out whether a defendant who made and lost a motion to dismiss for insufficient service of process can subsequently move to dismiss for failure to state a claim on which relief can be granted. You have found the following authority, all of which square-ly addresses your issue. Although the logic and wording of each authority will, of course, affect its weight, make a *preliminary* ranking of the following author-ities solely from the information provided here. (If you are not familiar with the boundaries of the federal circuits, see the map facing the title page in any volume of Federal Reporter, Second Series. Nevada is in the Ninth Circuit.)

Samuels v. Amundsen — 4th Circuit, 1990

Great Basin Realty Co. v. Rand — Nevada Supreme Court, 1986

Matthewson's treatise on Federal Courts (published last year) *TReatise = 2° Authority*

Wilkes v. Jae Sun Trading Corp. — 9th Circuit, 1963

Pincus v. McGrath — United States Supreme Court, 1949

Rule 12 of the Federal Rules of Civil Procedure (effective 1938) *Rule = 1° Authority*

Barlow v. Sepulveda — California Supreme Court, 1989

Garibaldi v. City of Boulder — 10th Circuit, 1982

Ott v. Frazier — 7th Circuit, 1931

11 Working with Precedent

§11.1 Eight Skills for Working with Precedent

Perhaps once in a blue moon, a lawyer might find that an issue is entirely resolved by mandatory precedent on point — precedent from a mandatory appellate court that has decided the same issue on mirrored facts. More often, the law is less certain, and the lawyer must construct an answer from more tangential precedent, using at least some of eight skills. They are (1) ranking precedent according to the hierarchy of authority and the principles that are derived from it; (2) formulating rules along a continuum from the broadest to the narrowest interpretations arguable from the facts and wording of precedent; (3) analogizing; (4) distinguishing; (5) eliciting policy; (6) synthesizing fragmented authority into a unified whole; (7) reconciling conflicting or adverse authority; and (8) testing the result of the first seven skills for realism and marketability to the judicial mind.[1]

In Chapter 10, you learned about the *hierarchy of authority* and the principles that are derived from it. The other skills are explained in this chapter.

---

§11.1 1. In this chapter, as in Chapter 10, the "precedential court" is the court that authored the precedent under discussion, and the "later court" or "decisional court" is the court that has been or could be asked to adjudicate a current controversy to which that precedent might be applied. Similarly, the "precedential facts" are the facts of the precedent itself (as opposed to the facts of the current case).

§11.2 Formulating a Variety of Rules from the Same Precedent

In §3.2, you learned something about *formulating rules along a continuum from the broadest to the narrowest interpretations.* For example:[1]

> *A*'s father induces her not to marry *B* as she promised to do. On a holding that the father is not liable to *B* for so doing, a gradation of widening propositions can be built, [the first of which is the following:]

1. Fathers are privileged to induce daughters to break promises to marry.

This would be a rule limited strictly to the precedential facts. How likely is it that the law would give fathers a privilege denied to others? What purpose might the law have had for doing such a thing? How likely is it that only daughters would be inducible within the scope of such a privilege? Why would the law have singled them out? And how likely is it that only promises to marry would be the object of such treatment? What reason might the law have to treat those kinds of promises specially? If you cannot answer these questions, one or more elements of this narrow formulation are inaccurate.

2. Parents are so privileged.

Here the father in the precedent is only an example of the class of privileged people. Even if the precedential court had written much about a special and valuable role for fathers in the family, that would not prevent a later court from deciding — in an era in which gender roles have come to be treated differently — that the rule privileges all parents, regardless of gender. A later court might do that overtly, by recognizing that the precedential court intended to limit the privilege to fathers and by deciding that such a limitation offends modern policy. Or a later court might do it more subtly, by concluding that the precedential court meant the privilege to extend to both parents and that the father was spoken of merely because he was the parent at issue in the precedent.

3. Parents are so privileged as to both daughters and sons.

Here the daughter in the precedent is only an example of the class of people who can be induced within the scope of the privilege. All that has been said about the father's gender applies equally to the daughter's.

4. All persons are so privileged as to promises to marry.

The father and daughter are no longer examples because the rule is not limited to classifications of people. Rather, the relationship between father and daughter would have been mere coincidence. This formulation is a

---

§11.2 1. The example and the sample rules derived from it are from Herman Oliphant, *A Return to Stare Decisis,* 14 A.B.A.J. 71, 72 (1928).

pretty drastic expansion of formulation 3. There could have been some intermediate steps: blood relatives are privileged to induce other blood relatives; relatives (blood or not) are privileged to induce other relatives; people who have reason to care about each other (friends, for example) are privileged to induce one another; and so on.

5. Parents are so privileged as to all promises made by their children.

We are back to parents and children, but now the contemplation of marriage has become coincidental: the promise might as well be one to buy a motorcycle or to climb the Himalayas. A later court might be wary of such a broad rule. Are there reasons why a parent should be privileged to induce a child to break *any* promise? How is society — or some valuable part of it — protected by such a privilege? Conversely, is there anything about a promise to marry that makes it fit for special treatment? (As you can see, policy considerations are important in selecting the most plausible rule formulation.)

THIS IS TOO BROAD

6. All persons are so privileged as to all promises made by anyone.

Under this formulation, no one can be liable for inducing another person to break a promise. If that were the rule, the law would have no need in this kind of controversy for a concept like a privilege. But the law has plainly used that concept, implying rather strongly that there is liability in some situations but not in others. Certainly, formulations 5 and 6 are so broad as to be unreasonable and unrealistic, just as formulations 1 and 2 are so narrow as to be unreasonable and unrealistic. The hard task is figuring out which of the other formulations is most likely to be adopted by a decisional court. Be careful when you consider such a question: you cannot do whatever you please. In predictive writing, formulate the rule as you believe the courts are most likely to in the case you are trying to predict. (And in persuasive writing, select a formulation that both favors your client and is likely to be accepted as valid by the court you are trying to persuade.) In addition, if the rule has been stated over and over again in many mandatory decisions and in pretty much the same wording, you do not have much room for interpretive maneuver. In fact, you might not have any at all. Your room for maneuver grows where the law has a gap: where the courts have implied but not fully stated the rule, where the decisions are inconsistent or sparse, and so forth.

§11.3 *Analogizing and Distinguishing*

An *analogy* is a demonstration that two situations are so parallel that the reasoning that justified the decision in one should do the same in the other. When a court is persuaded by an analogy to precedent, the court is said to "follow" the precedent. *Distinguishing* is the opposite of analogy: a demonstration that two situations are so fundamentally dissimilar that the same result should not occur in both. Analogizing and distinguishing have been two of the most important intellectual tools in the slow and gradual construction and evolution of the common law. Both help find and state the rule for which a precedent stands, together with something about how that rule is to be applied. (Distinguishing does so by showing what the rule is not and how it is not to be applied.) There are three steps in analogizing or distinguishing. First, make sure that the issue in the precedent is the same one you are trying to resolve. Second, identify the precedent's determinative facts. Do not look for mere coincidences between the precedent and the current case; look instead for facts that the precedential court treated as crucial and on which it really relied. Finally, compare the precedent's determinative facts to the facts you are trying to resolve. Although you should strongly consider what the precedential court has said about its reasoning, your conclusion need not necessarily be one that was within the stated or even conscious contemplation of the precedential court, since a court cannot always predict every one of the reasonable consequences of each precedent it sets. Your conclusion should, however, be the most logical and plausible one that is consistent with the heart of the precedential court's reasoning and with public policy. For example:

> Suppose a College Dean has a power to make and enforce rules of conduct in his College, and that he does not publish a set of carefully drafted rules, but applies a rough and ready doctrine of precedent. He fines Jones £5, and explains to him that he has done so because Jones kept Miss Doe, his girlfriend, in the College until 9:30, and that he has always fined undergraduates £5 if they allow ladies to stay in College after 9 P.M. Two days later he discovers that Smith allowed Miss Styles to remain in until 9:10 P.M. because she had been stung by a bee and was in considerable pain. It would surely be justifiable for the Dean to excuse Smith, and distinguish his earlier decision, without having to show that in Jones' case he emphasized the [good] health of Miss Doe, or treated it in any way material to the issue of Jones' guilt. For what he does in Smith's case is not to pretend that he previously regarded Miss Doe's health as material — which would be untrue — but only that in Smith's case he finds a circumstance which makes it very different from Jones' case, which is not in the least untrue, and indeed quite sensible of him.[1]

Several analogies are illustrated in the memorandum in Appendix C. (See the marginal notes there.)

§11.4   Eliciting Policy from Precedent

Policy is elicited from precedent that explains the underlying goals that the rules involved are intended to advance. Remember how revolting it was

---

§11.3   1. A. W. B. Simpson, *The Ratio Decidendi of a Case and the Doctrine of Binding Precedent*, in *Oxford Essays on Jurisprudence* 174 (A.G. Guest ed. 1961).

to Holmes, "to have no better reason for a rule of law than that so it was laid down in the time of Henry IV."[1] Not only is policy important in clearing up ambiguities in the law, but judges are guided by policy concerns even in applying law that seems on the surface to be unambiguous. A court needs confidence that a contemplated decision really is consistent with the law's goals. Thus, legal analysis persistently asks what the rules are meant to accomplish, whether the proposed result would accomplish that, and whether the rules and the result would create more problems than they would solve. And where a jurisdiction has no settled rule and therefore must choose between or among competing rules, the rule selected must be one that is consistent with the jurisdiction's policies. Although you may find policy openly stated in precedent, it is perhaps more often implied through the court's reasoning.

§11.5   Synthesis and Reconciliation

Synthesis is the binding together of several opinions into a whole that stands for a rule or an expression of policy. By focusing on the reasoning and generic facts that the cases have in common, synthesis finds and explains collective meaning that is not apparent from the individual cases themselves. As with analogizing and distinguishing, a synthesis must be realistic enough to work. Its plausibility will be measured by the extent to which it is logical, reasonable, and consistent with public policy. In predictive writing, a synthesis must be one the courts are likely to adopt. (And later, in persuasive writing, it must be both that and one favorable to your client. In persuasive writing, the essence of this skill is the turning of weakness into strength by looking beneath the surface of precedent to find underlying consistencies in reasoning and policy.)

Beginners sometimes think they have synthesized authority when in fact they have not. A passage does not explain a synthesis merely because several cases are mentioned, one after another. It is not a synthesis to describe Case A, describe Case B, describe Case C, describe Case D, and then stop. That is nothing more than an amplified list: the raw materials have been held up to view, but they have not been sewn together.

To turn it into a unified whole, step back and ask yourself what, under the surface, the cases really have in common. Identify the threads that appear in all four cases, tie the threads together, and organize the analysis around the threads themselves (rather than around the individual cases). The reader cares more about the threads than about the cases, and an individual case is important only to the extent that it teaches something about a thread. It may turn out that Case B sets out the most convincing proof of whatever is in question; Cases A and D agree and are the only out-of-state

---

§11.4   1. O.W. Holmes, *The Path of the Law,* 10 Harv. L. Rev. 457, 469 (1897). (See §10.6.)

cases to have decided the issue; and Case C is a much older decision standing for the same rule but on the basis of reasoning that is less complete than that expressed in Case B. An effective synthesis might explain Case B in full; use Cases A and D to show that foreign authority agrees; and then use Case C not at all (or only if needed to fill in a remaining gap). Your choice of a formula of synthesis like this one will depend on the issue and on the topography of authority available to you. That choice is an important decision, and you should be prepared to explain how you made it.

Some students go to all the trouble of working out a synthesis, but then fail to make the synthesis clear to the reader. First, state it in an opening sentence that includes the synthesized rule or statement of policy:

> Although the Supreme Court has not ruled on the question, the trend in the Courts of Appeal is to hold that such a prosecution is dismissable where any of four kinds of government misconduct has occurred: . . .

(A synthesis like this could take several pages to prove because, typically, no case will consider more than one form of misconduct.)

Second, organize your explanation around some variation of the paradigm for structuring proof of a conclusion of law (see §9.1), and use the techniques of forceful writing (see §15.3) to show the reader how the synthesis fits together. Remember that the reader will most easily understand the synthesis in the reverse of the order in which you developed it. Although in developing the synthesis in a first draft you might start from the case details and work up to a synthesized rule or statement of policy, things will be most clear to the reader in later drafts if you reorganize so that you start with the synthesized rule or policy and work down to the supporting details.

Finally, read over your explanation while pretending to be someone who does not know the cases or your synthesis. If the structure of your synthesis is not instantly clear to that kind of reader, find the problem and fix it.

Several syntheses are illustrated in the memoranda and briefs in Appendices C through F. (See the marginal notes there.)

A hybrid skill is that of *reconciliation*. If two decisions seem on the surface to be in conflict, you might be able to demonstrate that the conflict does not exist because on closer examination the two decisions actually stand for the same rule, espouse the same policy, or can be harmonized in some other way. Used in that way, reconciliation has much in common with synthesis. Similarly, a precedent might seem on the surface to conflict with a decision that would be favorable to your client in a current case. There you might be able to demonstrate that the seemingly adverse precedent does not actually conflict with the decision your client would prefer — and in some respects even supports a decision in your client's favor. (But the converse might also happen: if the precedent seems on the surface to be helpful to your client, your adversary might be able to demonstrate that it really stands for something entirely different and actually hurts your client and helps your adversary.) Reconciliation often uses other skills. For example, the seemingly adverse precedent might lose its adversity if it turns out to be distinguishable. Or it might actually reflect favorable policy.

§11.6 Testing for Realism and Marketability

The last skill is that of *testing the result of your reasoning for its realism and marketability to the judicial mind.* Whatever other skills you might use in assembling your analysis, step back from what you are doing and ask yourself whether the result will seem reasonable and just to the typical judge. The experience of adjudicating creates what Roscoe Pound called "the trained intuition of the judge,"[1] an instinct for how the law ought to treat each set of facts. If the result of your reasoning would strike the judicial mind as unrealistic and unreasonable, that mind will reject what you have done, even if you have used all the other skills with gymnastic agility. (That kind of analysis is called *formalistic* because it complies with the forms of the law but does nothing else.) Because the law is hardly ever certain, a judge can always fold back your reasoning and make other analogies, build other syntheses, and so forth — or, worse, adopt the analogies, syntheses, and other constructs proposed by your adversary. Karl Llewellyn wrote that "rules *guide*, but they do not *control* decision. There is no precedent that the judge may not at his need either file down to razor thinness or expand into a bludgeon."[2]

The skill of testing for realism and marketability requires that you have some understanding of how the judicial mind operates. That may take a long time to come to know fully, but you are learning it now through the decisions you read in casebooks and through the writing you do in this course. (Although lawyers often write arguments based on equity, justice, and reasonability, they *never write down* the kind of testing described here. It is easy to see why: how could you reduce to writing a test for realism? If a lawyer concludes that the result of his or her reasoning would offend the judge's trained intuition, the lawyer simply starts over again and builds another analysis.)

Instructions for Exercises I and II

The skills described in this chapter are individually difficult to master, but many students say that the harder part is using them together in an integrated way to resolve an issue. The exercises that follow will illustrate how to do that.

Make the prediction asked for in the exercise your teacher assigns. Assume that your library research shows that the prediction will depend on the decisions reproduced in the exercise.

§11.6 1. Roscoe Pound, *The Theory of Judicial Decision,* 36 Harv. L. Rev. 940, 951 (1923).
2. K. N. Llewellyn, *The Bramble Bush* 180 (1930).

A good way to work out your reasoning is to inventory your analytical resources:

1. identify the issues
2. analyze each issue
   ▶ identify the determinative facts
   ▶ for each precedent, consider
       ▷ likely rules for which the case stands (along a spectrum from broad to narrow)
       ▷ likely ways of analogizing and distinguishing
       ▷ policies for which the case stands
       ▷ likely syntheses with other cases
       ▷ likely reconciliations with inconsistent cases
       ▷ how the case fits into the hierarchy of authority
   ▶ test your analysis by
       ▷ counter-analyzing reasonable arguments that could challenge your prediction
       ▷ considering troublesome facts that would bother a judge
       ▷ asking whether your analysis will seem reasonable, just, and realistic to the judicial mind
   ▶ predict how the court will resolve the issue
3. predict how the court will resolve the entire controversy

While making this inventory, start with a lot of paper and leave much blank space because you will probably go back and forth, adding to what you have already done. Do not be afraid to change your mind as you go along.

Make an objective prediction and do not take sides. Your prediction is for the benefit of a supervisor, such as a senior partner, who really wants to know what will happen in court. You are not being asked for courtroom advocacy. (That will be covered in later chapters.)

If your teacher has assigned the exercise as preparation for a class, be prepared to speak in class from your inventory.

If, on the other hand, your teacher has assigned the exercise as work to be done entirely at home, complete the exercise by reorganizing your inventory into a writing outline based on some variation of the paradigm described in Chapter 9.

Exercise I.   *The Allegheny Steel Corporation*[1]

The Allegheny Steel Corporation (AlSteCorp) is a heavy metal rock band that specializes in laser and fog effects and which performed on July 25 in the new

---

1. See the instructions on page 125.

Nutmeg Dome in Bridgeport, Connecticut. This was the ninth of 16 concerts in AlSteCorp's North American tour, which began in June in Milwaukee. After the first concert was highly praised on MTV, all of the remaining performances — except Bridgeport — were sold out within hours after tickets became available.

Your client is the Bridgeport Cultural Authority (BCA), which owns the Nutmeg Dome and is now involved in a contract dispute with the Corvo Construction Company. BCA contracted with Corvo to build the Nutmeg Dome. Among other things, the contract required (in paragraph four) that Corvo build the Dome "so as to be ready for full use on or before the first day of July" of this year. Paragraph 51 of the contract provided as follows: "Because of the difficulty of determining lost income in the entertainment industry, in the event of Corvo's failure to perform its obligations according to the schedule set out herein, Corvo shall be liable to BCA in the amount of two thousand dollars for each day of delay."

The Dome consists of an auditorium and the offices and facilities needed to run it. BCA moved into the offices on July 1, and the July 25 concert was the first event scheduled in the Dome. The offices constitute six percent of the cubic feet in the building.

Corvo concedes that, due to its own fault, the electrical and ventilation systems were not installed according to the specifications set out in paragraphs 23 and 28 of the contract. Corvo further concedes that, as a result, it would have been unsafe to use AlSteCorp's fog effects on July 25 and there was inadequate electricity behind the stage on that date to use the group's laser effects.

These problems became apparent before the concert, and the local media reported throughout July that AlSteCorp might not be able to use its usual fog and laser effects. Eighteen hundred tickets went unsold, and BCA's profit from these tickets would have been $22,000. After the performance, AlSteCorp's lead guitarist told MTV,

> "What, ho, man, it was awful. After what we went through, no self-respecting creative artist would schedule a gig in this place. Can you imagine just standing on the stage and not being able to do anything but play the instruments? They must think we do grunge for a living. Is this Dome a hole, or what?"

On July 27, Corvo was able to complete the work to BCA's satisfaction. BCA believes that public confidence in the Nutmeg Dome is less that it would have been had Corvo performed on time, and that, to an unpredictable extent, it may become harder to book performances and to sell tickets than it otherwise would have been. BCA believes that performers' agents who might have considered booking into the Dome will now be reluctant to do so.

Before BCA decided to build the Dome, it studied the revenue generated by similar structures in other cities of comparable size. The study showed that these buildings have, on average, 12 to 15 bookings a month, of which two or three are concerts and the rest sports, convention, and community events. The profitability of a booking varies considerably, depending on the nature of the events. But the average net daily income of the buildings studied was $1,500. Net income is profit after all expenses (mortgage, salaries, etc.) have been paid. (Average daily income is 1/365 of annual income — *not* the average income generated by each event.)

Will BCA be able to recover from Corvo liquidated damages of $52,000 (26 days at $2,000 per day), or will recovery be limited to a lesser amount? (You are *not* being asked to determine the rights of the Allegheny Steel Corporation.)

BANTA v. STAMFORD MOTOR CO.
92 A. 665 (Conn. 1914)

Prentice, C.J. [Stamford Motor Co. contracted with Banta to build him a yacht for $5,500] to be paid in installments as the work of construction progressed. [If the yacht was not delivered by September 1, 1911, the contract provided that Stamford should pay Banta $15 in liquidated damages] for each day of delay. The boat was [delivered on] November 25, 1911.

[Banta paid Stamford for the yacht in installments as the work progressed, but Stamford refused to pay Banta $15 per day of delay, for which Banta now sues.]

The boat was . . . intended by the plaintiff for use by him in cruising in Chesapeake Bay during the months of October and November, and later for a pleasure trip in Florida waters. [Stamford knew this. Banta was unable to cruise in Chesapeake Bay. At the time, it would have cost $15 a day to rent a comparable yacht. Banta] did not rent another boat. . . .

[Stamford argues that the daily rate payable for delay is so disproportionate as to constitute a penalty and not liquidated damages. A predetermined damages provision in a contract is really a penalty if its purpose is to insure timely performance by putting the tardy party in fear. But such a provision is liquidated damages if its purpose is to compensate the other party for loss due to delay.]

"[P]arties are allowed to . . . fix beforehand the amount to be paid as damages for a breach . . . but the courts [will not enforce such a provision if the amount is so excessive that it is actually a penalty. When, on the other hand,] the amount of damages would be uncertain or difficult of proof, and the parties have beforehand expressly agreed upon the amount of damages, and that amount is not greatly disproportionate to the presumable loss, their expressed intent will be carried out." [Citation omitted.]

[To determine whether a sum agreed to be paid in the event of breach is an unenforceable penalty or enforceable liquidated damages, the law does not compare that sum with the loss the plaintiff actually suffered, but instead with the loss that the parties] might reasonably have anticipated at the time the contract was made. . . . [Banta is therefore] under no obligation to show actual damage suffered commensurate with the $15 a day rate. . . .

[Because Banta's injury was the loss of pleasure for a period of time, it would be difficult for a court to calculate an amount of money that would compensate for that loss. The parties agreed beforehand on an amount that would do that. And no fact indicates that this amount was greatly disproportionate to the possible loss which the parties imagined at the time they made the contract. Banta is entitled to liquidated damages of $15 per day of delay.]

HUNGERFORD CONSTRUCTION CO. v.
FLORIDA CITRUS EXPOSITION, INC.
410 F.2d 1229 (5th Cir.), cert. denied, 396 U.S. 928 (1969)

BELL, Circuit Judge.

[This diversity case concerns] the construction of a building at Winter Haven, Florida . . . which was to serve as an exhibition center for the citrus industry. . . . [The roof leaked, and acoustical plaster inside] was damaged. The damaged plaster was replaced by the contractor but subsequent leaks left it in a discolored condition. . . .

. . . The building owner was awarded [damages based on] a . . . provision in the contract [that provided for] liquidated damages in the amount of $200.00 per calendar day of delay [after the scheduled completion date. T]he building was delivered to the owner [on time and] was in continuous use thereafter. The owner contended that the liquidated damages clause was nevertheless applicable because of loss of secondary use due to the roof leak. . . .

. . . The building was to be used by the owner mainly for a year round office and for a citrus festival during February and March. [The owners also hoped to rent it for exhibitions, and to charge the public for tours of the structure.] . . .

[We conclude that under Florida law this liquidated damages clause is an unenforceable penalty clause if used] as a basis for damages for loss of secondary use under the facts here.

". . . [T]he courts . . . allow [parties] to agree upon such a sum as will probably be the fair compensation for the breach of a contract. But when they go beyond this, and . . . stipulate . . . a sum entirely disproportionate to the measure of liability which the law regards as compensatory, the courts will refuse to give effect to the stipulation and will confine the parties to such actual damages as may be pleaded and proved." [Citation omitted.]

. . . [Here, t]he evidence as to loss of secondary use was entirely speculative. One auto show may have been lost but there is no evidence as to the amount of rent which would have been realized out of this transaction or whether the loss occurred during the period in suit. The only other loss of use claimed was in the form of a daily admission charge to the public to see the building and its contents. [But there is no evidence that a significant number of people would actually have wanted to tour this building. This is] entirely disproportionate to the sum of $200.00 . . . per day. . . .

SIDES CONSTRUCTION CO. v. CITY OF SCOTT CITY
581 S.W.2d 443 (Mo. Ct. App. 1979)

GREENE, Judge.

Plaintiff [contracted to build a swimming complex for] defendant city. The contract provided [that if construction was completed after the scheduled delivery date, the plaintiff would be liable for liquidated damages of $50 per day of delay.] . . .

[T]he contract provided that [the liquidated damages were intended to compensate the city and the public] "for loss to the Owner and the public due to the obstruction of traffic, interference with use of existing or new facilities, and increased cost of engineering, administration, supervision, inspection, etc. . . ."

[The work was completed five and a half months late. The defendant deducted $50 per day from its payments to the plaintiff, which claims] that the liquidated damages provision in the contract was, in reality, a penalty since defendant failed to show that it sustained any actual damages by plaintiff's failure to complete the contract [on time]. . . .

The right to stipulate for liquidated damages for delay in completing construction of public works is generally recognized, and the stipulated amount may be recovered, if reasonable. Provisions for fixed per diem payments for delay in the performance of such contracts are usually construed as stipulations for liquidated damages, and not as penalties, where the actual damages are uncertain or are difficult of ascertainment, and where the stated sum is a reasonable estimate of probable damages or is reasonably proportionate to actual damages.

. . . Although we doubt . . . that any proof of actual damages were necessary to bring the liquidated damages provision to life, the defendant has shown damage by the necessity of having to hire additional engineering personnel to inspect the project; by being inconvenienced by the regrading of the parking lot; and, by the loss of interest on its capital investment during the delay period in question.

It is true that the precise amount of such damages is difficult to ascertain. That is why a liquidated damages provision in a construction contract is beneficial to both parties. It protects the owner from a future laborious recitation of item by item damage, and it protects the contractor from a potential lump sum claim of substantial sums of money in the event of breach of the completion provision. Here, . . . the amount of liquidated damages . . . was not greatly disproportionate . . . , and should not be considered as a penalty. . . .

Exercise II. Emil Risberg's Diary[1]

Returning from an expedition across the Arctic ice cap in the last century, Emil Risberg and his companions became stranded at the northern tip of Greenland. After several weeks they all died of scurvy and exposure. A few years later, their hut was found, their bodies were buried at sea, and their possessions were returned to their families. Emil Risberg's widow received, among other things, his diary.

Risberg had measured the group's geographic position every day during the expedition, and he recorded those measurements, as well as a mass of other detail, in his diary. His measurements showed that he and the group he led had travelled farther north than anyone else had gone at the time. The diary brought

1. See the instructions on page 125.

Risberg much posthumous fame, and it was not until early in this century that any explorer got closer to the north pole. The diary was passed on in Risberg's family through inheritance. Four years ago, when the diary became controversial, it was owned by Risberg's great-granddaughter, Olga Risberg.

The controversy began when a researcher named Sloan announced that Risberg had faked his measurements and that he could not possibly have gotten as far north as the diary showed. Sloan supported his argument with a large amount of scientific evidence involving things like the ocean currents that shift the ice pack and the distances that can be travelled in a day over ice. Olga Risberg took this very badly.

Within a month or two, she went to the officers of the New York Geographical Society, whom she had never met before, and gave them the diary, together with a letter that contained the following sentence:

> I donate my great-grandfather's diary to the Society because I believe the Society is best situated to evaluate the measurements recorded in it and to establish once and for all that Emil Risberg went where he claimed to have gone.

The Society had not asked Olga to make a gift of the diary, and no one at the Society said anything to her about conducting a study or about her motivation for the gift. At the time, the diary had an appraised value of $15,000.

The Society did nothing to evaluate the diary. Two years ago, Olga demanded that the Society either resolve the controversy or return the diary to her. The Society replied in a letter that, among other things, stated the following:

> When you donated the diary to the Society, you expressed some hope that it would be evaluated. But the Society made no promise — orally or in writing — to study the controversy surrounding the diary. If and when our board of directors chooses to go ahead with a study, we will do so, but you made a gift, which we accepted without conditions.

Sloan has just died. In his papers are notes showing that he had faked his own measurements, that he had started the controversy to build his reputation, and that all along he had believed that Risberg's diary was accurate. Olga has been besieged with offers to buy the diary from people who were unaware that she had donated it to the Society. All of the offers are well into six figures.

You have concluded that the gift cannot be set aside on the grounds of fraud. Will Olga Risberg be able to persuade a court to impose a constructive trust on the Society's title to the diary?

SHARP v. KOSMALSKI
351 N.E.2d 721 (N.Y. 1976)

GABRIELLI, J. . . .

Upon the death of his wife of 32 years, plaintiff, a 56-year-old dairy farmer whose education did not go beyond the eighth grade, developed a very close relationship with defendant, a school teacher and a woman 16 years his junior.... Plaintiff came to depend upon defendant's companionship and, eventually, declared his love for her, proposing marriage to her. Notwithstanding her refusal of his proposal of marriage, defendant continued her association with plaintiff and permitted him to shower her with many gifts, fanning his hope that he could induce defendant to alter her decision concerning his marriage proposal. Defendant was given access to plaintiff's bank account, from which it is not denied that she withdrew substantial amounts of money. Eventually, plaintiff ... executed a deed naming her a joint owner of his farm.... [N]umerous alterations ... were made to plaintiff's farmhouse in alleged furtherance of "domestic plans" made by plaintiff and defendant.

In September, 1971, while the renovations were still in progress, plaintiff transferred his remaining joint interest to defendant.... In February, 1973, the liaison between the parties was abruptly severed as defendant ordered plaintiff to move out of his home and vacate the farm. Defendant took possession of the home, the farm and all the equipment thereon, leaving plaintiff with assets of $300.

Generally, a constructive trust may be imposed "[w]hen property has been acquired in such circumstances that the holder of the legal title may not in good conscience retain the beneficial interest" [citations omitted]. In the development of the doctrine of constructive trust as a remedy available to courts of equity, the following four requirements were posited: (1) a confidential or fiduciary relation, (2) a promise, (3) a transfer in reliance thereon and (4) unjust enrichment [citations omitted].

... The record in this case clearly indicates that a relationship of trust and confidence did exist between the parties and, hence, the defendant must be charged with an obligation not to abuse the trust and confidence placed in her by the plaintiff....

... Even without an express promise ... courts of equity have imposed a constructive trust upon property transferred in reliance upon a confidential relationship. In such a situation, a promise may be implied or even inferred from the very transaction itself. As Judge Cardozo so eloquently observed: "Though a promise in words was lacking, the whole transaction, it might be found, was 'instinct with an obligation' imperfectly expressed (*Wood v. Duff-Gordon*, 222 N.Y. 88, 91)" (*Sinclair v. Purdy*, 235 N.Y. 245, 254 ...)....

... Indeed, in the case before us, it is inconceivable that plaintiff would convey all of his interest in property which was not only his abode but the very means of his livelihood without at least tacit consent upon the part of the defendant that she would permit him to continue to live on and operate the farm....

The salutary purpose of the constructive trust remedy is to prevent unjust enrichment.... A person may be deemed to be unjustly enriched if he (or she) has received a benefit, the retention of which would be unjust.... This case seems to present the classic example of a situation where equity should [impose a constructive trust in response to] a transaction pregnant with opportunity for abuse and unfairness....

SINCLAIR v. PURDY
139 N.E. 255 (N.Y. 1923)

CARDOZO, J. . . . Elijah F. Purdy [owned a half] interest in real estate in the city of New York. . . . Elijah was a clerk of what was then known as the Fifth District Court. His ownership of real estate subjected him to constant importunities to go bail for those in trouble. The desire to escape these importunities led him to execute a deed conveying his undivided half interest to his sister Elvira [who already owned the other half]. . . . The record does not make it plain whether at this time brother and sister made their home together. The relation between them in any event was one of harmony and affection, and so continued till the end. . . . There is evidence of repeated declarations by Elvira that, though the [whole] title was in her name, a half interest was his. . . . Elijah died at the age of 80 in 1914. [A niece, who would have inherited from Elijah, has brought this suit to establish a trust in favor of Elijah — and therefore in favor of the niece — over the property deeded to Elvira.]

. . . The sister's deposition shows that her brother disclosed his plan to her before the making of a deed. . . . It was an expedient adopted to save him the bother of going upon bonds. She does not remember that she made any promise in return. He trusted, as she puts it, to her sense of honor. A little later she learned that the title was in her name.

We think a confidential relation was the procuring cause of the conveyance. The grantor could not disclose the trust upon the face of the deed. If he had done so, he would have defeated the purpose of the transfer, which required that title, to outward appearance, be vested in another. He found, as he thought, in the bond of kinship a protection as potent as any that could be assured to him by covenants of title. . . . "The absence of a formal writing grew out of that very confidence and trust, and was occasioned by it." [Citation omitted.]

In such conditions, the rule in this state is settled that equity will grant relief. [Citations omitted.] . . .

. . . Here was a man transferring to his sister the only property he had in the world. . . . He was doing this, as she admits, in reliance upon her honor. Even if we were to accept her statement that there was no distinct promise to hold it for his benefit, the exaction of such a promise, in view of the relation, might well have seemed to be superfluous. . . . Though a promise in words was lacking, the whole transaction, it might be found, was "instinct with an obligation" imperfectly expressed *Wood v. Duff-Gordon*, 222 N.Y. 88, 91. It was to be interpreted, not literally or irrespective of its setting, but sensibly and broadly with all its human implications. . . .

TEBIN v. MOLDOCK
241 N.Y.S.2d 629 (App. Div. 1963)

BREITEL, J.P. . . . Plaintiffs are the son, sister and two brothers of a New York decedent, all of whom are residents of Poland. Defendant is decedent's niece, and a native-born American. Decedent emigrated to the United States from Poland in 1913. She died in 1956, a widow, leaving only plaintiff son as a surviving descendant. The action was to impose a constructive trust, in favor of plaintiffs, of certain funds deposited in savings institutions, and a multiple dwelling. The assets had once belonged to decedent but she, in the last five years of her life, had transferred them to defendant niece. . . .

[We hold that] a constructive trust [must] be imposed on the . . . assets of decedent in the hands of defendant niece. While the evidence does not establish fraud or undue influence, it does inescapably establish that the assets were transferred on certain promises to hold for the benefit of the son, which promises were made in a confidential relationship. These promises were relied upon, and for their breach equity is bound to provide appropriate relief.

Hermina Tebin, the decedent, was born in Poland in 1882. She married there, but later separated from her husband, left her two sons with her parents, and emigrated to the United States in 1913. One son died in 1920 without issue. The other, who was born in 1904, is the first-named plaintiff in this action.

Since coming to this country decedent lived in New York, earned her livelihood as a midwife, acquired the lower east side multiple dwelling in which she lived, and accumulated cash funds in the amount of about $19,000. During this period of over 40 years, she saw her son in Poland once when she travelled there in 1928, and stayed for some two months. She maintained an intermittent correspondence with him throughout and until the end of her life. . . .

In 1920, decedent brought her sister Aniela to the United States. . . . Defendant niece is Aniela's daughter, whom decedent knew as a growing child, befriended and assisted as a young woman training for an educational career, and who, in decedent's later years, handled her moneys and affairs when illness and age closed in.

[Decedent's health began to deteriorate in 1947. In 1951, she gave bank accounts and a deed to the multiple dwelling to the niece, who signed an] agreement [providing] that decedent should retain the use, free, of her apartment, and receive for her life the net income from the property less a management fee to the niece. The [agreement] recited that the niece was the sole and entire owner of the property.

In August, 1951 decedent made a will in which the niece was named as the sole beneficiary of her estate. It contained the following clause: "Third: I have given certain oral instructions to my said niece, with respect to my son Kazimierz Tebin, and having full faith and confidence in her honesty and integrity, I feel certain that she will carry out my instructions. Nonetheless, in the event that she fails to carry out my instructions, it shall be a matter for her own conscience and not otherwise."

As decedent's end approached, the niece handled more and more of the aunt's affairs, faithfully, and paid all her expenses of living, hospitalization and medical services, out of the funds theretofore transferred to the niece. After the aunt's death, the niece from the same sources paid the funeral expenses. . . .

Presently, the niece holds the real property and about $14,000 of roundly $19,000 transferred to her.

Plaintiffs assert that the niece and her mother frightened decedent with the representation that if any assets were ever received by the son, he being in a Communist country, the assets would be taken from him and that Stalin would kill him. . . .

Plaintiffs also claim that the assets were transferred to the niece on her promise that she would hold them for decedent's son and advance funds as he needed and could profitably use them.

The niece and her mother assert that the relation between the decedent and her son was not a close one, the decedent often complained of the greediness of the son and his persistent and exclusive interest in receiving remittances and gifts. Moreover, it is asserted that the niece was to send moneys to the son only in her exclusive discretion and judgment, and never in excess of $25 in any one month. . . .

In July, 1952 decedent came to Mr. Solon, a lawyer, and retained him to recover her property. . . . Decedent had told Mr. Solon the Stalin story and that she had transferred the assets to the niece to provide her lifetime needs and take care of her son. While there were some ensuing conversations about bringing a lawsuit nothing further was done to prosecute the matter. . . .

The niece testified that decedent told her: "that she was an older woman, that she wanted someone . . . who would look after her needs while she was alive [and] that all during her lifetime [her son] had always written to her and asked her to help, and that since she was giving me everything she had, she thought that he probably would, after her death, seek me out and ask me for help, and she asked me to see that he never got his hands on any lump sum of money. That is why she was giving it to me. But she knew that if he would write to me and ask me for help, and if I felt that he needed it, that I would help him.". . .

In August, 1952 decedent wrote to her son in Poland:

> I was very sick with my heart [because] Aniela and her daughter Janina scared me by telling me that if I leave my estate to you Stalin will take it away from you after I die and that . . . you may be shot to death. So I gave all to Janka — $14,000 and a house and now they are trying to commit me to an insane asylum so they could keep everything for themselves. I will try to have you come here and take it all back because they stole it from me by fraud and they bribed the lawyer.
>
> Keep this letter so that you could appear as a witness if necessary. . . .

It is evident . . . that a secret agreement had been effected between aunt and niece for the benefit of the aunt during her lifetime, and the son. . . .

[A constructive trust will be imposed where] the one who entrusted property did so because of certain understandings, and the one to whom the assets are given acquiesced even in silence (e.g., *Sinclair v. Purdy*, 235 N.Y. 245, 253-254 . . .). . . .

In dealing with the problem of a secret trust or the breach of a confidential relationship the ordinary rules imposed by the Statute of Frauds . . . are not applicable. Equity in this area has always reached beyond the facade of formal documents, absolute transfers, and even limiting statutes on the law side. . . .

Accordingly, the judgment . . . should [provide] for a constructive trust in [the son's] favor. . . .

TEBIN v. MOLDOCK
200 N.E.2d 216 (N.Y. 1964)

PER CURIAM. . . . The judgment should be modified to limit the scope of the constructive trust imposed on defendant Janina Moldock to an obligation to pay $25 a month for the benefit of Kazimierz Tebin. . . . [W]e conclude the record supports a finding that defendant, occupying a relationship of confidence and trust with decedent, undertook to devote a small part of the property given to her for the benefit of plaintiff. On the basis of defendant's own testimony this would approximate $25 a month. No such breach of confidence or of fiduciary obligation, either before or after decedent's death, has been established as would warrant forfeiture by defendant of the major interest in decedent's property which it was clearly decedent's intent that defendant should have.

12 Working with Statutes

§12.1 Ten Tools of Statutory Interpretation

Interpretation is the art of finding out . . . what [the drafter] intended to convey.

— *Francis Lieber*

I don't care what their intention was. I only want to know what the words mean.

— *Oliver Wendell Holmes*

As you have realized by now, "learning law" is less learning what the rules of law are (a body of information) than it is learning how to discover and use the rules (a repertory of intellectual skills). And you have learned that a common law country has two types of sources of law: judicial precedent, on one hand, and, on the other, statutes and statute-like material, such as constitutions, administrative regulations, and court rules. Chapter 11 described the skills used in writing about precedent. This chapter does the same thing for the tools used to interpret and explain statutes and statute-like material.

The two quotations at the beginning of this section might seem to express contradictory approaches to interpreting any source of law. The first focuses on what the lawmaker intended to do, and the second on what the lawmaker did. The first approach might use any reliable evidence of intent, but the second concentrates on the words actually used. This is a classic tension in statutory interpretation, and it grows partly out of a history of struggle — now mostly halted — between legislatures and courts. As you know, in

English common law, courts were the original lawmakers, and legislatures arose afterward, acquiring the power to make new law and to change law already made by courts. Courts, of course, retained the ultimate power to enforce all law. And, because interpretation is essential to enforcement, courts used their power to limit the effect of intrusive statutes, which judges treated with suspicion and even condescension until well into this century.[1]

Some practices of statutory construction grew out of this struggle and survive today because they still accomplish some logical purpose — although not necessarily the same purpose for which they were invented. For example, statutes in derogation of the common law are still strictly construed. Long ago, courts used this and other rules to limit the invasion of legislatures onto the courts' lawmaking turf. Today the reason is different: since the pre-statutory common law was a complete and fairly stable system of rules, one can fairly conclude that, unless a legislature announces otherwise, it intends to tinker with that system only in small ways.

The search for meaning or intent begins with the words of the statute. At one time, nearly every jurisdiction in the United States followed the "plain meaning" rule, which permits inquiry into other evidence of legislative intent only where the words of the statute do not plainly convey meaning. In recent decades, however, a number of courts have modified or abandoned the plain meaning rule and now search outside the statute for evidence of intent even where the statutory wording seems clear and unambiguous. Those courts that still adhere to the plain meaning rule do so not because they would rather not know how statutes or sausages are made,[2] but because they believe legislative intent can most efficiently be established by finding meaning in the words of the statute itself and by inquiring further only when those words are ambiguous. Those courts that examine other evidence of intent even when the statutory words are clear do so because they believe that the words' meaning is not good enough if other evidence shows that the legislature intended something else. (Are you beginning to understand the tension between what words mean and what their author intended them to mean? If the legislature wanted to communicate one thing but instead communicated another, which message should a court choose to receive — the one sent or the one intended to be sent?)

Aside from reading the statute, what kind of inquiry could a court make? You might think that the sensible thing would be to ask the legislature what it had in mind. But most state legislatures are made up of between 100 and 200 voting members, and Congress includes 100 Senators and 435 Representatives. Even if a group could have a collective state of mind, these groups are just too large to be able to tell you what, as groups, they were thinking some time before. In addition, legislatures consider such a stagger-

---

§12.1 1. There are many reasons why this kind of struggle is mostly behind us, but perhaps the most important is this: modern life is so complex and so difficult as to humble anyone who undertakes to make law, and judges today are grateful for a partnership with legislatures, which are better equipped to gather masses of detailed information and to work out compromises between competing interest groups.

2. "If you like laws or sausages, you should never watch either one being made" (attributed to Bismarck).

ing number of bills that most members are not likely to have clear memories of what they thought a bill meant when they voted for or against it. And even on the day of a vote, most legislators have no more understanding of a bill than they can get from a quick reading of it or — more likely — from reading a short synopsis of it. Finally, many questions of statutory interpretation arise long after enactment, when few of the enacting legislators are still in office or even alive.

How, then, can the meaning be found? Where the meaning of a statute has not been settled, courts use ten tools:

1. the *wording* of the statutory section at issue;
2. any *statutory context* that might indicate the legislature's intent: other sections of the same statute, other statutes addressed to the same subject matter, the heading of the section at issue, and the statute's title and preamble (if any);
3. the historical context: the *events and conditions* that might have *motivated* the legislature to act;
4. the context created by announcements of *public policy* in other statutes and in case law;
5. *interpretations of the statute by lower or collateral courts;*[3]
6. the statute's *legislative history,* which consists of the documents and records created by various parts of the legislature during the course of enactment;
7. a collection of maxims known as the *canons of statutory construction;*
8. *comparison with parallel statutes in other jurisdictions,* focusing on judicial interpretation of those statutes,[4] as well as the circumstances in which they were enacted;
9. *interpretations of the statute by administrative agencies* charged with enforcing the statute; and
10. *interpretations of the statute by scholars* who are recognized experts in the field.[5]

[handwritten margin note: HAVE THEY SEEN CITED IN OTHER CASES — HAVE THEY WRITTEN TREATISES? THAT DETERMINES HOW PERSUASIVE THIS CAN BE]

Beginners sometimes overlook the possibility that terminology in a particular section of a statute may be defined in another section of the same statute, or even in a definitions section that applies to an entire code. In addition, a relatively mundane word is sometimes defined, for the purposes of the statute, in a surprising way. And a term may have different meanings in different statutes. As versatile as the English language is, the number of ideas needing to be expressed seems to exceed the number of concise words and phrases available to be symbols for them, and some expressions have to do double or triple duty.

---

3. If the statute has been comprehensively interpreted by *higher* courts, its meaning would be settled through mandatory authority, and none of these tools would be needed.

4. See pages 109-10.

5. Mere publication of a law review article — without more — does not demonstrate recognized expertise. See page 106.

[handwritten marginalia in top margin]

For example, section 6-201 ("Franchises") of the Administrative Code of the City of New York defines "the streets of the city" as

> streets, avenues, highways, boulevards, concourses, driveways, bridges, tunnels, parks, parkways, waterways, docks, bulkheads, wharves, piers, and public grounds or waters within or belonging to the city

while section 16-101(3) ("Department of Sanitation") defines "street" to include any

[handwritten marginalia]

> street, avenue, road, alley, lane, highway, boulevard, concourse, driveway, culvert and crosswalk, and every class of road, square and place, and all parkways and through vehicular park drives except a road within any park or a wharf, pier, bulkhead, or slip by law committed to the custody, and control of the department of ports and terminals.

Why might a wharf be a "street" for one purpose, but not for another? In section 6-201, the word "street" is a symbol for a place where activity might require getting a franchise from the city. In section 16-101(3), the same word is a symbol for a place for which the Department of Sanitation has the responsibility for cleaning, sweeping, sanding, and removing ice, snow, and garbage.[6] In each case, the statute would be unreadable if the idea were fully described every time it is mentioned.

Beginners often make the mistake of focusing solely on a rule's phrasing (whether found in a statute or elsewhere) and ignoring the policies underlying the rule. The result is an overly mechanical application, often far from the contemplation of the legislature or the policies the rule is meant to advance. Remember that words are merely symbols for concepts, and that interpretation is the art of seeing through the words to locate the ideas represented. Courts will not mechanically apply a statute in a literal way if that would undermine the approach the legislature has taken to solving the problem in dispute. Learned Hand wrote that "statutes always have some purpose or object to accomplish, whose sympathetic and imaginative discovery is the surest guide to their meaning."[7]

Although legislative history is often resorted to and would seem to be the most direct evidence of the legislature's purpose, it is sometimes viewed with suspicion. It is often incomplete, especially with state statutes, and, because of the chaotic nature of legislative work, it can be internally contradictory. It is also vulnerable to manipulation by legislators who may not share the views of a majority of their colleagues. And the collective intent of a legislature (or any other large group of people) may simply be more a metaphysical idea than something ever provable through evidence. On the other hand, some portions of the typical legislative history tend to be viewed by the courts as particularly reliable. Those are the reports of the commit-

---

6. "A word is not a crystal, transparent and unchanged, it is the skin of a living thought and may vary greatly in color and content according to the circumstances and the time in which it is used." *Towne v. Eisner,* 245 U.S. 418, 425 (1918) (Holmes, J.).

7. *Cabell v. Markham,* 148 F.2d 737, 739 (2d Cir.), *aff'd,* 326 U.S. 404 (1945).

tees that considered and reported the bill and the floor comments of the sponsors of the bill, except as to amendments not considered by the committees and not endorsed by the sponsors.

Although scholars have frequently criticized many of the canons of construction, courts continue to use them regularly. It is certainly true, as Judge Posner has pointed out, that the courts have no way of knowing whether legislators have enacted a particular statute with the canons in mind, or even whether legislators have ever heard of the canons of construction.[8] It is also true, as Karl Llewellyn showed, that canons tend to be inconsistent with one another and that courts may invoke them to justify decisions rather than to help in making decisions.[9] On the other hand, few scholars would reject all the canons, and some canons are never criticized. Among this favored category are the following:

- A statute is to be construed in light of the harm the legislature meant to remedy.

- Statutory words and phrases are to be construed in the context of the entire statute of which they are a part.

- Statutes on the same subject (in Latin, *in pari materia*) are to be construed together.

- Where possible, statutes are to be construed so that their constitutionality is preserved.

- Penal statutes are to be narrowly construed.

- Statutes in derogation of the common law are to be narrowly construed.

In a less certain category are maxims — many of which contradict each other — on whether repeals by implication are favored; on whether the expression of one thing in a statute necessarily excludes another not mentioned; on the construction to be given to words of permission and to words of command; on whether words and phrases judicially construed in other contexts before enactment are to be given the same meaning in a statute; on the effect of grammar on interpretation; on the effect of statute titles, section headings, and preambles on interpretation; on the treatment to be given to legislative history; on the effect of interpretations by administrative agencies; on the effect of judicial interpretations in which the legislature, by not amending, might have acquiesced; and on a host of other issues.

Canons are rules of a sort and must be proved with authority, usually case law to be found in the digests under the topic heading of "Statutes." But be careful: the lawyer hurling a canon as an epithet is apt to find a contradictory one thrown right back. A convincing argument is instead a

---

8. Richard A. Posner, *Statutory Interpretation—in the Classroom and in the Courtroom,* 50 U. Chi. L. Rev. 800, 806 (1983).
9. Karl Nickerson Llewellyn, *The Common Law Tradition* 521-35 (1960).

thoughtful and thorough analysis of the statute. Canons play a part in that, but not the largest part.

Let us examine two decisions from a single litigation to see seven of the ten tools in operation.

McBOYLE v. UNITED STATES
43 F.2d 273 (10th Cir. 1930)

PHILLIPS, Circuit Judge. William W. McBoyle was convicted and sentenced for an alleged violation of the National Motor Vehicle Theft Act, section 408, title 18, U.S. Code. The indictment charged that on October 10, 1926, McBoyle caused to be transported in interstate commerce from Ottawa, Ill., to Guymon, Okl., one Waco airplane, . . . which was the property of the United States Aircraft Corporation and which had theretofore been stolen; and that McBoyle then and there knew it had been stolen. . . .

The primary question is whether an airplane comes within the purview of the National Motor Vehicle Theft Act. This act defines the term "motor vehicle," as follows:

> The term "motor vehicle" when used in this section shall include an automobile, automobile truck, automobile wagon, motor cycle, or any other self-propelled vehicle not designed for running on rails.

Counsel for McBoyle contend that the word "vehicle" includes only conveyances that travel on the ground; that an airplane is not a vehicle . . . ; and that, under the doctrine of ejusdem generis, the phrase "any other self-propelled vehicle" cannot be construed to include an airplane.

[In a passage deleted here, the court traces various meanings ascribed to the word "vehicle" in both legal and popular usage, quoting authorities that define a vehicle as an object that travels and carries things or people. One of the definitions specifies that a ship is a vehicle; according to another, a vehicle carries things or people, "especially on land."]

In the movies, when you hear someone say, "They've crossed the state line — call the FBI," this is the kind of statute that creates federal jurisdiction.

A *canon of construction:* Where general language follows a list of specific examples, the general language's meaning is limited to the same nature [*ejusdem generis*] as the specific, unless there are clear indications to the contrary.

The court focuses on the *words of the statute* and considers the canon of *ejusdem generis* only long enough to decide that the court's interpretation of the statute would not offend the canon.

142

Both the derivation and the definition of the word "vehicle" indicate that it is sufficiently broad to include any means or device by which persons or things are carried or transported, and it is not limited to instrumentalities used for traveling on land, although the latter may be the limited or special meaning of the word. We do not think it would be inaccurate to say that a ship or vessel is a vehicle of commerce.

An airplane is self-propelled [and] is designed to carry passengers and freight from place to place. It runs partly on the ground but principally in the air. It furnishes a rapid means for transportation of persons and comparatively light articles of freight and express. It therefore serves the same general purpose as an automobile, automobile truck, or motorcycle. It is of the same general kind or class as the motor vehicles specifically enumerated in the statutory definition and, therefore, construing an airplane to come within the general term, "any other self-propelled vehicle," does not offend against the maxim of ejusdem generis.

Furthermore, some meaning must be ascribed to [Congress's use of the] phrase "any other self-propelled vehicle" [immediately after Congress had specifically listed] all of the known self-propelled vehicles designed for running on land. . . .

We conclude that the phrase, "any other self-propelled vehicle," includes an airplane. . . .

Are you convinced by the court's interpretation of the statutory wording?

COTTERAL, Circuit Judge (dissenting). I feel bound to dissent on the ground that the National Motor Vehicle Theft Act should not be construed as relating to the transportation of airplanes.

A prevailing rule is that a penal statute is to be construed strictly against an offender and it must state clearly the persons and acts denounced. [Citations omitted.]

It would have been a simple matter in enacting the statute to insert, as descriptive words, airplanes, aircraft, or flying machines. If they had been in the legislative

Another *canon of construction*. The dissenter will soon try to link this one up with *ejusdem generis*.

Now the dissenter takes on the *words of the statute*, but in a way the court did not. The dissenter asks what Congress could have written into the statute but chose not to.

143

mind, the language would not have been expressed in such uncertainty as "any other self-propelled vehicle not designed for running on rails." The omission to definitely mention airplanes requires a construction that they were not included. Furthermore, by excepting vehicles running on rails, the meaning of the act is clarified. These words indicate it was meant to be confined to vehicles that *run,* but not on rails, and it did not extend to those that *fly.* . . .

The rule of ejusdem generis has special application to this statute. General words following a particular designation are usually presumed to be restricted so as to include only things or persons of the same kind, class, or nature, unless there is a clear manifestation of a contrary purpose. [Citation omitted.] The general description in this statute refers to vehicles of the same general class as those enumerated. We may assume an airplane is a vehicle, in being a means of transportation. And it has its own motive power. But is an airplane classified generally with "an automobile, automobile truck, automobile wagon, or motor cycle"? Are airplanes regarded as *other types of automobiles* and the like? A moment's reflection demonstrates the contrary.

Counsel for appellant have referred us to debates in Congress when the act was pending as persuasive of an interpretation in his favor. [Citations to the Congressional Record omitted.] . . . The discussions of the proposed measure are enlightening . . . in showing that the theft of automobiles was so prevalent over the land as to call for punitive restraint, but airplanes were never even mentioned.

It is familiar knowledge that the theft of automobiles had then become a public menace, but that airplanes had been rarely stolen if at all, and it is a most uncommon thing even at this date. The prevailing mischief sought to be corrected is an aid in the construction of a statute. [Citation omitted.] . . .

The dissenter turns to the *canon* considered in the court's opinion.

Because this question was not addressed in the reports of the committees that drafted the statute, the only relevant *legislative history* is the floor debates. Floor debates are a notoriously unreliable form of legislative history because they can include remarks by legislators who took no part in drafting the statute in committee, who might not have thought much about it, and who may not even have read it. But here the floor debates reveal surprising evidence of legislative intent: no legislator complained about a need to do something about airplane theft.

Finally, the dissenter takes up the *historical context.*

McBOYLE v. UNITED STATES
283 U.S. 25 (1931)

Mr. Justice HOLMES delivered the opinion of the Court. . . . The question is the meaning of the word "vehicle" in the phrase "any other self-propelled vehicle not designed for running on rails." No doubt etymologically it is possible to use the word to signify a conveyance working on land, water or air, and sometimes legislation extends the use in that direction, e.g., land and air, water being separately provided for, in the Tariff Act [of] 1922 [citation omitted]. But in everyday speech "vehicle" calls up the picture of a thing moving on land. Thus in Rev. Stats. § 4, intended, the Government suggests, rather to enlarge than to restrict the definition, vehicle includes every contrivance capable of being used "as a means of transportation on land." And this is repeated, expressly excluding aircraft, in the Tariff Act [of] 1930 [citation omitted]. So here, the phrase under discussion calls up the popular picture. For after including automobile truck, automobile wagon and motor cycle, the words "any other self-propelled vehicle not designed for running on rails" still indicate that a vehicle in the popular sense, that is a vehicle running on land, is the theme. It is a vehicle that runs, not something, not commonly called a vehicle, that flies. Airplanes were well known in 1919, when this statute was passed; but it is admitted that they were not mentioned in the reports or in the debates in Congress. It is impossible to read words that so carefully enumerate the different forms of motor vehicles and have no reference of any kind to aircraft, as including airplanes under a term that usage more and more confines to a different class. The counsel for the petitioner have shown that the phraseology of the statute as to motor vehicles follows that of earlier statutes of Connecticut, Delaware, Ohio, Michigan and Missouri, not to mention the late Regulations of Traffic for the District of Co-

While dissecting the words of the statute, Holmes considers *the statutory context.*

Historical context and *legislative history* are considered together.

Again, Holmes simultaneously uses two tools — this time *legislative history* and *comparison with parallel statutes.* The point is that Congress seems to have modelled the Act on statutes that clearly are not addressed to aircraft theft. The most telling comparison — and perhaps the most enjoyable for its irony — is with a *city's*

lumbia [citation omitted], none of which can be supposed to leave the earth.

. . . When a rule of conduct is laid down in words that evoke in the common mind only the picture of vehicles moving on land, the statute should not be extended to aircraft, simply because it may seem to us that a similar policy applies, or even upon the speculation that, if the legislature had thought of it, very likely broader words would have been used. [Citation omitted.]

Judgment reversed.

> traffic regulations, which certainly could not have been meant to penalize the stealing of airplanes.
>
> As important as *policy* is, it also has its limitations. Here Holmes notes that his court is permitted to construe the statute only to accomplish the goal Congress had selected for it — and not some other goal the court might think equally valid.

What idea or ideas — and which tools of statutory construction — most persuaded the Supreme Court to see the statute differently from the way the Tenth Circuit saw it?

Missing from these opinions are the three tools that use interpretations of the statute by others: by lower or collateral courts, by administrative agencies, and by scholars expert in the field. Each tool's absence has an explanation. First, the judges themselves tell us why they have no cases on point to guide them: airplane theft seems to have been exceedingly rare at the time. Second, no administrative agency would have had a reason to interpret the statute because no administrative agency was charged with enforcing it. And finally, the modern explosion in published scholarship on statutes had not yet begun when these opinions were written. Only a very few law reviews were then being published, and scholarship had not yet begun to concentrate on statutes, as it does today.

Parenthetically, Congress later amended the statute so that it now penalizes anyone who "transports in interstate or foreign commerce a motor vehicle *or aircraft,* knowing the same to have been stolen."[10] Having learned something about how overly specific wording can make a statute like this at least partially obsolete, Congress defined "aircraft" so that the statute could adapt to changing technology: "'Aircraft' means any contrivance now known

---

10. 18 U.S.C. § 2312 (1988 & Supp. IV 1992) (emphasis added). An adjacent section penalizes anyone who knowingly "receives, possesses, conceals, stores, barters, sells, or disposes of any motor vehicle *or aircraft,* which has crossed a State or United States boundary after being stolen." 18 U.S.C. § 2313(a) (1988 & Supp. IV 1992) (emphasis added). (Stealing a vehicle or an airplane would, of course, be punished under the law of the state where the theft took place. But once a stolen vehicle or airplane is moved out of state, it will be much harder for the local authorities to prosecute the thieves or those who received the stolen property from them. To make available the resources of the federal government, Congress made it a separate federal offense to move such stolen property across state lines.)

or hereafter invented . . . for flight in the air."[11] Although the amendment was enacted when airplanes were still powered by piston engines and propellers, it probably penalizes the act of knowingly moving a stolen space shuttle across a state line.

§12.2 How to Present Statutory Analysis

Writing about a statutory question focuses on the words of the statute because the words are what is to be interpreted. The crucial term or phrase should appear, inside quotation marks, when you state the issue, your conclusion, the rule on which you rely, and the most important steps of logic in the analysis:

> The question of whether the Interborough Repertory Theatre must get a franchise to present entertainment on the Staten Island ferry depends in part on whether the ferry is one of the "streets of the city" within the meaning of section 6-201.

But your obligation to tell the reader the *rule* on which you rely usually cannot be satisfied merely by quoting the statute in unedited form. Because statutes are drafted to govern wide ranges of factual possibilities, a rule expressed entirely in statutory language may need to be reformulated for practical application. If, for example, you are asked to determine whether moving a stolen "boat" across a state line violates the National Motor Vehicle Theft Act, you will not be able to express the controlling rule by quoting the statutory sentence on which your reasoning will be based: "The term 'motor vehicle' when used in this section shall include an automobile, automobile truck, automobile wagon, motor cycle, or any other self-propelled vehicle not designed for running on rails." For the purpose of resolving an issue like that, this sentence does not fully communicate the governing rule. It does not even contain a list of elements. A far more useful formulation, supportable by *McBoyle,* would be something like this: "For the purposes of the Act, a 'motor vehicle' is a conveyance that is 'self-propelled,' that operates primarily on land, and that does not run on rails." Do you see how much more practical and easy to apply this formulation is? A boat does not run on rails; it might be self-propelled; but, alas, it hardly ever transports things or people across land. What the reader needs is a statement of the rule *embodied* in the statute.

Do not be careless, however, in reformulating the statutory language into a useful expression of a rule: you want something that you can apply to facts, but you also want something that accurately pronounces the statute's meaning. If you oversimplify or distort, trouble awaits. It helps to use the key phrases of the statute. "Self-propelled" is a key phrase here because not

11. 18 U.S.C. § 2311 (1988) (emphasis added).

all boats are that. A barge, pushed by a tug, is not self-propelled. But what if the "boat" at issue is a rowboat, a canoe, or a kayak — powered by a person who rows or paddles? And if an ocean liner is permanently moored, with its engines removed, and used as a hotel, we would say it is no longer self-propelled — and probably not even a conveyance. But what about an ocean liner that sits at dockside as a derelict, its engines broken but repairable?

The two most important differences between the presentation of common law precedent and the presentation of statutory analysis are in the way the presentation is organized and in the role played by case law.

You already know that some precedent interprets the common law, while other precedent interprets statutes and statute-like authority. Interpretation of common law precedent focuses less on the intent of prior courts and more on reasonably applying rules that have been created through precedent. A court can thus make a significant change in the direction of the common law without invading the power of another branch of government. But a court's freedom of interpretive maneuver is more limited where a statute is involved because with statutes the aim is to discover the intent of the legislature. Not only is the legislature a coordinate branch of government with a right to have its enactments respected by the courts, but the legislature has the power to redraft a statute and thus obliterate judicial interpretations that the legislature finds annoying.

Some statutes are carefully drafted with the kind of explicitness that makes intent obvious and application relatively mechanical. But at times a legislature will deliberately leave gaps in a statute that the courts, through precedent, will be expected to fill. An example of the latter is 15 U.S.C. § 1, which prohibits any "combination . . . in restraint of trade." What do you think that means? Congress might have had a rough idea when it enacted the Sherman Anti-Trust Act in 1890, but it left to the courts the task of discovering the full sense of the phrase. In the West Publishing Company's annotated edition of the United States Code, over 500 pages in small print are devoted to notes of decisions in which courts have attempted to discover the precise meaning of these four words. On the other hand, 39 U.S.C. § 3009 provides that "unordered merchandise" received in the mail "may be treated as a gift by the recipient," and the statute defines "unordered merchandise" as "merchandise mailed without the prior expressed request or consent of the recipient." Here, perhaps because the subject matter is much more simple conceptually, politically, and economically, Congress left far fewer gaps in the enactment, although at least one appellate court has had to resolve the question of whether an offer to insure is "merchandise" within the meaning of the statute.[1]

Statutory and common law analysis differ in the way you organize authority in rule proof and in rule application.[2] If the issue is resolved purely by common law precedent, you might, for example, find one or more decisions that set out the fundamental rules, surrounded by an entourage of other decisions that each explain some specific aspect of a rule or its appli-

---

§12.2   1. *See Kipperman v. Academy Life Ins. Co.*, 554 F.2d 377 (9th Cir. 1977).
2. See Chapter 9.

cation — together with various relevant secondary authority, such as restatements, treatises, leading law review articles, and so forth. The
precedent at the center of this throng is the basic source for the overall rule
or rules, and parts of the entourage can be used to answer questions left
open after the overall rule is set out.

But if the issue is statutory, the central decisions are replaced by one or
more statutes, and the entourage is made up of decisions interpreting those
statutes, as well as any useful legislative history, interpretations by administrative agencies, decisions interpreting sufficiently similar statutes in other jurisdictions, commentaries by scholars and so forth. Some authority
appropriate to statutory analysis is inappropriate to common law analysis,
and vice versa. For example, if a state has codified a common law rule addressed in a restatement — and has done so in a way that is inconsistent
with the restatement's view — the restatement, to the extent of the incon-
sistency, is irrelevant to an interpretation of the statute.

Instructions for Exercises I and II

You have probably discovered that one of the harder things about legal writing
is organizing scattered insights into an integrated whole that resolves an issue.
The exercises in this chapter illustrate how to do that where an issue will be
determined at least partly on a statute.

Make the prediction asked for in the exercise your teacher assigns. Use the
statutory interpretation tools discussed in this chapter and the precedent skills
described in Chapter 11. Assume that your library research shows that the prediction will rest on the statutes and decisions reproduced in the exercise.

A good way to work out your reasoning is to inventory your analytical resources :

1. identify the issues
2. analyze each issue
   - ▶ identify the determinative facts
   - ▶ for each authority, consider
     - ▷ likely rules for which the authority
       stands (along a spectrum from broad
       to narrow)
     - ▷ policies for which the authority stands
     - ▷ (for statutes only:) events and condi-
       tions that motivated the legislature to
       act; legislative history; canons of con-
       struction; other tools of statutory con-
       struction
     - ▷ (for cases only:) likely ways of analog-
       izing and distinguishing
     - ▷ likely syntheses with other authorities
     - ▷ likely reconciliations with inconsistent
       authorities
     - ▷ how the authority fits into the hierarchy
       of authority

▶ test your analysis by

    ▷ counter-analyzing reasonable arguments that could challenge your prediction

    ▷ considering troublesome facts that would bother a judge

    ▷ asking whether your analysis will seem reasonable, just, and realistic to the judicial mind

▶ predict how the court will resolve the issue

3. predict how the court will resolve the entire controversy

While making the inventory, start with a lot of paper and leave much blank space because you will probably go back and forth, adding to what you have already done. Do not be afraid to change your mind as you go along.

Make an objective prediction and do not take sides. Your prediction is for the benefit of a supervisor, such as a senior partner, who really wants to know what will happen in court. You are not being asked for courtroom advocacy. (That will be covered in later chapters.)

If your teacher has assigned the exercise as preparation for a class, be prepared to speak in class from your inventory.

If, on the other hand, your teacher has assigned the exercise as work to be done entirely at home, complete the exercise by reorganizing your inventory into an outline for writing based on some variation of the paradigm described in Chapter 9.

Exercise I.   The Ironwood Tract[1]

Fourteen years ago, Palo Verde Development Corporation purchased a deed to an Arizona parcel known as the Ironwood tract. The tract is unimproved terrain and has never been fenced or built upon. It is one mile from a paved road and 65 miles from downtown Phoenix. Today, the nearest residential development is Verde River Estates, nine miles from the tract, toward Phoenix along the same road. From the date of the purchase until this past September, no employee of Palo Verde had set foot on the tract.

Palo Verde built Verde River Estates during the last two years. When the last units were sold in September, the company sent a surveying team to the Ironwood tract, but they were chased off the land by Homer Chesbro, whose Black Canyon Ranch adjoins the Ironwood tract. Chesbro bought the Ranch eleven years ago from a person who told him that he was buying both the Ranch and the tract. Although the metes and bounds description in Chesbro's deed does not include the tract, that and most of the rest of the deed is in language that non-

---

1. See the instructions on page 149.

lawyers would find incomprehensible. For the past eleven years, Chesbro and his employees have grazed cattle on the Ironwood tract two or three times a month throughout the year. The land cannot support more grazing, and the soil will not support farming or other intensive agriculture, although luxury housing could be built on it.

Chesbro had no idea that Palo Verde had a deed to the property. At the same time, Palo Verde did not know that Chesbro was using the tract or that he thought his deed included it.

If Chesbro claims that he acquired title by adverse possession, will Palo Verde succeed in an action to eject him and quiet its own title?

ARIZONA REVISED STATUTES

§ 12-521.   Definitions

A. In this article, unless the context otherwise requires:

1. "Adverse possession" means an actual and visible appropriation of the land, commenced and continued under a claim of right inconsistent with and hostile to the claim of another.

2. "Peaceable possession" means possession which is continuous, and not interrupted by an adverse action to recover the estate. . . .

§ 12-526.   Real Property in Adverse Possession and Use by Possessor; Ten-Year Limitation . . .

A. A person who has a cause of action for recovery of any lands, tenements or hereditaments from a person having peaceable and adverse possession thereof, cultivating, using and enjoying such property, shall commence an action therefor within ten years after the cause of action accrues, and not afterward. . . .

§ 12-527.   Effect of Limitation on Title

When an action for recovery of real property is barred by any provision of this article, the person who pleads and is entitled to the bar shall be held to have full title precluding all claims.

[These sections are descended from provisions in the Arizona Civil Code of 1901. The Arizona Supreme Court has held that what is now §12-527 provides a cause of action through which a person who occupies land through adverse possession can obtain title to it after the requisite number of years have passed. *Work v. United Globe Mines*, 100 P. 813 (Ariz. 1909), *aff'd*, 231 U.S. 595 (1914). Noting that the Arizona statutes reproduced on this page were modelled after Texas statutes, the court relied on a Texas case, *Moody v. Holcomb*, which interpreted those Texas statutes. *Moody* was decided before 1901. Compare *Work* to the first two cases below, *Arizona Superior Mining Co. v. Anderson* and *State v. McDonald.* Added together, these three cases tell you how the Arizona courts will react to the other out-of-state cases in this exercise.]

ARIZONA SUPERIOR MINING CO. v. ANDERSON
262 P. 489 (Ariz. 1927), error dismissed,
278 U.S. 578 (1929)

Ross, C.J. [The parties disagree over whether this case should be tried in Pima County or Maricopa County. The relevant Arizona statute is ambiguous.]

Counsel . . . have directed our attention to decisions [interpreting similar statutes in other states, but we are free to disregard precedent from states where] the language of the statute . . . is different from the language of our statute. . . . [The situation is different where the other state's statute is the one from which our statute is drawn. In adopting our statute] from another state, we took it with the construction theretofore placed upon it [by the courts of that state]. . . .

STATE v. McDONALD
352 P.2d 343 (Ariz. 1960)

Murry, J. [The issue is whether the plaintiff can be made to pay the fees and expenses of the defendant's expert witnesses. The governing Arizona statute, A.R.S. § 12-1128, is ambiguous.]

A.R.S. § 12-1128 was adopted from California [in 1901. After that date, two California cases interpreted the original California statute to mean] the usual costs attending trial allowed by statute. [Citations omitted.] . . .

Although we are not bound to follow the interpretation [subsequently] placed on a statute by a state from which our statute was adopted, it is persuasive. [Citation omitted.] . . .

ADAMS v. LAMICQ
221 P.2d 1037 (Utah 1950)

Wolfe, J. This action was commenced by the appellant to quiet title to an eighty acre tract of land in Duchesne County, Utah. . . .

. . . [T]he respondents claimed title to the land . . . by virtue of seven years' adverse possession[, during which they used the land as a winter range for sheep].

The . . . tract in question consisted of unbroken and unimproved brush lands suitable only for grazing. . . . The property was [not inclosed by a fence. T]he respondents during the winter grazed all of the eighty acres . . . , entering thereon in November and remaining until April, at which time they moved their sheep onto higher grazing lands in Colorado for the summer and early autumn. The respondents did not leave anyone upon or in charge of the eighty acres during the summer months while they were away. . . .

. . . Sec. 104-2-9, Utah Code Annotated 1943, provides: "For the purpose of constituting an adverse possession . . . , land is deemed to have been possessed and occupied in the following cases: . . . (3) Where, although not inclosed, it has been used for the supply of fuel, or of fencing timber for the purposes of husbandry, *or for pasturage*, or for the ordinary use of the occupant." (Italics added.)

In *Kellogg v. Huffman*, 137 Cal. App. 278, 30 P.2d 593, it was held under Sec. 323, subd. 3, Cal. Code Civ. Proc., which is identical to Section 104-2-9, subd. 3, quoted above, that pasturing during the entire grazing season of each year during which feed is available, if done to the exclusion of others, is a sufficient use and occupation of land, which is reasonably fit for grazing purposes only, to constitute the occupation and possession necessary to establish title by adverse possession. . . .

Thus we conclude that the respondents . . . had continuously claimed, occupied, and used [the property] for at least seven years prior to the commencement of this action. . . .

KELLOGG v. HUFFMAN
30 P.2d 593 (Cal. Ct. App. 1934)

BARNARD, P.J. This is an action to quiet title to 160 acres of land in the Kettleman Hills in Fresno county. . . . This property was rough and arid and was situated in what was, until about 1929, a sparsely settled country used only for grazing purposes. . . .

The appropriate portion of section 323 of the Code of Civil Procedure reads as follows: ". . . For the purpose of constituting an adverse possession . . . land is deemed to have been possessed and occupied in the following cases: . . . (3) Where, although not inclosed, it has been used for the supply of fuel, or of fencing-timber for the purposes of husbandry, or for pasturage, or for the ordinary use of the occupant."

. . . To establish adverse possession it is only necessary that land be put to such use as can reasonably be made thereof, and such a use is sufficiently continuous if, during the required time, it be so used at all times when it can be used for the purpose to which it is adapted. [Citations omitted.] It is well settled in this state that pasturing during the entire grazing season of each year during which feed is available, if done to the exclusion of others, is a sufficient use and occupation of land, which is reasonably fit only for pasturage purposes, to constitute the occupation and possession necessary to establish a title by adverse possession. [Citations omitted.] . . . ". . . It is sufficient that the use is in accordance with the usual course of husbandry in the locality." [Citation omitted.]

[There was ample evidence of adverse possession through use of the land for grazing purposes.]

DE LAS FUENTES v. MACDONELL
20 S.W. 43 (Tex. 1892)

GAINES, J. This was an action on trespass to try title. . . .

Appellants . . . complain that the court erred in sustaining the defendant's plea of the statute of limitations of five years. . . . The [land] was never inclosed [by fences]. It is fit only for grazing purposes. There have never been any houses upon it. No part of it has ever had any inclosures upon it, except small pens, made of posts and brush, for the purpose of penning sheep. These were renewed every year. . . . The land was used for "grazing and lambing purposes." How many sheep were kept upon it does not appear. One witness states that in 1871 there were 13,000 sheep upon the land. . . . Cattle belonging to others were permitted to graze upon the land. . . . There have been several cases decided in this court in which the effort has been made to show an adverse possession of land by merely grazing cattle and horses upon it, but it has uniformly been held that the possession was not sufficient to meet the requirements of the statute. [Citations omitted.] . . . [T]he mere occupancy of land by grazing live stock upon it, without substantial inclosures or other permanent improvements, is not sufficient to support a plea of limitation under our statutes. Uninclosed land, in this state, has ever been treated as commons for grazing purposes; and hence the mere holding of live stock upon it has not been deemed such exclusive occupancy as to constitute adverse possession. . . . There must be "an actual occupation of such nature and notoriety as the owner may be presumed to know that there is a possession of the land" [citation omitted]; "otherwise, a man may be disseised without his knowledge, and the statute of limitations run against him, while he has no ground to believe that his seizure has been interrupted" [citation omitted]. We think the testimony insufficient to show adverse possession. . . .

Exercise II. Pappas and Ziegler at Sal's Auto Parts[1]

Joel Pappas has been arrested in Connecticut for robbery. The police have a written statement from Jonathan Chen:

> I am employed at Sal's Auto Parts. I run the cash register. After 6 o'clock, I am the only employee there. I was at work at 6:30 P.M. last Tuesday. I was at the register when a man came in. This is the same man whom I have identified in a line-up and thereafter learned to be Joel Pappas.
>
> This man came up to the register, looked me straight in the eye, and said, "Open up the register and there won't be any trouble." He's a huge, musclebound guy and could easily have beaten me to a pulp. I opened up the register, and he scooped up all the bills and put them in a bag. He told me to lie down on the floor and count to a thousand. He said that if I stood up early, he'd pound my head into the countertop. I got down on the floor and counted to a thousand. Then I got up and called the police.

---

1. See the instructions on page 149.

No one else was in the store, and during this whole thing I could see only one other person. That was a woman standing on the sidewalk just outside the front door. I have also picked her out of a line-up and learned her name to be Gail Ziegler. The front of the store is a large picture window, and I could see that she was just standing there, looking out at the parking lot, as though she was waiting for a ride. She walked up to the front of the store three or four minutes before the defendant walked in. I did not see her leave. She was there when I hit the floor, and she was gone when I got up.

While this man was at the register, I didn't know why the woman was standing there. She could have been just hanging around, or she could have been helping him out somehow. At no time did I see the two of them talk or gesture to one another. All I knew at the time was that she wasn't going to help me. Even if she wasn't helping him, she wouldn't have been able to realize that I was being held up.

The distance between the register and the front door is 54 feet. When the police were in the store, I got a tape measure and measured it. The woman was at least a foot outside the door.

The police also have a statement from Ziegler:

At 6:30 last Tuesday, I was at Sal's Auto Parts. Joel was going to rob the place, and I was going to stand lookout at the front door. I walked up to the front of the store a few minutes before Joel walked in. I looked out at the parking lot to make sure nobody would walk in. If somebody did start to walk in, I was going to ask them for a lot of directions and act lost to keep them busy until Joel walked out. I left as soon as I saw the guy at the cash register disappear. Joel left about a minute later.

Joel is over six feet tall, and he works out with weights.

In Connecticut, robbery is classified in three degrees. The highest is first-degree robbery, which requires aggravating factors not present in Pappas's case. Third-degree robbery carries the least severe penalty, and the prosecution therefore would prefer a conviction for second-degree robbery.

If the evidence at trial coincides with the statements Chen and Ziegler have given the police, is Pappas likely to be convicted of second-degree robbery?

CONNECTICUT GENERAL STATUTES ANNOTATED

§ 53a-133. Robbery Defined

A person commits robbery when, in the course of committing a larceny, he uses or threatens the immediate use of physical force upon another person for the purpose of: (1) Preventing or overcoming resistance to the taking of the property or to the retention thereof immediately after the taking; or (2) compelling the owner of such property or another person to deliver up the property or to engage in other conduct which aids in the commission of the larceny.

§ 53a-135.   Robbery in the Second Degree . . .

(a) A person is guilty of robbery in the second degree when he commits robbery as defined in section 53a-133 . . . and (1) he is aided by another person actually present; or (2) in the course of the commission of the crime or of immediate flight therefrom he or another participant in the crime displays or threatens the use of what he represents by his words or conduct to be a deadly weapon or a dangerous instrument. . . .

§ 53a-136.   Robbery in the Third Degree . . .

(a) A person is guilty of robbery in the third degree when he commits robbery as defined in section 53a-133. . . .

Commission to Revise the Criminal Statutes: Comment on § 53a-135 (1971)

Robbery in the second degree makes the presence of an accomplice an aggravating factor. The rationale is that the accomplice is equal to a person armed and therefore would generate a higher degree of fear in the victim. Robbery in the second degree is also aimed at circumstances where the actor or accomplice, although not armed with a deadly instrument, purports or represents to be so armed and threatens its use. For example, the actor threatens to use what appears to be a gun he holds in his hand; in reality the gun is only a toy pistol.

STATE v. ANONYMOUS
427 A.2d 403 (Conn. 1980)

WRIGHT, J.

. . . The burden in a criminal case is placed squarely upon the prosecution to prove each essential element of the alleged crime beyond a reasonable doubt. . . .

STATE v. EDWARDS
513 A.2d 669 (Conn. 1986)

HEALEY, J. . . . The defendant . . . claims that . . . the state failed to prove beyond a reasonable doubt that [he] was guilty of being an accessory to robbery in the second degree. . . .

. . . [In a] supermarket parking lot, . . . Veda Johnson, seventy-eight years old, had just finished putting groceries from a shopping cart into her car when she heard footsteps behind her and was then pushed into the cart. At the same time, she felt someone tugging at the purse on her left arm and saw a man run toward the rear of the store. Johnson saw a car come from behind the supermarket building and slow down when it approached the man running toward it. The passenger door opened and the man entered a . . . station wagon. . . .

[While in custody, the defendant told the police that he had driven the station wagon and] that his partner had taken the pocketbook. . . .

General Statutes § 53a-135(a)(1) requires that the person who commits the robbery be "aided by another person *actually present.*" (Emphasis added.) The defendant claims that the driver of the getaway car, "whose very existence is unknown until *after* the commission of the crime," cannot be actually present during the crime as a matter of law. We agree with the defendant.

Penal statutes must be strictly construed [citations omitted]; but such construction must accord with common sense and commonly approved usage of the language. [Citations omitted.] The Commission to Revise the Criminal Statutes comments that § 53a-135 "makes the presence of an accomplice an aggravating factor. The rationale is that the accomplice is equal to a person armed and therefore would generate a higher degree of fear in the victim. . . ." [Citation omitted.] The Comment implies that the presence of the accomplice must be both temporarily and physically proximate to the robbery such that the victim is aware of the accomplice during the robbery. The state claims that there is "no suggestion in the language of the statute that the concept of actual presence hinges on the victim's perception of such presence." . . . [But the longer sentence of imprisonment] attached to robbery in the second degree indicates that the legislature considered it to be a more serious crime because it was likely to have a more severe effect upon the victim. . . . If the victim is unaware of the accomplice at the time of the robbery or the defendant is armed with a deadly weapon but does not display or threaten its use, then the aggravating factor enhancing the offense to robbery in the second degree is absent because there has been no additional effect upon the victim. . . .

. . . [W]e conclude that the defendant, as the driver of the getaway car, was not "actually present" . . . until sometime after the commission of the robbery. *Cf. State v. Miller,* 14 Or. App. 608, 513 P.2d 1199, 1201 (1973) (defendant guilty of robbery in the second degree; aided by individual standing in the parking lot twenty-five feet from the victim whom she observed *during the course of the attack*).

Because the element of actual presence was not proven, this case must be remanded. . . .

STATE v. ARCHAMBAULT
153 A.2d 451 (Conn. 1959)

MURPHY, J. . . . . While it is of course true that a penal statute should be strictly construed, it is not the purpose of the rule of strict construction to enable a person to avoid the clear import of a law through a mere technicality. To enforce the rule beyond its purpose would be to exalt technicalities above substance. [Citation omitted.]

HARRIS DATA COMMUNICATIONS, INC.
v. HEFFERNAN
438 A.2d 1178 (Conn. 1981)

SPEZIALE, J. [Harris Data seeks a refund of state sales and use taxes.]

[A statute] does not become ambiguous merely because the parties contend for differing meanings. [Citation omitted.] The intent of the legislature is to be found in the meaning of the words of the statute; that is, in what the legislature actually *did* say, not in what it *meant* to say. [Citations omitted.] Where the language of the statute is unambiguous, we are confined to the intention expressed in the actual words used and we will not search out any further intention of the legislature not expressed in the statute. [Citations omitted.] In the absence of ambiguity it is unnecessary to resort to principles of statutory construction such as the resolution of ambiguity in favor of the taxpayer. . . .

PEOPLE v. HEDGEMAN
517 N.E.2d 858 (N.Y. 1987)

HANCOCK, J. . . . [A] bank teller . . . testified that defendant came to her window [and] handed her a note which read: "Important. Follow to the letter. . . . Your life and others are in jeopardy. I have a bomb and demand the sum of $15,000. . . ." The teller informed defendant that she did not have that amount of money at her station and gave him the $200 in cash from her drawer. With the money in hand, defendant went out the front door. . . .

As defendant left, the teller [and] the assistant manager . . . went to the window . . . and observed defendant. He was walking along the sidewalk on that side of the bank, around the corner from the front door, towards an automobile parked at curbside by a parking meter. The automobile was 15 feet from the bank window. Sitting in the driver's seat was a person whose gender, age and race the teller could not determine. When defendant entered the automobile on the passenger side, it drove off. . . .

As defined in the Penal Law, a simple taking of property by force, without any aggravating circumstances such as physical injury to a nonparticipant or use of a weapon, constitutes robbery in the third degree. . . . When the commission of the offense includes circumstances which cause, threaten to cause, or increase the risk of physical injury to another, the Legislature has deemed the crime to be more serious and deserving of greater punishment. [Section 160.10 of the] Penal Law defines robbery in the second degree as follows:

> A person is guilty of robbery in the second degree when he forcibly steals property and when:
>> 1. He is *aided by another person actually present* [emphasis added]; or
>> 2. In the course of the commission of the crime or of the immediate flight therefrom, he or another participant in the crime:
>>> (a) Causes physical injury to any person who is not a participant in the crime; or

(b) Displays what appears to be a pistol, revolver, rifle, shotgun, machine gun or other firearm.

When the three aggravating factors in Penal Law § 160.10 are read together, they reflect a concern for the added element of physical harm, danger, and perceived threat of additional violence to the victims of the robbery. That concern is clearly present in situations involving physical injury or the apparent willingness to use a firearm. Likewise, it is present where the robber is joined by another in his use or threat of force or in his seizing or retaining another's property. No such concern exists, however, where the robber has but one accomplice, unknown and unseen to the victim at the time of the robbery, and limited in his participation to waiting for the robber and driving him from the area once the taking has been accomplished.

There is additional evidence in the statute that it was accessorial aid *at the crime scene* and not elsewhere which the Legislature considered sufficiently serious to be an aggravating factor. Two of the three aggravating factors, causing physical injury and displaying a firearm, operate to raise ordinary robbery to robbery in the second degree not only when the aggravating conduct occurs at the crime scene, but also when it occurs during the "immediate flight therefrom" (subd. [2]). By contrast, the aid rendered by an accomplice must, in order to operate as an aggravating factor, be rendered while that accomplice is *actually* present at the robbery (subd. [1]). Assistance rendered solely in the course of "flight therefrom" does not raise the offense to second degree robbery [citations omitted]. . . .

. . . [T]he Commission Staff Notes on the revised Penal Law . . . evince a legislative intent wholly consistent with the result we reach today. The use of a getaway car was included among the aggravating factors in the former robbery statute [citation omitted]. It was eliminated when the Penal Law was revised in 1965 because it was considered by the Legislature to be an insufficiently egregious factor to justify a more serious conviction and harsher sentence. The Commission Staff Notes explain that, where the robber acts alone, the use of an automobile simply does not seem "a highly significant item." And where the robber acts with "a group of bandits," regardless of whether an automobile is used, the robbery is *"in any event"* aggravated only "by virtue of the accomplice factor" [citation omitted]. The mere use of a driver, whose participation in a bank robbery is limited to waiting outside and operating the getaway vehicle, plainly does not constitute a "group of bandits." . . .

Here the evidence was that another person aided defendant in the course of his flight from the crime scene by driving him away. It showed nothing else. There was no suggestion that the driver was armed, prepared to assist defendant, or even observing defendant's actions, or that he was sufficiently close to defendant to be available to render him aid during the actual commission of the robbery. Under these facts, where there is no showing that the driver was ready, willing or able to aid defendant in the forcible stealing from the teller or the bank — let alone that he directly participated therein — it cannot be said that he was "actually present" within any fair construction of the statute.

. . . [The] defendant's conviction [should be] reduced to robbery in third degree, and the case remitted for resentencing.

STATE v. MILLER
513 P.2d 1199 (Or. Ct. App. 1973)

THORNTON, J. Defendant was convicted after jury trial of robbery in the second degree. ORS 164.405.[2] On appeal he contends that . . . the state failed to offer sufficient evidence to establish that he was aided by a second person actually present during the course of the robbery, a necessary element of the crime.

The victim of the robbery, an elderly woman, had parked her automobile in a lighted parking lot of a Portland restaurant, intending to enter the restaurant. She stepped from her car, closed the door, and was in the act of locking the car door with her key when she was grabbed from behind. She testified that her assailant threw her against the car door, struck her on the jaw with his fist, pulled her purse from her grasp and ran from the scene. She also testified that during the course of the attack she observed another young man standing across the parking lot approximately 25 feet from her, and that the second young man and her assailant ran from the scene together following the purse snatching. The victim testified that the defendant was the person who struck her with his fist and took her purse. . . .

The term "aided by another person actually present" as used in ORS 164.405 includes a person who is at hand, or within reach, sight or call, and who presents an added threat to the victim's safety. See Proposed Oregon Criminal Code . . . Commentary, §§ 148 to 150 (1970).

We conclude that the jury could legitimately infer that 25 feet away across a parking lot would constitute easy access to aid the defendant, if necessary, and would be in sufficient proximity . . . to support the finding of the jury that defendant was aided by a second person actually present. [Citation omitted.] . . .

Affirmed.

2. ORS 164.405 provides:
    (1) A person commits the crime of robbery in the second degree if he [commits robbery] and he:
        (a) Represents by word or conduct that he is armed with what purports to be a dangerous or deadly weapon; or
        (b) Is aided by another person actually present. . . .

13 Working with Facts

§13.1 What Is a Fact?

Consider the following statements:

1. *The plaintiff's complaint alleges* that, at a certain time and place, the defendant struck the plaintiff from behind with a stick.
2. At trial, *the plaintiff's principal witness testified* that, at the time and place specified in the complaint, the defendant struck the plaintiff from behind with a stick.
3. At the conclusion of the trial, *the jury found* that, at the time and place specified in the complaint, the defendant struck the plaintiff from behind with a stick.
4. At the time and place specified in the complaint, *the defendant struck* the plaintiff from behind with a stick.
5. At the time and place specified in the complaint, the defendant *brutally* struck the plaintiff from behind with a stick.
6. At the time and place specified in the complaint, the defendant *accidentally* struck the plaintiff from behind with a stick.
7. At the time and place specified in the complaint, the defendant *committed a battery* on the plaintiff.

Which of these statements expresses a fact?

Number 7 plainly does not: it states a *conclusion of law* because battery is a concept defined by the law, and you have learned that you can discover whether a battery occurred only by consulting one or more rules of law. Numbers 5 and 6, however, are a little harder to sort out.

161

Statement 6 includes the word *accidentally*. The defendant might have wanted to cause violence, or he might have struck the plaintiff only inadvertently and without any desire to do harm. With both possibilities, an observer might see pretty much the same actions: the stick being raised, the stick being lowered, the collision with the back. There might be small perceptible differences between the two — the defendant's facial expression, for example, or the words spoken immediately before and after the incident. But even those differences might not occur. A cunning defendant intent on harm, for example, can pretend to act inadvertently. The difference between the two possibilities is in what the defendant might have been thinking or feeling when he struck the plaintiff. If we say that the defendant struck the plaintiff "accidentally," we have made a conclusion about what the defendant was thinking at the time. That conclusion is a purely factual one — lawyers would say a *conclusion of fact*. (It would be a conclusion of law if it were framed in terms that the law defines, such as "intention to cause a contact with another person.") A conclusion of fact is not a fact: it is an inference derived from facts.

Statement 5 contains the word *brutally*, which is a value-based and subjective *characterization*. If one is shocked by the idea of a stick colliding with a human being — regardless of the speed and force involved — even a gentle tap with a stick might be characterized as brutal. (Conversely, an observer who is indifferent to suffering and violence might call repeated lacerations with a stick "playful.") And a friend of the plaintiff or an enemy of the defendant might construe whatever happened as "brutal," while an enemy of the plaintiff or a friend of the defendant might do the reverse. Assuming that we have not seen the incident ourselves, we should wonder whether the word *brutally* accurately summarizes what happened, or whether it instead reflects the value judgments and preferences of the person who has characterized the incident as brutal. A characterization is not a fact; it is only an opinion about a fact.

We are left with statements 1 through 4. Do any of them recite a fact? There are two ways of answering that question. Although the two might at first seem to contradict each other, they are actually consistent, and both answers are accurate, although in different ways.

One answer is that statements 1, 2, and 3 are layers surrounding a fact recited in statement number 4: number 1 is an allegation of a fact; number 2 is evidence offered in proof of the allegation; number 3 is a conclusion that the evidence proves the allegation; and number 4 is the fact itself. This is an answer that might be reached by a perceptive lay person who has noticed what you now know to be a sequence inherent to litigation: the party seeking a remedy first alleges, in a pleading, a collection of facts that, if proven, would merit a remedy, and that party later at trial submits evidence to persuade the finder of fact that the allegations are proven. Notice that this first answer is built on the ideas that a "fact" is part of an objective, discoverable truth and that the purpose of litigation is to find that truth.

The other answer is that numbers 1 through 4 all recite facts, the first three being procedural events of the kind described in §1.3. This answer is derived from the requirement, inherent to litigation, that the decisions of the finder of fact be based not on an objective "truth" that occurred out of court, but instead on whether *in court* a party has carried his or her burdens to make certain allegations and to submit a certain quantum of evidence in support of those allegations. Because it lacks omniscience, a court cannot decide on the basis of what is "true." In a procedural sense, litigation is less a search for truth than it is a test of whether each party has carried burdens of pleading, production, and persuasion that the law assigns to one party or another.[1] Because of the adversary system, the court is not permitted to investigate the controversy: it can do no more than passively weigh what is submitted to it, using as benchmarks the burdens set out in the law. Thus, if a party does not allege and prove a fact essential to that party's case, the court must decide that the fact does not exist. And this is so even if the fact does exist. That is why experienced lawyers tend to be more confident of their abilities to prove and disprove allegations than they are of their abilities to know the "real" truth about what happened between the parties before litigation began.

Both answers are correct, but their value to you will change as time goes on. Right now, the first answer gives you a model of how facts are processed in litigation. But soon the second answer will become increasingly important. That is because, as you learn lawyering, you will have to learn the ways in which the law compels lawyers to focus on whether a party can carry or has carried a burden of pleading, production, or persuasion.

The nonexistence of a fact can itself be a fact. For example, consider the following:

8. The plaintiff's complaint does not allege that the defendant struck the plaintiff with a malicious intent to cause injury.

Here the absence of an allegation is itself a fact. If the complaint demands not only compensatory damages (intended to compensate the plaintiff for his loss), but also punitive damages (additionally intended both to punish the defendant for the outrageousness of his conduct and to warn others like him), the defendant might win a motion to dismiss the demand for punitive damages. But that depends on whether local law treats malice as significant: if the jurisdiction allows punitive damages even in the absence of malice, the missing allegation means nothing.

9. At trial, no witness has testified that the plaintiff suffered any physical or psychological injury or even any indignity.

---

§13.1   1. These burdens are explained more fully in Chapter 20. For the moment, it will be enough to understand the following: A *burden of pleading* is a party's obligation to allege in a pleading facts that, if proven, would entitle the party to the relief sought. A *burden of production* is a party's obligation to come forward with enough evidence about a particular issue to warrant a trial of it. And a *burden of persuasion* is a party's obligation at trial to introduce enough evidence to persuade the trier of fact that the allegations are accurate. If a party fails to meet one of these burdens on a particular issue, the other party is considered the winner of that issue.

Now the absence of certain evidence is itself a fact. Consequently, the defendant might be entitled to a directed verdict[2] on the question of damages: the judge might instruct the jury that it is permitted to award only nominal damages, such as one dollar. But that depends on whether the jurisdiction limits recovery to injuries that require medical treatment, produce pain and suffering, or cause humiliation or other dignitary loss.

You might by now have begun to realize that facts are not as simple as they at first seem. Facts have subtleties that can entangle you if you are not careful. Beginners tend to have difficulties with four fact skills: (1) separating facts from other things; (2) separating determinative facts from other kinds of facts; (3) building inferences from facts; and (4) purging analysis of hidden and unsupportable factual assumptions. When you have mastered these skills, you will be able to make reasoned decisions about selecting and using facts. The last few pages have explained the first skill, and Exercise I at the end of this chapter develops it further. The remainder of this chapter considers each of the other skills in turn.

§13.2   Identifying Determinative Facts

Facts can be divided into three categories. The first category is made up of facts that are essential to a controversy because they will determine the court's decision: if a change in a fact would have caused the court to come to a different decision, that fact is determinative. The second is a category of explanatory facts that, while not determinative, are nevertheless useful because they help make sense out of a situation that would otherwise seem disjointed. The third category includes coincidental facts that have no relevance or usefulness at all: they merely happened. Part of life's charm is that all three categories of facts — the relevant and the irrelevant — occur mixed up together in a disorderly mess. And two of the most basic things lawyers do is to separate out the determinative facts and treat them as determinative.

You have already started learning how to do those things in this and other courses, mostly through the analysis of precedent. When, for example, you are asked to formulate the rule of a case, you have begun to develop the habit of isolating the facts the court considered determinative and then reformulating those facts into a list of generalities that — when they occur together again in the future — will produce the same result that happened in the reported opinion. But when you look at a given litigation through the lens of an opinion, you are looking at it *after* a court has already decided which facts are determinative: you are explicating the text of the opinion to learn what the court thought about the facts. We are concerned here with another skill: looking at the facts at the *beginning* of the case, before they are even put to a court, and predicting which facts the court will consider determinative.

2. In federal courts since 1991, directed verdicts have been called judgments as a matter of law. See Rule 50(a) of the Federal Rules of Civil Procedure.

Recall Welty's experience with Lutz, which you first considered in Chapter 2:

> Welty and Lutz are students who have rented apartments on the same floor of the same building. At midnight, Welty is studying, while Lutz is listening to a Stone Temple Pilots album with his new four-foot speakers. Welty has put up with this for two or three hours, and finally she pounds on Lutz's door. Lutz opens the door about six inches, and, when he realizes that he cannot hear what Welty is saying, he steps back into the room a few feet to turn the volume down, leaving the door open about six inches. Continuing to express outrage, Welty pushes the door completely open and strides into the room. Lutz turns on Welty and orders her to leave. Welty finds this to be too much and punches Lutz so hard that he suffers substantial injury. In this jurisdiction, the punch is a felonious assault. Is Welty also guilty of common law burglary?

You already know that common law burglary is the breaking and entering of the dwelling of another in the nighttime with intent to commit a felony therein. Whichever way a court rules, the size of the opening between Lutz's door and the door frame is going to be one of the determinative facts because the size of the opening helps to determine whether, at the moment Welty walked in, Lutz's dwelling was surrounded by the kind of enclosure that can be broken. Depending on one's theory, Lutz's activities before Welty knocked on the door could be either explanatory or determinative: they help make sense out of the situation, but they also help explain Welty's actions and intent, which go to other elements of the test for burglary. But you have not been told that Lutz only recently got into hard rock and that previously he had been a devotee of country music; those facts are omitted because they are purely coincidental and do not help you understand the issues.

Of the four fact skills considered in this chapter, isolating the determinative facts is probably the one that seems most obvious from your law school work generally. The first few months of law school are designed to teach two things that are the heart of this skill: rule analysis and a heightened sense of relevance.

§13.3 Building Inferences from Facts

> The main part of intellectual education is . . . learning how to make facts live.
>
> — *Oliver Wendell Holmes*

We will continue a bit further with Welty and Lutz.

One of the elements of burglary is the intent to commit a felony within the dwelling. In the jurisdiction where Welty and Lutz live, that element can be satisfied only if a defendant had that intent at the time that any breaking and entering might have occurred. If the defendant formed the intent for the first time only after entering the dwelling, the element is not satisfied. Assuming for the moment that Welty broke and entered Lutz's apartment when she opened the door further and walked in,[1] did she — at the instant she stepped inside — intend to commit a felony there?

Your response may be "Well, let's ask Welty — she's the one who would really know." But things are not so easy. If you are the prosecutor, you may find that the police have already asked her that question and that she has refused to answer or has given an answer that the police consider self-serving. In fact, one rarely has direct evidence of a person's state of mind: people do not carry electronic signboards on their foreheads on which their thoughts can be read at moments the law considers important. Instead, as prosecutor you would have to prove Welty's state of mind through the surrounding circumstances — for example, through the things she did or did not do, as well as the things she knew other people had or had not done.[2] Although her state of mind would be easier to determine if she had appeared at Lutz's door with an arsenal of weaponry — or, in another situation, with safecracking tools — inferences can be built from circumstances even without such dramatic displays of intent.

Even if you are Welty's defense lawyer and can freely ask her when she formed an intent to hit Lutz, you might not be much better off than the prosecutor. She might tell you something like the following:

> I don't know when I decided to punch him. I had to listen to his loud music on his four-foot speakers for two or three hours while I was trying to study for civil procedure. At least once or twice during that time, I thought that it might be nice to punch his lights out, but I don't know that I had decided then to do it. When I knocked on his door, I thought, "This guy had better be reasonable, or else" — but at that instant I don't know whether I was committed to punching him. When I pushed the door open and stepped inside, I thought, "This joker might learn a little respect for the rest of us if something very emphatic happened to him — something that might help him remember in the future that other people have needs and that he shouldn't be so self-centered." Even then, I wasn't certain that I was going to do anything

---

§13.3   1. The breaking and entering issues may not be easy to resolve. See Chapter 8. Let us focus here, however, only on the state-of-mind element: whether, at the time of any breaking and entering that *might* have occurred, she intended to commit a felony inside.

2. Once again, the nonexistence of a fact can be treated as a fact, as with the dog that did not bark:

> "Is there any other point to which you wish to draw my attention?"
> "To the curious incident of the dog in the night-time."
> "The dog did nothing in the night-time."
> "That was the curious incident," remarked Sherlock Holmes. . . . "Obviously the midnight visitor was someone the dog knew well."

Arthur Conan Doyle, *Silver Blaze*, in *The Memoirs of Sherlock Holmes* 27 (1893).

except try to reason with him. And when he ordered me out, I decked him. Nobody told me that I was supposed to make sure that my thoughts fit into this "state of mind" thing you're telling me about. I have no idea when I "formed an intent" to hit him. I can only tell you what my thoughts were at each step in the story. You're the lawyer. You tell me when I "formed an intent."

Now the problem is something else: a party's thoughts do not mesh nicely with the law's categories of states of mind. Welty's sequence of emotions somehow culminated in an action, but there seems to have been no magical moment at which anger crystallized into a decision that the law might recognize as "intent." A defense lawyer handles this problem in the same way that a prosecutor deals with the absence of direct evidence: each lawyer will build inferences from the circumstances surrounding Welty's actions. As Welty sees the arguments unfold, she might conclude that the law is doing strange and perhaps arbitrary things in categorizing her thoughts. But the law must have a way of judging states of mind, and it relies heavily on circumstances.

Albert Moore has used the term *inferential stream* to refer to the sequence of circumstantial conclusions that can grow out of a fact or piece of evidence.[3] Circumstantial evidence does not necessarily lead to only one stream of inferences. Consider the evidence in *Smith v. Jones,* where Smith claims that Jones caused an accident by running a red light:

Jones testifies that his two children, ages five and six, were arguing in the back seat of his car just before the accident occurred. [This] is circumstantial propositional evidence that Jones entered the intersection against the red light because there is a series of valid generalizations that connects this evidence to the factual proposition in question. These generalizations might be stated as follows:

Generalization 1: People driving with children arguing in the back seat of the car sometimes pay attention to what is happening in the back seat.

Generalization 2: People who are paying attention to what is happening in the back seat of the car are sometimes momentarily distracted from what is happening on the road in front of them.

Generalization 3: People who are momentarily distracted from what is happening on the road in front of them sometimes enter an intersection against the red light.

Conclusion: Jones entered the intersection against the red light.

Based on the foregoing, one might conclude that this circumstantial evidence tends to prove only that Jones entered the intersection against the red light. One could also, however, conclude that this evidence tends to disprove

---

3. Albert J. Moore, *Inferential Streams: The Articulation and Illustration of the Advocate's Evidentiary Intuitions,* 34 UCLA L. Rev. 611 (1987).

that Jones entered the intersection against the red light. This conclusion might be based on the following analysis:

> *Generalization 4:* People driving with children arguing in the back seat are sometimes conscious of the presence of children in the car.
>
> *Generalization 5:* People who are conscious of children in their car sometimes drive cautiously.
>
> *Generalization 6:* People who drive cautiously sometimes pay close attention to the road.
>
> *Generalization 7:* People who pay close attention to the road sometimes do not enter an intersection against the red light.
>
> *Conclusion:* Jones did not enter the intersection against the red light.

In *Smith v. Jones,* therefore, the evidence that Jones' children were arguing in the back of the car just before the accident, by itself, may tend to prove or disprove that Jones entered the intersection against the red light, depending on which set of generalizations is viewed as more reliable and accurate. . . . Thus, circumstantial propositional evidence may "cut both ways" in two situations: when the same evidence tends to prove or disprove the same factual proposition; or when it tends to prove one factual proposition while also tending to disprove another.[4]

§13.4 Identifying Hidden and Unsupportable Factual Assumptions

As David Binder and Paul Bergman have pointed out, "[i]f in medieval times there was 'trial by combat,' then today we have 'trial by inference.'"[1] Your adversary and the court will mercilessly challenge your inferential streams, looking for weaknesses in the way they were put together. Consequently, you must purge your analysis of hidden assumptions that will not stand up to scrutiny when exposed. Consider the following:

> Detective Fenton Tracem rushes breathlessly into the office of the local prosecutor, Les Gettem, eager to persuade Les to issue an indictment. Fenton describes the evidence he has uncovered:
>
> > Les, we've got a good case for bank robbery against Clyde. The gun the robber used and dropped at the door was originally purchased by Clyde. The owner of A-1 Guns can definitely identify Clyde as the purchaser and the teller can identify the gun. Moreover, the day after the $10,000 was taken, Clyde deposits $7,000 cash in a bank account using the fictitious name of Dillinger. A teller at the bank can definitely identify Clyde. Then later that day, Clyde buys a $1,500 gold watch and pays for

4. *Id.* at 625-27.
§13.4   1. David A. Binder & Paul Bergman, *Fact Investigation: From Hypothesis to Proof* 82 (1984).

it in cash. The owner of A-2 Jewelry can also identify him. Finally, the next day — two days after the robbery — Clyde moves out without giving Ness, his landlord, his two neighbors, Capone and Siegel, or the post office his new address. Ness, Capone, Siegel and the post office clerk are all willing to testify. Les, we're rock-solid on this one.

The detective has disgorged a mass of circumstantial evidence which appears in the aggregate to be quite convincing. The prosecutor cannot, however, be content to rely on this presentation. In order to analyze the probative value of the evidence, Gettem must first expressly articulate the generalization which links each item of evidence to an element. . . . [E]xpressly articulating generalizations is the key to determining just how strong a piece of evidence is.

Consider, therefore, the generalization the prosecutor might articulate for the first piece of evidence, that the gun used and dropped by the robber was originally purchased by Clyde. The generalization might be something like, "People who have purchased a gun subsequently used in a robbery are more likely to have participated in the robbery than people who have not."[2]

How accurate is this generalization? See what happens when you compare it with *either* of two strings of other generalizations. Here is the first one: "Robbers do not feel morally compelled to pay for what they acquire, and because guns can be stolen, a robber does not have even a practical need to pay for a gun." This is the second string: "Robbers tend to plan their crimes with at least some amount of forethought; some forethought would cause a robber to foresee that he or she might lose control of a gun during the robbery; other forethought would cause a robber to foresee that a gun legally purchased from a merchant might be traced back to the robber; Clyde is bright enough to have come to both of these foresights." Both strings seem more believable than "People who have purchased a gun subsequently used in a robbery are more likely to have participated in the robbery than people who have not" — and *either* string might overcome and negate the generalization on which the detective relies.

> In the beginning years of practice, one must force oneself to articulate explicitly the generalizations on which one relies, for it is not a skill practiced in everyday life. In fact, there is a word for people who state the generalizations underlying all inferences they make: bores. But in the privacy of one's office, one should expressly identify the premises on which one relies [because] by articulating the underlying generalization one can consciously consider the question of how strongly it is supported by common experience.
>
> This point may be seen more clearly if one is asked to evaluate another of Det. Tracem's pieces of evidence without the aid of an expressed generalization. "The day after the $10,000 was taken, Clyde deposits $7,000 cash in a bank account using the fictitious name of Dillinger." As D.A. Les Gettem, one is asked how strongly suggestive of Clyde's guilt this piece of evidence is. . . .

---

2. *Id.* at 92-93.

. . . If your answer is something like, "The evidence is strongly indicative of guilt" (or "isn't too probative of guilt"), you have had a knee-jerk reaction to the evidence. Undoubtedly some accumulation of common experience was implicit in whatever conclusion you reached. But unless the common experience is crystallized in an explicitly stated generalization, one has no focal point for considering how uniformly common experience supports the generalization.

If your conclusion did include a generalization, it may have been something like, "People who deposit $7,000 in a bank account under a fictitious name are likely to have gotten the money illegally." With this generalization explicitly stated, one has a basis for gauging with some degree of accuracy the probative value of the fictitious bank account evidence. One has an explicit premise which can be tested according to one's own and a factfinder's probable views as to how the world operates. . . .

There are other reasons for articulating generalizations. Their articulation may bring to mind potential exceptions. . . . [O]ne method of testing the degree to which common experience uniformly supports a generalization is to add "except when" to a generalization, and see how many reasonable exceptions one can identify. . . .

[For example, consider] a generalization that one might make in Clyde's case: "People who move without leaving a forwarding address are usually trying to avoid detection." By adding "except when," one sees that this generalization is subject to many exceptions and is therefore less likely to be persuasive. People may be trying to avoid detection, except when they simply forget to leave a forwarding address, or except when they do not yet know the permanent address to which they will be moving, or except when they will be moving around for a time and will not have a permanent address.[3]

As Binder and Bergman point out, only bores recite for the benefit of others all the generalizations underlying their inferences. Thus, when you build and test your own inferences, you will not commit to paper much of the analysis Binder and Bergman describe. As they suggest, it is thinking reserved for the privacy of your own office.

But things are different when you attack your adversary's inferences. If Clyde becomes your client, you might argue that a directed verdict should be — or, on appeal, should have been — granted because a rational jury would not be able to find guilt beyond a reasonable doubt. In a supporting memorandum or in an appellate brief, you might write, "The evidence that he moved without leaving a forwarding address does not tend to prove guilty flight. It could just as easily prove that he forgot to leave a forwarding address, or that he did not yet know his new permanent address when he moved, or that he would be moving around for a time without a permanent address."

Exercise I.   The Menu at the Courthouse Cafe

The following appear on the menu at the Courthouse Cafe. Decide what is a fact, what is a characterization, and what is a conclusion of fact. (If part of an

3. *Id.* at 93-96.

item is factual and part is not, decide exactly where the fact ends and the non-fact begins.)

Hot, steaming coffee

Healthful oat bran muffins

Pure beef hot dogs

Garden-fresh vegetables

Hand-picked huckleberries

Home-made huckleberry pie

Delicious peanut butter ice cream

Exercise II.   Welty's State of Mind

Complete the first part of this exercise before doing any portion of the second.

1. Develop whatever streams of inferences are necessary to determine Welty's state of mind from the facts given on pages 165-67. Write out each fact on which you rely and each inference in the stream flowing from that fact.

2. You are now no longer the person who completed the first part of this exercise. You are somebody else, and you have been hired to attack each of the inferential streams developed in the first part of the exercise. Write down every hidden assumption you can find in those inferential streams, and decide whether each assumption is probable enough to support the inferences that flow from it.

14

Paragraphing

§14.1 How Paragraphing Reveals Your Organization

Before law school, you might have paragraphed by writing until you seemed to have written a lot, stopping, starting a new paragraph, and then going through the cycle all over again. But in law, paragraphs put together that way will confound and annoy readers who must find your meaning quickly.

Most readers unconsciously use paragraph divisions to learn how a writer's thoughts fit together. They assume that each paragraph substantiates or explores a separate and distinct idea or subject. They also assume that the first or second sentence in each paragraph states or implies that idea or subject and, if necessary, shows how it is related to matters already discussed. To the extent that you frustrate these assumptions, your writing will be less helpful to the reader and therefore less influential.

Paragraphing has three goals. The most obvious is to break your material up into digestible chunks. The second is to help you discipline yourself to confront and develop each theme inherent in the material. The third is to tell the reader where he or she is in your logic, how that place was arrived at, and where you are headed — in other words, to make your organization apparent. If the reader feels lost or does not immediately know what the paragraph's thesis or topic is or how it differs from that of the preceding paragraph, there is something wrong with the paragraph's length or structure or with the wording of individual sentences. As you will see in §14.4, the paragraph's first sentence is the one most often botched.

How can you tell the difference between a paragraph that accomplishes these goals and one that does not? An effective paragraph has five characteristics. First, it has *unity:* it proves one proposition or covers one subject. Material that is more relevant to other propositions or subjects has

173

been removed and placed elsewhere. Second, an effective paragraph has *completeness:* it includes whatever is necessary to prove the proposition or cover the subject. Third, an effective paragraph has *internal coherence:* ideas are expressed in a logical sequence that the reader is able to follow without having to edit the paragraph mentally while reading. Fourth, an effective paragraph is of *readable length:* it is neither so long that the reader gets lost nor so short that valuable material is underdeveloped or trivialized. Fifth, an effective paragraph *announces or implies its purpose* at the outset: its first or second sentence states its thesis or topic and, if necessary, makes a transition from the preceding material.

Ineffective paragraphing is related to incomplete analysis. When you set out to fix problem paragraphs, you will often find yourself fixing analytical problems as well.

§14.2 Probative Paragraphs and Descriptive Paragraphs

Some paragraphs merely *describe* conditions or events; they convey information without analysis. But in legal writing, most paragraphs are expected to do more than that: they *prove* propositions that help resolve issues. In descriptive writing, the paragraph states information, and the first or second sentence tells the reader the paragraph's topic or theme, to the extent that is not already evident from the context. But in probative writing, the paragraph exists to prove its first or second sentence, which states the paragraph's *thesis.*

A topic is merely a category of information ("weather in Death Valley"), but a thesis is a proposition capable of proof or disproof ("the climate of Death Valley is brutal"):

Descriptive

In January in Death Valley, the average high temperature is about 65°, and the average low is about 37°. Spring and fall temperatures approximate summer temperatures elsewhere. In April and in October, for example, the average high is about 90°, and the average low about 60°. July is the hottest month, with an average high of about 116° and an average low of about 87°. The highest temperature ever recorded in Death Valley was 134°F on July 10, 1913. Average annual rainfall is about 1½ inches.

Probative

The climate in Death Valley is brutal. At Furnace Creek Ranch, the highest summer temperature each year reaches at least 120° and in many years at least 125°. The highest temperature recorded in Death Valley — 134° — is also the highest recorded in the Western Hemisphere and the second highest recorded anywhere on earth. (The highest is 136° — in the Sahara.) In the summer sun, a person can lose four gallons of perspiration a day and — in 3% humidity — die of dehydration.

174

A confused reader of descriptive writing might ask, "What is this paragraph about?" But a confused reader of probative writing asks instead, "What is this writer trying to prove?"

Probative and descriptive writing can occur in the same document. In college writing, you might typically have written many descriptive paragraphs setting out an abundance of raw data and then concluded with a short passage expressing one or more inferences that the data supported.[1] Although the document as a whole might tend to support the inferences, probative writing in college tends to be limited to the final passage — if it occurs even there.[2] But in a Discussion (or Argument in a motion memorandum or appellate brief), the writing should be largely probative, with only occasional digressions into description. Some other parts of a memorandum or brief, however, are predominantly description. The best examples are the Statement of Facts in an office memorandum and the Preliminary Statement in a motion memorandum or appellate brief.

§14.3 Thesis Sentences, Topic Sentences, and Transition Sentences

A probative paragraph states its thesis in its first or second sentence, and that sentence is the *thesis sentence*.[1] A descriptive paragraph does the same with its *topic* unless the topic is implied by the context. Although in descriptive writing a topic can often be implied, probative writing has more force if a thesis is always expressly stated. (Remember that a practical reader needs to know your purpose in saying things before you start saying them.) With either type of paragraph, a *transition sentence* helps show the reader how the paragraph is connected to the material before it or the material after it.[2]

Thesis, topic, and transition sentences can be worked into a paragraph in several different ways. A transition sentence most often appears at the

§14.2 1. As you learned in Chapters 8 and 9, in law that kind of organization will frustrate your readers to the point of impatience. The law-trained reader needs to learn *at the beginning* what you intend to prove and needs to be told, at *each* step along the way, *how* the data support the proposition you are trying to prove.

2. Unless the reader is told *how* the data support the inference, the writing is not probative. A mere recitation of data is not a proof. Proof is an explanation of *how* the data support the inference.

§14.3 1. In college, "thesis sentence" is sometimes used to refer to a sentence that sums up the meaning of an entire essay. Here, it has a different meaning.

2. This is a descriptive paragraph. Its topic is the three kinds of sentences that tell a reader a paragraph's purpose and relationship to its surroundings. Although the paragraph could have begun with a sentence expressing that, the topic sentence was omitted on the grounds that it would have blocked the flow into the paragraph; that too many announcements of paragraphs' topics can become tedious; and that this paragraph's purpose is implied by the context. From your point of view as the reader, was that the best writing decision? Does the context make the topic clear enough without a topic sentence? Or would you rather have been told at the beginning what the paragraph is about?

beginning of a paragraph, less often at the end (as a bridge into the next paragraph), rarely in the middle, and not at all if a transition is unnecessary. The first sentence in a paragraph can often do double duty. It might state a thesis or topic and — perhaps in a dependent clause — make a transition. Or a transition sentence at the beginning of a paragraph can imply a topic while making a transition from the previous paragraph. If the paragraph begins with a transition sentence that does not also state a thesis or state or imply a topic, the paragraph's second sentence can express either. Where a paragraph's thesis or topic is complex, the paragraph might end with a closure sentence that ties up loose ends.

§14.4 The Two Most Common Ways of Botching the Beginning of a Paragraph

The two most common ways of botching the beginning of a paragraph are (1) omitting entirely any statement of the thesis or topic, and (2) using a topic sentence to begin a probative paragraph (which should have a thesis sentence instead). Either problem can force a judge to read the paragraph two or three times to figure out its purpose, unless that is clear from the context.

Botching the beginning by omitting any statement of the thesis or topic: The habit of announcing or alluding to a para-graph's purpose at the beginning is a kind of self-discipline. Because it forces you to articulate the paragraph's reason for being, it will encourage you — especially during rewriting — to limit the paragraph to one thesis or topic (unity), to do whatever is necessary inside the paragraph to prove that thesis or cover that topic (completeness), and to express the ideas in the paragraph in a sequence appropriate to the thesis or topic (coherence). If a statement of the topic or thesis is missing, that often means that you do not yet know what the paragraph is supposed to accomplish — which can lead to conversations like this:

(a) Instructor identifies a murky paragraph in student writing.

(b) Instructor asks student, "Tell me in a sentence what you are trying to say in this paragraph."

(c) Student reads paragraph — ponders — and, generally, comes up with a one-sentence statement.

(d) Instructor says, "Well, would it help the reader if you *said that* at the front end of the paragraph?"

(e) Light bulb flashes over student's head.

(f) Instructor then asks, "Now if that's your main idea, how does *this* sentence [indicating one whose function is unclear] tie in to that idea?"

(g) If the student suggests a function, the instructor asks, "Is there any way you could make that function clearer to the reader?"

(h) If the student does not see a function, the instructor asks, "Does that sentence belong in the paragraph?"

As the author of this familiar scene concludes, *"There is no reason why you, the writer, cannot carry on that conversation inside your own head as you [rewrite]."*[1]

Botching the beginning by using a topic sentence to begin a probative paragraph: Consider this probative paragraph, which begins with an unhelpful topic sentence:

> The federal bank robbery statute penalizes obtaining anything of value from a bank "by force and violence, or by intimidation." 18 U.S.C. § 2113 (1982). Several cases have defined the term "intimidation." For example, a defendant takes by intimidation when he hands a bank teller a note reading "Put all your money in this bag and nobody will get hurt." *United States v. Epps*, 438 F.2d 1192 (4th Cir. 1971). The same is true where a defendant, while holding his hand in his pocket to suggest that he has a weapon, hands a teller a note reading, "This is a holdup." *United States v. Harris*, 530 F.2d 576 (4th Cir. 1976). And even where a teller never sees a weapon, intimidation is proved where a defendant produces a note stating, "I have a gun. Give me all the bills or I will shoot you." *United States v. Jacquillon*, 469 F.2d 380 (5th Cir. 1972), *cert. denied*, 410 U.S. 938 (1973).

This is *not* a descriptive paragraph. Its purpose is to prove a definition of "intimidation." But the first sentence does not tell you what the definition is and therefore it is not a thesis sentence. The first sentence announces only a topic — the federal bank robbery statute — and thus does not communicate what the paragraph is meant to prove. In fact, *no* sentence in the paragraph sets out the definition that the paragraph is intended to prove. To the reader who needs to know what "intimidation" is, a paragraph like this one is frustrating to the point of impatience. Not only does the reader need to know exactly what you are trying to prove, but he or she needs to know it *before proof begins*. Most of the problem could be solved with an accurate thesis sentence like this:

> Under the federal bank robbery statute, 18 U.S.C. § 2113 — which penalizes obtaining anything of value from a bank "by force and violence, or by intimidation" — the courts have defined "intimidation" as conduct reasonably calculated to produce fear, even in the complete absence of physical violence. . . .

The last fourteen words of this sentence give the whole paragraph meaning because they synthesize the holdings of the cases into a definition that the paragraph proves to be accurate.

Once you have replaced a topic sentence with a thesis sentence, some rewording and reordering of other sentences might be needed to give the paragraph coherence — to show, in other words, *how* the rest of the para-

---

§14.4 1. Peter W. Gross, *California Western Law School's First-Year Course in Legal Skills,* 44 Alb. L. Rev. 369, 389-90 (1980).

graph proves the thesis. Notice how the earlier version has been changed here so that it seems to flow straight from the new thesis sentence:

> *Writer HAS / synthesized — he's not just describing*

> Under the federal bank robbery statute, 18 U.S.C. § 2113 — which penalizes obtaining anything of value from a bank "by force and violence, or by intimidation" — the courts have defined "intimidation" as conduct reasonably calculated to produce fear, even in the complete absence of physical violence. For example, even where a teller never actually sees a weapon, intimidation is proved where a defendant produces a note stating, "I have a gun. Give me all the bills or I will shoot you." *United States v. Jacquillon*, 469 F.2d 380 (5th Cir. 1972), *cert. denied*, 410 U.S. 938 (1973). More vaguely expressed threats are treated the same way. A defendant takes by intimidation when he hands a bank teller a note reading, "Put all your money in this bag and nobody will get hurt." *United States v. Epps*, 438 F.2d 1192 (4th Cir. 1971). And the result is the same even where the threat is entirely implied — for example, where a defendant, while holding his hand in his pocket to suggest that he has a weapon, hands a teller a note reading, "This is a holdup." *United States v. Harris*, 530 F.2d 576 (4th Cir. 1976).

If your prior writing experience has primarily been descriptive — and that is true of most law students — you will have to discipline yourself to see the difference between a descriptive paragraph and a probative one. And you will have to be careful to begin a probative paragraph with a thesis sentence. You will probably find that this kind of self-discipline forces you to make your meaning more clear to the reader throughout the paragraph — and that consequently you will analyze more deeply.

Both of these problems occur for pretty much the same reason. When you begin a probative paragraph with a topic sentence — or when you write a paragraph that has no thesis or topic sentence at all — in all likelihood you did not know when you began to write the paragraph what you intended to prove or describe within it. In a first draft, there is nothing wrong with that. The purpose of a first draft, after all, is to get the material out in the open so that you can finish analyzing it. But during rewriting, when you find a topic sentence atop a probative paragraph — or when you find a paragraph with no thesis or topic sentence at all — that is often a clue that you have not yet begun to articulate *even to yourself* what you are trying to accomplish in the paragraph. But this problem is miraculously easy to solve: merely asking yourself "What am I trying to prove here?" often produces almost instantly a thesis sentence that gives the whole paragraph meaning and relevance.

§14.5   How to Test Your Writing for Effective Paragraphing

In first drafts, paragraphs are seldom put together well. Instead, the work of paragraphing generally occurs during re-writing, when you should be trying to find paragraphs that do not accurately reflect the structure of your analysis. To identify the paragraphs in need of rehabilitation, ask yourself the following questions.[1]

Have you told the reader, near the beginning of each paragraph, the paragraph's thesis (if the paragraph is probative) or its topic ⎡**14-A**⎤ **(if the paragraph is descriptive)?** If the reader does not learn the paragraph thesis or topic at the beginning, the reader will have to read the paragraph two or three times to figure out its purpose. (See pages 175-78.) The only time you are exempt from this requirement is where the topic or thesis is clearly implied by the context.

Have you gotten rid of throat-clearing introductory sentences, which bump into the paragraph's thesis or topic backward? ⎡**14-B**⎤ For example:

> The Court of Appeals considered this question in *Bellamy.* There, the court held that, under some circumstances, a promissory note can be a security subject to regulation under this state's Blue Sky Law.

You can combine these two sentences into a single thesis or topic sentence that goes straight to the point:

> The Court of Appeals held in *Bellamy* that, under some circumstances, a promissory note can be a security subject to regulation under this state's Blue Sky Law.

Have you given each paragraph a unified purpose? Prove one proposition or cover one subject. Remove and place elsewhere ⎡**14-C**⎤ material that is more relevant to other propositions or subjects.

Within each paragraph, have you expressed your ideas in a logical and effective sequence? Where a paragraph is confusing ⎡**14-D**⎤ but nothing is wrong with its size or with the wording of individual sentences, the problem is usually that the paragraph lacks internal coherence. That happens when ideas within the paragraph are presented in a sequence that makes it hard for the reader to understand them or how they fit together to prove the thesis or illuminate the topic.

Have you broken up paragraphs that were so large that the reader would have gotten lost? Although there are no set rules ⎡**14-E**⎤ on paragraph length, paragraphs that wander aimlessly or endlessly do not accomplish the goals of paragraphing. Where that happens, you have probably tried to develop two or more complex and separable themes in a single paragraph, perhaps without being aware of it. The cure is to identify the

---

§**14.5** 1. When marking up your work, your teacher might refer to these questions by using the number-letter codes that appear next to each question here.

individual themes and then break up the material accordingly into digestible chunks (which become separate paragraphs).

14-F | **Have you rewritten paragraphs that were so short that no thesis or topic is developed?** Generally, one- and two-sentence paragraphs are ineffective unless you have a special reason for emphasizing something or for separating out uncomplicated material. One- or two-sentence paragraphs can be used to good effect in clearing up matters that are preliminary (such as identifying the procedural posture) or ancillary (such as identifying issues that are not presently before the court). When used carefully, short paragraphs can also emphasize some memorable aspect of the material. In many other situations, however, a short paragraph leaves the reader hungry for a more satisfying explanation of some important point. If a paragraph is so short that no thesis or topic is developed, ask yourself whether (1) you might have missed the complexities of the thesis or topic, or (2) the thesis or topic might be so simple that it does not merit treatment in a separate paragraph because it is actually part of some other thesis or topic.

14-G | **Have you shown the reader how each paragraph is related to the surrounding material (unless the relationship is implied by the context)?** There are several ways of doing this. The paragraph can begin with a transition sentence. Or it can begin with a sentence that both makes a transition and states a thesis or topic. Or the last sentence of the preceding paragraph can build a bridge between the two paragraphs: that sentence can raise an expectation, for example, that the second paragraph satisfies.

Exercise I.   The First Weeks of Law School (Probative and Descriptive Paragraphs)

Write two paragraphs — one descriptive and the other probative — about the first weeks of law school.

Descriptive paragraph: Summarize what happened during your first weeks in law school. Describe only things you saw, heard, read, and wrote. Do not try to prove any belief you might have about the first weeks of law school.

Probative paragraph: The opening sentence of this paragraph should be "The first weeks of law school are hard" (or "puzzling" or "exciting" or "cruel" or "challenging" or any other characterization you choose) "because" — and here you complete the sentence by stating whatever you believe to be the cause of your characterization. The rest of the paragraph should prove the thesis expressed in this sentence.

Exercise II.   Maldonado's Citrus Croissants (Thesis and Topic Sentences, Paragraph Coherence)

Is the paragraph below probative or descriptive? What is the thesis or topic? Is it adequately expressed in the first or second sentence? If not, write an appropriate thesis or topic sentence or find a sentence already in the paragraph that states its thesis or topic. Within the paragraph, are ideas expressed in a logical sequence so that you do not have to edit the paragraph mentally while reading? If you believe the sentences in the paragraph should appear in a different order, rearrange them and write out separately your reasons for doing so. Decide whether any sentence's wording should be altered to improve the flow from sentence to sentence and from idea to idea. (Each sentence is preceded by a letter in brackets so that you can refer to it in class without having to read the sentence aloud.)

[A] A matter of general knowledge within an industry lacks a trade secret's novelty or uniqueness and therefore is not protectable as a trade secret. *Wright v. Palmer*, 11 Ariz. App. 292, 464 P.2d 363 (1970); Restatement of Torts § 757 comment *b* (1939). [B] If an examination of a product "completely disclose[s]" the process through which it was made, that process by definition is not a secret. Restatement § 757 comment *b*. [C] Maldonado's Citrus Croissants recipe is not a trade secret. [D] Although the recipe for Citrus Croissants was unique and novel and had not been developed by any other baker, anyone in the baking industry could have purchased Citrus Croissants from a store and discovered their ingredients and baking process through reverse engineering, a relatively time-consuming and expensive process. [E] Thus, the recipe could have been discovered, although not easily. [F] Since the recipe could have been disclosed through marketed croissants, it does not constitute a trade secret.

Exercise III.   *Escape from Prison (Paragraph Unity, Coherence, and Length)*

Is the paragraph below limited to proving a single proposition or covering a single subject? If not, what material is extraneous? Is the paragraph of appropriate size? If you believe it is too long, how should the problem be solved? Are the ideas expressed in a sequence that enables you to understand the meaning of the paragraph without reading it twice? If not, what sequence would be better? Edit the paragraph in light of your answers to these questions. Add any thesis, topic, or transition sentences that you think are needed. Bring your work to class and be prepared to explain your thinking. (Each sentence is preceded by a letter in brackets so that you can refer to it in class without having to read the sentence aloud.)

[A] A prisoner who leaves a prison without permission is guilty of a crime of escape. [B] Until relatively recently, the defense of necessity was not available in California to a prisoner who claimed that prison conditions were so intolerable as to require escape. [C] An early case, for example, affirmed a conviction for escape, conceding that "if the facts were as stated by the defendant, he was subjected to brutal treatment of extreme atrocity" in a "remote" mountain prison camp far from any authorities to whom he might complain. *People v. Whipple*, 100 Cal. App. 261, 266, 279 P.2d 1008, 1010 (2d Dist. 1929). [D] And a more recent case affirmed a conviction where the defendant offered evidence that other prisoners had threatened to kill him, and that prison guards had refused to protect him. *People v. Richardson,* 269 Cal. App. 2d 768, 75 Cal. Rptr. 597 (1st Dist. 1969). [E] Both *Whipple* and *Richardson* cited 1 Hale P.C. 611 for the proposition that escape from prison can be excused only to avoid death as immediate as that threatened when the prison itself is engulfed in fire. [F] But drawing on decisions from other jurisdictions, the Court of Appeal for the Fourth District has held that, through a "limited defense of necessity," a prisoner can defeat a prosecution for escape if the prisoner can demonstrate (1) that he or she was "faced with a specific threat of death, forcible sexual attack or substantial bodily injury in the immediate future," (2) that a complaint to the authorities would have been futile or not possible, (3) that the same was true regarding resort to the courts, (4) that the prisoner used no "force or violence" in escaping, and (5) that the prisoner surrendered to the authorities "when he [had] attained a position of safety from the immediate threat." *People v. Lover-camp,* 43 Cal. App. 3d 823, 831-32, 118 Cal. Rptr. 110, 115 (4th Dist. 1974). [G] Even under this test, Victor Minskov does not have a defense to the charge of escape. [H] He had been beaten twice by a group of prisoners who threatened to attack him as long as he remained in the same prison. [I] He scaled the prison wall at 4 A.M. immediately after the second beating and while being chased by the same group. [J] After the first beating, he had complained to prison guards, who laughed at him, and during the second beating his cries for help brought no response. [K] The courts would not have been able to protect him from such an assault, and he used no force or violence in escaping. [L] But after leaving the prison he hid under an assumed name for 16 months and was finally captured at the Los Angeles airport trying to leave the country. [M] Thus, he will not be able to show that he complied with the last element of the *Lovercamp* test by surrendering to the authorities upon attaining "a position of safety from the immediate threat."

15 Effective Style

JAMES P. DEGNAN, THE PH.D. ILLITERATE
The Washington Post, Sept. 12, 1976

The scene is my office, and I am at work, doing what must be done if one is to assist in the cure of a disease I have come to call straight-A illiteracy. I am interrogating, I am cross-examining, I am prying and probing for the meaning of a student's paper. The student is a college senior with a straight-A average, an extremely bright, highly articulate student who has just been awarded a coveted fellowship to one of the nation's outstanding graduate schools. He and I have been going over his paper sentence by sentence, word by word, for an hour.

"The choice of exogenous variables in relation to multi-colinearity," I hear myself reading from his paper, "is contingent upon the derivations of certain multiple correlation coefficients." I pause to catch my breath. "Now that statement," I address the student — whom I shall call, allegorically, Mr. Bright — "that statement, Mr. Bright — what on earth does it mean?" Mr. Bright, his brow furrowed, tries mightily. Finally, with both of us combining our linguistic and imaginative resources, we decode it. We decide exactly what it is that Mr. Bright is trying to say, which is: "Supply determines demand."

Bright's disease attacks the best minds and gradually destroys the critical facilities, making it impossible for the sufferer to detect gibberish in his own writing or in that of others. During the years of higher education it grows worse, reaching its terminal stage, typically, when its victim receives his Ph.D.

The ordinary illiterate — perhaps providentially protected from college and graduate school — might say: "Them people down at the

183

shop better stock up on what our customers need, or we ain't gonna be in business long." Not our man. Taking his cue from years of higher education, years of reading the textbooks and professional journals that are the major sources of his affliction, he writes: "The focus of concentration must rest upon objectives centered around the knowledge of customer areas so that a sophisticated awareness of those areas can serve as an entrepreneurial filter to screen what is relevant from what is irrelevant to future commitments."

---

§15.1   Clarity and Vividness

Degnan does not misuse the term *illiterate*. It means a person who lacks the ability to communicate through the written word, and that is true of the student described. What causes such a condition in an educated person? Three things combine.

First, there are more words in English than in almost any other language on earth. That is because English inherited two storehouses of vocabulary. One came from the Anglo-Saxon and Scandinavian languages; the other from Latin and French. These alternative storehouses give English an almost unique capacity to express with precision a wide range of nuance if you are skilled enough to find the "right" word. But — by their sheer size — the alternative storehouses create abundant opportunities to select the "wrong" word — the one that blurs meaning, rather than sharpening it.

Second, many people feel compelled to go straight for the "wrong" word because the storehouses are assumed to have different statuses. The Latin/French vocabulary has traditionally been considered to have a higher status because it derived in part from the language spoken the Norman French ruling class in medieval England and in part from the Latin used in the medieval churches and universities. The Anglo-Saxon/Scandinavian vocabulary, on the other hand, is sometimes felt to be vulgar and undignified, the words of people who are neither subtle nor influential: construction workers *sweat* (from Anglo-Saxon), while people who ride to the hounds *perspire* (from Latin).

But in many languages the verbiage of the governors tends to become euphemistic and fuzzy, while the vocabulary of the governed remains crisp and vivid.[1] You might be tempted to sound like a lawyer but fail to *communicate* like one — for example by writing "ingested" (an impressive but vague word from Latin) instead of a word that would tell exactly what happened, such as "ate," "drank," or "swallowed" (all from Anglo-Saxon).

---

§15.1   1. Both tendencies are described in George Orwell's most famous essay, *Politics and the English Language*.

Because law depends on clarity, precision, and readability, judges and senior lawyers want to read straightforward English. Not only will they be frustrated and confused by pretentiously vague diction, but they also treat it as evidence of the writer's mediocrity. In one experiment, appellate judges and their law clerks were asked to appraise material written in a contorted style that might be called "legalese," while other judges and their law clerks were asked to evaluate the same material rewritten into straightforward "plain English." They considered the original legalese "substantively weaker and less persuasive than the plain English versions."[2] And the judges and law clerks assumed that the traditional legalese had been written by lawyers working in low-prestige jobs.[3]

The third cause of educated illiteracy is fear. The insecure writer who is not sure what to say may try to hide that insecurity in a fog of convoluted constructions, writing

> the above captioned appeal is maintained by the defendant as a direct result of

rather than

> the defendant appeals because

But this kind of camouflage does not actually reduce a writer's fear. The only real way to allay fear is to figure out exactly what should be said and then to say precisely that.

To understand the importance of clarity in law, recall two things. First, you must prove everything you say, because the law-trained mind considers every unsupported assertion to be untrue. Second, no matter how important the issue, your reader will be able to spare only a very limited amount of time to ponder what you write. The more time that must be spent trying to figure out what you are saying, the less time the reader will have left to think about your message and to consider agreeing with it. Where poor writing obscures the message or makes the reading troublesome, you may get rejection even if entitled to agreement. "[A] cardinal principle of good writing [is] that no one should ever have to read a sentence twice because of the way it is put together."[4]

When it comes to clarity, *you will never get the benefit of doubt*. As Donald McCloskey puts it, the reader is always right: "If the reader thinks something you wrote is unclear, then it is, by definition. Quit arguing."[5]

2. Robert W. Benson & Joan B. Kessler, *Legalese v. Plain English: An Empirical Study of Persuasion and Credibility in Appellate Brief Writing*, 20 Loyola L.A. L. Rev. 301, 301 (1987).

3. *Id.* at 301-02.

4. Wilson Follett, *Modern American Usage* 480 (1974).

5. Donald McCloskey, *The Writing of Economics* 7 (1987).

§15.2   Conciseness

> The present letter is a very long one simply because I had no time to make it shorter.
>
> — *Pascal*

First drafts are not lean. Rewriting is the program of exercise and diet that trims a passage down to something easily read and understood. And conciseness is an important issue in legal writing for three reasons. First, concise writing is by nature more clear and often more precise. Second, the typical reader of legal writing has no time to spare and either will resent inflated verbiage or will simply refuse to read it. Third, something about legal work paradoxically creates a temptation to swell a simple expression into something ponderous and pretentious.

For example, compare two versions of the same analysis:

It is important to note that, at the time when the parties entered into the agreement of purchase and sale, neither of them had knowledge of the cow's pregnant condition.

When the parties agreed to the sale, neither knew the cow was pregnant.

Because of the fact that the cow, previous to the contract, had not become pregnant, despite planned and observed exposure to bulls whose reproductive capacities had been demonstrated through past experience, the seller had made the assumption that the cow would not be able to produce offspring.

The seller had assumed that the cow was infertile because she had not become pregnant when he tried to breed her with known stud bulls.

Due to the fact that the seller had made a statement to the buyer describing the cow's opportunities to reproduce and the failures thereof, there would have been, in the buyer's thinking, no purpose to any further investigation or inspection he might have considered making.

Because the seller had told the buyer about the cow's history, the buyer did not investigate further.

For these reasons, the contract did not include a provision for an upward modification in the payments to be made by the buyer to the seller in the event that the cow should later prove to be capable of reproduction.

Thus, the contract did not provide for an increase in the purchase price if the cow should turn out to be fertile.

How did the verbose rough draft on the left become the concise, finished product on the right?

First, some sentences were rewritten so that a person or a thing did something. Although the verbose draft is weighted down with modifiers, the concise version focuses on carefully chosen nouns and verbs, and many modifiers became unnecessary because their meaning has been incorporated into nouns and verbs (and sometimes into more succinct modifiers):

the cow's pregnant condition	*became*	the cow was pregnant
despite planned and observed exposure to bulls whose reproductive capacities had been demonstrated through past experience	*became*	when he tried to breed her with known stud bulls
there would have been, in the buyer's thinking, no purpose to any further investigation or inspection he might have considered making	*became*	the buyer did not investigate further

Second, words and phrases were eliminated if they could not justify themselves:

It is important to note that	*was deleted because the "importance" is communicated by the sentence's placement and, ironically, by the rewritten version's brevity*
previous to the contract	*was deleted because it is communicated by the context*

Third, each word and phrase was weighed to see if the same thing could be said in fewer words:

at the time when	*became*	when

187

entered into the agreement of purchase and sale	*became*	agreed to the sale
neither of them	*became*	neither
had knowledge of	*became*	knew
Because of the fact that	*became*	because
had made the assumption	*became*	assumed
would not be able to produce offspring	*became*	was infertile
Due to the fact that	*became*	Because
had made a statement to	*became*	told
describing the cow's opportunities to reproduce and the failures thereof	*became*	about the cow's history
For these reasons	*became*	Thus
include a provision for	*became*	provide for
an upward modification in the payments to be made by the buyer to the seller	*became*	an increase in the purchase price
in the event that	*became*	if
the cow should later prove to be capable of reproducing	*became*	the cow should turn out to be fertile

Be careful, however, not to edit out needed meaning. In the material above, it would be folly to eliminate so much verbiage that a reader would not know that the cow was pregnant when sold; that the parties did not know of the pregnancy at the time; how each party acquired his ignorance; that the contract did not provide for an adjusted price; and why it did not do so. But not all meaning is needed: "an upward modification in the *payments* to be made by the buyer to the seller" tells us that the money was to be tendered in installments, but that meaning does not survive into the rewritten version because it has nothing to do with the issue under discussion.

§15.3   *Forcefulness*

Forcefulness is not a writer's version of table-pounding. Instead, forceful writing leads the reader through ideas by specifying their relationships with one another and by identifying the ideas that are most important or compelling.

Specifying relationships. Transitional words and phrases, such as the following, can very economically show relationships between ideas:

accordingly	in fact
additionally	(in order) to
although	in spite of
analogously	in that event
as a result	instead
because	moreover
but	nevertheless
consequently	not only . . . , but also
conversely	on the contrary
despite	on the other hand
even if	on these facts
even though	rather
finally	similarly
for example	since
for instance	specifically
for that reason	such as
furthermore	there
hence	therefore
here	thus
however	under these circumstances
in addition (to)	while
in contrast	

[handwritten note in margin: GIVES A PRECISE STATEMENT]

Some transitional words and phrases are stronger than others. Be careful to select those that accurately represent the relationship at hand and that claim neither too little nor too much.

For example, some words are better than others at showing causation. *Because* and *since* do a much better job than *as* and *so*. Both *as* and *so* can confuse a reader who sees them used much more often — and much more effectively — to join contemporaneous events ("the driver accelerated *as* the child ran into the street") or to emphasize the abundance of some fact ("the explosion was *so* loud that . . ."). In describing causation in a rough draft, you might use *as* or *so* just to get onto the page a sentence that is forming in your mind:

> The magistrate who issued the arrest warrant was able to evaluate the reasonableness of Det. Bloom's conclusion that the defendant was

hiding in his friend's home, so the arrest warrant was sufficient authority, under the rule of *Commonwealth v. Sadowski*, for the police to search that home.

But in rewriting, you should notice that the limp, little word *so* will not catch the judge's attention the way *because* would. To figure out how to rewrite the sentence, first decide whether you want to emphasize the facts (the first example below) or the conclusion you draw from them (the second below).

> Because the magistrate who issued the arrest warrant was able to evaluate the reasonableness of Det. Bloom's conclusion that the defendant was hiding in his friend's home, the arrest warrant was sufficient authority, under the rule of *Commonwealth v. Sadowski*, for the police to search that home.

> The arrest warrant was sufficient authority, under the rule of *Commonwealth v. Sadowski*, for the police to search the home of the defendant's friend because the magistrate who issued the warrant was able to evaluate the reasonableness of Det. Bloom's conclusion that the defendant was hiding there.

The word *since* is an acceptable synonym for *because*, especially in passages where one word or the other must be used several times. But "since" is the weaker of the two, and it causes confusion if the reader does not know immediately from the context whether it refers to causation or to time:

> Because the defendant spent the marital assets of extravagances, the plaintiff has no money for attorney's fees.

If this had begun with "since," you would not have known until near the end of the sentence whether the dependent clause introduced causation or marked a point in time ("Since the defendant spent . . .").

Some words and sentence structures show contrast better than others do. Consider this:

> The Court of Appeal has held that the objection is waived if not made at trial, but it has also held that, even without an objection, a conviction should be reversed where a prosecutor's conduct was as inflammatory as it was here.

The word *but*, buried in the middle of a long sentence, only weakly alerts the judge that one idea (the rule about waiver) is being knocked down by another (the exception for inflammatory prosecutorial conduct). Everybody writes this kind of thing in rough drafts, but it should be recognized and cured during rewriting:

> Although the Court of Appeal has held that the objection is waived if not made at trial, it has also held that, even without an objection, a

conviction should be reversed where a prosecutor's conduct was as inflammatory as it was here.

Although tells the reader from the very beginning of the sentence that the first clause (however damning) will be shown, before the sentence is over, not to matter. Because of its placement, and because it is a larger and less commonly used word, *although* will usually show contrast more clearly than *but*. If handled carefully, however, *but* can still do the job well:

> The Court of Appeal has held that the objection is waived if not made at trial. But it has also held that, even without an objection, a conviction should be reversed where a prosecutor's conduct was as inflammatory as it was here.

This solves the problem in a different way. The sentence has been broken in two, and the new second sentence begins with *But*. (Despite common belief, no rule of grammar forbids starting a sentence with a conjunction.)

Where several ideas are discussed collectively, the reader is forcefully led if that is made clear, perhaps through some sort of textual list. The list need not be diagrammed. In fact, it is usually more economical to incorporate a list into the text with a transition sentence ("There are four reasons why . . ."), followed by sentences or paragraphs coordinated to the transition sentence ("First . . . " or "The first reason . . .").

Logical relationships can also be shown through demonstrative sentence structure:

> The amended court rule provides for attorney sanctions, *which eliminates the need to rely on any inherent powers the court might or might not have to punish attorneys whose procedural misconduct multiplies the court's work.*

Here, the italicized[1] dependent clause, when joined to the main clause of the sentence, aggressively ties together the ideas that sanctions are now provided for by court rule and that the court therefore need not face the difficult issue of whether it has an inherent power to punish (even without a court rule).

Identifying the ideas that are most important or compelling. There are several ways of accomplishing that. One is simply to say it:

> This attorney's most reprehensible act was to make a motion for a preliminary injunction where his clients were not in any way threatened with harm.

---

§15.3   1. Italics appear in these examples only to identify parts of the sentences for discussion, not to suggest that you italicize (or underline) for emphasis. Although italics or underlining for emphasis can be effective if done sparingly and carefully, it is too easily overdone and seldom has the desired effect on a reader.

Other methods are more subtle. An emphasized idea can be placed at the beginning of a sentence, paragraph, or passage, where it will be most quickly noticed. Or a series of sentences can be arranged so that the shortest and simplest of them conveys the emphasized idea:

> This attorney served and filed a pleading alleging extremely unlikely facts without making any factual investigation and under circumstances indicating that his clients' only motive for litigation was harassment. He made numerous frivolous motions, including one for a preliminary injunction where his clients were in no way threatened with harm. He has now brought an appeal without any basis in statute or precedent, and he has submitted a record and brief not in compliance with the court's rules. *He has thoroughly disregarded the professional obligations of an attorney.*

Notice the differences in tone between the last example and the two that preceded it. The paragraph quoted immediately above might be appropriate for a brief in which an adversary urges that the attorney be punished or that a punishment meted out below be sustained; it might also be appropriate to an opinion in which a court justifies a punishment. The tone is one intended to convince. Although the two preceding examples address the same subject, they are expressed in a more objective tone in which analysis is merely reported (although those two examples might also appear in a persuasive or justifying document to provide a foundation for other, more rhetorical statements).

Although forcefulness is desirable in all legal writing — simply to help the reader understand what is important and how ideas are related — a rhetorical tone is reserved for documents intended to persuade or justify and is inappropriate where you are asked — in predictive writing — merely to report how the law will resolve a given set of facts.

§15.4 Punctuation and Other Rules of Grammar

In re HAWKINS
502 N.W.2d 770 (Minn. 1978)

[The Lawyers Professional Responsibility Board petitioned the court for an order disciplining the respondent lawyer for unethical conduct.]

The referee . . . found that respondent's failure to comply with [certain court rules] and his repeated filing of documents rendered unintelligible by numerous spelling, grammatical, and typographical errors were sufficiently serious that they amounted to incompetent representation. . . .

It is apparent to us that [respondent's] repeated disregard of [court rules], coupled with the incomprehensibility of his correspondence and documentation, constitutes a violation of Rule 1.1 of the Minnesota Rules of Professional Conduct.[1] . . .

. . . Public confidence in the legal system is shaken when lawyers disregard the rules of court and when a lawyer's correspondence and legal documents are so filled with spelling, grammatical, and typographical errors that they are virtually incomprehensible. . . .

Respondent . . . is hereby publicly reprimanded for unprofessional conduct [and ordered, among other things, to participate in a program of writing instruction].

In another case, a trucking company and the Interstate Commerce Commission battled for 19 years over the confusion caused by the absence of a single comma in an administrative order.[1] And in yet another case, the Maine Supreme Court had to write a two-thousand word decision to untangle the mess created by two commas that somehow ended up in the wrong place in a statute.[2]

Correct punctuation makes writing clear and easier to understand. It is not mere decoration. A lawyer cannot excuse a poorly punctuated sentence by arguing that the reader would be able to understand it if only he or she would think about it. The antagonistic reader can make much trouble out of ambiguity caused by bad punctuation. And even where a reader is neutral or friendly, the lawyer's job is to make meaning so plain that the reader need not read the sentence twice.

Not only are punctuation and other grammar skills essential to conveying meaning clearly and precisely, but they have an important effect on your credibility and reputation. Readers — including readers of law school examinations — will question your analytical abilities and general competence if you do not observe the accepted rules of English grammar. "Where lumps and infelicities occur," the novelist John Gardner wrote, "the sensitive reader shrinks away a little, as we do when an interesting conversationalist picks his nose."[3]

Thus, if you have not already mastered the rules of punctuation and of grammar generally, you will have to do so in this course. Now and while writing and rewriting, consult Appendix B, which summarizes the more important rules of punctuation. Make sure that you understand *every* rule in

---

§15.4   1. [*Court's footnote.*] Rule 1.1 . . . provides as follows: "A lawyer shall provide competent representation to a client. Competent representation requires the legal knowledge, skill, thoroughness and preparation reasonably necessary to the representation."

1. *T. I. McCormack Trucking Co. v. United States,* 298 F. Supp. 39 (D.N.J. 1969).

2. *Sawyer v. State,* 382 A.2d 1039 (Me. 1978).

3. John Gardner, *The Art of Fiction: Notes on Craft for Young Writers* 99 (1984).

Appendix B: your law school writing will be scrutinized for solid grammar in a way that you might not have experienced before.

§15.5 How to Test Your Writing for Effective Style

> In any language, it is a struggle to make a sentence say exactly what you mean.
>
> — *Arthur Koestler*

In first drafts — even by the best writers — style is usually pretty awful. Effective style is really achieved through rewriting, as you spot style problems and fix them. During rewriting, ask yourself the following questions.[1]

| **15-A** | **Have you used nouns and verbs that let the reader see the action?** Consider two examples: |

wrong: In *Smith*, there was no withdrawal of the guilty plea, based on the court's determination of a lack of evidence of coercion.

right: In *Smith*, the court denied the defendant's motion to withdraw her guilty plea because she submitted no evidence that the plea had been coerced.

In the "wrong" example, you can hardly tell who has done what to whom because the pontifical tone obscures the action, and because the nouns and verbs are vague and lazy. They do not stand out, take charge, and create action. The "right" example is more vivid and easier to understand. You immediately know what is going on and do not have to read the same words twice.

In law, people do things to other people and to ideas and objects. The only way to describe that is with nouns and verbs that are straightforward and often fairly plain and simple. As with so many other legal writing problems, rewriting is the key to solving this one. Your early drafts might have sentences like the "wrong" example above, but your final drafts should more closely resemble the "right" one. Here is how to do it:

Nouns: As you rewrite, figure out who is doing things and make those people and organizations the subject of sentences and clauses. Grammatically, only the subject gets to act. In the examples above, the main event was what the court did, which is why the court had to become the subject of the sentence. But the defendant did something, too, (or, more accurately,

---

§15.5   1. When marking up your work, your teacher might refer to these questions by using the number-letter codes that appear next to each question here.

failed to do something), and she thus became the subject of a clause inside the sentence.

Verbs: As you rewrite, do two things: *(1)* Wherever possible, replace the verb *to be* with a verb of action. The principal forms of the verb *to be* are "is," "are," "am," "was," "were," and "will be." They do a good job of describing condition or status ("the defendant is guilty"). But they are not verbs of action. In fact, they obscure action. Consider ways of eliminating variations on *there is* (such as *there were* and *it is*). Sometimes these constructions are helpful or even unavoidable ("there are four reasons why the plaintiff will not be able to recover. . . ."). At other times, however, they hide your message in a fog of pretentious verbiage. *(2)* Replace *nominalizations* with real verbs. A nominalization is a phrase that is built around a noun but is asked to do a verb's work. "The search *was a violation of* the defendant's rights" should become "the search *violated* the defendant's rights." The nominalized phrase *was a violation of* is weaker and wordier than the blunt and vivid verb *violated*. The same problem occurs when you ask an adjective to do a verb's job ("was violative of"). Some other examples:

cross out	*and replace it with*
is able to	can
enter into an agreement	agree
make the argument that	argue that
make the assumption that	assume that
is aware of	knows
is binding on	binds
give consideration to	consider
make an objection	object
make payment to	pay
make provision	provide

Have you used verbs that communicate the precise relationship between subjects and objects?   For example:

15-B

[handwritten: better]
[handwritten: ct held that defendant did not commit common law larceny]

> **wrong:**   The court *dealt with* common law larceny.

What did the court do to larceny? Define it? Define only one of the elements? Clarify the difference between larceny and false pretenses? Decide that there is no longer an offense by that name because the legislature has replaced it with the statutory crime of theft? The sentence would be much better with a verb that tells the reader precisely what happened.

> **wrong:**   The defendant *indicated* that he was interested in buying hashish.

How did he do that? By nodding affirmatively when asked if that was his desire? By asking "Is hashish sold in this neighborhood?"? By stating "I want to buy some hash"? (Depending on the surrounding facts and on local law, a court might treat these three possibilities very differently.)

How? Very ambiguous

> **wrong:**   The Freedom of Information Act *applies* to this
>   case.

Does the Act require that the document at issue be published in the *Federal Register*? Does it require that the document be given to anyone who asks for a copy? Does it require that the document be available for photocopying, but not at government expense? Or does it give the government permission to refuse to do any of these things? The quoted sentence would be much more helpful if *applies* were replaced with a verb or a verbal phrase that communicates exactly what the Act does.

> **wrong:**   Section 452(a) *involves* the Rule Against Perpetui-
>   ties.

Here, *involves* communicates only that § 452(a) has some connection with the Rule Against Perpetuities. Has § 452(a) codified the Rule? Modified it? Abolished it?

The four verbs illustrated here — "deal with," "indicate," "apply," and "involve" — rarely communicate a precise relationship between a subject and an object.

15-C **Have you brought the reader to the verb quickly?** Consider this:

> The defendant's solicitation of contributions through an organization with a misleading name, immediate deposit of the funds in a bank account in the Bahamas, and eventual use of the money to buy a vacation home in his own name constitutes fraud.

The verb is what ties an English sentence together. In fact, a sentence is incomprehensible until the reader has identified both a subject *and* a verb. And the most easily understood sentences in English bring the reader to the verb as quickly as possible. The example above cannot be understood in a single reading because it is "front-loaded." The verb and object ("constitutes fraud") are not reached until after the reader has plowed through a subject that is 39 words long.

Sentences like that are caused by automatically making whatever you want to talk about the subject of the sentence. "What shall I talk about next?" you ask yourself and then write down the answer. That becomes the subject of a sentence, no matter how unreadable the result. In first drafts, you cannot avoid doing this, but in later drafts you should be able to recognize the problem and correct it.

There are two easy ways to fix a front-loaded sentence. The first is to find a way to make the subject simple, thus bringing the reader to the verb quickly:

> The defendant committed fraud by soliciting contributions through an organization with a misleading name, immediately depositing them

in a Bahamian bank account, and eventually using the money to buy a vacation home in his own name.

The other cure, sometimes a little less effective, is to break the original sentence in two:

> The defendant solicited contributions through an organization with a misleading name, immediately deposited them in a Bahamian bank account, and eventually used the money to buy a vacation home in his own name. This was fraud.

You will lose control of your sentences if you just let them happen. Each sentence must be *built* if it is to communicate well.

Have you put the verb near the subject and the object near the verb? A sentence is hard to understand if you insert a clause or phrase between a subject and a verb or between a verb and an object:

⬛ **15-D**

> Federenko, since her attorney neither requested an instruction on self-defense nor objected to the instruction that was actually given, cannot complain on appeal that the jury was improperly instructed.

> Myers was awarded, after four years of litigation involving two trials and an appeal, damages that equalled only half his losses.

The solution is to move the clause or phrase to the end or to the beginning of the sentence, leaving the subject and verb (or the verb and object) relatively close together:

dependent clause AFTER subject and verb	Federenko cannot complain on appeal that the jury was improperly instructed, since her attorney neither requested an instruction on self-defense nor objected to the instruction that was actually given.
dependent clause BEFORE subject and verb	Because her attorney neither requested an instruction on self-defense nor objected to the instruction that was actually given, Federenko cannot complain on appeal that the jury was improperly instructed.
phrase BEFORE subject and verb	After four years of litigation involving two trials and an appeal, Myers was awarded damages that equalled only half his losses.
phrase AFTER subject and verb	Myers was awarded damages that equalled only half his losses, after four years of litigation involving two trials and an appeal.

The clause or phrase should begin the sentence only if you want to emphasize it. Federenko's dependent clause belongs at the end of the sentence because it deserves less emphasis than the subject and verb. Where should the phrase in Myers' sentence go?

15-E **Have you used transitional words and phrases to show how ideas are related?** Beginners often underestimate the reader's need to be told explicitly how ideas fit together or contrast with one another. You can do this economically with transitional words and phrases. See those listed in §15.3.

15-F **Have you streamlined unnecessarily wordy phrases?** Good rewriting pares a convoluted phrase down to something straightforward:

cross out	*and replace it with*
because of the fact that	because
during such time as	during
for the purpose of	to
for the reason that	because
in the situation where	where
in the case of	in
in the event that	if
make a motion	move
subsequent to	after
take into consideration	consider
until such time as	until
with regard to	regarding
with the exception of	except

15-G **Have you deleted throat-clearing phrases (also known as "long windups")?** Phrases like the following waste words, divert the reader from your real message, and introduce a shade of doubt and an impression of insecurity:

It is significant that . . .

The defendant submits that . . .

It is important to note that . . .

The next issue is . . .

Of the two examples below, why would the plaintiff's attorney feel more comfortable writing the first than the second?

The plaintiff submits that the judgment should be reversed because . . .

The judgment should be reversed because . . .

The superfluous words in the first example shift emphasis from the idea propounded and to the obvious but irrelevant fact that the writer is the one doing the propounding. (But it is *not* ineffectual to begin an attack on an adversary's argument by beginning with phrasing like "Although the defendant has argued. . . .")

Have you broken up or streamlined unnecessarily long sentences? They obscure meaning. If a sentence is too long to be | **15-H** |
understood easily on the first reading, express the sentence's ideas in fewer words, or split the sentence into two (or more) shorter sentences, or do both. If you decide to reduce the sentence's verbiage, see questions 15-A, 15-F, and 15-G and review §15.2. If you decide to break up the sentence, be sure to avoid the "sing-songy" style described in question 15-I.

Have you rewritten sentences so that none are "sing-songy"? | **15-I** |
For example:

> The defendant solicited contributions through an organization with a misleading name. He immediately deposited the funds in a bank account in the Bahamas. Eventually, he used them to buy a vacation home in his own name. This was fraud.

These are four simple sentences, three of them beginning with a subject. Not only does the passage sound naive, it is also likely to bore the reader. The cause is a tendency to write down one thing at a time, without describing the relationships between or among the things mentioned. At its most extreme, the result is a series of simple sentences, all beginning with the subject.

There are two kinds of cure. One is to focus on the relationships, especially causal ones, using some of the transitional words and phrases listed in §15.3:

> Not only did the defendant solicit contributions through an organization with a misleading name, but he immediately deposited the funds in a bank account in the Bahamas. Moreover, he used them to buy a vacation home in his own name. Therefore, he has committed fraud.

The other cure is to vary three things periodically: the types of sentences (some simple, some compound, some complex); the lengths of sentences (some long, some short, some medium); and the way sentences begin (some with the subject, some with a prefatory word or phrase, some with a dependent clause). Closely related material can be combined into fewer sentences, where the sentence structure itself can demonstrate relationships between ideas:

> Having solicited contributions through an organization with a misleading name and deposited them in a Bahamian bank account, the defendant used the funds to buy a vacation home in his own name. This was fraud.

This example uses a subordinate sentence element ("Having solicited . . . bank account") to achieve the desired effect.

To avoid the sing-songy effect, you must understand and be able to use the full range of sentence structures available in English.

IMPORTANT →

15-J **Have you avoided the passive voice unless you have a good reason for using it?**   In the active voice, the subject of the sentence acts ("Maguire sued Schultz"), but in the passive voice the subject of the sentence is acted upon ("Schultz was sued by Maguire"). More often than not, the passive is best avoided because of its three disadvantages: it is often more verbose; it tends to vagueness; and it is usually weaker and more boring to read.

But the passive may be the more effective voice where the identity of the actor is unknown, unimportant, or better left unemphasized. For example, compare the following:

> Ms. Blitzstein's aid-to-dependent-family benefits have been wrongfully terminated fourteen times in the last six years.

> The Department of Public Welfare has wrongfully terminated Ms. Blitzstein's aid-to-dependent-family benefits fourteen times in the last six years.

Here the passive is actually more concise. Depending on the context, the passive might not be vague because the reader might be likely to know that the Department is the only agency capable of terminating aid-to-dependent-family benefits, or at least that the Department is being accused of doing so in this instance. And, again depending on the context, the passive sentence may be the stronger and more interesting of the two. If the reader is a judge who is being asked to order the Department to stop this nonsense, the passive will be the stronger sentence because it emphasizes the more appealing idea. (Generally, a judge is more likely to sympathize with a victim of bureaucratic snafus than to condemn a government agency for viciousness or incompetence.)

In some circumstances, the passive voice is also a good way of avoiding sexist pronouns. See question 15-S.

15-K **Have you avoided placing modifiers so that the reader will wonder what they modify?**   In speech, modifiers tend to wander all over sentences, regardless of what they are intended to modify. But in formal writing, more precision is required. These sentences all mean different things:

> The police are authorized to arrest *only* the person named in the warrant.
>   [They are not authorized to arrest anyone else.]

> The police are authorized *only* to arrest the person named in the warrant.
>   [They are not authorized to torture or deport him.]

200

> The police are *only* authorized to arrest the person named in the warrant.
>
> [They have the right to arrest him, but they do not have to. The warrant gives them some discretion.]
>
> *Only* the police are authorized to arrest the person named in the warrant.
>
> [Civilians are not so authorized.]

Make sure that the modifier's placement communicates what you really want to say, and do not assume that a busy reader will be willing or even able to figure out the meaning from the context.

Have you used parallel constructions when expressing a list? **15-L** Even implied lists should be expressed in some sort of consistent structure. Each item or idea must be phrased in the same grammatical format. Consider the following:

> This attorney should be disbarred because of his neglect of a matter entrusted to him, for pleading guilty to the felony of suborning perjury, and because he disclosed a client's confidences without the client's consent.

Here, the first listed item is expressed as a noun possessed by a pronoun ("his neglect"); the second as an unpossessed gerund ("for pleading"); and the third as a dependent clause, complete with subject, verb, and object ("because he disclosed confidences"). Although the first and third items are preceded by the word "because," the second is not. Isolated from the others, each form alone would be grammatical. But the inconsistencies among them make the whole sentence sound inarticulate. That would not have been true if each item in the list were expressed in the same format:

> This attorney should be disbarred because he neglected a matter entrusted to him, pleaded guilty to the felony of suborning perjury, and disclosed a client's confidences without the client's consent.

Be careful also about the introduction to the list: it must be phrased so that it is appropriate to each item listed.

Have you used terms of art where appropriate? Where an idea **15-M** peculiar to the law is customarily expressed through a term of art, that term should be used because it conveys the idea as precisely as the law can manage and often makes long and convoluted explanations unnecessary. Do not write "the plaintiff asked the court to tell the defendants to stop building the highway." It is much more precise to write "the plaintiff moved for an order preliminarily enjoining. . . ."

But do not confuse terms of art with legal argot. A term of art is the law's symbol for an idea that usually cannot be expressed with precision in any other way. Legal argot, on the other hand, has no special meaning peculiar to the law. Instead, it is pretentious verbiage used for everyday concepts by a writer who wants to sound like a lawyer but instead creates an impression of mediocrity. (See question 15-O.)

15-N **Have you edited out inappropriately used terms of art?** Terms of art ought to be used only to convey the precise meaning the law holds for them. Where you use a term of art (perhaps because it sounds lawyer-like) but do not really intend to communicate the idea the term of art stands for, the reader will assume that you do not know what you are talking about.

15-O **Have you edited out imitations of lawyer noises?** Said noises found in and about a lawyer's writing have heretofore caused, resulted in, and led to grievous injury with respect to said lawyer's readers, clients, and/or repute, to wit: by compelling the aforesaid readers to suffer confusion and/or consternation at the expense of the aforementioned clients and consequently rendering said repute to become null, void, and nugatory.

Good legal writing and good writing in other fields have the same characteristics of clarity and smoothness in reading. Thinking like a lawyer is not the same as imitating lawyer noises. Expressions like "to wit," "hereinbefore," and "aforesaid" are argot — not terms of art (see question 15-M) — and they do not convey anything that ordinary English cannot communicate more clearly and less awkwardly. The most influential memos and the most persuasive briefs are written in the real English language.

15-P **Have you edited out contractions and other conversational language?** They may be appropriate to a note to a friend, but they have no place in lawyerly documents.

15-Q **Have you edited out inappropriate abbreviations?** In formal documents, a lawyer does not write "the N.C. Supreme Court has held. . . ." Spell words out unless the abbreviation is generally used at least as often as the full name (for example, "NAACP" and "FCC"). Otherwise, abbreviate only in citations.

15-R **Have you avoided rhetorical questions?** They are ineffective. Your job is to lead — not jab — the reader.

15-S **Have you avoided sexist wording?** In the way all languages evolve, English is now shedding many centuries of sexist phrasing. Perhaps a decade or two from now, English might settle into phrasings that are both gender-neutral and fluid. In the meantime, writers must struggle a bit.

The thorniest problem is English's use of the pronouns *he, his,* and *him* to refer generally to people of either gender. The problem would not exist if English had a third-person pronoun that meant "any person," regardless of gender. But English lacks that. The ersatz pronoun *s/he* has not gained acceptance, and it offends most readers. The ritual incantations *he or she, his or her,* and *him or her* are wordy and, if repeated often, tedious.

The best solution is to eliminate the need for a pronoun. If that cannot be done, recast both the pronoun *and* its noun in the plural. Often, that also makes the writing more concise:

	To calendar a motion, an attorney must file *his* moving papers with the clerk.
pronoun replaced with "the"	To calendar a motion, an attorney must file *the* moving papers with the clerk.
actor made plural	To calendar motions, attorneys must file *their* moving papers with the clerk.
actor eliminated from sentence	A motion is calendared by filing the motion papers with the clerk.

With these sentences, the most concise solution is to eliminate the actor entirely and cast the sentence in the passive voice. But that may not be true with other examples. And even here, the most concise solution might not be the best one. If the sentence is meant to warn the kind of lawyers who forget to file their moving papers, that point is lost if the attorneys themselves are not even mentioned.

Make sure that the remedy you choose makes sense in the context. For example, substituting "the" for "his" works here only because the moving attorney would be the only one to calendar the motion. And if you recast in the plural, recast the whole construction that way. The following is wrong because the pronoun is plural but the noun to which it refers is singular:

> To calendar a motion, an attorney must file their moving papers with the clerk.

As a last resort, you can fall back on "he or she."

Gender-biased nouns are usually easier to avoid. The "reasonable man" in negligence law can as easily be the "reasonable person"; a "juryman" is better as a "juror" anyway; and, depending on the context, "manpower" might be replaced with "effort," "personnel," "workers," or something else. Some nouns, such as "businessman," are harder, however. Unless gender truly matters ("the corporation specializes in the manufacture of business-women's clothing"), it is sexist to refer to a woman in business as a "businesswoman." (She is a person in business. What has her gender got to do with it?) Unless the awkward term "businessperson" gains acceptance, the only solution is to rephrase the sentence so that you do not need a word like "businessman" or "businesswoman."

Exercise I.   Kalmar's Driveway (Clarity and Conciseness)

Rewrite the following sentences around nouns and verbs that describe action. Make sure that each sentence is of comprehensible length. Eliminate throat-clearing phrases, and replace nominalizations, unnecessary passives, and unnecessarily wordy constructions. (See §§15.1, 15.2, and 15.5.) You will find this easier if you read the whole exercise before starting to rewrite.

1. It is evident that Kalmar is likely to be convicted of accepting a bribe because all the elements of bribery are susceptible of proof beyond a reasonable doubt.

2. A person is guilty of accepting a bribe if that person is an employee of the government and "requests or receives from any other person anything of value, knowing it to be a reward or inducement for an official act," Crim. Code § 702, and a conviction may occur only if evidence is presented by the prosecution that persuades the finder of fact beyond a reasonable doubt that the defendant is guilty.

3. The initial element that can be established is that Kalmar is an employee of the government.

4. The facts indicate that in his capacity as Roads Commissioner, Kalmar had occasion from time to time to purchase, on behalf of the government, quantities of cement, asphalt, and other road construction materials from Phelps, who caused these materials to be delivered to road-repair sites on trucks owned by Phelps.

5. Kalmar had need for a new driveway at his own home, and he made a request to Phelps for a recommendation of a contractor who would do a good job at a reasonable price.

6. Phelps told Kalmar that she would look into the matter, but, without Kalmar's knowledge, a new driveway was built at his home by her employees the next day.

7. The circumstances fit into a pattern showing that Kalmar had knowledge that he was being offered a reward or inducement by Phelps for official acts directly relating to his job, and although the statute does not specify that a defendant must know at the time the thing of value is actually delivered or physically taken that it is a reward for official acts, Kalmar both accepted and continued to receive the bribe when, according to the facts, he did not undertake any effort to compensate Phelps for the cost of the driveway.

8. Because the cost involved is such that it could not have been accidentally overlooked by Kalmar, there can be no innocent explanation for the fact that he had an opportunity every day to see that he had a new driveway

for which nothing had been paid, and there is therefore no reasonable doubt about his guilt.

Exercise II. Smolensky at the Plate (Clarity and Forcefulness)

Rewrite the following to bring the reader to the verb quickly and use transitional words and phrases to show how ideas are related. Avoid "sing-songy" sentences and make sure that subjects, verbs, objects, and modifiers are appropriately placed. (See §§15.1, 15.3, and §15.5.) You will find this easier if you read the whole exercise before starting to rewrite.

1. Vargas, when Smolensky, who was batting, turned around and attacked him with a baseball bat, was playing catcher.

2. In *Crawford v. Bender*, the Court of Appeals held that a person who engages in a sport, has an opportunity to know beforehand of the types of bodily contact customary in that sport, and suffers an injury as a result of such a contact, cannot recover damages.

3. Some physical contact is inevitable in athletics. Assault is not inevitable and is prohibited by the rules of virtually every team sport.

4. Vargas participated in the game of baseball. He consented to those bodily contacts that are customary in baseball or permitted by the rules of the game. Baseball players are rarely beaten with baseball bats. In the past, Vargas has only been hit with a bat by accident. League Rule 19 specifically prohibits "striking another player."

5. To hold that Vargas will not be able to recover when Smolensky will not be able to offer any evidence that would show that Vargas intended to consent to be attacked with a bat would be inconsistent with the rule of *Crawford*.

16 Citations and Quotations

§16.1 A Tour of the Bluebook

Legal writing has unique citation rules because the typical reader of legal writing needs very specific information about each authority and needs it expressed precisely and succinctly in "citation language" that can be quickly skimmed and understood. A properly constructed legal citation conveys a large amount of information in a very small space. Bad citation form, on the other hand, is instantly noticed and causes a reader to suspect that the writer is sloppy or ignorant — and therefore unreliable. Letter-perfect citation form not only provides necessary information unambiguously, but it also helps to create an impression of meticulousness and dependability.

From a citation, a reader expects to learn (1) *where* the authority can be found, (2) the authority's *weight* (whether it is mandatory and, if not, some of the factors on which its persuasiveness can be judged, such as its date and the name of the court that decided it); and (3) *your purpose* in using the authority. To show the reader where authority can be found, citations include, in formulated abbreviations, the names of publications, as well as volume numbers and page, section, or paragraph numbers. To show the weight of authority, citations identify courts and jurisdictions and include dates, subsequent histories, and explanatory parentheticals. And if the surrounding text does not make your purpose clear, the citation can include a signal defining the relationship between the text and the cited authority (although, as you will see, signals are disfavored in memoranda and briefs). All of these things are accomplished through *citation grammar:* words, abbreviations, and numbers that, when expressed in proper order, have precise meaning for the reader.

The Bluebook is a codification of the most commonly followed rules of legal citation.[1] The Bluebook is divided into the following parts:[2]

The *Introduction* explains and illustrates the structure of citations. (When you are just getting started with citations, the diagrams here can be quite helpful.)

Practitioners' Notes (printed on blue paper) show you how to adapt Bluebook rules for practical writing in briefs and memoranda. (Throughout the Bluebook are cross-references to the Practitioners' Notes. For example, if you see "P.4" in the margin of a Bluebook page, the rule you are looking at is modified by practitioners' note 4.)

General Rules of Citation and Style (rules 1 through 9) govern matters common to all citations, regardless of the type of authority involved. Examples include citation structure, signals, short-form citations, quotations, and the like.

Citations to particular types of authority are explained under *Cases* (rule 10); *Constitutions, Statutes, and Legislative, Administrative, and Executive Materials* (rules 11- 14); *Books, Periodical Materials, and Other Secondary Sources* (rules 15-17); *Services* (rule 18); *Foreign Materials* (rule 19); and *International Materials* (rule 20). In the first year of law school, you will refer often to rules 10 and 12 and sometimes to rules 15 and 16.

The *Tables* (printed on blue paper) give you special citation rules for each jurisdiction (tables 1-4) and the standard abbreviations used in legal writing (tables 5-17). From table 1, you can learn the citation form for each state's statutory code, the names and abbreviations of the reporters to which a particular court's decisions must be cited, and even some details about the history of a state's court system. (Check Kentucky, for example.) Tables 6 through 17 show you how to abbreviate things like the names of cases, courts, and law reviews.

On the *inside back cover* of the Bluebook are quick reference examples drawn from the Practitioners' Notes. These can be helpful when you are writing your own citations. (On the inside *front* cover are quick reference examples for law review footnotes, but you will not need them during the first year of law school.)

Two kinds of tasks confront you in using the Bluebook: finding the applicable citation rule (which can be like statutory research) and discovering its meaning (which can be like statutory interpretation). The research is not as hard as it looks. If you use the descriptive word method (in the Bluebook index) and the topic method (in the table of contents) — just as in researching any other kind of code — you can find the rules that govern the citation you are trying to put together. Until you have a good "feel" for the Bluebook, try the index before the table of contents (just as you would with an unfamiliar statutory codification).

Be careful about the following:

First, you will read many citations that would violate Bluebook rules. You can see from cases excerpted into your casebooks that some states follow

§16.1   1. You will understand this chapter more easily if you read each Bluebook rule in the Bluebook (15th edition) as it is mentioned here.
2. Look at the Bluebook's table of contents to follow the organization explained here.

citation rules that differ from those in the Bluebook. And several publishers of reporters, digests, and annotation and looseleaf services have developed their own citation styles, which differ from Bluebook rules. In addition, some important Bluebook rules were changed in 1991, which means that material published earlier might have used citation formats that are now in disfavor. But because the Bluebook's rules coincide with state and federal rules much more often than not, and because it is the most complete citation code, it is used nationally by law reviews and in legal writing courses. And as long as you are required to follow Bluebook rules — which will last throughout law school and probably afterward — you assume a risk whenever you copy a citation out of a library book without asking yourself whether you have first converted it into Bluebook form. The experienced reader will quickly spot a nonconforming citation and can often tell which publication led the writer astray.

The second problem may arise if you later practice in a state where courts require a citation format different from Bluebook rules. When — in a clinical program or after graduation — you first begin preparing documents to be filed in a real court, you would be wise to discover the extent, if any, to which local requirements differ from Bluebook form.

The third problem concerns typefaces. The Bluebook was designed primarily to govern law review footnotes, and most examples in the Bluebook are therefore printed in typefaces appropriate to footnotes. In brief and memo writing, however, different typeface conventions prevail. In addition, some law review footnote practices, such as large and small capitals, cannot be produced with a standard typewriter or computer printer. Practitioners' Note 1 explains how to adapt Bluebook rules and examples to citations in the briefs and memoranda you will write.

The rest of this chapter explains some rules that are not entirely clear in the Bluebook. As mere commentary, these explanations are, of course, only secondary authority, the Bluebook itself being the primary authority.

§16.2   Citation to Specific Types of Authority

You will cite most often to cases (rule 10) and statutes (rule 12), and those citations can be a bit more complicated than others.

§16.2.1   Citation to Cases

Aside from a signal (rules 1.2 through 1.4) or any explanatory parenthetical (rules 1.5 and 10.6), a case citation has six components, which must appear in the following order:

1. the *case name* (rule 10.2);
2. the *official reporter,* if required (practitioners' note 3 and rule 10.3);

3. an *unofficial reporter,* if required (practitioners' note 3, rule 10.3, and table 1);
4. the *court,* if its identity is not "conveyed unambiguously" by the name of the official reporter (rule 10.4);
5. the *date* of the decision (rule 10.5); and
6. the *subsequent history,* if any (rule 10.7).

For example, this citation might appear in a brief or memorandum submitted to a New York court:

> *People v. Onofre,* 51 N.Y.2d 476, 415 N.E.2d 936, 434 N.Y.S.2d 947 (1980), *cert. denied,* 451 U.S. 987 (1981).

Here are the citation's component parts:

1. **case name**   *People v. Onofre*

2. **official reporter**   51 N.Y.2d 476

3. **unofficial (regional) reporter**   415 N.E.2d 936

3. **unofficial (state) reporter**[3]   434 N.Y.S.2d 947

4. **court**   [not specified because N.Y.2d reports only cases from the New York Court of Appeals]

5. **date**   (1980)

6. **subsequent history**   *cert. denied,* 451 U.S. 987 (1981) [in 1981, the United States Supreme Court denied a petition for a writ of certiorari]

"N.Y.2d" is the second series of New York Reports. "N.E.2d" is the second series of North Eastern Reporter. And "N.Y.S.2d" is the second series of New York Supplement. The number before the abbreviation is the volume. The number after is the page on which the opinion begins.

If the same case were cited in any document other than a brief or memorandum submitted to a New York court — see rule 10.3.1(b) and practi-

---

3. California and New York are the only states with unofficial state reporters. See practitioners' note 3 and Bluebook table 1.

tioners' note 3 — only the regional reporter (N.E.2d) would be referred to, and the court and jurisdiction would be identified in the parenthetical (see rule 10.4):

> *People v. Onofre,* 415 N.E.2d 936 (N.Y. 1980), *cert. denied,* 451 U.S. 987 (1981).

Here, an official reporter (N.Y.2d) and an unofficial state reporter (N.Y.S.2d) have been removed. And the notation "N.Y." has been added in the parenthetical because wherever an official reporter is omitted — here under rule 10.3.1(b) — you must identify the court in the parenthetical pursuant to rule 10.4(b). (The cite must tell the reader which court decided the case.)

There are other reasons why a cite might not have all six components. For instance, there is no subsequent history if, after the decision cited to, no further appeal was taken (see rule 10.7). As in the first example above, the court need not be specified if the official reporter is included and if it publishes the decisions of only one court (see rule 10.4). In federal cases, citations to unofficial reporters do not appear unless the official citation is not yet available because the official reporter has not yet published the opinion (see rule 10.3.1). A citation to a state's official reporter might not appear for that reason or where the state has stopped publishing its official reporter (see table 1 to find out).

Three aspects of rule 10.4 sometimes prove troublesome for beginners. First, because the reader needs to know exactly which court rendered the decision, it is not enough merely to name the *type* of court: the *specific* court itself must be identified. Thus, "U.S. Ct. App." does not tell the reader which of the thirteen circuits was responsible for the decision. One of the approved abbreviations (such as "8th Cir.") must be used instead. Similarly, "U.S. Dist. Ct." is not sufficient for the United States District Court for the Eastern District of Pennsylvania; "E.D. Pa." tells the reader exactly which court made the decision.

Second, although rules 10.4 and 10.5 do not explicitly allow it, you can omit the court or the date from the citation where the same information is included in the preceding text:

> As long ago as 1897, the New York Court of Appeals held that . . . *People v. Conroy,* 151 N.Y. 543, 45 N.E. 946.

If a decision's weight depends in some *significant* way on the identity of the court or the date, you can thus stress either or both of those things in the text. For example, if the rule you state is a surprising one and likely to excite aggressive skepticism, you might want to relax the reader a bit by making clear at the outset that you are relying on top-quality authority. Or you might want to do it where it is important for the reader to understand that you are relying on a long and well-established line of cases, or — at the opposite extreme — that, although the rule you state is an antique, it was enforced just last year by an appellate court in your jurisdiction.

Third, although rule 10.4(b) prohibits identification of the subdivision of an intermediate state court except where that is "of particular relevance," the geographic subdivision is frequently "of particular relevance" in states where the intermediate appellate court is segmented geographically — such as New York and California — because the subdivision can affect the authoritative value of the decision. For example, in New York the intermediate appellate court is the Appellate Division of the state's Supreme Court, which is divided into four Departments. Even where an Appellate Division decision is cited as persuasive authority outside New York State, the identity of the Department can be of "particular relevance." In a defamation case being litigated in Colorado, for instance, an opinion from the First Department (which includes Manhattan) may have added weight because the concentration of publishers and broadcasting media in New York City has given the First Department a fair amount of experience in the field. This problem does not, of course, arise in states, such as Pennsylvania and Maryland, where the jurisdiction of the intermediate appellate court is not geographically segmented.

Case names are regulated in citations by rule 10.2.2 and in textual references by rule 10.2.1. Although the rules are not simple, the Bluebook explanation is straightforward. (If you are not sure what a textual reference is, see the first sentence of §16.3.)

The subsequent history of a decision is set out according to rule 10.7. The subsequent history includes only the result of appeals from the decision cited to. (The *prior* history is cited to only in the circumstances described in the second paragraph of rule 10.7.) Where there is a subsequent history — and there often is not — the years of both lower and appellate decisions are included if they are different (as they were in *Onofre*). If both decisions date from the same year, that year is listed only at the end of the citation and not elsewhere. Rule 10.7.2 governs the situation where the case name changed during the appeal.

§16.2.2   Citation to Statutes

Aside from the signal and any explanatory parenthetical, a citation to a statute currently in force has four components:

1. the *name* of the statute as it was originally enacted, if the statute is still known by that name;
2. the *section* being cited to, as numbered in the *original* enactment — if the statute is still known by its enacted name;
3. a reference to the *current codification,* providing title, article, chapter, and section numbers, to the extent required by rules 12.1, 12.2.1, 12.3.1 and using information provided in the Bluebook tables; and
4. the *date* (and supplement, if any), as determined under rule 12.3.2.

For example, this citation

Wilderness Act, § 2(b), 16 U.S.C. § 1131(b) (1988)

is made up of the following parts:

1. **statute name**   Wilderness Act

2. **section in original enactment**   § 2(b)

3. **current codification**   16 U.S.C. § 1131(b)

4. **date of code**   (1988)

Generally speaking, the third component is the most important; the rest of the citation is built around it.

Most statutes are no longer known by the names under which they were originally enacted. Sometimes, that is because the statute has been recodified so many times that its enacted name has been forgotten. Just as often, the statute was a routine enactment in the first place and never had a name, or at least not one worth remembering. Where the section being cited to in the code is thus no longer identified with the session law in which it was originally enacted, the citation consists only of the third and fourth components:

18 U.S.C. § 4 (1988).

In some instances, additional material is required; rules 12.6 and 12.7 tell you when and what to add. As with cases, any signal and explanatory parenthetical appear, respectively, at the beginning and end of the citation. Forms for textual references to statutes are suggested in rule 12.9.

Rules 3.4 and 6.2(b) regulate citation to specific sections of a statute. Rules 12.2 and 12.4 explain the differences between citations to codifications and citations to session laws, as well as the uses of each. Rule 12.2.1 governs citation to statutes no longer in force, and rule 12.2.2(a) describes how to cite both a statute and its amendments where they are not published in the same place.

Under rules 3.4 and 6.2(b), use a section symbol ("§") in citations (full or short-form); the word "section" in textual references to state statutes and regulations; and either the word or the symbol in textual references to federal statutes and regulations. (The symbol can begin a citation sentence but never a textual sentence.) Readers will expect to see the "§" symbol even if you are not sure how to make one with your typewriter or word-processing equipment.[1]

§16.3   Rules Governing All Citations

Authority can be referred to in three different ways: a full citation ("*Terry v. Ohio,* 392 U.S. 1 (1968)"), a short-form citation ("*Id.* at 14"), or a textual reference ("In *Terry,* the Supreme Court ruled . . .").

Full citations: A full citation should be used whenever you first mention an authority and wherever clarity would be promoted by communicating all the information found in a full citation. Generally, the worst place for a full citation is near the beginning of a sentence: *it interrupts flow*

> In *Curley v. United States,* 160 F.2d 229, 233-34 (1947), the D.C. Circuit held that a trial judge should grant a motion for a directed verdict of acquittal where the evidence would necessarily cause reasonable jurors to entertain a reasonable doubt about the defendant's guilt.

Here you have to climb over the citation just to find out what the rest of the sentence is about. Either of the following would be better:

state the rule for which the authority stands and then follow with a citation	A trial judge should grant a motion for a directed verdict of acquittal where the evidence would necessarily cause reasonable jurors to entertain a reasonable doubt about the defendant's guilt. *Curley v. United States,* 160 F.2d 229, 233–34 (D.C. Cir. 1947).
if the source of the authority should be emphasized, it can be referred to in the sentence preceding the citation	The D.C. Circuit has held that a trial judge should grant a motion for a directed verdict of acquittal where the evidence would necessarily cause reasonable jurors to entertain a reasonable doubt about the defendant's guilt. *Curley v. United States,* 160 F.2d 229, 233-34 (1947).

§16.2 1. If you are using a typewriter without a "§" key, you can solve this problem in either of two ways. The first is to type a lowercase *s* and then type another *s* about a third of a line directly above the first, so that the upper loop of the first interlocks with the lower loop of the second. (This is approximately how the symbol was created in the first place.) The other solution is to leave space while typing so that you can add the "§" in pen while proofreading.

If you are using a computer, read your software manual to find out how to use the "§" sign even though it is not on your keyboard. For example, in Wordperfect 5.1, while holding down the "Ctrl" key, press "2" (not F2). Then type "4,6" (do not type the quote marks) and press the "Enter" key. You will not see "2" or "4,6" on the monitor screen. But after you hit "Enter," the "§" sign will appear. (Be careful: type "4 *comma* 6" and not "4 *period* 6" or 4 *comma space* 6.")

Full citations to cases (rule 10) and statutes (rule 12) have been explained in the preceding pages. The Bluebook has elaborate rules in its specific part governing full citations to every other kind of authority (rules 11 and 13 through 19).

Short-form citations are governed by practitioners' note 4 and by rules 4 (short-forms generally), 10.9 (cases), 12.9 (statutes), 13.7 (legislative materials), 14.9 (regulations), 15.8 (books), 16.6 (periodicals), and so on. Short-form cites may be used at any time after authority has been introduced with a complete citation, except where a short form would cause confusion. Confusion would occur, for example, if a short-form citation were to appear many pages after the full citation.

Beginners tend to encounter two problems with short-form citations. One arises from the once permitted but now prohibited practice of using "*supra*" with primary authority (see rule 4.2). Since so much previously published material follows the old rule, the second sentence of rule 4.2 is sometimes overlooked by students.

The other problem is that rule 4.1 and practitioners' note 4 are often misunderstood. Taken together, they amount to the following for citation of cases in briefs and legal memoranda: Short-form citations to cases include the name of only the first party, or, if the first party is a frequent litigant — such as "United States," "California," or "State" — the name of the second party instead. If the citation should refer to a specific page in the decision, the following information is added: volume number, name of reporter, and the page referred to (the last preceded by "at"). The first page number of the decision does not appear in a short-form citation. In this example, both official and unofficial reporters are cited to:

> *Beshada,* 90 N.J. at 200, 447 A.2d at 544.

Just to show you what is missing in a short-form cite, the following would be the corresponding full citation:

> *Beshada v. Johns-Manville Products Corp.,* 90 N.J. 191, 200, 447 A.2d 539, 544 (1982).

If the immediately preceding citation is to the same case, "*Id.*" should be used in a short-form cite instead of the name of the first party, even if the preceding citation is also in short form. Be careful to "[i]ndicate any particular" (rule 4.1) in which the second citation is meant to differ from the first. Thus, where "*Id.* at 414" is followed simply by "*Id.*," the reader has in both instances been referred to page 414. Where "*Id.*" is used and a page number inside the case is to be indicated, the name and volume number of the official reporter are omitted, but that is not true where a party's name is used. Thus,

> *Id.* at 200, 447 A.2d at 544.

but

> *Beshada,* 90 N.J. at 200, 447 A.2d at 544.

There is no logical reason for the distinction, but it is clearly made in the examples in practitioners' note 4.

Textual references: A textual reference is the mention of authority in text without the formalities of either a long- or short-form Bluebook citation. There are two textual references in the following sentence, one to a case and the other to a statute:

> In *Sanders,* the Supreme Court held that § 10 of the Administrative Procedure Act does not provide . . .

The integration of a Bluebook citation into a sentence is not a textual reference. The following includes a full citation and no textual reference:

> Since 5 U.S.C. §§ 701-706 (1988) does not so provide, jurisdiction depends instead on . . .

A textual reference, if written unambiguously, is an appropriate device where discussing authority previously cited in full. But many students do not realize that because, although some Bluebook rules, such as 12.9 and 6.2(b), are based on the use of textual references, no rule overtly regulates them.

Citation sentences and clauses: Citations, whether full or short form, are arranged in citation sentences and clauses according to rule 1.1. Where an authority supports an entire sentence of your text, you must put the citation in a separate citation sentence:

> A defamation defendant enjoys an absolute privilege for expressions of mere opinion. *Gertz v. Robert Welch, Inc.,* 418 U.S. 323 (1974).

On the other hand, where an authority supports only part of a sentence, the citation is interpolated into the textual sentence as a citation clause:

> A defamation defendant enjoys an absolute privilege for expressions of mere opinion, *Gertz v. Robert Welch, Inc.,* 418 U.S. 323, 339-40 (1974), and it is a question of law, to be determined by the court and not the jury, whether a statement at issue is one of fact or of opinion, *Information Control Corp. v. Genesis One Computer Corp.,* 611 F.2d 781, 783 (9th Cir. 1980).

This is a densely packed sentence, full of citation clutter, but it is one that many lawyers would write. You probably found it a bit hard to climb over the *Gertz* cite so you could get to the rest of the sentence. The following is a little better:

> A defamation defendant enjoys an absolute privilege for expressions of mere opinion. *Gertz v. Robert Welch, Inc.,* 418 U.S. 323, 339-40 (1974). And it is a question of law, to be determined by the court and not the jury, whether a statement at issue is one of fact or of opinion. *Information Control Corp. v. Genesis One Computer Corp.,* 611 F.2d 781, 783 (9th Cir. 1980).

Where several authorities are cited for the same point, the order in which they appear in citation sentences and clauses is governed by rule 1.4.

Signals: Depending in part on whether you are doing practical or academic writing, your purpose in citing an authority could be communicated either through your own discussion of the authority or through signals (rules 1.2 and 1.3) at the beginning of the citation. Although signals are essential to the massive compression in law review footnotes and in other kinds of scholarly writing, they cannot communicate the type of precise information needed by the reader of a brief or memorandum. In those documents, your purpose must be communicated through your own explanations of the authorities. Thus, although the Bluebook has much to say about signals, the only signal that should appear frequently in practical writing is the invisible one: under rule 1.2(a), the *absence* of a signal at the beginning of a citation is itself a signal telling the reader that the authority "(i) *clearly* states the proposition, (ii) identifies the source of a quotation, or (iii) identifies an authority referred to in text." The Bluebook italicizes "clearly" to stress that if a proposition is not plain from a reading of the authority cited, you should explain the reasoning through which you inferred it.

Subdivisions and abbreviations: Rule 3 governs citation to pages, sections, volumes, and other subdivisions of an authority. Rule 3.3 explains how to direct a reader to a specific page in an authority in what is called a "pinpoint cite" or a "jump cite." But rule 3.3 does not tell you when that must be done. A quotation *must* be cited to a specific page. Where you refer to only part of a sizeable opinion — even without quoting — a reader is entitled to know which pages you have in mind. To many lawyers, "sizeable" means four pages or more in a West reporter or the equivalent amount of text in another publication. (To some lawyers, it means two pages or more.)

Four provisions of Rule 6 (abbreviations and symbols) might seem perplexing in the beginning. First, under rule 6.1(a), no space appears between initials or between initials and numbers, although a space must appear between "longer abbreviations" and anything else. Thus: "S.W.2d," but "Cal. 3d" and "F. Supp." Second, under rule 6.1(b), where an abbreviation is formed by deleting part of the middle of a word and leaving part of the beginning and end, an apostrophe is inserted where the deletion was made. "Aff'd" and "Dep't" are correct, but "affd." and "Dept." are not. Third, examples throughout the Bluebook use "2d" and "3d" — and *not* "2nd" and "3rd." Finally, you must add a space between initials that stand for "the name of a geographic or institutional entity" and initials that stand for other things. Thus:

wrong: N.C.L. Rev.

right: N.C. L. Rev.

(North Carolina is, of course, a "geographic entity.")

Parentheticals: There are two kinds of parentheticals in legal citations. The first is an integral part of the citation and provides required information, such as the court and year for a case (Bluebook rules 10.4 and 10.5), the code year for a statute (rule 12.3.2), the edition and publication year for a book (rule 15.4), and any notation about alterations in the quotation (rule 5.2).

The second kind is an explanatory parenthetical that provides information that could be expressed in the writer's text but for economy might instead be compressed into the citation. (See rules 10.6 for cases and 12.7 for statutes.) Some of this information is a technical comment on the authority and is usually better placed in a citation parenthetical unless you want it emphasized in the text:

in citation: *Carey v. Population Services Int'l,* 431 U.S. 678, 691-99 (1977) (plurality opinion).

emphasized in text: Although a majority of seven justices struck down that portion of the statute which prohibited distribution of nonprescription contraceptives to persons under the age of 16, only four justices supported the rationale now urged in this court. *See Carey v. Population Services Int'l,* 431 U.S. 678, 691-99, 702-03, 707-08, 713-16 (1977).

You will run into trouble, however, if you go overboard trying to express the *substance* of an authority in explanatory parentheticals:

Carey v. Population Services Int'l, 431 U.S. 678, 691-99 (1977) (state statute prohibiting distribution of nonprescription contraceptives to persons under 16 years old is unconstitutional because sexual activity may not be constitutionally deterred by increasing its hazards).

Not only is the explanatory parenthetical here awkward and hard to read, but it oversimplifies and inevitably misrepresents the material in order to pack it into parenthetical form.

If the material is complicated and important to the issue, explain it in text. Use an explanatory parenthetical only for information that is simple and not an important part of your discussion or argument. And resist the temptation to use explanatory parentheticals to avoid the hard work of explaining complicated and important authority.

§16.4   Bluebook Rules on Quotations

Beginners have many more problems with quotations than they think they will. This section explains the complex Bluebook rules on quotation format. Section 16.5 explains how to avoid faults like overquoting, unnecessarily long quotations, and quoting out of context.

Bluebook rule 5 governs the format of quotations. The provisions on quotation alterations and omissions (rules 5.2 and 5.3) are not as clearly set out in the Bluebook as they might be. These are the most essential requirements:

Use brackets to enclose additions and substitutions that you place inside quotation marks, including the transformation of a lowercase letter into a capital or vice versa (rule 5.2). Parentheses and brackets convey different messages, and one cannot substitute for the other. If you are using a typewriter that cannot make brackets, leave space and pen them in while proofreading.

If you incorporate a quote with capitalized words into a sentence of your own, the capital letter must be reduced to a lowercase letter unless the capital denotes a proper name. For example:

wrong:	The court **held** "Unconscionability includes an absence of meaningful choice."
wrong:	The court **held,** "Unconscionability includes an absence of meaningful choice."[1]
right:	The court **held that** "[u]nconscionability includes an absence of meaningful choice."

[handwritten note: Altering what was in original]

If you omit citations from a quote, or if you add or delete italics or underlining, you must communicate that in a parenthetical following the citation (rule 5.2). The following is an example in the correct format:

> In order to obtain the names of a defamation defendant's confidential sources, a plaintiff must prove that he or she has "*independently* attempted to obtain the information elsewhere and has been unsuccessful." *Silkwood v. Kerr-McGee Corp.*, 563 F.2d 433, 438 (10th Cir. 1977) (emphasis added).

Under rule 5.3, if you delete words (other than a citation) from a quote, you must indicate that by an ellipsis (". . .").[2] There are two exceptions. First, where you incorporate a quotation into a sentence of your own composition — as in the unconscionability and *Silkwood* examples above — do

[handwritten note: Ellipsis never goes at beginning of a quotation]

---

§16.4   1. This form works for dialogue in a novel, but not when analyzing the words of a court.

2. When the final words of a sentence are omitted, the sentence ends with *four* periods—three for the ellipsis and one to stop the sentence (rule 5.3(b)(iii)).

not place an ellipsis at the beginning or the end of the quotation. The incorporation itself suggests the possibility that something might have been omitted. Second, do not place an ellipsis at the beginning of a quotation, even if you intend the quote to stand on its own as a complete sentence. If the quote is not incorporated into a sentence you have written and if the first letter of the quote was not capitalized in the original, capitalize that letter and place it in brackets to indicate an alteration.

A quotation of 50 words or more belongs in a single-spaced, indented quotation block (rule 5.1). A block quote should *not* begin and end with quotation marks. (The indentation alone tells the reader that it is a quote.) And the citation to the quote's source does not go at the end of the quotation block (rule 5.1(a)). It goes instead in your text, usually at the beginning of the next line you write. The first example below is wrong on both counts:

wrong: The court distinguished *Norton v. Franz.*

                    "[block quote from case]" [citation to case]

                    Thus, . . .

right: The court distinguished *Norton v. Franz.*

                              [block quote from case]

                    [citation to case] Thus, . . .

But many block quotations should not exist in the first place. See question 16-A in §16.5.

§16.5 How to Test Your Writing for Effective Use of Quotations

While writing — and rewriting — ask yourself the following questions.[1]

16-A **Have you quoted only the essential words?** A busy reader tends to skim over — or skip — large quotations because the perceived value of the quotation rarely seems to outweigh the tedious business of finding the juicy words hidden inside it.

Generally speaking, quoted words should not appear in your work unless they fit into one of the following categories:

1. words that must be *interpreted* in order to resolve the issue;
2. words that are so closely identified with the topic under discussion that they are *inseparable* from it;

---

§16.5 1. When marking up your work, your teacher might refer to these questions by using the number-letter codes that appear next to each question here.

3. words that, *with remarkable economy,* put the reader in touch with the thinking of a court, legislature, or expert in the field; or
4. words that are the *most eloquent and succinct conceivable* expression of an important idea.

Beginners are too quick to think that words, merely because they are printed in a book, can satisfy the third or fourth criteria. That kind of awe causes a student to write a sentence like the following:

> The court relied on "[w]ell-established jurisprudence of our sister states . . . holding that baseball is a strenuous game involving danger to . . . players . . . and that one who, with full knowledge of this danger, attends . . . and places himself in a position of danger, assumes the risks inherent in the game." *Gaspard v. Grain Dealers Mut. Ins. Co.,* 131 So. 2d 831, 834 (La. Ct. App. 1961).

The writer of this sentence did some editing, but the quoted words are really worth no more than the following:

> Relying on "[w]ell-established" precedent in other states holding baseball to be a dangerous game, the court concluded that anyone who knows of that danger and nevertheless plays baseball "assumes the risks inherent in the game." *Gaspard v. Grain Dealers Mut. Ins. Co.,* 131 So. 2d 831, 834 (La. Ct. App. 1961).

The most convincing descriptions of precedent are written almost entirely in your own words, punctuated with very few and very short quotations that convey the essence of the court's approach.

Block quotations are especially troublesome. The best you can usually hope for with a block quotation is that the reader will actually read the first sentence, skim the second, and skip the rest unless the first two sentences are gripping. Readers feel that block quotations are obstacles that have to be climbed over. The more of them you use, the more quickly a reader will refuse to read any of them. And judges and supervising attorneys view large quotations as evidence of a writer's laziness. They think that your job is to find the essential words, isolate them, and concisely paraphrase the rest. When you throw a big block quotation at a reader, you are asking the reader to do some of your work.

How do you cut a block quotation down to size? Assume that, in a first draft, you have written the following:

> Although in *Roth* the Supreme Court held that a government could, without satisfying the traditional clear-and-present-danger test, restrict public distribution of obscene material, it came to the opposite conclusion when faced with a statute that punished private possession of obscene materials in one's own home:
>
> > It is true that in *Roth* this Court rejected the necessity of proving that exposure to obscene material would create a clear and present danger

SINGLE SPACE {
of antisocial conduct or would probably induce its recipients to such conduct. . . . But that case dealt with public distribution of obscene materials and such distribution is subject to different objections. For example, there is always the danger that obscene material might fall into the hands of children . . . or that it might intrude upon the sensibilities or privacy of the general public.

DOUBLE SPACE

Stanley v. Georgia, 394 U.S. 557, 567 (1969). A number of the Court's later right-to-privacy rulings have been based in part on *Stanley*.

First drafts are full of passages like this, and in a first draft they cause no real harm. But in later drafts, you should realize that the block quote will repel the reader. Ask yourself "Why do I want this quote? What words inside it satisfy one or more of the four criteria?"

The answer might be that no words in the quote satisfy those criteria, but that the quote does contain ideas that you want the reader to know about. If so, rewrite all of it in your own words. If you do this well — and it requires effort — your words will be better than anyone else's because your words will *fit* better.

On the other hand, the answer might be that some words are too valuable to give up. Here, "might fall into the hands of children" creates an image that economically reflects the Court's thinking (criterion 3), and "intrude upon the sensibilities or privacy of the general public" sets out a standard that will need to be interpreted (criterion 1). Isolate words like that, and rewrite everything else, condensing in the process. You might come up with something like this:

> Although in *Roth* the Supreme Court held that a government could, without satisfying the traditional clear-and-present-danger test, restrict public distribution of obscene material, it came to the opposite conclusion when faced with a statute that punished private possession of obscene materials in one's own home. In *Stanley v. Georgia*, 394 U.S. 557 (1969), the Court struck down such a statute and distinguished *Roth* because publicly distributed pornography "might fall into the hands of children" or "intrude upon the sensibilities or privacy of the general public." *Id*. at 567. A number of the court's later right-to-privacy rulings have been based in part on *Stanley*.

This is shorter; it flows better; and it makes the meaning much more clear than the block quote did. The reader's attention is taken straight to the essential words, which stand out when integrated into your own text.

To do this kind of thing, you do not have to be a better writer than a Supreme Court justice was. The justice who wrote *Stanley* had the task of justifying a significant decision of constitutional law. The writer of the passage above had a smaller job: explaining, as concisely as possible, the difference between *Roth* and *Stanley*. The smaller job simply takes fewer words.

A writer whose quotations are too long and too many is sometimes called a "cut-and-paste artist" because the product is not really writing at all. Little thought goes into it, and readers have no confidence in it because what they want is your analysis, which comes only with hard work — not scissors and glue.

Have you been careful not to quote out of context? Readers of legal writing are professional skeptics who often verify context. | 16-B | "Sentences out of context rarely mean what they seem to say, and nobody in the whole world knows that better than the appellate judge. He has learned it by the torturing experience of hearing his own sentences read back to him."[2]

Have you quoted and cited whenever you use the words of others? Whether done out of sloppiness or out of an intent to deceive, | 16-C | this is treated as plagiarism. One attorney was professionally disciplined because he plagiarized large portions of a thesis he submitted while enrolled in a law school's postgraduate degree program. The court held that the plagiarism constituted "conduct involving dishonesty, fraud, deceit or misrepresentation" in violation of DR 1-102(A)(4) of the Code of Professional Responsibility.[3] The court was unpersuaded by the attorney's defense that his plagiarism was unintentional, "the result of academic laziness and . . . not . . . an intentional effort to deceive his thesis examiners."[4] A disciplinary hearing board found — and the court agreed — that "it is inconceivable . . . that a person who has completed undergraduate school and law school would not know that representing extensively copied material as one's own work constitutes plagiarism."[5]

Have you quoted accurately? Reading a case, a student spots language that may be quotable. The student starts to copy it out, | 16-D | and — although the student does not realize it at the time — some of the words written down are not the same as those that appear in the case. But the words written down are the ones that eventually appear in the student's memorandum or brief. You will be surprised at how easily supervisors, judges, and teachers can spot this, and it usually causes them to lose some confidence in the writer. You may also be surprised at how easily you can make this sort of mistake. The cause is often a natural and unconscious tendency to rewrite quotes into your own style while copying them. The best prevention is to proofread your notes while you still have the original source in front of you.

Have you placed quotation marks exactly where they belong? The most common problems are (1) omitting the quotation | 16-E | marks that close a quotation, even though the opening quotation marks are included ("Where does the quote end?" writes the teacher in the margin);

2. E. Barrett Prettyman, *Some Observations Concerning Appellate Advocacy,* 39 Va. L. Rev. 285, 295 (1953).
3. *In re Lamberis,* 93 Ill. 2d 222, 443 N.E.2d 549 (1982).
4. *Id.* at 225-26, 443 N.E.2d at 550.
5. *Id.* at 226, 443 N.E.2d at 551.

(2) omitting the quotation marks that open a quotation, even though the closing marks are present ("Where does the quote begin?" writes the teacher); and (3) where there is a quote within a quote, failing to change the double quotation marks of the original to single marks.

16-F **Have you been careful not to quote from a headnote?** A court's opinion is limited to the text appearing in the reporter *after* the name of the judge who wrote it. The one- or two-sentence headnotes that appear between the case's name and the opinion itself are supplied by the publisher and are not written by the court. Those headnotes may be useful in research, but they are not part of the opinion and have no authoritative value, even if they resemble parts of the opinion. Moreover, the headnotes are written in a distinct style, instantly recognizable by the experienced reader. For example:

> That portion of award of double costs and attorney fees imposed upon counsel would be imposed upon counsel personally, even though client was responsible for pursuing litigation, where client received bad legal advice.[6]

This is typical of headnote style. Every "the," "a," and "an" has been omitted. More important, the sentence is so terse that a reader has only the barest idea of what the court might actually have decided.

Compare the headnote with the heart of the passage it tries to summarize:

> In sum, this appeal rests on a serious misstatement of state law. It is hard to imagine that a lawyer could advise a client to defy an outstanding judgment on the ground that an application for a stay had been filed but had not been granted, or that a lawyer could inform us — without a shred of authority — that in Illinois an application for a stay has the effect of a stay itself. . . . [A]n advocate must represent his client within the existing structure of the law, and not some imagined version of it. . . .
>
> Rule 11 requires counsel to study the law before representing its contents to a federal court. An empty head but a pure heart is no defense. . . . Counsel who puts the burden of study and illumination on the defendants or the court must expect to pay attorneys' fees under the Rule. . . .
>
> . . . Ordinarily we impose attorneys' fees on the party, leaving party and lawyer to settle accounts. But we do not suppose that the representations about state law were approved by [this lawyer's client] personally; . . . she has received bad legal advice. We therefore impose part of the award on counsel personally.[7]

Between the headnote and the opinion itself, the difference — both in style and in substance — is unmistakable. The reader will instantly spot it, feel cheated of a direct description of the case, and think the writer lazy and unreliable.

---

6. Publisher's headnote to *Thorton v. Wahl*, 787 F.2d 1151, 1152 (7th Cir. 1986).
7. *Thorton v. Wahl*, 787 F.2d 1151, 1154 (7th Cir. 1986) (text of court's opinion).

The solution is not to quote the entire longer passage from the opinion. Instead, explain the case in your own words, quoting from the court only to the extent necessary according to the criteria set out in question 16-A.

Exercise I.   The First Amendment (Quotations)

1. You are in the midst of writing a memorandum involving the right-of-assembly clause — and no other part of the First Amendment. You intend to quote the words to be interpreted. This is the text of the entire amendment:

> Congress shall make no law respecting an establishment of religion, or prohibiting the free exercise thereof; of abridging the freedom of speech, or of the press; or the right of the people peaceably to assemble, and to petition the Government for a redress of grievances.

Using words from the Amendment, complete the following sentence: "The First Amendment provides . . ."

2. Do the same for a memorandum involving the freedom-of-speech clause.

Exercise II.   The Separation of Powers
(Citations and Quotations)

Correct the following passage for incorrect use of quotations and citations. Correct every error you can find, adding and subtracting to the citations as necessary. If a Bluebook rule requires a change, write the rule's number in the margin. Be prepared to explain your work in class.

> The constitutional doctrine of separation-of-powers precludes judicial review of prosecutorial discretion. *Pugach v. Klein,* 193 F. Supp. 630 (U.S. Dist. Ct.) *Powell v. Katzenbach,* 359 f.2d 234 (D.C.Cir. 1965), certiorari denied 384 US 906 (1965) reh. den. 384 US 967 (1966); *Inmates of Attica Correctional Facility, et al. v. Rockefeller,* 477 F. 2nd 375 (U.S.Ct.App. 1973). These decisions are based on the ideas that "(t)he discretion of the Attorney General in choosing whether to prosecute or not to prosecute, or to abandon a prosecution already started, is absolute," Smith v. United States, 375 F.2d at 247, cert. denied 389 U.S. 841 (1967), and that "it is not the function of the judiciary to review the exercise of executive discretion." Newman v. U.S., 382 F.2d 479, p. 482 (U.S.Ct. App. 1967. Nevertheless, it has been clear since *Yick Woo v. Hopkins,* 118 U.S. 356, 6 S.Ct. 1064, 30 L. Ed. 220 (1886) (discriminatory enforcement violates equal protection) that prosecutorial discretion is not absolute. The United States Supreme Court has, however, spoken approvingly of plea bargaining while not taking any position on whether the separation of powers precludes judicial review.
>
> Generally, prosecutorial discretion is not supervised by state courts. "District Attorney has broad discretion in determining when and in what manner to prosecute a suspected offender." *People v. DiFalco,* 406 N.Y.S.2d 279, 44 N.Y. 482, 377 N. E. 2nd 732. "Prosecutor is allowed broad discretion in

law enforcement and is not obliged to treat two similarly situated defendants alike. *Ward v. State,* (Del. 1980) 414 A.2d 499, 500.
Consequently,

> "prosecutors are not insulated against ulterior influence. . . . They are free to avoid investigating any case, and they are free to refuse to act on evidence found when they do investigate. They are never required to state findings of fact, . . . never required to follow their own precedents or to explain departures from them, and are never required to discuss publicly their policy positions." 2 DAVIS ADMINISTRATIVE LAW TREATISE 224 (1979 2d ed.)

NOTE: The passage below appears on page 224, volume 2, of Kenneth Culp Davis's *Administrative Law Treatise:*

> Over nearly two centuries, both legislators and executives have generally ignored the manner in which prosecutors have exercised their discretion, and the judicial doors have been generally closed to those who want to assert that discretion has been abused. Unlike judges, prosecutors are not insulated against ulterior influence. Their discretion is unguided by statutory standards, and it is unguided by rules which the prosecutors themselves might make. They are free not to investigate in any case, and they are free to refuse to act on the evidence found when they do investigate. They are never required to state findings of fact, never required to explain decisions made on questions of law, never required to follow their own precedents or to explain departures from them, and never required to discuss publicly their policy positions. They are free, if they choose, to accept a plea of guilty in return for charging a lesser crime, no matter how easily they can prove the serious crime. They are not required to act openly, and many of their most important decisions are kept secret. The victim of a crime typically has no remedy even if he can prove that failure to prosecute is an abuse of discretion.

IV

LAW SCHOOL EXAMINATIONS

17 How to Write Examinations

§17.1 How Examination Answers Differ from Other Forms of Legal Writing

A supervising lawyer or a judge reads your work for the purpose of deciding what to do in the client's case. But a teacher reads your exam answers to decide something else: how much you have learned in the course. Many students assume that teachers want to know how well students have memorized rules of law. But that is only part of it. A teacher is also interested — and often *more* interested — in your understanding of how to use the rules and what the law is trying to accomplish with them.

To get credit for what you know about these things, you have to structure your exam answers in a way that tells the teacher what he or she needs to know about you.

Compare a law school examination to a computerized cash register in a grocery store. The cashier places each item above an electronic "eye" that "sees" the item's universal product code and rings up the price. If the cashier does not hold an item at exactly the proper angle, the eye sees nothing and registers nothing. The cashier is able to try again and again and, if necessary, can even ring up a purchase manually. Like the electronic eye, the teacher will give you credit for what you show in the proper form, but, unlike the cashier, you get only one chance.

§17.2   Answering Essay Questions

The traditional law school examination question contains a story, which you are asked to analyze in terms of the field of law covered by the course. This is called an essay question, even though a good answer to it could not accurately be called an essay.

You are graded on how well you identify the real issues in the story, identify the governing rules, state those rules accurately, and apply the rules to the facts. The teacher is less interested in your conclusions than in the analytical skills and understanding you display in arriving at and explaining those conclusions. In answering an essay question, the most effective organization is one that clearly shows the teacher the things he or she is grading: issue spotting, knowledge of legal rules, and the ability to analyze and solve a legal problem in depth. (As you will see in a moment, that will differ from the paradigm described in Chapter 9.)

There are many effective methods of producing an answer to an essay question. Here is one:

Start by reading the question once from beginning to end without using a pen for any reason. Just read, so that you see the big picture. Then read the question again, underlining important things or making notes in the margin. Then read it a third time — but while doing so, make a list on scratch paper of all the issues you see in the question. (Leave plenty of blank space between issues.) Whenever you see a fact relevant to a particular issue, make a note of that fact under the issue in your list of issues.

Now focus on the list of issues. Look at each issue individually. What rules are necessary to resolve it? Make a note of each rule in the blank space under the issue. What policy considerations would help resolve the issue? Make a note of them as well. If you think of anything else relevant to the issue, make a note of that as well. In what sequence should the issues be discussed in your answer? Write "1" next to the one that should be discussed first, "2" next to the one that should come second, and so on.

You have just made an outline of your answer. Under exam conditions, you do not have time to make an extensive formal outline, but the one that grew out of your list of issues will be good enough.

Most teachers will tell you, in one way or another, approximately how much time you should spend answering each question on the exam. Do not be afraid to spend half that time reading the question and making an outline. If you do that well, you will have everything you need to write a good answer.

Now write. For each issue, use the following permutation of the paradigm described in Chapter 9:

1. Since the teacher is more interested in your issue-spotting ability than in your conclusion, start by stating the *issue*.
2. The governing *rule or rules* should normally follow. Use some judgment about this. If the rule is very basic — such as the four elements

of negligence — it might not be necessary to state it because if you do a good job of applying a rule that the whole class knows, the teacher could reasonably conclude that you know it, too. But often the teacher is specifically trying to find out whether you know a rule. If on a civil procedure exam, you realize that the court plainly lacks subject matter jurisdiction but the defendant fails to raise the issue, the teacher is trying to find out whether you know that defects in subject matter jurisdiction can never be waived.

3. Proof of a rule is usually not necessary (because the teacher is in part testing your ability to remember rules that have been more or less proven in class) and often not possible (because the facts are frequently set in mythical jurisdictions). However, in some subjects dominated by uniform or federal statutes, the teacher may be willing to give you a little credit if you are able to refer to specific sections of a code, although such a teacher will not give you credit for good citation form.

4. Having stated the rule, *apply* it to the facts. Use additional rules as you need them. You can show intellectual depth by explaining how your analysis is consistent with the policy behind these rules. You can also show intellectual depth by including a counter-analysis. (Most of the time, you cannot get full credit without policy discussions and counter-analyses.)

5. If you have not already done so, state your *conclusion* before moving on to the next issue.

Students have traditionally tried to remember this formula by calling it "IRAC": *I*ssue, *R*ule, *A*nalysis/counter-analysis, *C*onclusion. Your answer to each essay question will include several IRAC-structured discussions — one for each issue you identify. But limit the IRAC formula to exam-taking: it does not work well in office memoranda, motion memoranda, or appellate briefs.

As you use each fact, rule, or policy consideration, cross it off your checklist. Do the same for each issue as you finish it. When you have finished the last issue, go on to the next question. (If you have time after answering all the questions, go back and proofread what you wrote.)

§17.3 Other Types of Questions

There is a non-story variant of the essay question. The teacher might describe a proposed statute and ask you to comment on it. There are no characters and no plot. Here, a good answer might in fact resemble an essay. Figure out how the proposal would alter the way the law functions, and decide whether that would be beneficial or detrimental, remembering the public policy considerations that were stressed in class and in the casebook.

Then write an answer in which you state your conclusion and substantiate it by analyzing the proposal in policy terms.

Some law school exams include short-answer questions. Several of them might be based on a single set of facts. Each question poses a specific and narrowly framed inquiry, such as "Did the defendant waive defects in personal jurisdiction?" You are given a small space — perhaps enough for a paragraph — in which to give your answer and the reasons for it.

§17.4   General Suggestions for Taking Examinations

Start preparing for exams long before the end of classes. The best preparation is to make your *own* course outline during the semester from your class notes and from the portions of the text covered by the teacher. The act of making the outline is an irreplaceable self-teaching experience. In structuring the course outline, the casebook's table of contents is more helpful than you might suppose.

Teachers differ from one another on examination philosophy, and most teachers tell their classes something of their own views on examinations and grading. Take seriously what each teacher tells you.

During the examination, budget your time carefully. One of the tragedies of the examination room is the student who spends so much time on one question that the others cannot be handled adequately.

Read the instructions carefully. Before beginning to answer a question, be sure that you understand the role you have been assigned. Are you being asked to analyze objectively the rights and liabilities of various characters in a story? To state the legal advice you would give to one of the characters if that person were your client? To make arguments on behalf on one character and against others? To write a judicial opinion?

Do not waste time writing about background matters — like the historical evolution of the rules you are using — unless they truly help you resolve the issues in the exam. Most teachers will give you credit only for finding issues and analyzing them.

Your goal is not to find the largest number of issues in each question. It is to identify the issues actually in the question — no more and no less. You will, of course, lose credit for missing issues. But many teachers will also reduce your grade if you "find" issues that are not reasonably suggested by the facts.

Analyze every genuine issue, even if you believe that your analysis of one issue would make all the others moot. Not only must you do that in law practice anyway, but you cannot get full credit on examinations without doing it.

Many — perhaps most — exam issues can reasonably be resolved in more than one way. Remember that the teacher is most interested in the quality of your reasoning (and often less interested in the result of that reasoning). It is not unusual for two students to get full credit for a given issue while coming to opposite conclusions about it. They deserve full credit because both conclusions are reasonable and arguable, and because both students supply knowledgeable and perceptive supporting analyses. But that does not mean that you can adopt any conclusion you please. Some conclusions are more reasonable and easier to prove than others. And a few issues on an exam have only one correct answer. (That usually happens when the teacher wants to know whether you have understood some very basic concept in the course.)

It is, however, never enough to state the arguments for each side and then waffle or avoid stating a conclusion. Take a position and support it with analysis. That is what lawyers are paid to do and what your teachers hope you are learning how to do.

If you make an assumption in answering a question, say so. A sloppy mind mushes over a gap in the facts without realizing that the gap is there. A precise mind recognizes the gap, defines it exactly, and offers a resolution of the issue while taking the gap into account. (But make assumptions only where there truly is a gap in the facts. Do not invent far-fetched facts of your own that distort the question the teacher wants you to answer. The teacher will see that as an attempt to avoid facing the hard aspects of the exam.)

Use terms of art properly. Misuse of a term of art implies that the student's knowledge of the subject is superficial.

Teachers justifiably hate gimmicks in exam answers. Simply write down — in a business-like manner — what the teacher must see if you are to get credit.

The teacher will give you credit only for what is plainly written in the examination booklet. You will get no credit for things that you know but do not expressly state. And you will get no credit for things that you expressly state in handwriting that the teacher cannot read.

Finally, learn from your examinations. Most teachers will let you read your examination after final grades are posted. Many are willing to talk with you individually about what you did well or badly. Some provide written post-mortems (sometimes called model answers) that explain the issues on the exam. Take advantage of all of these things. Sometimes, you will learn more about the subject matter of the course (which may be tested again on the bar examination and in any event will help you later as a lawyer). And sometimes you will learn how to write examination answers more effectively.

V
THE SHIFT TO PERSUASION

18 Developing a Persuasive Theory

§18.1 Introduction

Persuasive writing aims to convince judges to do what your client wants. Whether you are writing a motion memorandum or an appellate brief, the ability to persuade centers on three skills: developing a persuasive theory (explained in this chapter), developing persuasive arguments (see Chapter 19), and working within a procedural posture (see Chapter 20).

§18.2 Strategic Thinking

> There are 55 reasons why I shouldn't have pitched him, but 56 why I should.
>
> — *Casey Stengel, New York Yankees manager, on why he started Ed Lopat in the final game of the 1952 World Series*

My main objection to Lou was that he managed by hunch and desperation. You ask Casey Stengel why he made a certain move and he will tell you about a roommate he had in 1919 who demonstrated some principle Casey was now putting into effect. You ask Lou and he will say, "The way we're going, we had to do *something*." If there is a better formula for making a bad situation worse, I have never heard it.

> — *Bill Veeck, owner of the Cleveland Indians, on why he wanted to fire manager Lou Boudreau and hire Casey Stengel in 1946*

A strategy is a plan for causing a particular result. The desired result is your goal.

In litigation writing, a lawyer develops strategies by identifying goals (such as persuading a court to adopt rule X or to find fact Y) and then by generating a list of possible methods of accomplishing each goal. In imagining these alternative strategies, the lawyer asks him- or herself, "What would *cause* a court to decide in my favor?" After predicting each strategy's risks and chances of success, the lawyer selects the best one for each goal.

If a professional is asked why he or she did a particular thing and can answer only "It seemed like a good idea at the time," people will assume that the professional did not really think through the problem. In post-mortems of your work, a supervising lawyer or a teacher might ask you a litany of questions about strategy:

What was your goal?

What was your strategy?

What other possible strategies did you consider and reject?

For each rejected strategy, why was it inferior to the one you did choose?

What led you to believe that the strategy you chose would actually achieve the ultimate goal?

Did you do all the things necessary to execute the strategy you chose?

Did you do anything that impeded that strategy?

If the goal was not achieved, why not?

Supervisors and teachers ask these questions because a lawyer's job is *to make desired things happen.* The supervisor or teacher will be trying to make sure that your planning is free of the kinds of thinking that prevents strategy, such as overlooking opportunities, relying on unrealistic assumptions, and engaging in wishful thinking and other forms of self-deception.

The first sophisticated strategic decisions that you will make in law are the development of a theory that will persuade a court to rule in your client's favor (explained in this chapter) and the development of arguments to support that theory (explained in Chapter 19). Later in this chapter, you will learn what theories are and how they work. But first, let us consider the creative process through which all effective strategy decisions are made.

§18.3 Professional Creativity

Effective professional work usually progresses through the six stages of the creative process:[1]

1. *Problem-identification:* Identifying a problem that must be solved or some other situation in which a decision must be made.
2. *Gathering and evaluating information and raw materials:* Learning about the relevant law and facts in a fairly open-ended manner.
3. *Solution-generation:* Thinking up the largest reasonable number of potential solutions.
4. *Solution-evaluation:* Testing potential solutions to see how well they would work.
5. *Decision:* Comparing the evaluated solutions and choosing the most effective one.
6. *Action:* If the decision is a prediction, action means reporting it and the reasons for it in an office memorandum. If the decision is selection of a strategy, action means using the strategy in a motion memorandum or an appellate brief.

Frequently, these stages overlap, and at least some parts of them occur unconsciously. You might, for example, find yourself thinking up arguments (which is a form of *solution-generation*) while reading cases in the library (*gathering and evaluating information and raw materials*). And you might unexpectedly make a decision — perhaps while washing dishes or driving a car — on the basis of some unconscious solution-evaluation that occurred during the preceding hours or days.

When you make a predictive judgment, you realize that you need to know the future behavior of courts (*problem-identification*), and you read cases and statutes in the library (*gathering and evaluating information and raw materials*), develop arguments for each side (*solution-generation*), test each argument for the likehood of its adoption by a court (*solution-evaluation*), formulate a prediction based on the most likely arguments (*decision*), and record that prediction in an office memorandum (*action*).[2]

You are now learning another level of lawyerly analysis: strategizing. And the process here follows a similar pattern. When you create a strategy, you notice a need to cause a particular event (*problem-identification*), and you find the helpful and harmful authorities and facts (*gathering and evaluating information and raw materials*), think up the largest reasonable number of competing strategies (*solution-generation*), assess each strategy for

§18.3 1. *See, e.g.,* Teresa M. Amabile, *The Social Psychology of Creativity* 79–81 (1983); Silvano Arieti, *Creativity: The Magic Synthesis* 15-18 (1976); John Dewey, *How We Think* 12-15 (1933); Graham Wallas, *The Art of Thought* 80–82 (1926). (Researchers use different names for these stages. The ones used here were mostly suggested by Steven Jamar.)

2. See §8.1.

its effectiveness (*solution-evaluation*), choose the most effective strategy (*decision*), and execute it in a motion memorandum or appellate brief (*action*).

These sequences of thought all rest on habits of *disciplined curiosity*. Problem-identification, for example, requires the ability to spot quickly what John Dewey called a "forked-road situation . . . that is ambiguous, that presents a dilemma, that proposes alternatives"[3] — a place, in other words, where your thinking can make a difference and cause things to happen. Problem-identification thus is the opposite of passivity, which always sends you down the easier or more obvious road without considering the one less often taken.

Solution-generation and solution-evaluation pose the greatest challenges for students, in part because they require contrary skills. To think up the largest number of reasonable alternatives for solution-generation, you must be willing to look below the surface of the facts and law for deeper possibilities and meaning. (See §6.2 for an example.) Solution-generation requires temporarily suspending judgment. That is because workable ideas tend to arrive in one's mind mixed together with unworkable ones. The poet Schiller wrote that solution-generation becomes blocked

> if the intellect examines too closely the ideas already pouring in. . . . Regarded in isolation, an idea may be insignificant, and venturesome in the extreme, but it may acquire importance from an idea which follows it; perhaps, in a certain collation with other ideas, which may seem equally absurd, it may be capable of furnishing a very serviceable link. The intellect cannot judge all these ideas unless it can retain them until [all can be seen together. When many ideas are being collected,] the intellect has withdrawn its [guards] from the gates, and the ideas rush in pell-mell, and only then does it review and inspect the multitude. [People who are ineffective at solution-generation] reject too soon. . . .[4]

The key is to avoid premature judgment, to defer evaluation until after you have developed an array of alternatives. This can be constricted by snap evaluation of ideas as soon as they are expressed, by verbal aggression (yours or other people's), by a desire to conform, or by what Kenney Hegland calls the "fear of making a fool of yourself."[5] Lon Fuller, the great contracts scholar, wrote that solution-generation does not easily happen when you ask yourself "anxiously at every turn that most inhibitive of questions, *'What will other people think?'* "[6]

Paradoxically, solution-evaluation needs the qualities that would impoverish solution-generation: ruthless skepticism, fear that an idea might truly

3. John Dewey, *How We Think* 15 (1933).
4. Quoted at Morris I. Stein, *Creativity as Intra- and Inter-Personal Process,* in *The Creative Encounter* 21-22 (Rosemary Holsinger, Camille Jordan & Leon Levenson eds. 1971).
5. Kenney F. Hegland, *Trial and Practice Skills* 181 (1978).
6. Lon L. Fuller, *On Teaching Law,* 3 Stan. L. Rev. 35, 43 (1950) (emphasis in original).

be foolish, a pragmatic sense of the realistic, a precise ability to calculate risk. The trick is to turn those qualities off while thinking up solutions and then to turn them back on once you have assembled a full range of solutions and are ready to start evaluating them. During solution-generation, you will do best if you think with intellectual freedom and a tolerance for chaos, but during solution-evaluation you must become a completely different kind of person, viewing things with the cold-blooded realism of a person who must take responsibility for success or failure. The critical thinking on which solution-evaluation depends is taught aggressively throughout the law school curriculum. But because solution-generation and solution-evaluation depend on contrary qualities, you must be careful not to let that critical skepticism — of which we teach so much — overwhelm your ability to imagine the widest range of possibilities.

Only rarely does a person come to law school already skilled at both solution-generation and solution-evaluation. Most law students need substantial improvement in both, but — because those two stages require such contrary states of mind — you might start off with more ability at one than the other. There are, however, many effective ways of generating and evaluating solutions. As you become a professional, you will develop styles of generating and styles of evaluating that best make use of the person you are, taking advantage of your strengths while controlling your weaknesses.

§18.4 Theories: Of the Case, of the Motion, of the Appeal

To make their decisions, judges need more than raw information about the law and the facts. They make decisions by choosing between *theories,* and you will lose if your adversary's theory is more attractive than yours is.

Think back to the last major decision you had to make — perhaps the choice of a career, the selection of a law school, a decision about where to live, or the purchase of a car or an appliance. If your decision-making was conscious and deliberative — as judges hope their decisions are — you can probably recall an idea — or a small number of related ideas — that caused you to choose one career over another, one law school over another, and so forth. And if your decision-making was conscious and deliberative, there was probably a moment when you first identified and appreciated this idea (or small group of ideas). At that moment, you probably also realized that one of the alternatives had become inevitable. Some people who specialize in sales work call this moment the "selling point" because the decision to buy becomes inevitable once the selling idea is fully appreciated by the buyer.

Persuading is selling, and judges have accurately been described as "professional buyers of ideas."[1] Judges have their selling points, and both lawyers and judges use the word *theory* to refer to the collection of ideas that, in a given case, a lawyer offers for purchase. At trial, each lawyer propounds a *theory of the case.* Where the court is to decide a motion or an appeal, the phrases *theory of the motion* or *theory of the appeal* might be used instead. Each lawyer proposes a theory, and the court chooses between them, or — if neither theory is satisfactory — the court may fashion one of its own, often causing unhappiness to both sides.

A theory, then, is an idea on which a decision can be based. A persuasive theory is a view of the facts and law — intertwined together — that justifies a decision in the client's favor and motivates a court to make that decision. A persuasive theory "explains not only *what* happened but also *why*" through a compelling story that "has both rational and psychological appeal" and thus is "persuasive both to the mind and to the heart."[2]

For example, if Welty is prosecuted for burglarizing Lutz's apartment (see pages 165-67), the prosecution's theory of burglary might be that Lutz's conduct did not imply permission to break the threshold and enter the apartment, and that Welty's actions show beyond a reasonable doubt that — when she stepped into the apartment — she had already formed an intent to assault Lutz.[3] To prove the element of a breaking, for example, the prosecutor might point to four facts: (1) Lutz opened the door only six inches, (2) he never told Welty she could enter, (3) his only reason for stepping away from the door was to turn down the volume on his stereo so that he could hear what Welty was already saying while she was outside the apartment, and (4) as soon as Lutz discovered that Welty had entered the apartment, he ordered her to leave. To prove the element of "intent to commit a felony therein," the prosecutor might focus — in a way you have already explored in Chapter 8 — on Welty's anger at the time she entered the apartment.

On the other hand, Welty's attorney might develop the theory that the evidence creates reasonable doubt about whether she broke through a threshold to get into Lutz's apartment and about whether, at the instant she walked through the door, she intended to strike him. To substantiate this theory, Welty's attorney might argue that there was nothing to break once the door was open; that Lutz's actions could reasonably have been understood by Welty to have implied permission to enter and continue the conversation inside the apartment; and that Welty's actions before she was ordered to leave are consistent with an innocent intent to persuade Lutz to behave in a more neighborly fashion. If believed, this theory should cause an acquittal on the charge of burglary.[4]

---

§18.4   1. Girvan Peck, *Strategy of the Brief,* Litigation, Winter 1984, at 26, 27.

2. David Binder & Paul Bergman, *Fact Investigation: From Hypothesis to Proof* 140, 184 (1984).

3. The other elements of common law burglary would not be hard to prove: Welty did, in the nighttime, enter the dwelling of another. See §8.1.

4. For the separate charge of assault, the lawyer might have to ask some questions to develop a further theory: for example, if Welty struck Lutz because she thought he had

Although both theories address the facts in terms of the law of burglary and of the prosecution's obligation to persuade beyond a reasonable doubt, one theory favors the prosecution and the other favors the defendant. You might see something of how hard adjudicating is by putting yourself in the position of the judge and jury in this case, and by considering the consequences if you make a mistake: either an innocent person could be punished or a person could go free despite evidence of guilt beyond a reasonable doubt.[5] You might also understand some of the difficulties of advocacy by putting yourself in the position of each of the lawyers and asking yourself how you would go about persuading the decision-makers to adopt your theory *and to reject the other one,* both on the facts and on the law.

§18.5 Characteristics of a Persuasive Theory

A theory's success is measured, of course, by the likelihood of its adoption by the adjudicator. A theory is worth arguing if it stands a significant chance of being adopted by a fair-minded and reasonable person who must make the adjudicator's decision. George Vetter[1] has formulated six "bench marks" through which the marketability of a theory can be predicted:

First, the theory must have a firm foundation in strong facts and the fair inferences to be drawn from the facts.

And it must also have a firm foundation in law. A foundation can be firm even though the law is not yet settled through mandatory authority: what is needed is the likelihood that the law will, in the end, favor the theory.

Second, if possible, the theory should be built around the so-called "high cards" of litigation, incontestable or virtually incontestable facts, such as self-certifying documents, . . . admissions against interest, the testimony of independent witnesses, clear scientific facts, and so on.

Third, and as a corollary of the second bench mark, the theory should not be inconsistent with, or fly in the face of, incontestable facts.

---

become so angry that he might strike her, she might — to the charge of assault (but not burglary) — argue self-defense.

5. For centuries under the common law, the rule has been that a guilty person *must* go unpunished if the prosecution cannot prove guilt beyond a reasonable doubt. That is because our culture considers it more horrible to punish the innocent than to free the guilty, and our law therefore imposes on the prosecution a burden of persuasion heavy enough to create confidence that innocent people are not being punished. Thus, a prosecution theory must do more than show the likelihood of guilt: it must exclude every reasonable explanation of innocence. And a criminal defense theory is not necessarily a theory that the defendant is innocent: if the evidence of guilt is not overwhelming, the defense theory would be that the evidence does not exclude every reasonable possibility of innocence.

§18.5 1. George Vetter, *Successful Civil Litigation* 30-31 (1977).

Use the "high cards" as a foundation and avoid fighting with incontrovertible facts because that is exactly what the adjudicator — whether judge or jury — will do. In court, ambiguous evidence and debatable inferences are usually resolved in whatever way is most consistent with the evidence that cannot be questioned. When the time for decision arrives, the adjudicator's natural tendency is to say, "Let's start with what we *do* know."

> Fourth, the theory should explain away in a plausible manner as many unfavorable facts as it can. . . .
>
> Fifth, the theory should be down to earth and have a common-sense appeal. . . .

All other things being equal, a simple theory is more down-to-earth than a complex one, although even a simple theory must address all the facts. A theory has a commonsense appeal if its internal logic is consistent, if it is realistic, if its explanations are compatible with the adjudicator's experiences in life, and if it reflects the adjudicator's values and morality and the values and morality of the community to which the adjudicator feels answerable. If a theory assumes that the parties behaved quite differently from the way people normally do in similar circumstances, the theory is not commonsensical unless it includes a very persuasive reason for the difference. Theories that impute deceit to disinterested witnesses, for example, are less attractive than those that suggest honest but faulty abilities to observe and remember. Innocent misunderstandings are much more common than lying and stealing.

> Sixth, the theory cannot be based on wishful thinking about any phase of the case.

It helps to develop contradictory theories together — to develop, in other words, your adversary's most likely theory while creating your own. If you look at the case as your adversary will see it and if you hypothetically work up a theory for your adversary to argue, you will be able to identify the weaknesses in your theory. Otherwise, you will look at the controversy one-sidedly, and your theories will be wishful and too one-dimensional to withstand attack.

A judge looks for reliability in a theory, in its supporting arguments, and in the lawyer who is trying to sell the whole package. Like any other kind of consumer, a judge buys only when struck with a feeling of confidence that the purchase will turn out well, without causing injustice or embarrassment on appeal or before the public. Like most people who have had much opportunity to observe human nature, judges become fairly astute at surmising how various kinds of people behave under given circumstances. And like most people with substantial responsibilities, judges see the world as a place that works well when people are reasonable, rather than extreme. Judges also feel safer when they can make narrow decisions, rather than earth-shaking ones, because earth-shaking decisions provide more room for error. Thus, the most easily sold theories are those that are based on reasonable and believable interpretations of the evidence and the authorities; that would lead to reasonable results; that do not ask a judge to believe that people have behaved in improbable ways; and that do not ask the judge to change the law more than absolutely necessary.

A theory that sells in an appellate court necessarily has a flavor different from one that seems attractive to a trial court. That is because trial judges and appellate judges do not see their work in precisely the same way. A trial court is a place of routine, and trial judges want to make decisions the way they are usually made and not in ways that would greatly disturb the world. Although trial judges sometimes try to avoid the full impact of appellate authority, the rulings of the courts to which a trial judge's decision could be appealed are like orders from a superior, and the trial judge needs and wants to know — through those rulings — what the supervising courts expect. In contrast, appellate judges are conscious of their responsibility to see the bigger picture and to keep the law fair and reasonable, even if that requires modifying the common law now and then to fit changes in society. Judicial circumspection and the doctrine of stare decisis keep these changes in direction to a minimum, however, and appellate courts generally presume the decision below to be correct, reversing only if deeply troubled by what happened in the lower court. Generally, theories presented to high appellate courts are more policy-oriented than theories presented to trial courts.

§18.6 Designing a Theory

> Luck is the residue of design.
>
> — *Branch Rickey*

Before the memorandum in Appendix D was written, Goslin undoubtedly showed his lawyer a deed that, on its surface, seemed to give the nephew every right to have Goslin and his belongings removed. A lawyer who lacks the skill of theory design might say to such a client something like this: "Well, Mr. Goslin, you made a mistake. In future, don't give a deed without securing some rights for yourself, either by making a collateral contract or by taking payment for your equity. In the meantime, I think you'll have to move out."

Another — and better — lawyer might look under the surface for possibilities: at the time of the deed, did Goslin believe he was giving up all his property rights? Did he think he was going to continue to live in the house? Had the nephew said or done anything that would show that the nephew thought Goslin was making a gift or was going to move out? Is there anything in the history of this uncle and this nephew on which some sort of reliance theory might be based? Since people tend not to negotiate with their relatives at arm's-length or with written contracts, and since people do turn on each other even in family relationships, might some part of the law go so far as to enforce understandings between relatives, even if those understandings have never been spoken or written down? Notice the technique: first, open doors to factual possibilities; then discover how the law treats those possibilities and find out whether there is evidence to prove them.

A theory will not spring forth in final form from your mind. Instead, a germ first occurs and then grows as new information is learned and more law researched. Although research guides the growth of the theory, the theory also guides the course of the research, each filling in the gaps of the other. Sometimes, there is rapid progress; at other times, it may be painfully slow. More than at any other time in legal writing, this is when you depend on the creative process described in §18.3.

George Vetter[1] has described a sequence of steps in the development of a theory of the case:

> First, isolate the legal and factual issues in the case. Be sure about the nodes on which the case will turn. . . .

What will really matter to the court? Every case has some aspects that have distressed the client or the attorney but will be greeted in court with profound boredom. There are certain kinds of suffering that — for good reasons or bad — have no effect whatever on the typical judge. Some suffering can be dismissed on the ground that it is too small to merit judicial intervention, or that it is as much the client's own fault as anybody else's, or that it represents problems courts cannot solve. Conversely, every case has some aspects that both client and attorney would like to forget but will nevertheless strongly influence a judge. The client may have suffered a wrong, for example, but only while doing something that judges find grossly unacceptable. Or the other side might enjoy one of the traditional advantages in court: it might, for instance, be engaged in one of those industries that courts like to protect. Every theory has to take these into account. Omit things that courts will ignore anyway, and find ways of explaining away things that otherwise would harm the client's case.

> Next, take an objective look at the proof pro and con on these issues.

What propositions of law and fact will you be able to prove to the satisfaction of the court? And what propositions of law and fact will your adversary be able to demonstrate (and in so doing, damage you)? Be realistic about the people in the courthouse and the way they are likely to deal with your case.

> Third, pin-point the critical areas. This means assessing and weighing the results of the analysis on the first two points. . . . At this stage, you must begin to think about how to exploit your strong points and your opponent's weak points, and how to shore up your weak points and attack your opponent's strong points.

---

§18.6   1. George Vetter, *Successful Civil Litigation* 32-33 (1977).

What are your best facts? What facts cause you anxiety? What are your strongest and weakest points in the law? In procedure? In policy? And in the human equities of the situation?

> Fourth, come up with a tentative theory and check it against the . . . bench marks [in §18.5]. If it falls way below the marks, scrap it. If it partially passes muster, set about strengthening it. . . .

This step is a transition between solution-generation and solution-evaluation (see §18.3). The best way to make an objective assessment is to pretend to be the adjudicator and to ask yourself how persuaded you would be by the theory you are considering. Forget that it is your own theory you are judging, and be as skeptical, impatient, and pragmatic as the typical judge can be.

> Fifth, as you strengthen and develop the theory, keep checking it against the bench marks.

Now you are moving back and forth between solution-generation and solution-evaluation. As evaluation reveals problems, generation is used to find solutions.

> Finally, from the time you begin to develop a theory, try it out on a colleague. It is too easy to miss the forest for the trees deep in the preparation of a case.

This process of theory development is the most important — and perhaps the most satisfying — form of creativity in a litigator's work.

§18.7 Imagery and Story-Telling

Imagery has a powerful effect in theory development. That is because the process of finding solutions is filled with "inner monologues, crystallized concepts, reveries, fleeting as well as generic images, abstract pictures, visualized movements, and subjective feelings."[1] Thinking in images helps to find new ways of looking at things that would otherwise be iron-bound givens.

A truck runs off the highway, through a farmer's fence, and over the farmer's cow. The truck driver's insurance company wants to pay as little as possible for this cow, and the farmer, of course, wants more.

The insurance company's lawyer wants to treat the cow as "a unit of livestock" or "a farm asset." The insurance company would be much better off litigating this as a question about how much money the farmer is entitled

§18.7 1. Vera John-Steiner, *Notebooks of the Mind: Explorations of Thinking* 87 (1985).

to for the replacement of a machine-like object that consumes grass as fuel to produce milk and an occasional calf. The farmer's books can be gone over to determine the productivity of this object, its purchase price, depreciation, useful life remaining at the time of its destruction, etc.

The farmer's lawyer, on the other hand, wants to know if the cow had any other value. The lawyer asks the farmer some questions. "That wasn't just any cow," replies the farmer.

> That was Bessie! She was the only Guernsey cow left in this county. She didn't give that thin milk you get out of a Holstein. She gave the thickest, most flavorful milk you ever tasted. We didn't sell it to the dairy. We drank it ourselves and made the best butter and cheese out of it. And Guernseys are smaller cows. They're friendly, like pets, and Bessie was like part of our family.

The persuasive weight of each of these theories is in the imagery of what we *see*. The farmer's lawyer wants us to see a big pair of Guernsey eyes in a head that is nudging the farmer with affection — a loss to the farmer's family that includes but is greater than the loss of a grass-to-milk machine. The insurance company's lawyer wants us to see the farmer's balance sheet, where a certain item of livestock is carried as an asset valued at a certain number of dollars. In any writing that grows out of this controversy, the farmer's lawyer probably will not mention Bessie's head nudging the farmer, and the insurance company's lawyer probably will not mention the balance sheet — because those things are not, strictly speaking, relevant to the legal controversy. But if they are good writers, these lawyers will include enough relevant detail so that we will see these scenes anyway because they are implied.

If you develop an eye for revealing detail, your theories will much more quickly come to life as vivid, compelling stories. Vividness not only helps the reader remember the story (and the theory it embodies), but it makes the story and the theory more believable. Imagery makes a theory real.

Exercise.   Escape from Prison? (Developing a Theory)

Orville Bradwyn is charged with the crime of escape from prison. The state's sole witness was Benjamin Tunmeyer, a prison guard, who testified as follows.

Q: Please tell the court what you observed and did at 6:30 in the evening on the sixth of July.

A: I was checking prisoners in the dinner line. Prisoners are required to be in there at that time, and any prisoner who has not shown up for dinner is considered missing. The defendant did not appear. I then checked his cell. Some material had been put in his bed, bunched up so that it looked like somebody was asleep there. His radio had been left on. But he was gone.

Q: What did you do?

A: We searched the grounds outside the prison. We didn't find the defendant there, so we searched inside the prison — first the perimeter, and then the inside of buildings and containers where someone might hide. We finally found him in the laundry room at 7:39 P.M.

Q: What did he have with him?

A: All of his clothing.

Q: Does the prison wash the laundry of any other institution?

A: Yes, we do the laundry for the state hospital down the road. It's done in the same laundry room where we found the defendant.

Q: How is the hospital's laundry transported to and from the prison?

A: By truck. The hospital's truck brings in it in the morning and picks it up at about 8 P.M.

Q: Are prisoners permitted in the laundry room in the evening?

A: No prisoner is allowed in that room after 5 P.M. Hiding in one of the hospital's laundry bags is an obvious way to escape from the prison.

Q: What precautions are taken to prevent that?

A: At 5 P.M., a guard makes sure all prisoners assigned to work in the laundry have left, and then the door is locked. In addition, the guard opens up each laundry bag that goes to the state hospital and makes sure it has only laundry in it. Then he locks up the room and locks another door on the corridor leading to the laundry room. Nobody is inside those doors until the hospital's truck arrives about three hours later.

Q: What guard was assigned that responsibility on the night in question.

A: Me. I sent out all the prisoners and satisfactorily inspected the state hospital's bags. Then, I locked the doors and left.

Q: Was Mr. Bradwyn assigned to work in the laundry?

A: Yes. But he was not scheduled to work in the laundry room on the day in question.

Cross-examination:

Q: Are you familiar with Mr. Bradwyn's reputation among other prisoners and among corrections officers?

A: He is an exceptionally tidy person.

Q: Were there any prior occasions on which you and Mr. Bradwyn had shouting matches?

A: Yes. It's almost impossible to inspect his cell. He starts yelling the minute you touch any of his things. He says he doesn't like them moved.

Q: What was the defendant doing when you found him?

A: He was washing his clothes. No, actually, he was drying them. They were in the dryer.

Q: What items of clothing were in the dryer?

A: Both of his prison uniforms — prisoners are issued two — socks, undershirts, undershorts. They were still wet.

Q: What did you find when you searched Mr. Bradwyn's cell?

A: Letters from his family, personal photographs, letters from his lawyer, an address book.

Q: Before dinner, prisoners are free to move about outside their cells, aren't they?

A: Yes.

Q: And the same is true after dinner, isn't it?
A: Until 7:30.

After this testimony, the prosecution rested. Bradwyn moved to dismiss on the ground that the prosecution had presented insufficient evidence to convict.

Develop two theories that satisfy the criteria in §18.5. One theory should support Bradwyn and his motion. The other should support the prosecution and oppose the motion. Use the method outlined in §18.6.

The relevant statute and cases interpreting it appear below:

CRIMINAL CODE § 745

If any person committed to prison shall break and escape therefrom or shall escape or leave without authority any building, camp, or any place whatsoever in which he is placed or to which he is directed to go or in which he is allowed to be, he shall be deemed guilty of an escape and shall be punished by imprisonment for a term not to exceed five years, to commence immediately upon the expiration of the term of his previous sentence.

STATE v. HORSTMAN

The crime of escape is established by proof that the defendant was confined in a prison and escaped from such confinement or departed without authority from a place to which he or she was duly assigned. Unauthorized departure is the gravamen of the offense.

STATE v. CAHILL

While incarcerated, the defendant was placed in solitary confinement for fighting with another prisoner. A guard inadvertently left the cell door unlocked. The defendant got out and was apprehended on top of the prison wall.

The defendant argues that the evidence does not prove that he committed the crime of escape because there is no evidence that he escaped from the custody of the Department of Prisons. He argues that, at most, he is guilty of the lesser crime of attempted escape.

The crime of escape was complete, however, when the defendant got out of his cell. The crime can be committed without leaving the prison as a whole. It is enough that the defendant left a place where he was confined within the prison.

STATE v. LIGGETT

The defendant was incarcerated and assigned to work in the prison shop manufacturing auto license plates. On the day in question, the defendant was reported absent from his shift in the license plate shop. After a prolonged search, he was found inside a machine in the prison cannery, using a pillow, and reading a novel.

The evidence does not prove beyond a reasonable doubt that the defendant committed the crime of escape. He failed to report for work in one part of the prison and, without authorization, spent the time in another part. That might violate prison rules and merit internal prison discipline, but it is not the crime of escape.

19 Developing Persuasive Arguments

§19.1 What Judges Expect from Written Argumentation

You already know some things about how judges think: in our system of litigation the lawyers — and not the judge — frame the issues, develop the theories and arguments, and adduce the evidence. Judges are busy people who view any assertion skeptically and who must make many decisions in limited periods of time. Thus, they need complete but concise arguments that can be quickly understood.

In addition, there is so much litigation now that courts are increasingly dependent on written arguments submitted by attorneys. Many — perhaps most — appeals today are decided without oral argument and without any other personal contact between attorneys and judges. On appeal the written brief bears the primary burden of persuading the court. A similar evolution is occurring in trial courts. It is not unusual today for a judge to complete a case without a trial, without a hearing, without an oral argument, without a conference in chambers, and solely on the basis of the attorneys' written submissions in connection with a motion to dismiss or a motion for summary judgment.

Judges are evaluated on their skill at the art of judging — not on whether they know all the law. Although judges know a great deal about rules of procedure (which they use constantly), they usually know less about individual rules of substantive law (which come up less often). And in most courts judges cannot specialize in particular areas of substantive law: they must decide any case you bring before them. Unless a case turns on parts of the law about which a judge has thought deeply lately, the judge depends on the attorneys to show what the law is and how it governs the case. And a judge knows nothing at all about the facts of a case except for what can be learned through the attorneys and their evidence.

Judges will want you to *teach* them your case. Think of a motion memorandum or appellate brief as a *manual on how to make a particular decision* (and — by implication — how to write the opinion that justifies that decision). Because important decisions are hard to make and can worry the decision-maker, a lawyer who can show the court how the decision should be made, laying out all the steps of logic, stands a much better chance of influencing the result.

If done in a respectful tone, this is not as presumptuous as you might think. If you have prepared properly, you will know much more about the decision than the judge will. But you must teach the court without insulting its intelligence, and you must do so in the clearest and most concise manner possible. Judges will find it hard to rule in your favor if you are condescending or if you waste their time.

§19.2 Argumentation Techniques

A carefully prepared, carefully stated, lawyer-like written argument is a work of art and a joy forever.

— *E. Barrett Prettyman*

Argumentation is not the pushy expression of one's opinions. (Many people are eager to state their views, but only some are able to do so persuasively.) Nor is it a random collection of stray comments that sound good for the arguer's client. Those kinds of comments might be useful raw materials, but they become an argument only when they coalesce into a coherent presentation that *influences* the audience.

Argumentation should *affect* the reader. Good argumentation leads readers through reasoning so convincingly that they are pleased to be persuaded. In designing an argument,[1] your initial question should be "What will make the reader want to agree with me?"

This section explains some of the basic argumentation techniques:

1. Design a compelling theory and back it up with compelling arguments.
2. Include both motivating arguments and justifying arguments.
3. Limit your contentions to those that have a reasonable chance of persuading the court.
4. Organize to emphasize the ideas that are most likely to persuade.

§19.2 1. Uncapitalized, "argument" means a contention designed to persuade. Capitalized, it means the largest portion of a motion memorandum or appellate brief. There might be many arguments in an Argument.

5. Make your organization obvious.
6. Give the court a clear statement of the rule or rules on which the case turns.
7. Rely on an appropriate amount of authority with appropriate amounts of explanation.
8. Explain exactly and in detail how the law governs the facts.
9. To the extent they advance the theory, make the facts and people involved come alive on the written page.
10. Show the judge how you should prevail from a policy standpoint.
11. Reinforce the theory with carefully chosen wording.
12. Confront the weaknesses in your case openly.
13. Enhance your credibility through careful editing and through the appearance of the memorandum or brief.
14. Make it easy for the judge to rule in your favor.

Each of these techniques requires strategic decisions on your part. If you think these decisions through carefully, you should be able to explain your work by answering the litany of strategy questions in §18.2.

You will find the following material easier to understand if you read the motion memorandum in Appendix D before continuing here.

1. Design a compelling theory and back it up with compelling arguments. Until you provide proof, a judge will not believe anything you say. In litigation writing, proof is a well-argued theory that compels a decision favorable to your client. You can develop a theory through the process described in §§18.6-18.7. And the quality of your theory can be measured by the criteria set out in §18.5. But even a good theory does not sell unless it is argued.

A persuasive argument is neither extravagant nor belligerent. To a judge, extreme statements sound unreliable. Because judges are experienced, professional skeptics, they are rarely fooled by inaccurate or farfetched statements, and when they find such a statement in an argument, in their view a dust of untrustworthiness settles over the theory and the lawyer involved. Judges usually have what Hemingway, in another context, called "a built-in, shock-proof, shit detector."[2] Because you cannot afford to be seen as unreliable, you need to be similarly equipped so that you can examine — with a judge's skepticism — each statement you contemplate making. In addition to the skills explained here, it helps to have a mature and thorough understanding of human nature (some of which can be acquired in law school, even if it is not listed in the catalog).

It is not enough that everything you say is believable. You might be so reasonable that you cannot win because — although the judge might believe all you say — your individual statements, even when taken together, do not add up to proof that your client is entitled to what you have asked for. A good theory and good arguments are reasonable and accurate, appear reliable, and make your client's victory appear *inevitable* — either because the

---

2. *Writers At Work: The Paris Review Interviews, Second Series* 239 (George Plimpton ed. 1965).

higher courts will reverse any other result, or because it is the only right thing to do, or both. The feeling of inevitability is a judge's selling point. It is reached by laying out for the judge every step of logic so that the advocate's conclusion becomes more and more irresistible as the argument proceeds. A judge knows when the selling point approaches, because the job of deciding seems to grow easier.

2. *Include both motivating arguments and justifying arguments.* Both are needed to persuade.

A motivating argument is one that causes a judge to *want* to decide a case in a particular way. It causes the judge to feel that any other decision would be unjust. Motivating arguments tend to be centered on facts or a combination of facts and policy. Greatly oversimplified, the following are the primary motivating arguments in the sample motion memorandum and appellate briefs in the appendices:

Appendix D:	A manipulative nephew should not be allowed to cheat his generous and trusting uncle in this way.
Appendix E:	The defendant was only following accepted medical treatment for a recognized illness, and the law should leave her alone.
Appendix F:	The defendant and his friends had misrepresented their true identities, and a crime-ridden society is threatened when people do that.

(In all three appendices, notes in the margins show you where motivating arguments are being made.)

A justifying argument is one that shows that the law either requires or permits the result urged by the arguer. Justifying arguments are centered on legal rules or on a combination of rules and policy. Again oversimplified, the following are the main justifying arguments in the sample motion memo and briefs in the appendices:

Appendix D:	These facts satisfy the test for a constructive trust.
Appendix E:	The defendant was not disguised within the meaning of the statute. And if she was, the statute would violate the constitutional right to privacy.
Appendix F:	The defendant was disguised within the meaning of the statute. And the statute does not violate the constitutional right to privacy.

The first-year of law school is designed, among other things, to teach you how to make justifying arguments. (You probably understood something of motivating arguments even before you came to law school, although you will learn more about making them.)

In judicial opinions, justifying arguments are usually developed in much detail while motivating arguments are only hinted at. The hints are found most often in the court's recitations of the facts. Have you had the feeling, while reading the first few paragraphs of an opinion, that you knew how the case would be decided before the court had told you — and even before the court had begun to discuss the law? If so, it was probably because you noticed in the fact recitation clues about which facts had motivated the court.

Why do you need both motivating arguments and justifying arguments? A motivating argument alone is not enough because even a motivated judge is not supposed to act without a solid legal justification. Judges understandably want to feel that they are doing a professional job of judging, and they can be reversed on appeal if they fail to justify their actions within the law.

And a justifying argument alone is not enough because, in a large number of cases, a justifying argument, without more, will not persuade. The law can usually be interpreted in more than one reasonable way. When a judge is given a choice between two conflicting justifying arguments, each of which is reasonable, the judge will take the one he or she is motivated to take. (Judges are, after all, human.)

Remember what Karl Llewellyn wrote: "rules *guide*, but they do not *control* decision. There is no precedent the judge may not at his need either file down to razor thinness or expand into a bludgeon."[3] (See §11.6.)

3. Limit your contentions to those that have a reasonable chance of persuading the court.

You might be tempted to throw in every good thing you can think of about your theory and every bad thing about your adversary's theory, assuming that all this cannot hurt and might help. That is "shotgun" writing, and it hurts more than it helps. Instead, focus sharply on the strong contentions. Develop them fully, and leave out the weak ones. As Holmes put it: "strike for the jugular and let the rest go."[4] That creates a document that is more compact but, paradoxically, explores more deeply the ideas on which the decision will be based.

A good argument begins by subduing the judge's skepticism into a general feeling of *confidence* that the theory can be relied on, and then, on that foundation of confidence, it builds a feeling that your client is the *inevitable* winner. Weak contentions interfere with this. They excite skepticism, rather than quieting it. If a judge believes that you have indiscriminately mixed unreliable contentions with seemingly attractive ones, the judge's natural temptation is to dismiss the whole lot as not worthy of confidence, for the same reason that a person considering the purchase of a house justifiably suspects the integrity of the entire structure after cracked beams are found in the attic. Just as it is the builder's job to select only sturdy materials, so it is the lawyer's job — and not the judge's — to separate out the weak ideas

3. K. N. Llewellyn, *The Bramble Bush* 180 (1930).
4. Oliver Wendell Holmes, *Speeches* 77 (1934).

before the memorandum or brief is submitted. A judge has neither the time nor the inclination to delete all the suspect material and then reassemble the remainder into something sturdier.

When you determine whether a contention has a reasonable chance to persuade, you are, of course, making a predictive judgment. A "reasonable chance" does not mean certainty and might not even mean probability. To be worth making, however, a contention should have the capacity to seem tempting and attractive to a judge.

4. Organize to emphasize the ideas that are most likely to persuade.

Remember that you will make both motivating arguments and justifying arguments. Justifying arguments can be organized through the paradigm structures you have already learned because they are conventional proofs of a conclusion of law. Motivating arguments, on the other hand, are more often appeals to a human sense of justice or pragmatic policy needs. When you add motivating arguments, you may vary the paradigm structure in radical ways (many of which would not work in predictive writing). In part, that is because motivating arguments should be introduced very early in a presentation, preferably in the first paragraph.

To merge motivating and justifying arguments, do this: First, write a justifying argument structured in the paradigm format you have already learned. Then start adding motivating arguments wherever they seem relevant to what you have already written. Finally, write an opening paragraph that sums up your motivating arguments.[5] (This is illustrated in the memorandum in Appendix D and in the appellate briefs in Appendices E and F. See the notes in the appendix margins.)

The opening paragraph that introduces the motivating argument should precede all statements of rules, proof of those rules, and rule application. Word for word, the opening paragraph is the most powerful argumentative passage you can write. It is worth rewriting and rewriting many times until it introduces your motivating arguments in the most persuasive way.

Why is it so important to introduce the motivating arguments first? There are several reasons. Most importantly, it tracks the way many judges think. They act on what motivates them unless it cannot be justified. Motivation is established first, the need to justify afterward. Moreover, early impressions tend to color how later material is read, and, like most people, a judge reads most carefully at the beginning. In addition, because judges are so busy, they expect the strongest material first. If they find themselves reading weak material early, they assume that nothing better follows and stop reading altogether.

(You probably read a newspaper in the same way: you expect the most important or most entertaining material near the beginning of a story, and when you have had enough, you stop reading and go on to something else. Newspaper editors know that, and newspaper stories are written with the

---

5. With more experience, you will be able to write motivating and justifying arguments at the same time, or even to write the motivating argument before you write the justifying argument.

least valuable material at the end, so that readers can decide how much of a story to read. Just as your method of reading a newspaper would be thrown off if the most valuable material were strewn randomly throughout the story, so a judge's method of reading a memorandum or a brief would become muddled if the strongest arguments might appear anywhere.)

Thus, judges will expect you to get immediately to the point. A judge quickly becomes impatient with long prefatory passages of historical background because that kind of material is rarely useful in making a decision. Even in a constitutional case where the issue is the drafters' intent one or two centuries ago, the historical material is part of the argument, not a preface to it. An argument — and even a predictive memorandum — written in the style of a law review article is considered especially offensive because law review writing aims to be densely encyclopedic and is not focused to assist decision-making.

Michael Fontham has said that the "best strategy is to strike quickly, establish momentum, and maintain the advantage through a forceful presentation of contentions selected for their persuasive effect."[6] Focus the reader's thoughts on the ideas that can cause you to win.

In general, the most persuasive sequence is to present first the issues on which you are most likely to win; within issues, to make your strongest arguments first; and, within arguments, to make your strongest contentions and use your best authority first.

For example, if your adversary must prove that a five-element test has been satisfied, and if you think that your adversary's proof is weakest on element number three, do not argue the elements in the order in which they are listed in the controlling statute. Argue number three first because as far as you are concerned, it is the controlling element. (Your adversary, however, might do either of two things. She might argue them in exactly the order listed in the statute, to build a feeling of cumulating persuasion. Or if some elements are extremely easy to prove, she might get them out of the way first and then concentrate on the ones where the battle is concentrated.)

Sometimes, however, the logic of the dispute requires that the strongest material be delayed to avoid confusing the court. Some arguments are simply hard to understand unless preceded by less punchy material. In these situations, you must weigh your need for clarity against your need to show merit from the start.

5. *Make your organization obvious.* You cannot afford to let the judge grope for clues about how your contentions are related to each other. Instead, use the techniques of forceful writing[7] to help the judge see your focus. Very soon after you begin to discuss each issue, tell the judge exactly what your theory is. Use a thesis sentence to state each contention before you begin to prove it. And use transitional words and phrases to show how your contentions are cumulative:

6. Michael R. Fontham, *Written and Oral Advocacy* 108 (1985).
7. See §15.3.

There are three reasons why ... First, ... Second, ... And finally, ...

Not only has the defendant violated ... , but she has also ...

6. Give the court a clear statement of the rule or rules on which the case turns. That rule might not be exactly as stated in the cases to which you cite. In fact, the cases might enforce the rule without stating it at all, and you might have to figure out what the rule is from the court's reasoning, particularly the way it treats the facts. (See §3.2.)

The judge who reads your Argument needs what Karl Llewellyn called the advocate's "own clean phrasing of the rule," together with "a passage which so clearly and rightly states and crystallizes the background and the result that it is *recognized* on sight as doing the needed work and as practically demanding to be lifted into the opinion."[8] Particularly in appellate courts, judges know that they will have to write an opinion justifying their decision, and that the opinion should be as convincing as possible to the parties, to the bar, to the public, and to any still higher court to which the decision could be appealed. That is a hard task where a gap in the law must be filled. The judge who asks in oral argument in a gap-filling case, "Counselor, what rule would you have us enforce?" really wants to know how — if the lawyer prevails — the court should word the second component of the paradigm when it writes the opinion.

As you already know, for any given rule, the authority can usually be interpreted to support several different formulations from broad to narrow. In choosing one formulation over another, balance two separate factors. First, out of any given set of authority, some rule formulations are more likely than others to be accepted by a court. And second, some formulations more logically support the client's position. The trick is to find a formulation that does both.

7. Rely on an appropriate amount of authority with appropriate amounts of explanation. To rule in your favor, a court would need to believe that you have provided sufficient authority, although the typical judge is unwilling to tolerate an exhaustive explanation of every case you cite. How do you steer a middle course between underciting and overciting and between underexplaining and overexplaining?

Begin by predicting the amount of citation and explanation a skeptical but busy judge would need. Then carefully study the available authorities. Place in a "major authority" category those that are likely to *influence* the court and in a "peripheral" category those that are merely somewhat related to the issue. Think in terms of cause and effect: if you had to make the judge's decision, which authorities would be most likely to have an effect on you, *even an effect adverse to your clients' position*? Those are the authorities you must discuss, and many of them are best discussed in detail. Pe-

---

8. Karl Nickerson Llewellyn, *The Common Law Tradition: Deciding Appeals* 241 (1960) (emphasis in original).

ripheral authorities should eventually be discarded unless they are needed to fill holes in your argument not settled by the major authorities.

The quantity of authority and the volume of explanation will depend on how much is needed to clarify the issue involved, how disputed that issue is, and how important it is to your theory. At one extreme, an idea may be so complex, so disputed, and so critical that it must be supported by a comprehensive explanation, filling many pages, of major authorities. At the other extreme, if the court is apt to be satisfied with a mere conclusory explanation, you should limit citation to one or, at the very most, two cases. If an idea is undisputed and routine, such as an uncontested procedural test,[9] it should be enough to cite, with little or no explanation, the most recent decision from the highest court in the jurisdiction that has invoked the test.

The point is to give the court confidence that you are right without tiring its patience.

8. Explain exactly and in detail how the law governs the facts.

A court rules for one party over another not merely because the law is abstractly favorable, but, more importantly, because the law and facts *combine* favorably. The judge often reaches the selling point only where the law and facts are finally combined — woven together — to show that what the writer wants is inevitable. Beginners sometimes devote so much attention to the law that they overlook the final step of arguing the facts — weaving the law into the facts to show the court precisely how the decision should be made. After all the work of explaining the law, a beginner might assume that the application to the facts is obvious, but it hardly ever is. Do not assume that merely mentioning the facts is enough: *show* the court exactly how the determinative facts require the decision you seek.

9. To the extent they advance the theory, make the facts and people involved come alive on the written page.

As the judge looks at the facts of your case, you want him or her to see more than "a narrative of events arranged in their time-sequence."[10] You want the judge to see something that reveals character and causality. In fiction, the standard illustration of the difference is from E. M. Forster's classic lectures.[11] When we read "The king died, and then the queen died," we might see in the mind's eye either no image or at best an image of stick-like figures without personality. But when we read "The king died, and then the queen died of grief," we see instead an image of at least one real human being: she may be wearing fairy-tale-like clothing, but she is genuinely suffering as real people do.

When a judge, reading an argument, visualizes stick figures or no image at all, the case seems boring and unimportant, and the judge is not moti-

9. Notice, for example, how the test for a preliminary injunction is proved in the memorandum in Appendix D.

10. E. M. Forster, *Aspects of the Novel* 86 (1927).

11. *Id.*

vated to rule in your favor. But the judge begins to take sides if he or she can visualize real people doing real things to each other. When you read the Argument in the memorandum in Appendix D, you probably took sides at some point. Start reading the argument from the beginning until you find the place at which you began to favor either Goslin or his nephew. What was it that got to you? Was it the *picture* of a 74-year-old man in the home he had lived in for 24 years being treated harshly by younger people who had moved in and were trying to throw him out? If this or similar scenes were to appear in a judge's mind, they would have extraordinary power over the disposition of Goslin's motion because they show who deserves to win and who deserves to lose. In the memorandum in Appendix D, how are mental images created? Find the passages that put them into your mind. What did the writer do to help you see them?

Before you begin to write, make a list on scratch paper of the determinative facts. You will have to discuss those facts to make your argument, and that is where your opportunities occur. For each fact, ask yourself what the fact illustrates about the *people* involved: does it show who is an innocent victim, who is predatory, who is inexcusably foolish, and so forth. For each fact, ask yourself further what the fact illustrates about *what happened:* does it show the events to have been accidental, caused by one person's carelessness, the result of another's greed and cunning, and so on. Only by knowing what each fact reveals can you turn a story into a plot.

When you describe these facts in your writing, do not characterize them with emotion-laden verbiage. Although a fact is determinative because the law coldly makes it so, a judge is capable of forming a human reaction to it. That is not merely because the judge is human, but also because the judge prefers to make decisions that are fundamentally fair. On the other hand, a judge's professional self-image is naturally offended by an argument that reads like political oratory or a story in a tabloid newspaper. *Vividness,* which causes the effect in Goslin's memorandum, is not the same as luridness, which demeans an argument and the judge who reads it. If a fact will seem compelling to a court, that fact will speak for itself. All you will need is a calm description of the fact, in simple words and with enough detail to make the picture vivid. When reading Goslin's Argument, you may have thought that his nephew was deceitful, irresponsible, selfish, manipulative, and cruel — but the writer never called him any of those things. Instead, the writer simply described what happened in such a way that *you* formed those opinions. (Forster did not say that the queen loved the king. He only told you why she died.)

10. Show the judge how you should prevail from a policy standpoint.   Not only must you show the court that your client deserves individually to win, but you also must demonstrate that what you want makes sense in other cases as well. In a system of precedent where rules are to be applied even-handedly, judges want confidence that society will be protected if other like cases are decided as you want your client's case resolved. If a court must choose between competing rules, for example, you should spend more than a little effort showing that the rule you urge is better than others. Even where the rule is settled and the issue is how it should be applied, a court is still less likely to rule in your favor if it is not confident that what you want is, in a very general sense, a good idea.

Policy must be proved with authority. Some policy is openly announced in decisions and statutes, but more often it is implied. Some policy considerations can be found in every era in every American jurisdiction. For example, courts everywhere like solutions that are easily enforceable, promote clarity in the law, are not needlessly complex, and do not allow true wrongdoers to profit from illegal acts. Other policy considerations may differ from state to state. In states such as Arizona, for example, public policy strongly disfavors solutions that interfere with land development, while in states like Vermont policy prefers agriculture, conservation, and the environment. Some states favor providing tort remedies even at some risk to judicial efficiency, although in others the reverse is true. Still other policy considerations differ from era to era. Some activities once greatly favored in the law — such as the building and operation of railroads in the last century — now enjoy no special treatment, while other things — such as a woman's reproductive control over her own body — are now protected in a way they once were not.

Lawyers tend to introduce policy-based arguments with phrasings like the following:

> This court should reject the rule urged by the defendant because it would cause . . .

> Automobile rental companies [or some other category of litigants] should bear the risk of loss because . . .

> Not only is the order requested by the plaintiff not sanctioned by this state's case law, but such an order would violate public policy because . . .

Remember, however, that policy arguments are used to reinforce argument from authority. Only where authority is unusually sparse should policy arguments play the predominant role in a theory.

11. Reinforce the theory with carefully chosen wording. Choose words in part for the effect they should have on the reader.

The careful use of words can advance the ideas that make up your theory. For example, in the memorandum in Appendix D, the transaction between Goslin and his nephew is called a "transfer" infrequently, and then only because it is absolutely necessary in satisfying the third element of the test for a constructive trust. Otherwise, "deed" is used because the writer's theory is that Goslin continues to hold certain property rights to his home, the deed being only partial evidence of what really happened. The continual use of "deed" reminds the judge of the writer's limited interpretation of the transaction: Goslin gave his nephew a piece of paper that transferred legal but not equitable ownership. If used often, "transfer" would have implied a concession psychologically, and perhaps intellectually as well.

Notice also that, although the writer says the nephew has "not yet recip-rocated" the tuition help he received from Goslin, the writer does not argue that the nephew has failed to "repay." If a sum has not been "repaid," it is borrowed money, and there is no evidence that the tuition money was a loan. The writer's theory is instead that the nephew's moral obligation to help a relative was heightened by the earlier tuition assistance, and that Goslin reasonably thought "at the time of the deed" that his nephew was trying to help him keep — rather than lose — his property. To call it "re-payment" would only arouse the court's skepticism. The idea of "recipro-cation" does the same job without running that risk.

Do you begin to see how carefully you must choose words to advance your theory precisely and not to confuse it?

Within limits, you can even advance the theory through the way you refer to the parties. Whenever the reader meets the plaintiff in the memorandum in Appendix D, the latter appears with dignity as "Mr. Goslin." Even if his neighbors might know him to treat people and pets vilely and to have vicious opinions that offend all decent-minded folk, he is a sympathetic figure in litigation as long as the court knows him to be "Mr. Goslin," the elderly widower who only wants to live out his last days in his own home. Herbert Skeffington, however, is always "the nephew" or "the defendant," with no dignity other than his role as nephew and with no personality other than what he reveals about himself through the way he treats his uncle. While he is the shadowy "nephew," it is easier to think him capable of deceit, greed, and cold-bloodedness. But if the judge were to think of him as Mr. Skeffing-ton — and to think of the other interlopers as Mr. Skeffington's wife Amelia and their children Wendy and Tom, aged respectively eight and four — it is a little harder to think ill of them.[12]

Simple, concrete words can paint the pictures on which your theory is based. In the memorandum in Appendix D, notice how facts are described almost entirely in short, everyday words with very specific meanings. That is so not only of Goslin's facts, but also of the facts of the precedents on which the argument is based.

But readers see scenes only where writers have given some concrete de-scriptions to build on. The knack is, first, to isolate the very few facts that are determinative under the law and therefore essential to the scene, and then to describe those facts in words that are simple and concrete enough

---

12. Here are the customs on referring to parties in persuasive writing: In civil cases, you can try to humanize the client by using his or her name while depersonalizing the opposing party by referring instead to that party's status out of court ("the airline"), or in court ("the plaintiff"), or both ("the defendant insurance company"). If the opposing party already has a well-defined identity, you might refer to both parties by name ("Pennzoil has sued Texaco because . . ."). Appellate courts, however, will become confused if you refer to the parties as "the appellant" or "the appellee," and many prohibit it, preferring instead references to the parties' statuses in the trial court ("plaintiff," "defendant") or to the identities on which the dispute is based ("the city," "the employee"). *See, e.g.,* Rule 28(d) of the Federal Rules of Appellate Procedure. Virtually all courts — trial and appellate — will allow you to refer to your own client by name. In criminal cases, the prosecution usually refers to the other party as "the defendant," or — if there are more than one — "defendant Brooks" and "de-fendant Martini." The defendant's attorney, on the other hand, will generally use the defen-dant's name: "Mr. Brooks" or "Mrs. Martini."

for the desired image to come quickly into the reader's mind. This is simple and concrete:

> The two had seen each other at least monthly since the nephew was a boy.

This is not:

> The two had occasion to come together for social and family purposes on a periodic and regular basis of at least once each month since the nephew's extreme youth.

Did you see an image when you read the first example? Maybe a front door opened; people greeted each other as they do at family gatherings; and so on. Did you see an equally vivid image when you read the second example?

You can do harm with words that claim too much. The first example below is actually less persuasive than the second:

> It is obvious, therefore, that the defendant clearly understood the consequences of his acts.

> Therefore, the defendant understood the consequences of his acts.

In the first example, "It is obvious" and "clearly" supply no extra meaning. Instead, they divert the reader's attention from the message of the sentence. Judges assume that expressions like these are used to cover up a lack of logical proof.

12. Confront the weaknesses in your case openly. Hiding from problems will not make them go away. You have to confront and defeat them. "Be truthful in exposing . . . the difficulties in your case," an appellate judge has written. "Tell us what they are and how you expect to deal with them."[13] If you do not do that, the court will assume that you have no arguments worth making on the subject. Section 19.4 explains how to confront your problems and overcome them.

13. Enhance your credibility through careful editing and through the appearance of the memorandum or brief. Help the judge to trust you. Understandably, judges do not trust easily. Their decisions are important ones, and you will always face at least one competing attorney with another theory to sell. A judge will more readily trust you if you appear to be careful, thorough, and professional. For that reason, a document is more persuasive if its appearance is flawless.

Edit out every form of intellectual sloppiness: inaccuracies; imprecision; incorrectly used terms of art; errors with citations and other matters of format and layout; mistakes with the English language, its spelling and punc-

---

13. Roger J. Miner, *Twenty-five "Dos" for Appellate Brief Writers*, 3 Scribes J. Leg. Writing 19, 24 (1992).

tuation; typographical errors; invective and unnecessary personal statements about parties, attorneys, or judges; and empty remarks that do not
advance the argument (such as rhetorical questions and irrelevant histories
of the law). Any of those would suggest a lawyer who cannot be relied on —
and judges will be quick to draw that inference.

14. Make it easy for the judge to rule in your favor. Judges are
overburdened with so many cases that you must assume a certain amount
of fatigue. If a memorandum or brief is frustrating, it will be ignored. Instead, submit a document that is ingratiatingly easy to read and use. Think
about the problems a judge would have with the document, and solve
them before submission. Not only should the writing be clear, concise,
and focused sharply on the issue at hand, but the type should be easy
to read; margins should be large enough that each page does not look op-
pressively dense; and headings should look like headings (and not like
part of the text). A visually inviting document is more likely to be read with
care.

§19.3   Argumentation Ethics

Advocacy is not a free-for-all. The rules of professional ethics[1] place limits
on what a lawyer is permitted to do in argument.

First and most basically, a lawyer is forbidden to "[k]nowingly make a
false statement of law or fact" to a court.[2] The whole system of adjudication
would break down if lawyers did not speak honestly to courts.

Second, a lawyer is required to inform a court of "legal authority *in the
controlling jurisdiction* known to the lawyer to be *directly adverse* to the
position of the [lawyer's] client and not disclosed by opposing counsel."[3] The
system of adjudication would suffer immeasurably if courts could not depend on lawyers to give a full account of controlling law. (Section 19.4 explores ways to comply with this requirement while least damaging your
case.)

---

§19.3   1. Nearly every state has adopted one or the other of two model codes on professional ethics drafted by the American Bar Association. The older of the two is the Model
Code of Professional Responsibility, which dates from 1969. The newer is the 1983 Model
Rules of Professional Conduct. The usual method of adoption is by incorporation into the
state's court rules. Many states have made changes, small or large, in whichever code they
have adopted. California has rejected both ABA codes and written its own set of rules. A
lawyer who violates the applicable code can be censured, suspended, or disbarred. A state's
code of professional ethics is statute-like, with a body of interpretive case law.
  2. Model Code of Professional Responsibility, DR 7-102(A)(5). The same prohibition, in
virtually the same words, appears in Rule 3.3(a)(1) of the Model Rules of Professional Conduct.
  3. Model Rules of Professional Conduct, Rule 3.3(a)(3) (emphasis added). The same requirement, in virtually the same words, appears in Disciplinary Rule 7-106(B)(1) of the
Model Code of Professional Responsibility.

Third, a lawyer is not permitted to advance a theory or argument that is "frivolous"[4] or "unwarranted under existing law,"[5] except that a lawyer may make a "good faith argument for an extension, modification or reversal of existing law."[6] In a legal system like ours, where "the law is not always clear and never is static," the rules of ethics permit a lawyer to advance theories and arguments that take advantage "of the law's ambiguities and potential for change."[7] But a frivolous theory or argument — one that stands little chance of being adopted by a court — is unfair to courts and to opposing parties because it wastes their time, effort, and resources.

Separate court rules — procedural, rather than ethical in nature — also punish lawyers who make frivolous arguments. In federal trial courts, for example, every "written motion, or other paper" must be signed by an attorney, whose signature certifies "that to the best of the [signer's] knowledge, information, and belief, formed after inquiry reasonable under the circumstances . . . the claims, defenses, and other legal contentions therein are warranted by existing law or by a nonfrivolous argument for the extension, modification, or reversal of existing law or the establishment of new law."[8] Where that standard is violated, the court has the power to impose monetary fines on the offending lawyer.[9] Similar rules govern in appellate courts.[10]

§19.4 What to Do About Adverse Authority and Arguments

Adverse authority will not go away just because you ignore it: if the court does not find it, opposing counsel probably will. There are, in fact, a number of reasons for you to address adverse authority. First, as you have just read, the ethical rules require it. Second, a lawyer who ignores adverse authority is seen by courts as unreliable and unpersuasive, while a lawyer who speaks with candor is more easily trusted and respected by the bench. Third, a lawyer who ignores adverse authority throws away the opportunity — often the only opportunity — to give the court reasons for not following it. The first reason applies only to authority within "the controlling jurisdiction," but the others apply to any adverse authority that can be predicted to influence the court, even precedent from other jurisdictions.

---

4. Model Rules of Professional Conduct, Rule 3.1.
5. Model Code of Professional Responsibility, DR 7-102(A)(2).
6. These words appear in both codes. Model Rules of Professional Conduct, Rule 3.1; Model Code of Professional Responsibility, DR 7-102(A)(2).
7. Drafters' comment to Model Rules of Professional Conduct, Rule 3.1.
8. Fed. R. Civ. P. 11.
9. *Id.*
10. For example: "If a court of appeals shall determine that an appeal is frivolous, it may award just damages and single or double costs to the appellee." Fed. R. App. P. 38.

If the authority is a statute, court rule, or administrative regulation, you must show that the provision was not intended to govern the controversy, or that it was intended to govern it but favorably to your client, or that the provision itself is not law. The last is the least often successful. Although it may seem tempting to argue, for example, that a statute you do not like is unconstitutional, courts rarely sustain such attacks. In fact, if a statute or similar provision is susceptible to more than one meaning, courts are obliged to choose one that would not violate a controlling constitution. You should frontally attack a statute only if there is significant doubt — shared by respected lawyers — about its validity.

If the adverse authority is precedent, consider distinguishing it, focusing on significant — and not merely coincidental — differences between the precedent and your case. Be careful. The differences on which you rely should be important enough to impress a skeptical judge who is looking for the basis of a decision, and hypertechnical discrepancies and minor factual variations are not persuasive. Another approach might be to reconcile the precedent with your case, showing that — although the precedent seems superficially adverse — its underlying policy would actually be furthered by the ruling you want from the court. Still another approach is to attack the precedent head-on, challenging its validity on the grounds that it is poorly reasoned or that changes in society or in public policy have made it unworkable. Although the doctrine of stare decisis does not absolutely forbid the overruling of precedent, a frontal attack on mandatory case law is nearly always an uphill fight, to be attempted only when there is very serious doubt — again shared by at least some respected lawyers — about the precedent's viability. In general, do not ask a court to overrule mandatory authority if you can win through distinguishing, reconciliation, or some other skill of precedent analysis. Judges simply prefer distinguishing and reconciling precedent to overruling it. But things are different where local law has a gap and where the challenged authority is not mandatory: if a judge must choose between competing out-of-state rules, he or she will not be able to decide without rejecting at least some precedent as ill-founded.

With both precedent and statutes, you might consider taking more than one approach, arguing in the alternative — but only if neither alternative would weaken the persuasive force of the other. It is not illogical, for example, to argue, first, that a statute was not intended to govern the facts before the court and, alternatively, that, if the statute is interpreted otherwise, it should be held unconstitutional.[1] It is illogical, however, to argue, first, that the statute was not intended to govern the facts and, alternatively, that it should be construed to provide a benefit and not a detriment to the client.

Attack an opposing argument if it has been made by your adversary, or if there is a reasonable possibility that the court might think of it and be persuaded by it. Otherwise, the court will assume that you have no defense to such an argument. But make your own arguments first. Your theory will be

---

§19.4   1. For an example of exactly these alternative arguments, see the brief in Appendix E.

more easily understood if you argue it before you attack opposing arguments. Generally, you can win more easily if the court's dominant impression is that you deserve to win, rather than that your adversary deserves to lose. And a defensive tone can undermine an otherwise worthwhile argument.

If you are responding to a memorandum or brief that your adversary has already propounded,[2] you know most of the arguments that threaten you because they will appear in the document to which you are responding. The court might itself think up other arguments not mentioned by your adversary. Even if an argument has not been mentioned by your adversary, attack it if it has a reasonable chance of occurring to and persuading the court. (In nonresponsive writing, where you will not see your adversary's writing before submitting your own, use this criterion for all opposing arguments.)

How much emphasis should you give to an attack on an adverse argument or authority? Give it as much emphasis as necessary to convince the judge not to rule against you. Little treatment is necessary if the point is minor and if the argument or authority is easily rebutted. You will, of course, need to say more if the point is more significant or if your counter-analysis is more complex. You cannot reduce the force of adverse arguments and authorities by giving them minimal treatment in your own writing: they have lives and voices of their own.

Beginners often have difficulty writing the thesis and transition sentences that introduce attacks on opposing arguments. In responsive writing, it is enough to refer to what opposing counsel has said and then to get on with the counter-argument. Here are two examples:

> The plaintiff misconstrues § 401(d)(1). Four other circuits have already decided that § 401(d)(1) provides for X and not, as the plaintiff contends, for Y. [*Follow with an analysis of the circuit cases.*]

> No appellate court has held to the contrary, and the few district court decisions cited to by the plaintiff are all distinguishable. [*Follow with an analysis of the district court cases.*]

> The legislative history also demonstrates that Congress intended to provide for X and not for Y. [*Follow with an analysis of the legislative history.*]

These opening sentences are written so that opposing counsel's contention is surrounded by the writer's counter-contention and the beginning of the counter-contention's proof. The effect is to argue affirmatively and not defensively. This is much weaker:

---

2. The attorney going forward—the movant in a trial court or the appellant on appeal — submits a memorandum or brief. Then the opposing attorney submits an answering memorandum or brief. The first attorney may complete the exchange with a reply memorandum or brief. This is called *responsive* writing. In some situations — usually in trial courts — the attorneys submit their documents simultaneously each without having seen the other's writing. Most law school persuasive writing assignments are *non*responsive.

The plaintiff has argued that § 401(d)(1) provides for Y, but . . .

In nonresponsive situations — where you suspect but do not actually know which arguments your adversary will make — begin simply by denying the contention while emphasizing your counter-contention:

Section 401(d)(1) provides for X and not for Y.

The following sounds defensive and almost silly:

Opposing counsel might argue that § 401(d)(1) provides for Y, but . . .

Opposing counsel might never argue it, but it may occur to the judge or to the judge's law clerk.

Both in responsive and in nonresponsive writing, a dependent clause can be useful in thesis and transition sentences:

Although the House Judiciary Committee report states that its bill would have provided for Y, § 401(d)(1) more closely tracks the bill drafted in the Senate Judiciary Committee. Both that committee's report and the conference committee report flatly state that § 401(d)(1) provides for X.

Be careful, however, not to use a dependent clause to make a relatively minor problem look like a major one. For example, compare

Although a few district courts have held that § 401(d)(1) provides for Y, every circuit that has faced the question has held the contrary.

with

Every circuit that has faced the question has held that § 401(d)(1) provides for X. [*Analysis of circuit cases.*] The few district court cases to the contrary are distinguishable.

20 Handling the Procedural Posture

§20.1 Why Procedural Postures Matter

The procedural posture is the procedural event or events — such as a motion — that places an issue before the court. For example, if you were asked to give the procedural posture in the trial court in *Meints v. Huntington*,[1] a reasonable answer might begin like this: "The defendants requested that the jury be instructed that . . ."

In trial courts, an attorney requests a judicial order by making a motion for it, and most procedural postures are defined in terms of the motion that has been made. Each type of motion is governed by rules that govern how the motion is to be decided. If you move for summary judgment, for example, you must satisfy the test for summary judgment, and your arguments ought to be designed to satisfy that test.

In a motion memorandum or an appellate brief, the procedural posture governs the arguments you can make. It also governs how you use and describe facts. That is because courts see the facts through filters that differ from one posture to another.

§20.2 Types of Procedural Postures

Trial court motions fall into four very generalized categories: (1) motions that challenge the quality of an adversary's allegations (in a pleading); (2)

---

§20.1 1. See page 28.

other motions that challenge the manner in which the litigation began; (3) motions that challenge the quality of a party's evidence; and (4) a large catch-all category of miscellaneous case management motions.[1] When a trial court's decision is appealed, the case moves into yet another procedural posture, where the trial judge's decision is evaluated according to a standard of review.

§20.2.1   Motions Challenging the Quality of a Party's Allegations

The *burden of pleading* is a party's obligation to allege, in its pleading, facts that, if proven, would entitle the party to the judgment it seeks. In a civil case, the plaintiff's complaint must allege facts that, if proven, would constitute a cause of action. If a defendant pleads a counterclaim or an affirmative defense in the answer, that answer must allege facts that, if proven, would substantiate a counterclaim or affirmative defense. And in a criminal case, the government's indictment or information must allege facts that, if proven, would be a crime.[2]

In a civil action, a defendant can, before answering a complaint, move to dismiss it for failure to state a cause of action. Because this motion tests the sufficiency of allegations (and nothing more), the record is limited to the four corners of the complaint. The question is not whether either party has proved anything. Instead, the court assumes — for the purpose of the motion only — that the factual allegations in the complaint can be proven, and the court then decides whether, if proven, those allegations would amount to a cause of action. If the court concludes that they could not, it strikes the cause of action from the pleading. If the court strikes all the causes of action pleaded in a complaint, the complaint itself is dismissed and the litigation is terminated unless the plaintiff can serve and file an amended complaint with additional or reformulated allegations that would survive a motion to dismiss.

Similarly, a plaintiff can move to dismiss a counterclaim or an affirmative defense pleaded in the defendant's answer. And in a criminal case a defendant can move to dismiss one or more counts in the indictment or information, or the entire indictment or information.

Because, at this stage in litigation, no evidence has been submitted, lawyers do not describe the "facts" alleged in the pleadings as things that ac-

---

§20.2   1. You will find this material easier if you review §1.3. Rules governing how motions are decided may differ from state to state. Check the rules that govern the court for which you are writing a memorandum or brief, as well as the precedent interpreting those rules. That takes time and thought in the library. Guessing about local rules frequently leads to grief.

2. Criminal defendants do not file written answers to indictments or informations. Criminal defendants cannot constitutionally be required to make statements about the events at issue. Instead, a criminal defendant pleads only "guilty" or "not guilty," orally in court and without saying more.

tually happened. Until it receives evidence later in the case, the court has no idea whether the alleged "facts" happened, and the "facts" therefore are described purely as allegations:

> Although the plaintiff has alleged that the defendant struck him from behind with a stick, he has not alleged that the defendant intended to cause him injury.

In this procedural posture, you cannot accurately write the following:

> Although the defendant struck the plaintiff from behind with a stick, the defendant did not intend to cause the plaintiff injury.

We will find out later — after evidence has been produced — whether the defendant struck the plaintiff or intended to cause injury.

There is an exception to all this. If the defendant admits, in the answer, an allegation made in the complaint, the allegation is considered established without need of evidence. The event alleged and admitted might be described as a fact ("The defendant struck the plaintiff") because the admission makes it as good as proved. Or it might be described as a conceded allegation ("The defendant admits that he struck the plaintiff").

§20.2.2 Motions Challenging Other Aspects of the Way in Which the Litigation Began

A defendant might move to dismiss an action on the ground that the court lacks jurisdiction over the subject matter, or that it lacks personal jurisdiction over the defendant, or that venue is improper, or that the summons did not include all the information required, or that it was improperly served, or that some persons who must be made parties have not been,[3] and so on.

Like motions challenging the quality of allegations, these seek dismissal of the action, and they are made after the plaintiff serves a summons and complaint and before the defendant serves an answer.[4] (Actually, an answer would be served only if the motion is denied.) But these motions are different in one important respect: they are not limited to the contents of the complaint. In fact, the contents of the complaint might be irrelevant to the motion. If the defendant asserts that the summons was improperly served, for example, the court would ignore the contents of the complaint and would instead hear testimony from the server and from the defendant about how the summons was delivered to the defendant.

---

3. See Rule 12(b)(1)-(5) and (7) of the Federal Rules of Civil Procedure.
4. Several of them are waived unless made during that period. *See, e.g.,* Rule 12(b) and (h) of the Federal Rules of Civil Procedure.

§20.2.3 Motions Challenging the Quality of a Party's Evidence

These include (1) motions for summary judgment; (2) motions for directed verdict (or in federal courts, motions for judgment as a matter of law[5]); and (3) motions for judgment notwithstanding the verdict (in federal courts, renewed motions for judgment as a matter of law[6]). In contrast to the motions testing allegations in pleadings, these require the court to decide whether a party has sustained a burden to produce evidence. There are also (4) motions for a new trial, which are analytically different from the other three (and therefore explained near the end of this section).

Do not confuse the *burden of production* with the *burden of persuasion*. The burden of persuasion is the obligation to persuade the trier of fact that a particular allegation ultimately is true. The burden of production (often called the burden of going forward) is the threshold obligation to satisfy the judge (even in cases where the actual trier of fact is a jury) that the party who must shoulder the burden can provide enough evidence about a particular allegation to make it worth putting the question to the trier of fact.

The law has good reasons to avoid putting an issue to a trier of fact unless the party with the burden of production has at least a threshold quantum of evidence. First, putting a question to a trier of fact, in a trial or hearing, is expensive and time-consuming. Second, it might also be unnecessary. The only purpose of a trial is to ascertain the facts from conflicting evidence. If the evidence is not really in conflict, the court can adjudicate without a trial. Third, there are certain risks where the trier of fact is a jury. Although the right to trial by jury is one of the foundations of common law procedure — treasured as a vehicle for limiting the authority of government — jurors with no training in law are so capable of misunderstandings that many of the rules of evidence and procedure are designed to limit what juries can see, hear, and decide.

Although the difference between a burden of persuasion and a burden of production may seem technical, it is important in practice and in practical legal writing. A beginner may be confused not only because the two burdens at first seem similar, but also because the term *burden of proof* is occasionally but confusingly applied to both burdens collectively. You will be able to differentiate between them, however, if you remember some of the basic concepts of each burden.

You already know all of the following: When a civil case is tried, the plaintiff has the burden of persuading the fact finder of the existence of facts that substantiate each element of a cause of action pleaded in the complaint.

---

5. In federal courts since 1991, motions for directed verdict have been known as motions for judgment as a matter of law. See Rule 50(a) of the Federal Rules of Civil Procedure. Despite the change of name, these motions continue to function just as they did when they were called motions for directed verdict. In state courts, they will still be known by the traditional name unless the state amends its rules to conform with the new federal practice.

6. In federal courts since 1991, motions for judgment notwithstanding the verdict have been known as renewed motions for judgment as a matter of law. See Rule 50(b) of the Federal Rules of Civil Procedure. Despite the change of name, these motions continue to function as they did when called by the traditional name, which will still be used in state courts unless the state amends its rules to conform with federal practice.

The defendant can try to prevent the plaintiff from carrying that burden, or the defendant can raise one or more affirmative defenses, or the defendant can do both. A defendant who pleads an affirmative defense assumes the burden of persuading the fact finder of the existence of facts that substantiate each element of that defense. In criminal cases the prosecution must carry a burden of persuasion as to every element of the crime, and the defendant assumes a similar burden for each element of any asserted affirmative defense.[7] The trier of fact determines whether these burdens have been carried, and the trier does so only at the end of the trial. The trier of fact should find against a defendant if the plaintiff or prosecution has carried its burden of persuasion and if the defendant has not done so with an affirmative defense. But the trier of fact should find for a defendant if the defendant has substantiated an affirmative defense, even if the plaintiff or prosecution has carried all its burdens. In any event, if the trier of fact is a jury, the result is a verdict, and if the trier is a judge, the result is the judge's findings of fact.

The concept that may now seem odd to you is that the parties might not even be allowed to try to carry these burdens of persuasion unless they have already shown that they can satisfy their burdens of production. The burden of production requires the party shouldering it to come forward with a minimum, threshold quantum of evidence, defined by the relevant rules of procedure and by the case law interpreting those rules. The question of whether a party has carried a burden of production is generally put to a judge through one of the three motions that challenge the quality of the other party's evidence.

Motions for summary judgment,[8] for directed verdict,[9] and for judgment notwithstanding the verdict[10] exist so that parties, lawyers, and judges can avoid, where possible and appropriate, the effort and expense of trial, as well as the perils of juries. A motion for summary judgment can be made before trial. A motion for a directed verdict can be made during trial, after the adversary has rested (finished presenting evidence) and before the jury has begun to deliberate. And a motion for judgment notwithstanding the verdict is made — as its name suggests — after the jury has returned a verdict. (In criminal cases, there are no summary judgments, and only the defendant can move for a directed verdict or for judgment notwithstanding the verdict.[11])

---

7. Some criminal defenses are called "affirmative" even if conceptually they are not. By definition, an affirmative defense is one for which the defendant assumes a burden of persuasion. Local law, however, might label a defense "affirmative" if the defendant assumes a burden of production, but not the burden of persuasion (which the prosecution must carry).

8. *See* Rule 56 of the Federal Rules of Civil Procedure.

9. *See* Rule 50(a) of the Federal Rules of Civil Procedure (motion for judgment as a matter of law).

10. *See* Rule 50(b) of the Federal Rules of Civil Procedure (renewed motion for judgment as a matter of law).

11. Our constitutional concepts of procedural due process would not tolerate granting any of these motions to the prosecution. In many jurisdictions, a criminal case will be dismissed unless the government can carry a burden of production at a preliminary hearing. Analytically, this operates like a summary judgment motion, except for two things. First, at a preliminary hearing the court receives evidence primarily through oral testimony in the

Although these motions are governed by different procedural rules, all three are decided according to approximately the same logic: the motion should be granted if the opposing party has failed to satisfy a burden of production and if the law is such that the movant is entitled to a favorable judgment.

Measuring whether a party has satisfied a burden of production requires taking into account the amount of evidence that would be required at trial to carry a burden of persuasion. In the overwhelming majority of civil actions, the party charged with a burden of persuasion must satisfy it by a *preponderance of the evidence:* by evidence showing more likely than not that the alleged facts are true. A few burdens of persuasion are heavier and must be carried by *clear and convincing evidence.* And in criminal cases, the prosecution must prove guilt *beyond a reasonable doubt*, which is the heaviest burden known to the law.

For example, if a party must at trial prove a fact by clear and convincing evidence, that party will lose one of these motions unless he or she can produce (in response to a summary judgment motion) or has already produced (at trial before one of the other motions is made) evidence that would give a reasonable jury a basis for deciding that the fact has been proved by clear and convincing evidence. The burden of production would be less onerous in a case where the burden of persuasion is a preponderance of the evidence. And it would be more onerous in a case where the burden of persuasion is proof beyond a reasonable doubt.

Although motions for summary judgment occur often in civil practice, they may at first perplex you. The judgment is "summary" because there is no trial. The evidence is not put before the court through testimony in a courtroom, but instead through the parties' written submissions, which can include affidavits, deposition transcripts, exhibits, and answers to interrogatories. In virtually every American jurisdiction, the moving party is entitled to summary judgment if none of the material facts are genuinely disputed and if that party is entitled to judgment as a matter of law.[12]

Be careful: although this seems like a simple, two-element test, it has some deceptive subtleties. First, a fact is not material merely because it is logically connected to the controversy. A fact is material in this sense only if it is truly determinative or, put another way, capable "of *altering the outcome* of the litigation."[13]

Second, a fact is not genuinely disputed just because the parties have different opinions about it. On a motion for summary judgment, an alleged fact is genuinely at issue only if a jury could reasonably decide either that the fact did happen or that it did not. If reasonable jurors could go either way, then the case deserves a trial and deliberation by a trier of fact.

Third, most motions for summary judgment are made by the party that does not have the burden of persuasion at trial. In federal courts, the non-

---

courtroom and not through the written submissions used in summary judgment motions. And second, the prosecution cannot obtain a judgment from a preliminary hearing.

12. *See, e.g.,* Rule 56 of the Federal Rules of Civil Procedure.

13. *Rivera-Muriente v. Agosto-Alicea*, 959 F.2d 349, 352 (1st Cir. 1992).

moving party in that situation will lose the motion (and the case) if unable to present evidence sufficient at least to satisfy the burden of production.[14] (In other words, that nonmoving party would have to demonstrate a genuine dispute about a material fact.) Many states do not follow this principle. They instead require the moving party to prove the absence of a dispute about each material fact. You can rarely figure out the jurisdiction's practice on this point by reading its rules of procedure.[15] It takes a careful reading of the jurisdiction's recent cases on summary judgment.[16]

Finally, the second element of the test for summary judgment incorporates the relevant substantive rules at issue — primarily, the rules defining the cause of action and any affirmative defenses — because the only way a court can determine whether a party is entitled to judgment as a matter of law is to apply the substantive rules that define the parties' rights and obligations. If you move for summary judgment in a products liability case, the second element incorporates every part of the law of products liability that happens to be relevant to your case.

Unlike the three motions just described, the motion for a new trial does not test whether a party has carried a burden of production. A new trial can be granted on two kinds of grounds: (1) if the jury's verdict is seriously tainted through procedural faults such as erroneously admitted evidence or inaccurate jury instructions, or (2) if the verdict was against the overwhelming weight of the evidence. The first category obviously does not test the quality of a party's evidence. The second does but by examining the extent to which a burden of persuasion (rather than a burden of production) has been carried. A new trial is not granted merely because the judge would have come to a different verdict if he or she had been the trier of fact. But it can be granted if the overwhelming weight of the evidence is on one side of the case and the jury returned a verdict for the other side.

In any of these procedural postures, a description of the facts is framed in terms of the evidence submitted:

> The plaintiff testified that he was struck in the back and that the defendant was the only person who was behind him at the time. The defendant does not deny that he struck the plaintiff or that he used a stick to do it. Aside from the stick, the only evidence that might conceivably show that the defendant intended to cause injury is a letter, dated two days before the incident, in which the defendant complained that the plaintiff "had better keep his cattle off my land or I'll have to do something."

Notice how each fact is connected with evidence so that the reader can judge whether the evidence really proves it. That is because the provability

---

14. *See Celotex Corp. v. Catrett*, 477 U.S. 317 (1986); *Anderson v. Liberty Lobby, Inc.*, 477 U.S. 242 (1986); *Matsushita Elec. Industrial Co. v. Zenith Radio Corp.*, 475 U.S. 574 (1986).

15. It would not be clear from reading Rule 56 of the Federal Rules of Civil Procedure.

16. You might look for local cases citing to *Celotex, Anderson,* and *Matsushita* to see if the state has reacted to the changes in federal law.

of facts is at issue. In these procedural postures, the only facts that can accurately be stated without any reference to evidence are those that are "true" because the parties do not disagree about them.

§20.2.4   Miscellaneous Case Management Motions

These are housekeeping motions, used to manage the progress of litigation, such as motions in discovery; motions for preliminary injunctions; and suppression motions in criminal cases.[17] What makes these motions different from the ones you have just read about is that the granting of a management motion does not terminate the litigation; instead, management motions regulate the litigation's progress. Burdens of production and burdens of persuasion are so effective at helping a court structure its decision-making that they are used not just to award judgments, but also to decide many of these motions as well.

For example, before trial, a criminal defendant who gave the police a statement might move to suppress it, arguing that the police wrongfully obtained the statement by failing to inform him of his constitutional right to remain silent. If the court grants the motion, the statement cannot be used as evidence at trial. At or before the hearing on the motion, the defendant must carry a burden of production by submitting at least some evidence that he made a statement. That is a relatively easy burden for the defendant to satisfy,[18] especially because the prosecution is not likely to deny it. Once the burden of production has been met, however, the prosecution must shoulder a much heavier one: the prosecution must show beyond a reasonable doubt that the defendant was warned, in language he could understand, that he need not say anything to the police, that anything he says may be held against him, that he has a right to an attorney present during interrogation, and that if he cannot pay for an attorney, one would be appointed for him at government expense.[19]

Because these miscellaneous motions are generally decided on the basis of evidence, the facts are described in the same way as with motions for summary judgment, for directed verdict, and for judgment notwithstanding the verdict.

§20.2.5   Appeal

On appeal, a standard of review is applied to the decision below. Standards of review are explained in §27.3.

---

17. Although a request for jury instructions is not called a motion, in a technical sense it is one—and it is of the case management variety.
18. The defendant can carry the burden of production simply by stating in an affidavit or in testimony that he made a statement to the police.
19. *See Miranda v. Arizona,* 384 U.S. 436 (1966).

§20.3 Writing in a Procedural Posture

Because most of a legal education is spent studying the substantive law of torts, property, and so on, you might tend to view issues in the abstract ("should the plaintiff win?"). But judges see issues in terms of the motion context in which they are raised.

If, for example, a defendant moves for summary judgment, you are wrong if you define the issue as whether the defendant should win the case. The issues the judge will see are whether there is a material dispute of fact and whether the defendant is entitled to judgment as a matter of law. The judge's view is the correct and more precisely focused one because a summary judgment can be granted only if the answer to both these questions is yes.

Similarly, on appeal the question is not whether the appellant should have won in the trial court, but instead whether the trial court's ruling was error as defined by the applicable standard of review.[1]

Because the procedural posture and the rules governing it control the way the judge will make the decision, you must show the judge how to decide within the procedural rules he or she must follow. How can you do that in writing?

First, remember that in a motion or appeal the threshold rule is *not* the rule of substantive law that provides the remedy sued for. The threshold rules are procedural. In a trial court, the threshold rules are the rules that govern how the motion is to be decided. On appeal, the threshold rules are the ones that govern the trial court's decision plus the appellate court's standard of review.

For example, the memorandum in Appendix D has been submitted in support of a motion for a preliminary injunction in a suit to enforce a constructive trust. In deciding the motion, the court will evaluate the record in terms of the elements of the test for a preliminary injunction: likelihood of success on the merits, threatened irreparable harm, and a balancing of the equities. And — appropriately — that test is invoked very early in Goslin's Argument.

Second, recall that some procedural tests contain an element that incorporates the underlying substantive rules on which the litigation as a whole is based. In the test for a summary judgment, that happens through the element requiring entitlement to judgment as a matter of law.[2] In the test for a preliminary injunction, it is done through the element requiring likelihood of success on the merits. In the memorandum in Appendix D, Goslin can demonstrate likelihood of success on the merits only by showing that the record before the court contains all the elements of the test for a constructive trust — and that concern occupies the largest part of Goslin's Argument.

§20.3   1. See §27.3.
2. See §20.2.3.

279

Be careful about these incorporation elements: they can include *all* the substantive rules that could determine the ultimate judgment in the case at hand, including defenses. For example, if the nephew had raised the affirmative defense of unclean hands, Goslin would be able to demonstrate likelihood of success on the merits only by showing *both* that the record contains all the elements of a constructive trust (his cause of action) *and* that the record will not satisfy the test for unclean hands (the nephew's affirmative defense).

Third, organize your paradigm variations around the procedural test. If the procedural test incorporates a substantive test, the substantive test operates as a sub-rule. To see how that is done, study Goslin's Argument, which includes several paradigmed proofs inside the organization of an umbrella paradigm. The umbrella structure — through which the entire Argument is organized — is built on the test for a preliminary injunction. Each element of the test is proved through a distinct paradigmed proof:

> *Umbrella Paradigm:* proof — supplied element-by-element (below) —that Goslin is entitled to a preliminary injunction

A. paradigmed proof that Goslin is likely to succeed on the merits (i.e., that he will eventually be able to prove a constructive trust)

  1. paradigmed proof of a confidential relationship

  2. paradigmed proof of an implied promise

  3. paradigmed proof of a transfer

  4. paradigmed proof of unjust enrichment

B. paradigmed proof that Goslin is threatened with irreparable harm

C. paradigmed proof that equity favors an injunction

Because the first element (likelihood of success on the merits) incorporates a rule of substantive law (the test for a constructive trust), it includes paradigmed proofs (one for each element of the test for a constructive trust) inside a larger paradigmed proof (likelihood of success on the merits), which is in turn inside yet another paradigmed proof (the test for a preliminary injunction).

Although that may all sound complicated, it is the precise sequence of logic that a judge would need to go through in order to decide whether Goslin should be granted a preliminary injunction. The judge would have to decide whether Goslin has carried his burden of persuasion as to each of the elements of the test for a preliminary injunction, including all the elements of the constructive trust test, which is incorporated into the element of likelihood of success on the merits. An argument carefully organized in this way can systematically demolish a judge's skepticism because it demonstrates, element by element, how a party has carried — or, if you are arguing the other side, failed to carry — a burden.

Finally, do not go overboard in citing to authority for the procedural test. Procedural tests are routine rules that judges use constantly and generally know by heart. A conclusory explanation[3] is usually sufficient for rule proof. (And that is all that was needed at the beginning of Goslin's Argument in Appendix D.) You should provide more only in two situations. The first is where authority will help you guide the court in rule application. (That is done at certain points later in Goslin's Argument.) And the second is where the parties disagree about the proper formulation of the procedural rule. The second situation occurs very infrequently.

§20.4   Researching to Account for Your Case's Procedural Posture

In the library, you are looking for two kinds of rules:

First, you are, of course, searching for the rules that govern the *substance* of the controversy — definitions of causes of action, crimes, affirmative defenses, and other forms of rights and obligations like the ones you have already studied in the courses on torts, property, contracts, and criminal law. This is by far the larger research task in nearly all instances.

Second, you are looking for the *procedural* rules that govern how the court's decision is to be made. Some examples are

1. rules setting out the tests for granting various motions ("Summary judgment is appropriate if there is no genuine issue of material fact and if the moving party is entitled to judgment as a matter of law");
2. rules controlling how the court must evaluate the record before it on the motion to be decided ("In deciding a motion for summary judgment, the court views the evidence in the light most favorable to the party opposing the motion");

3. See §9.3.2.

3. if an appeal has been taken, the rule defining the standard of review in the appellate court ("On appeal, a grant of summary judgment is reviewed de novo").

A court evaluates the record differently for different types of motions. And the standard of review differs from one kind of appeal to another.

Much time will be saved in the library if you first identify the type of motion involved and then look in the procedural statutes and court rules and in the digests for procedural rules that govern the motion's disposition. For any given motion, you will probably find part of the procedural law in a statute or court rule and the rest in interpretive case law.

If you find the procedural rules in a procedural statute or court rule, the language may be subtle, but it will not be terribly hard to recognize. The section heading alone will usually announce that you have arrived at the right place. In case law, when a court mentions the rules governing how a motion is to be decided, it usually does so immediately after reciting the facts and immediately before beginning the legal analysis (just as it was done in Goslin's memorandum[1]). That is because the procedural rules are a threshold through which the court must pass in order to begin the analysis. This is typical of the kind of language you will find:

> A complaint should not be dismissed for failure to state a claim unless it appears beyond a doubt that plaintiffs can prove no set of facts in support of their claim which would entitle them to relief. [Citations omitted.] The allegations of plaintiffs' complaint must be assumed to be true, and further, must be construed in [the plaintiffs'] favor. [Citations omitted.] The issue is not whether plaintiffs will ultimately prevail, but rather whether they are entitled to offer evidence in support of their claims. [Citation omitted.][2]

The first sentence is the test that must be satisfied before the motion can be granted. The rest are some of the rules that govern how the court is to evaluate the record before it on this particular type of motion.

Exercise.   Welty's Facts at Various Procedural Postures

Welty has been indicted for burglary. The indictment alleges the events on page 20. She has moved to dismiss the indictment.

1. Write a description of the facts in this procedural posture. (See §20.2.1.)

2. How is that fact description different from the one you would write if Welty were to move for a directed verdict during the trial? (See §20.2.3.)

---

§20.4   1. See Appendix D.

2. *United States v. Aceto Agric. Chems. Corp.*, 872 F.2d 1373, 1376 (8th Cir. 1989).

VI
MOTION
MEMORANDA

21 Motion Memoranda

§21.1 Motion Memorandum Format

When a motion is made, each party may submit a memorandum. A plaintiff moving for a preliminary injunction, for example, submits a document that might be titled "Memorandum in Support of Plaintiff's Motion to Dismiss," and the opposing party's document might be titled "Memorandum in Opposition to Plaintiff's Motion to Dismiss."

This chapter describes the format of a motion memorandum and the process of writing one. Chapters 18 and 19 explain how to develop a persuasive motion theory and persuasive arguments. And Chapter 20 explains how to handle the motion's procedural posture. In addition, many of skills used in writing an office memorandum are valuable here: organizing proof of a conclusion of law (Chapter 9), selecting authority (Chapter 10), analyzing precedent and statutes (Chapters 11-12), analyzing facts (Chapter 13), paragraphing (Chapter 14), style (Chapter 15), and citing and quoting properly (Chapter 16).

Like the reader of an office memorandum, the judge (and the judge's law clerk) may look at each memorandum more than once. Depending on the judge's work habits and on the nature of the motion, at least some part of the memorandum might be read once for an understanding of the issues involved, a second time in preparation for a hearing or oral argument on the motion, a third time while deciding the motion, and a fourth time while writing an opinion. Thus, you cannot assume that a memorandum will be read from front to back or at one sitting.

Although conventions differ from jurisdiction to jurisdiction, generally the components of a memorandum of law are the following:

1. a cover page
2. a Table of Contents
3. a Table of Authorities
4. a Preliminary Statement
5. a Question Presented (or Questions Presented if the motion is sufficiently complex)[1]
6. a Statement of the Case[2]
7. an Argument, broken up by point headings
8. a Conclusion
9. an indorsement (and, in some courts, the attorney's signature)

If local court rules permit, you can vary the format according to your assessment of the complexity of the motion and the most persuasive way to present your theory. In a short memorandum, the Table of Authorities is probably not needed. Some lawyers omit the Table of Contents in short memoranda, but if you have several point headings or sub-headings, that would be a mistake. (Chapter 22 explains why.) And some motions do not lend themselves to a Question Presented.

(The rest of this chapter is easier to follow if you look to the memorandum in Appendix D for illustration as you read the description below of each of these components.)

The *cover page* includes a caption and title, which correspond to the memorandum heading at the beginning of an office memorandum. The caption identifies the court and the parties, specifying their procedural designations (plaintiff, defendant, etc.). In a criminal case, the prosecution is called, depending on the jurisdiction, "State," "Commonwealth," "People," or "United States," and no procedural designation follows those terms in the caption. The title identifies the memorandum and the purpose of its submission ("Memorandum in Opposition to Defendant's Motion to Dismiss").

The *Table of Contents* begins on the page after the cover page, and the *Table of Authorities* appears on the first page after the Table of Contents. The tables are put together and paginated just as they would be in an appellate brief. They are explained in Chapter 26 (on appellate brief writing) because they are often omitted from law school memorandum assignments. (See pages 340-41).

The *Preliminary Statement* briefly sets out the case's procedural posture by identifying the parties (to the extent that is necessary); explaining the nature of the litigation; listing the relevant procedural events; and describing the motion before the court and the relief sought. If it can be done very concisely, the Preliminary Statement might also summarize the parties' contentions. The point is to tell the judge why the matter is before the court and to specify the type of decision the judge will have to make. That can usually be done in less than a page.

---

§21.1 1. In some jurisdictions, these are called "Issues Presented" or just "Issues."

2. In some jurisdictions, the Preliminary Statement is called the "Statement of the Case," and the component that elsewhere is known as a Statement of the Case is instead called the "Statement of Facts." This is only a confusion of names. The contents are the same regardless of what the components are called.

Although a persuasive *Question Presented* is at least superficially similar to the Issue in an office memorandum, here the Question should persuade as well as inform. A convincing Question Presented is — for the small number of words involved — one of the most difficult drafting tasks in legal writing. Chapter 24 explains how to do it.

The *Statement of the Case* corresponds to the Facts in an office memorandum, but there are differences in substance and in drafting technique. Chapter 23 explains how to write a Statement of the Case.

The *Argument* corresponds to the Discussion in an office memorandum, but here the goal is to persuade as well as to explain. An Argument is organized into *points*, each of which is a single, complete, and independent ground for relief. Each point has a heading and may have sub-headings, all of which are reproduced verbatim in the table of contents. Chapter 22 explains how to construct point headings and sub-headings. The Argument is the most complex component of a motion memorandum, but you have already learned many of the skills required. Chapters 9-13 explained how to organize proof of a conclusion of law and use authority and facts. Additionally, you will need to know how to develop theories (Chapter 18) and arguments (Chapter 19); and how to work with a procedural posture (Chapter 20).

In a motion memorandum, the *Conclusion* is intended only to remind the reader of what you seek (or oppose), with an allusion to your theory, if that can be compressed into one or two sentences. Although a Conclusion in a persuasive document is shorter than a Conclusion in an office memorandum, it cannot persuade if it is cut to the bone. Compare the following:

CONCLUSION

For all these reasons, this court should preliminarily enjoin construction of the logging roads here at issue.

CONCLUSION

Thus, the Forest Service's authorization of these logging roads violates the National Environmental Policy Act, the Administrative Procedure Act, and the enabling legislation of the Forest Service. The harm would be irreparable, and an injunction would promote the public interest. This court should therefore preliminarily enjoin the Forest Service from building the roads.

The second example does a much better job of reminding the court, in just a few sentences, of precisely what the writer wants and why it should be done.

The *indorsement,* like the signature in an office memorandum, appears under a line reading "Respectfully submitted." The indorsement, however, is entirely typewritten and includes the attorney's name, an indication of which party the attorney represents, and the attorney's office address and telephone number. In some jurisdictions, the attorney also signs the memorandum.[3]

§21.2 Writing a Motion Memorandum

As with office memoranda, lawyers differ about which part of a motion memorandum they draft first. But virtually every lawyer modifies his or her habits somewhat from document to document, simply because a practice that works well in one instance might not work well in another.

Many lawyers start by writing the Preliminary Statement because it is not hard to do and is a convenient way to get going. Then they turn to the heart of the job, which is the Statement of the Case and the Argument.

Some lawyers write the Argument before they write the Statement of the Case because writing the Argument shows them what to do with the facts. Other lawyers might write the Argument and the Statement of the Case simultaneously. Some might outline the Statement of the Case while writing the Argument.

Some lawyers write the point headings and sub-headings before starting to write the Argument. Others might write an outline of the Argument and gradually convert the outline into headings and sub-headings. (Even in a finished memorandum, the headings and sub-headings *are* an outline of the Argument.)

The Question Presented is usually best written after the Argument and the Statement of the Case. The Question Presented compresses into a very small space ideas that are usually developed while writing the Argument and Statement.

The Conclusion, the Tables, and the indorsement are best done last. The cover page can be done any time.

While putting the memorandum through further drafts, ask yourself the questions in the checklists on the inside front and back covers.

3. *See, e.g.,* Rule 11 of the Federal Rules of Civil Procedure.

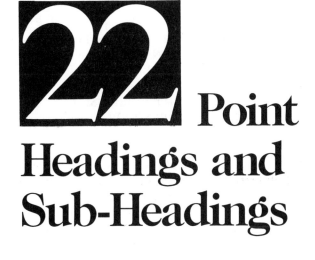 Point
Headings and Sub-Headings

§22.1 How Points and Headings Work

In a motion memorandum or appellate brief, the Argument is divided into points. Each point is given a heading and may be divided by sub-headings.[1]

A point is an independent, complete, and free-standing ground for a ruling in your favor on a Question Presented. If only one ground would support a favorable ruling on the Question, you have only one point for that Question and only one point heading, although the point itself could be broken up into sub-headings to the extent that would help the reader. If, on the other hand, you have two or more favorable theories, each of which could stand alone as a *complete* and *independent* ground for relief, each theory is a separate point and is to be summarized in a separate heading.

How could you have more than one complete and independent reason for a ruling in your favor? Take a motion to dismiss at the commencement of an action. As they would appear in the Table of Contents, the movant's point headings might read as follows:

---

§22.1 1. You will understand this material more easily if, before reading this chapter, you read the point headings and sub-headings in the Tables of Contents of the memorandum in Appendix D and the briefs in Appendices E and F.

II.   THE ACTION SHOULD BE DISMISSED BECAUSE THE SUMMONS WAS IMPROPERLY SERVED ON THE DEFENDANT.

III.   THE ACTION SHOULD BE DISMISSED ON THE GROUND OF RES JUDICATA.

IV.   THE ACTION SHOULD BE DISMISSED ON THE GROUND THAT THE PLAINTIFF'S TIME TO SUE HAS EXPIRED.

If true, any one of these should justify granting the motion. A complaint that fails to set out a cause of action should be dismissed even if properly served and even if the action is not barred by res judicata or the statute of limitations. An action should be dismissed if the summons was not properly served, even if the complaint does state a cause of action — and so on.

Sub-headings can be used to develop a point heading:

I.   THE COMPLAINT SHOULD BE DISMISSED FOR FAILURE TO STATE A CAUSE OF ACTION.

    A.   The plaintiff claims only that the defendant School District did not "adequately" teach him.

    B.   Virtually every jurisdiction that has considered the question has refused to recognize a tort of "educational malpractice."

    C.   Because an education is the result of the efforts of both student and teachers, a failure to learn cannot be attributed solely to the school.

    D.   A tort of "educational malpractice" would disrupt the public schools.

        1.   Scarce educational resources would be diverted to pay damages or insurance premiums.

        2.   A litigious atmosphere would interfere with teaching and learning.

II.   THE ACTION SHOULD BE DISMISSED BECAUSE THE SUMMONS WAS IMPROPERLY SERVED ON THE DEFENDANT.

The numbering and lettering sequence is the same as with a formal outline:

      I. [point heading]

          A. [sub-heading]

              1. [secondary sub-heading]

              2. [secondary sub-heading]

          B. [sub-heading]

      II. [point heading]

A solitary sub-heading is inappropriate. If you find yourself with an "A" but no "B," either create a "B" or incorporate the substance of "A" into the point heading itself.

Before you have completed your research, you can start to outline the Argument by rough-drafting the point headings and sub-headings. In fact, your rough draft of the headings can be part of your outline.

When you set up headings and sub-headings in a Table of Contents and in an Argument, study the examples in Appendices D, E, and F for format. In the Argument (but not in the Table of Contents, where they are printed verbatim), point headings appear entirely in capital letters. Sub-headings are underlined in the Argument but not in the Table of Contents. And in both places, all headings and sub-headings are single-spaced. In the Argument, headings and sub-headings are centered with extra margins on both sides and white space above and below. Headings and sub-headings should be obvious to a reader who is skimming. That reader does not easily notice this:

I. THE COMPLAINT SHOULD BE DISMISSED FOR FAILURE TO
STATE A CAUSE OF ACTION.

But a better layout on the page has a more arresting effect:

      I.   THE COMPLAINT SHOULD BE DISMISSED
          FOR FAILURE TO STATE A CAUSE OF
          ACTION.

If you have only an inch or two left at the bottom of a page in the Argument, do not put a heading there; put it instead at the top of the next page. For the same reason that newspaper headlines do not appear at the bottom of a newspaper page, point headings and sub-headings look silly if they appear at the bottom of an Argument page without any text underneath.

§22.2   How to Evaluate Your Headings and Sub-Headings for Effectiveness

The effectiveness of your point headings and sub-headings can be judged by the following criteria:

1. When collected in the Table of Contents, the headings and sub-headings should lay out a complete and persuasive outline of your theory.
2. Each point should be an independent, complete, and freestanding ground for a ruling in your favor.
3. Headings and sub-headings should not assume information that a judge would lack when reading the Table of Contents.
4. The sub-headings should be neither too many nor too few.
5. Each heading and sub-heading should be a single sentence that can be immediately understood.
6. Each point heading should identify the ruling you want.
7. The controlling rules should be identified in the headings or sub-headings.
8. The one, two, or three most determinative facts should at least be alluded to in either the headings or sub-headings.
9. Headings and sub-headings should be forceful and argumentative.

1. When collected in the Table of Contents, the headings and sub-headings should lay out a complete and persuasive outline of your theory.   Many judges read the point headings in the Table of Contents before reading any other part of the memo or brief. The point headings are thus your opportunity to introduce and outline your theory. Although the reader would have to study the Argument to learn how the theory works, the headings — when read together in the Table of Contents — should lay out the significant steps of logic on which the theory is based, outlining a paradigm-structured argument, with rule proof and rule application and perhaps with policy arguments and counter-analyses. (Notice how that is done with the headings and sub-headings in §22.1.) If you draft the headings after you write the Argument, be sure that the headings and sub-headings present a complete and coherent picture of your theory when they are isolated in the Table of Contents. When you compile the headings and sub-headings in the Table of Contents, you may find that you have to redraft them because only then might you discover gaps or inconsistencies not apparent when the headings are scattered in the Argument.

Look at the Tables of Contents of the memorandum in Appendix D and in the briefs in Appendices E and F. Read the headings and sub-headings there as a judge would on first opening each document. From the headings, can you understand each writer's theory? Why or why not?

2. Each point should be an independent, complete, and free-standing ground for a ruling in your favor.   A careless beginner might write four or five "point" headings for material that will yield only one or two genuine points. This is caused by confusing a point with a contention. Check yourself in the following way: if you have several point headings, look at each one in isolation. If the court were to believe everything you say in and under that heading, but were to believe absolutely nothing else in the Argument, would you win? If the answer is no, the "point" cannot stand on its own, and you have fewer points than you thought you did. You have a real point only if the court can make some ruling in your favor based on what is in and under that heading alone.

Beginners sometimes make the opposite error of grouping several points under one heading. This happens most often where the writer's adversary is the one charged with a burden of pleading, production, or persuasion. If the adversary must carry a burden for several elements, the failure to support any element creates a complete and independent ground for a ruling against the adversary (and therefore a separate point).

For example, in the memorandum in Appendix D, Goslin is entitled to a preliminary injunction only if he can show (1) that he is likely to succeed ultimately on the merits, (2) that he would suffer irreparable harm without a preliminary injunction, and (3) that a balancing of the equities favors an injunction. Goslin has only one point because he must prove all those elements to win. But the nephew can win if he can show that Goslin is not likely to succeed on the merits, *or* that Goslin is not threatened with irreparable harm, *or* that the equities run against an injunction. If the nephew makes all three of these arguments, he would have three separate points because any one of them would support a decision against Goslin.

3. Headings and sub-headings should not assume information that a judge would lack when reading the Table of Contents.

Put yourself in the judge's position. When turning to the Table of Contents for the first time, the judge knows nothing of the case. How would you react to this heading?

> I. THE MOTION TO QUASH BECAUSE OF
> THE FIRST AMENDMENT SHOULD BE
> DENIED.

Quash what? What does the First Amendment have to do with this? The following is better:

> I. THE MOTION TO QUASH A DEPOSITION
> SUBPOENA SHOULD BE DENIED BE-
> CAUSE THE SUBPOENA DOES NOT VIO-
> LATE THE JOURNALIST WITNESS'S FIRST
> AMENDMENT RIGHT TO MAINTAIN THE
> CONFIDENTIALITY OF HIS SOURCES.

4. The sub-headings should be neither too many nor too few.

For each point, the number of sub-headings should equal the number of *significant* steps of logic inherent in the argument. For example, the failure-to-state-a-cause-of-action point on page 290 depends on the following steps of logic:

- The complaint alleges only educational malpractice. Because the complaint cannot be interpreted to allege any other kind of claim, it can survive a motion to dismiss only if this state were to recognize a cause of action for educational malpractice.
- The idea of recovering for educational malpractice has been scorned by other courts.
- Such a tort is impractical because a court would not be able to determine how much of the fault was the student's and how much was the school's.
- Such a tort would damage schools by disrupting the educational process.

These are the very steps represented in the sub-headings on page 290. More sub-headings would have fragmented the argument so much that the reader would not quickly see how it fits together. Fewer sub-headings would have hidden the logic.

5. Each heading and sub-heading should be a single sentence that can be immediately understood. What does this heading mean?

> I. BECAUSE THIS STATE'S SHIELD LAW
> PROVIDES NO EXPLICIT PROTECTION
> FOR THE MEDIA AGAINST REVEALING
> NONCONFIDENTIAL INFORMATION OR
> SOURCES AND BECAUSE THE LEGISLA-
> TIVE HISTORY IS SILENT, THE SCOPE OF
> ART. 9, SECTION 765 IS LIMITED TO PRO-
> TECTING ONLY CONFIDENTIAL INFOR-
> MATION OR SOURCES, AND THIS COURT
> SHOULD THEREFORE QUASH A SUB-
> POENA THAT SOUGHT INFORMATION
> THAT THE MOVANT, A NEWSPAPER RE-
> PORTER, HAD OBTAINED THROUGH CON-
> VERSATIONS IN WHICH HE HAD NOT
> PROMISED TO KEEP HIS INFORMANTS'
> IDENTITIES IN CONFIDENCE.

A monster like this has two parents. One is the urge to put everything in the point heading and save nothing for the sub-headings. The other is simple verbosity: even more than elsewhere, conciseness is a real premium in a heading. Rewriting can produce something like this:

> I. THE DEPOSITION SUBPOENA SHOULD BE
> QUASHED BECAUSE THE EVIDENCE

SOUGHT IS NOT CONFIDENTIAL AND IS
THEREFORE NOT PROTECTED BY THIS
STATE'S MEDIA SHIELD LAW.

A. Art. 9, Section 765 permits a litigant
    to obtain information that the media
    has not treated as confidential.

B. The appellant journalist concedes that
    he did not promise confidentiality
    to his sources.

6. Each point heading should identify the ruling you want.   A
point heading fails this criterion if it leaves a judge wondering "What do you
want me to do?" In a trial court, you can tell the judge what you want by
identifying the order or judgment that you argue should be granted or denied. (On appeal, you can do the same thing by identifying the order or
judgment appealed from and by calling it either correct or erroneous —
which implies whether you want it affirmed or reversed.) To all of the following headings (from three different cases), a judge's reaction would be
"What do you want from me?":

Case A: I.   THE PARTIES NEVER FORMED A CON-
                 TRACT TO MERGE.

Case B: I.   THE COMPLAINT DOES NOT STATE A
                 CAUSE OF ACTION.

Case C: I.   THE EVIDENCE SOUGHT IS NOT PRO-
                 TECTED BY A PRIVILEGE.

In a trial court, the following would at least tell the judge what you want:

Case A: I.   THE DEFENDANT'S MOTION FOR SUM-
                 MARY JUDGMENT SHOULD BE GRANTED
                 BECAUSE THE PARTIES NEVER FORMED
                 A CONTRACT TO MERGE.

Case B: I.   THE COMPLAINT STATES A CAUSE OF
                 ACTION AND SHOULD NOT BE
                 DISMISSED.

Case C: I.   THE MOTION TO QUASH SHOULD BE DE-
                 NIED BECAUSE THE EVIDENCE SOUGHT
                 IS NOT PROTECTED BY A PRIVILEGE.

Later, if there were an appeal, the headings below would do the same job. Notice how each heading identifies the ruling appealed from:

Appeal A: I.   BECAUSE THE PARTIES NEVER FORMED A CONTRACT TO MERGE, THE CIRCUIT COURT SHOULD HAVE GRANTED THE DEFENDANT'S MOTION FOR SUMMARY JUDGMENT.

Appeal B: I.   THE COMPLAINT STATES A CAUSE OF ACTION, AND THE DISTRICT COURT ERRED IN DISMISSING IT.

Appeal C: I.   THE SUPERIOR COURT PROPERLY REFUSED TO QUASH A SUBPOENA FOR EVIDENCE NOT PROTECTED BY A PRIVILEGE.

Be careful about two things. First, this criterion applies only to *point* headings, not sub-headings. Second, the examples above satisfy this criterion *but not the next two.*

7. The controlling rules should be identified in the headings or sub-headings.   A reader who must make a decision is not influenced until the governing rules are set out. Compare the examples at the bottom of page 295 with the following:

Case A: I.   THE DEFENDANT'S MOTION FOR SUMMARY JUDGMENT SHOULD BE GRANTED BECAUSE THE PARTIES NEVER FORMED A CONTRACT TO MERGE.

     A.   In an action for breach of contract, a defendant is entitled to summary judgment where the plaintiff is not able to produce evidence of the existence of a contract.

Case B: I.   THE COMPLAINT STATES A CAUSE OF ACTION AND SHOULD NOT BE DISMISSED.

     A.   This state has recognized the tort of wrongful discharge.

Case C: I.   THE MOTION TO QUASH SHOULD BE DE-
NIED BECAUSE THE EVIDENCE SOUGHT
IS NOT PROTECTED BY A PRIVILEGE.

     A.   The First Amendment does not pro-
tect evidence in the possession of a
journalist where the journalist did
not obtain it under a promise of confidentiality and where the evidence
cannot be obtained elsewhere.

Be careful: the examples above satisfy this criterion *but not the next one.*

**8. The one, two, or three most determinative facts should at
least be alluded to in either the headings or sub-headings.**   This is
what pins down for the reader how the rules entitle you to what you want.
Compare the examples in the preceding criterion with the following:

Case A: I.   THE DEFENDANT'S MOTION FOR SUM-
MARY JUDGMENT SHOULD BE GRANTED
BECAUSE THE PARTIES NEVER FORMED
A CONTRACT TO MERGE.

     A.   In an action for breach of contract, a
defendant is entitled to summary
judgment where the plaintiff is not
able to produce evidence of the
existence of a contract.

     B.   The written contract was never
signed, and there was no evidence of
an oral understanding that could
survive the Statute of Frauds.

Case B: I.   THE COMPLAINT STATES A CAUSE OF
ACTION AND SHOULD NOT BE DIS-
MISSED.

     A.   This court has recognized the tort of
wrongful discharge.

     B.   The complaint alleges that the plain-
tiff was discharged solely because he
questioned the defendant employer's
corrupt contributions to political
campaigns.

Case C: I.   THE MOTION TO QUASH SHOULD BE DE-
                 NIED BECAUSE THE EVIDENCE SOUGHT
                 IS NOT PROTECTED BY A PRIVILEGE.

             A.   The First Amendment does not pro-
                  tect evidence in the possession of a
                  journalist where the journalist did
                  not obtain it under a promise of con-
                  fidentiality and where the evidence
                  cannot be obtained elsewhere.

             B.   This journalist did not promise his
                  source confidentiality, and his
                  source did not request it.

             C.   The evidence sought cannot be
                  obtained elsewhere because the
                  journalist's source has died.

Each of the examples above reflects a paradigm-structured argument, with a conclusion, a rule, an implied rule proof, and an express rule application. (Rule proof can be implied because the reader will understand that where a rule is stated in a heading, the proof will appear in the Argument under that heading.)

9. Headings and sub-headings should be forceful and argumentative.   Each heading and sub-heading should state an essential idea in an assertive way and show how that idea fits into your theory. The two faults to avoid are topic headings and headings with a tone of weakness or neutrality. These headings are topical:

Disruption in the public schools.

Absence of a contract to merge.

Wrongful discharge.

Confidentiality.

But these are argumentative:

The public schools would be disrupted if this court were
to recognize a tort of educational malpractice.

The parties made no contract to merge.

The complaint states a cause of action in
wrongful discharge.

The journalist neither promised confidentiality
nor was asked for it.

This heading sounds weak and almost neutral:

> Arbitration was ordered by the Superior Court
> incorrectly, no agreement to arbitrate having
> been made.

This is more argumentative:

> Because the parties never agreed to arbitrate,
> the Superior Court should not have granted an
> order compelling arbitration.

Exercise. Point Headings and Sub-Headings

Draft two sets of point headings and sub-headings — one favoring each party — using the facts and authority either from an exercise of your teacher's choice in Chapter 11 or Chapter 12 or from a writing assignment that you have previously completed in this course.

23 Statements of the Case

§23.1　How a Statement of the Case Works

> There is nothing more horrible than the murder of a beautiful theory
> by a brutal gang of facts.
>
> — *La Rochefoucald*

"It may sound paradoxical," wrote Justice Jackson, "but most contentions of law are won or lost on the facts."[1] And in a motion memorandum or an appellate brief, the judge learns of the facts in the Statement of the Case, which has two purposes.[2] The ostensible purpose is to summarize the factual record relevant to the decision the court has been asked to make. The ulterior purpose is to imply your motivating arguments[3] through the way the facts are presented. (Motivating arguments, after all, grow out of the facts.)

Statements of the Case are subject to some rather strict rules.

You must recite in the Statement all facts that you mention elsewhere in your motion memorandum or appellate brief. You must also recite in the Statement all facts on which your adversary relies. The judge is entitled to a place in the document where all the legally significant facts can be seen together.

---

§23.1　1. Robert H. Jackson, *Advocacy Before the Supreme Court: Suggestions for Effective Case Presentations,* 37 A.B.A. J. 801, 803 (1951).

2. You will understand this chapter more easily if, before continuing here, you read the Statements of the Case in the motion memorandum in Appendix D and in the appellate briefs in Appendices E and F.

3. See pages 256-57.

You must provide a citation to a page in the record for every fact in the Statement. (See §23.4.) The judge is entitled to an easy method of checking what you say.

You are not allowed to argue, analyze law, draw factual inferences, or even characterize[4] the facts. It is called a *Statement* of the Case because the facts are *stated* there and analyzed elsewhere. Inferences and characterizations of facts belong in the Argument because they are argument. (You are, however, allowed to report the inferences witnesses drew and the characterizations they spoke. And you are allowed to state inferences that your adversary is certain not to contest (because an undisputed inference will be treated as a fact.)

You are not allowed to discuss facts that are outside the record. (See §23.4.) A Statement of the Case describes only procedural facts: allegations in pleadings, testimony, other evidence, and so on. Other facts must be excluded, a process called *limiting the Statement to the record*. It is called a Statement of the *Case* because the only facts allowed are the ones that have been put before the court through appropriate procedural means. (It could more accurately be called a "Summary of the Record," although nobody uses that term.) However, the *absence* from the record of a particular allegation or piece of evidence can itself be a fact. And you can describe such a gap in the record ("no witness identified the defendant") if it demonstrates that the opposing party has failed to carry some burden of pleading, production, or proof.

Finally, you are not allowed to misrepresent the facts, either overtly or by omission. (See §23.3.)

If you cannot argue, characterize, or state inferences in a Statement of the Case, how can you persuade there? The most effective Statements of the Case persuade through organization that emphasizes favorable facts and through word choice that affects the reader while saying nothing that the adversary could reasonably claim to be inaccurate. In other words, a persuasive Statement of the case is *descriptive in form but probative in substance*.

Consider two examples, each the beginning passage of a Statement of the Case. Assume that the plaintiffs are suing a backcountry hiking guide for negligence after the guide led them into disaster. (Citations to the record have been deleted.)

On June 11, the plaintiffs asked in Stove Pipe Springs whether there was a backcountry guide who could lead them through certain parts of Death Valley. After some discussion, they hired the defendant to take them on a full-day hike the next day.

The climate in Death Valley is one of the hottest and driest known. The highest temperature recorded each year reaches at least 120° and in many years at least 125°. The highest temperature recorded in Death Valley — 134° — is also the highest recorded in the

---

4. See §13.1.

When they started out, the defendant carried a compass and map. Each plaintiff carried sunglasses, a large-brim hat, and a quart of water.

At trial, a climatologist testified about the climate in Death Valley. Occasionally, winter temperatures fall below freezing, but there is no water to freeze. Spring and fall temperatures approximate summer temperatures elsewhere. July is the hottest month, with an average high of about 116° and an average low of about 87°. The highest temperature ever recorded in Death Valley was 134°. (The highest recorded on earth was 136°.) Reports by early explorers of temperatures above 150° have not been confirmed or repeated through official measurements. Average annual rainfall is about 1½ inches, and the number of days on which precipitation falls in an average year is eight.

Western Hemisphere and the second highest recorded anywhere on earth. (The highest was only two degrees hotter and was recorded in the Sahara desert.) The rainfall is only 1½ inches per year — the lowest in the Western Hemisphere — and in a few years no rain falls at all.

In the summer sun there, a person can lose four gallons of perspiration a day and — in 3% humidity — die of dehydration unless the lost water is quickly replaced. A person becomes delirious after two gallons are lost. At that heat and humidity, unprotected wood can split open spontaneously.

The defendant advertised himself as a professional and experienced backcountry guide. He was hired by the plaintiffs and then took them into Death Valley for a full-day hike on a June day with a quart of water each.

After reading the example on the right you are prepared to believe that this hike was madness, and that the guide was responsible for it. But in early drafts, many beginners instinctively produce a Statement like the one on the left, which does not convince you that the guide did anything alarming. It fails because it is descriptive *both* in form *and in substance*. After you complete your first-draft Statement, your goal will be to rewrite it until you have something that more closely approximates the example on the right, which is descriptive in form but *probative* in substance.

How did the example on the right persuade you?

First, you were given no marginal facts — such as the temperatures in other months or the unverified reports by explorers — that would have obscured the information that is critical. You were not even told the precise date because only the month or season matters. And each fact was given a prominence corresponding to the fact's value.

Second, the writer selected facts that would illustrate the theory: you will lose four gallons of water a day in such a place. After two gallons, you will become delirious. This was a full-day hike. The plaintiffs had a quart of water each. The defendant claimed to be a professional and experienced guide. As each of these facts is added, the logic of the theory unfolds.

Third, the relationship between each fact and the theory was pointed out to you. You were told, for example, why these temperatures should have suggested caution to the guide: they were "the highest recorded in the Western Hemisphere and the second highest recorded anywhere on earth," and the only higher temperature "was recorded in the Sahara desert."

Finally, you were given the kind of vivid details that make a theory come alive: the delirium, for example, and the wood splitting open. (See §18.7.)

But the example on the right appears to be nothing more than a description of the relevant facts. Nothing in it could reasonably be challenged as untrue by an adversary. Each fact is objectively verifiable in the record. The only characterization ("one of the hottest and driest known") was testified to by an expert witness (the climatologist). And — most importantly — the writer never expressed inferences. *You drew all of them yourself.*

§23.2   How to State Facts Persuasively

> If you want to win a case, paint the Judge a *picture* and keep it simple.
>
> — *John W. Davis*

Here is how to paint the picture in the Statement of the Case:

1.   Reflect your theory throughout the Statement.
2.   Breathe life into the facts by telling a compelling story about people.
3.   Choose the method of organization that tells the story most persuasively.
4.   Start with a punch.
5.   Focus on facts that would show that you have satisfied a procedural burden (or that your adversary has failed to do so).
6.   Emphasize favorable facts.
7.   Neutralize unfavorable facts.
8.   Humanize your client.

1. Reflect your theory throughout the Statement.   Tightly focus the Statement of the Case on facts that advance your theory. If the Statement wanders aimlessly and indiscriminately through the facts, the reader will not grasp your theory and may not even understand the story.

Every word should be selected to make the theory more clear. In the Statement in Appendix E, you learn that the defendant "suffers from gender dysphoria syndrome," while the prosecution's Statement in Appendix F instead says the defendant "planned to undergo surgery" to alter gender. Do these phrasings advance the theories? How? When referring to the defendant, the prosecution's Statement uses the words "he," "him," and "her." The defendant's Statement, on the other hand, uses feminine pronouns and calls the defendant "*Ms.* Bresnahan." Is any of that unethical?[1] Would the court

---

§23.2   1. See §§19.3 and 23.3.

be misled? Has either attorney risked credibility? Or do these phrasings reflect legitimate differences in the parties' theories?

If you focus the Statement in this way, it might be surprisingly short. For example, consider the following from one of Cardozo's opinions (surely, a model of brevity):

> A radiator placed about ten or twelve inches from the edge of an unprotected hoistway and parallel thereto fell down the shaft and killed a man below.[2]

The only other facts we need to know are the identity of the parties. After reading this we are prepared to hold liable whoever put the radiator there, whoever knocked it over, and whoever failed to put a protective screen over the top of the shaft. Imagine the facts *not* mentioned: why the radiator was put there, where it came from, where it was supposed to go afterward, why the man was below, and so on. None would have advanced the theory, and all would have distracted the reader.

Throughout the Statement, the reader should be conscious — from the way the facts are cast — of whom you represent. If the reader wonders about that, even for a paragraph or two, you have probably written an unpersuasive Statement.

2. Breathe life into the facts by telling a compelling story about people.
You can make the story come alive by setting out the facts that show who has behaved properly and who has not, letting the facts themselves make your case. A simple narrative with vivid nouns and verbs does this best. For example, *Hatahley v. United States*[3]

> involved, on its face, cold jurisdictional and legal problems: Were rights under the Taylor Grazing Act, a federal law, affected by a state law regulating abandoned horses? Had there in any event been compliance with the state statute's terms? Did the Federal Torts Claims Act cover intentional trespasses within the scope of federal agents' authority? The injuries for which redress were sought were the carrying off of horses and mules belonging to the plaintiffs, who were Navaho Indians.
> . . . Here is how the facts were set forth in [the plaintiffs'] brief:
>
>> The animals were rounded up on the range and were either driven or hauled in trucks to a Government-owned or controlled corral 45 miles away. Horses which could not be so handled were shot and killed by the Government's agents on the spot. . . . [T]he horses were so jammed together in the trucks that some died as a result, and, in one instance, the leg of a horse that inconveniently protruded through the truck body was sawed off by a federal employee. . . . (Fdg. 23, 25; R. 33-34.) Later, the animals were taken in trucks to Provo, Utah, a distance of 350 miles, where they were sold to a glue factory and horse meat plant for about $1,700 — at about 3 cents a pound (R. 93, 293) — no part of which was received by petitioners (Fdg. 24; R. 34).[4]

---

2. *DeHaen v. Rockwood Sprinkler Co.*, 179 N.E.2d 764, 765 (N.Y. 1932).

3. 351 U.S. 173 (1956).

4. Frederick Bernays Wiener, *Briefing and Arguing Federal Appeals* 58-59 (1967). (The references to "Fdg." and to "R." are citations to the record. Section 23.4 explains what a record is and how to cite to it.)

The Supreme Court held that "[t]hese acts were wrongful trespasses not involving discretion on the part of the agents, and they do give rise to a claim compensable under the Federal Tort Claims Act."[5] On this fact description, does the result surprise you?

After reading the Statement of the Case for the movant or for the appellant, the judge should be left with the feeling that something is unacceptably wrong with what has happened. The movant or the appellant, after all, wants the judge to *do* something about the facts. But after reading the Statement of the Case of an appellee or a party opposing a motion, the judge should instead believe the facts are fair and just — or at least that they are not so unjust as to call for judicial intervention. One way to arouse those feelings is to show how the facts are vividly, even interestingly, just or unjust. Can you still see in your mind trucks, horses, a corral, a man with a saw? Does that scene sum up what *Hatahley* was all about?

3. Choose the method of organization that tells the story most persuasively.

The first step in organizing a Statement of the Case is to make a list of the facts that are — according to your theory — determinative. Add explanatory facts only if needed to avoid confusion or to tell the story coherently. Omit the coincidental facts.[6] Include dates only if they are determinative or are needed to avoid confusion.[7] Include the identity of the witness who is the source of the fact only if that truly adds to the story. (Identifying every witness clutters up the Statement and gets in the way of the story you want to tell.[8]) Be careful to note each fact's citation to the record (see §23.4).

The second step is to make an outline that would set out the determinative and explanatory facts in a sequence both persuasive and easily understandable. Sometimes — but not often — the most effective sequence is chronological. More frequently, a topical organization works better because you can use the way you organize the facts to imply the logical relationships between them. In some cases, you might try a topical organization that breaks into a chronological narrative where it is important for the reader to understand the sequence in which events happened. Often, the Statement

---

5. *Hatahley*, 351 U.S. at 181.

6. See §13.2 for more on determinative facts, explanatory facts, and coincidental facts.

7. Beginners tend to include every available date because dates are the easiest of all facts to state. But irrelevant dates clutter up the Statement and thus obscure the truly important facts. And if time is not an issue, they can mislead the reader by implying that it is. For example, where the first sentence in a Statement is "The summons and complaint were served on February 1, 1988," the reader will get the impression that the controversy is about a statute of limitations or some other issue involving time.

8. The identity of a witness could be valuable if the fact is an admission ("the plaintiff admitted that he was not wearing his seat belt"); if the witness is impressively authoritative ("four professors of engineering all testified that the dam broke because"); or if the fact is part of the witness's state of mind ("the defendant testified that she intended to sell only the frame and not the painting"). And if the fact is contested — for example, one witness says the traffic light was green while another says it was red — you probably need to identify the witnesses because you will try to show that one is more credible than the other. If the record includes affidavits, the names of the affiants will unavoidably appear in citations to the record (see §23.4).

can be made more accessible by breaking it up with sub-headings that are reprinted verbatim in the table of contents.

4. Start with a punch.   Begin the Statement with a short passage — one or two paragraphs — summarizing your most compelling facts so that the judge understands the heart of your theory. Then tell the whole story, explaining along the way and in detail the facts that you summarized at the beginning. Never begin the Statement with neutral facts, unfavorable facts, or unimportant facts.

The opening passage is the most important part of the Statement. If written well, it puts the judge in a receptive frame of mind; tells the judge what facts to look for later; and creates a lasting impression. The opening passage is usually the hardest part of the Statement to write. But the extra time and effort are an excellent investment.

In the memorandum in Appendix D and in the briefs in Appendices E and F, notice how each Statement begins with a passage like the one described here.

5. Focus on facts that would show that you have satisfied a procedural burden (or that your adversary has failed to do so).   If you must carry a burden of pleading, production, or persuasion, you can emphasize in the Statement of the Case the facts that you will later use in the Argument to show that you have discharged the burden. If any of those facts are undisputed, you can point that out:

> Dr. Charbonneau testified without contradiction that Ms. Leyland's injuries could have been caused only by a blow from a long, thin object "about the size and shape of a nightstick." (T. at 97.)

Regardless of which party has a burden, you can also point to inconsistencies in the evidence and things that are missing from the record:

> Although Officer Joyner testified that Ms. Leyland was assaulted by another prisoner in her cell (T. at 178), he could not name or describe that prisoner (T. at 187), and there is no evidence anywhere in the record that another prisoner was at any point assigned to or given access to her cell. Moreover, although the warden of the county jail testified that arresting officers are not normally permitted in cell blocks (T. at 245), Officer Joyner was the sole witness who claimed to have seen an assault in Ms. Leyland's cell.

Who do you think beat up Leyland? Every word in this passage is value-neutral, and none of the evidence is interpreted or characterized. Although it persuades, the passage sounds clinically objective. The writer has merely brought together facts that had been scattered about in the record. And the writer has refrained from stating inferences — such as "Officer Joyner should not be believed" — that should be left for the Argument.

6. Emphasize favorable facts.   That can be done through organization. Readers tend to be most attentive at the beginning, less attentive at the end, and least attentive in the middle. It can also be done by describing favorable facts in detail and by omitting unnecessary facts that cloud the picture you want the reader to see. Notice, for example, that the name of the warden is missing from the example above: the essential fact is the warden's official position, and the name would have no effect on the court. Specifics about dates, times, and places can be seductively concrete when you are writing, but to a reader they can also obscure what really happened. Compare these:

At 2:10 A.M., on Tuesday, September 2, 1986, Officer Joyner was told by his dispatcher to investigate a disturbance on the fourth floor of the building at 642 Sutherland Street. (T. at 162.) There he took a complaint from Kenneth Novak, a tenant in apartment 4-C, and, as a result, arrested Ms. Leyland, who lives in apartment 4-E. (T. at 163-65.) Officer Joyner was not able to leave the building with Ms. Leyland until 2:45 A.M. because she had been asleep and needed to dress. (T. at 166-67.) Ms. Leyland testified that she was so tired that she fell asleep in the police car during the drive to the precinct station. (T. at 14.) Cynthia Scollard, a police booking clerk, testified that she was on duty at about 3:05 A.M. on September 2, when she heard a commotion in the precinct parking lot. (T. at 145.) Ms. Scollard further testified that she noticed Ms. Leyland's injuries as soon as Officer Joyner turned Ms. Leyland over to her, and that Ms. Leyland appeared to be very tired at the time. (T. at 147-49.)

Ms. Leyland was awakened and arrested by Officer Joyner at her apartment shortly after 2 A.M. on the day she was beaten. (T. at 162-67.) A police booking clerk testified that she heard "a man yelling in the parking lot" just before Officer Joyner brought Ms. Leyland into the precinct station. (T. at 145.) The booking clerk also testified that she immediately noticed bleeding from Ms. Leyland's lip and from the side of her head (T. at 147-48), and that Ms. Leyland's face began to swell during booking (T. at 148-49).

In the passage on the left, the date, the address, the precise times, the booking clerk's name, and the details about Leyland's tired state are all clutter. The passage on the right omits the unnecessary, opening up room to dwell on the details that are truly essential. And the carefully edited quotation in the passage on the right brings the story to life.

7. *Neutralize unfavorable facts.* The most effective method is to juxtapose an unfavorable fact with other facts that explain, counter-balance, or justify it:

> Even though the booking clerk testified that Ms. Leyland did not complain to her that she had been beaten by Officer Joyner, the booking clerk also testified that Officer Joyner stood next to Ms. Leyland throughout the booking procedure. (T. at 166-69.) Ms. Leyland testified that she had no memory of being booked (T. at 32), and Dr. Charbonneau testified that persons who suffer a head injury like Ms. Leyland's are often "stunned and impassive" immediately afterward. (T. at 104.)

The most effective juxtapositions are often found in sentences structured around an "even though" contrast (like the first sentence in the paragraph above). A far less effective method is to de-emphasize an unfavorable fact by tucking it into an obscure part of the Statement of the Case and summarizing it without much detail. Hiding an unfavorable fact will not make it go away. And if you seem to be trying to ignore the fact, you will not be viewed as credible and reliable. If you do not try to neutralize it, you forfeit an opportunity to persuade.

8. *Humanize your client.* Be careful about how you refer to the parties. In an appellate brief, you only cause confusion if you refer to them continually as "appellant" and "appellee" because these designations tell the reader nothing more than who lost below.[9] The procedural designations from the trial court are more clear: "the plaintiff" and "the defendant" in a civil case or, in a criminal case, "the defendant" and "the State" (or "the People," "the Government," or "the Commonwealth"). More still can be conveyed by using some generic factual designation related to the issues: "the buyer" and "the seller" in a commercial dispute or "the employer" and "the employee" in a discrimination case. But, unless it would be confusing, your client's real name is often the best tactical choice. The passages on the preceding pages would lose much of their liveliness if "Ms. Leyland" were reduced to "the plaintiff." The same thing would happen if Officer Joyner were to gain anonymity as "the arresting officer," although in many other cases a depersonalized opposing party would seem easier to dislike ("the insurance company," "the union," "the hospital").

---

9. In many courts, you are not permitted to use these designations in the body of the brief, although they will naturally appear on the cover page. *See, e.g.*, Rule 28(d) of the Federal Rules of Appellate Procedure.

§23.3   Fact Ethics

As you know, a lawyer is forbidden to "[k]nowingly make a false statement of law or fact" to a court.[1] In §19.3, we explored the consequences of a false statement of law. Courts react just as harshly to false statements of fact.

There are three kinds of false statements that will incur the fury of a court. One is a flat-out misrepresentation: making a statement about a fact that is unsupported by the actual record. The second is misrepresentation by omission: presenting a version of the record that ignores facts favoring the opposing party.[2] The third is misrepresentation by describing inferences as though they were facts. (In the Statement of the Case, only facts may be described.[3] In the Argument, you may draw inferences from the facts, but they should be presented as that — and argued because the court can reject them and draw contrary inferences.)

Even if it were not unethical, factual misrepresentation never fools a court and hurts only the misrepresenting lawyer and that lawyer's client. Misrepresentations are quickly spotted by opposing attorneys, and once a misrepresentation is pointed out to a court, the entire memorandum or brief is treated with deep suspicion.

§23.4   The Record

Court rules virtually everywhere require that each fact be cited to a specific page in the record — not only when you recite the fact in the Statement of the Case, but also when you analyze it in the Argument.[1] (The judge should not have to go back to the Statement to find the citation.) Court rules aside, citations have a persuasive effect of their own. Thorough citations, by their appearance alone, create confidence that every fact recited in the Statement is fully supported in the record, while spotty or absent citations arouse a court's skepticism. And thorough record citations add to your own credibility by creating an impression of carefulness.

---

§23.3   1. Model Code of Professional Responsibility, DR 7-102(A)(5). The same prohibition, in virtually the same words, appears in Rule 3.3(a)(1) of the Model Rules of Professional Conduct.

2. "[T]he court is not impressed by a statement of facts which completely ignores the evidence produced by the other side." *Manteca Veal Co. v. Corbari,* 116 Cal. App. 2d 896, 898, 254 P.2d 884, 885 (1st Dist. 1953).

3. But as §23.1 explains, inferences drawn by witnesses and inferences the other side will not dispute are both treated as facts.

§23.4   1. *See, e.g.,* Rules 28(a)(4) and (e) of the Federal Rules of Appellate Procedure. The type of opening passage described on page 307 is usually considered exempt from this requirement because facts summarized there will be explained in detail later in the Statement.

The record might include any or all of the following: (1) the pleadings;[2] (2) evidence in the form of testimony, affidavits, and exhibits; and (3) prior court orders, judicial opinions, and, on appeal, the judgment below.

The Bluebook provides some record citation rules in practitioners' note 7[3] and some abbreviations for court documents in table 8. In addition, every jurisdiction has rules and customs of its own.[4] In a motion memorandum, cite to specific documents within the record, such as "Compl. ¶ 22" (complaint at paragraph 22), "T. at 98" (transcript at page 98), or "Myers Reply Aff. ¶ 12" (Myers reply affidavit at paragraph 12). On appeal, cite to the record as a whole ("R. at 393") or to the joint appendix[5] ("JA at 99"). In any event, the citation is placed in a parenthetical:

> The plaintiff alleged only that the goods were not delivered on time. (Compl. ¶ 22.)

Remember that a citation proves no more than the sentence that precedes it and, if the citation is placed inside a sentence, the citation proves only the portion of the sentence that precedes it.

> Although Officer Joyner wrote in an incident report that Ms. Leyland was injured when she resisted arrest (R. at 98), he testified at trial that she was injured when assaulted by another prisoner in her cell (R. at 178).

The citation ends with a period if it stands alone as a citation sentence, but not if it is interpolated into a textual sentence.

Exercise I.   What Is a Fact? (Reprise)

Of the nine events listed in §13.1, which can be mentioned in a Statement of the Case?

---

2. Remember that pleadings are not evidence. If the issue before the court is whether a burden of pleading has been carried, the pleadings are the only source of "facts," and the "facts" must be described as allegations. On a motion to dismiss a complaint in a wrongful death action, it is wrong to write "The deceased was run over by the defendant's truck." See §20.2.1 for why. You do not, however, have to begin every factual sentence with "The complaint alleges." It is enough to begin the Statement of the Case with this: "The complaint alleges the following:". If, on the other hand, the issue is whether a burden of production or persuasion has been carried, the source of facts must be evidentiary (not pleadings) because the burden at issue is an evidentiary one. See §20.2.3.

3. One of the Bluebook rules is routinely ignored in the practice of law. When a record cite appears inside a sentence, practitioners' note 7 purportedly requires that it be surrounded *both* with parentheses *and* with commas. That is redundant, and lawyers generally do not do it.

4. Local rules and custom usually allow some latitude in the use of abbreviations when citing to the record. If you use abbreviations that might be unfamiliar to the court, include a footnote near the beginning of the Statement of the Case, explaining what the abbreviations mean.

5. The joint appendix is an abbreviated form of the record on appeal. See §25.2.

Exercise II.   Topical Organization v. Chronological Organization

For each Statement of the Case in Appendices D, E, and F, decide whether the organization is topical, chronological, or a combination. For each, is the organization effective or ineffective? Why?

Exercise III.   Escape from Prison? (Rewriting Statements of the Case)

Orville Bradwyn is being tried for attempted escape from prison. Below is a Statement of the Case for the prosecution, followed by one for the defense. (Citations to the record have been omitted.)

Rewrite each Statement.

For the prosecution:

The defendant is a prisoner at the Simmonsville Penitentiary. On July 6, he was not in the dinner line where he was required to be, and Sgt. Tunmeyer, the prosecution's sole witness, organized a search for him. According to Sgt. Tunmeyer, no prisoner is allowed in the laundry room after 5 P.M., and the defendant was found in the laundry room at 7:39 P.M. The reason for this rule is that the laundry room is an obvious place from which to escape. The prison does the laundry of the state hospital nearby, and hospital trucks pick up hospital laundry directly from the prison laundry room. At 5 P.M., Sgt. Tunmeyer checked the laundry room thoroughly, did not see anyone, and subsequently locked the door. Even though the defendant had been assigned to work in the laundry, he was not on duty when he was found in the laundry. Before and after dinner, prisoners are free to move about outside their cells. When the defendant's cell was checked, many of his personal belongings were found. In fact, the defendant had a reputation for being tidy and was drying all of his clothes when found in the laundry at 7:39 P.M. However, when his cell was checked his radio had been left on, and some material had been left under the covers of his bed to make it look like someone was asleep there.

For the defendant:

Mr. Bradwyn is an inmate at the Simmonsville Penitentiary. At this prison, inmates are free to move about outside the cells before and after dinner, which is from 6:00 to 7:00 P.M. The prisoners are counted each day in the dinner line, and when Mr. Bradwyn was not present, he was considered missing. Prisoners are not allowed in the laundry after 5 P.M. because the laundry room provides an obvious escape route on the truck the state hospital sends at 8 P.M. each night to pick up its laundry. Sgt. Tunmeyer testified that he checked the laundry at 5 P.M. and locked it up without seeing Mr. Bradwyn there.

When Mr. Bradwyn was discovered to be absent from the dinner line, Sgt. Tunmeyer organized a search and found him in the laundry room at

7:39 P.M., where Mr. Bradwyn was drying his prison uniforms. There was no testimony about how Mr. Bradwyn could have entered the laundry room, which Sgt. Tunmeyer claims to have locked. Mr. Bradwyn is one of the prisoners assigned to work in the laundry. Sgt. Tunmeyer admits to past quarrels with Mr. Bradwyn, and that Mr. Bradwyn had filed a complaint against him for beating him. He also admitted that Mr. Bradwyn is an unusually tidy person who does not like other people to touch his things, and that at 7:39 P.M. all of Mr. Bradwyn's clothing was in a dryer.

The state has not introduced any evidence that Mr. Bradwyn was not on duty earlier in the day. Nor has it introduced any evidence that Mr. Bradwyn could not have been locked in the laundry room accidentally by Sgt. Tunmeyer at 5 P.M.

Exercise IV.   *Drafting Statements of the Case*

Draft two Statements of the Case — one favoring each party — using the facts and authority either from an exercise of your teacher's choice in either of Chapter 11 or Chapter 12 or from a writing assignment that you have previously completed in this course.

24 Questions Presented

§24.1 The Purpose and Structure of a Question Presented

A Question Presented has two functions.[1] First, it defines the decision that the court is asked to make. And second, within limits, you can use the Question to persuade by framing it in terms of the facts at the core of your theory. If the Question defines the decision objectively, it does not perform the second function of a persuasive Question Presented. And if it argues the case, it does not fulfill the first. The solution is to persuade through juxtaposition and careful word choice — just as you do in a Statement of the Case, but much more concisely.

Structurally, a Question Presented is an inquiry plus a list of the most determinative facts and an allusion to the body of law that would govern the result:

> Is the manufacturer of an acoustical keyboard liable under an implied warranty of fitness for purpose to a purchaser in whose hands the keyboard exploded the first time it was plugged in?

The determinative facts and the allusion to the governing body of law define the issue so that, as a matter of legal inquiry, it becomes the question "presented" by the situation. "Is a manufacturer liable to a purchaser?" may be a question, but it is not a Question Presented.

§24.1 1. You will understand this chapter more easily if you read the Questions Presented in the memorandum in Appendix D and in the briefs in Appendices E and F.

The inquiry can begin with whatever verb is most appropriate to the issue:

Does the First Amendment allow . . . ?

Is the manufacturer of an acoustical keyboard liable . . . ?

Or the inquiry can instead begin with the word *whether* — even though the result is not a grammatically complete sentence:

Whether the First Amendment allows . . .

Whether the manufacturer of an acoustical keyboard is liable . . .

But "whether" Questions often strike the reader as weaker and more tedious than Questions that begin with a verb.

Facts that do not fit naturally into the inquiry can be attached at the end in clauses beginning with "where" or "when":

Is the manufacturer of an acoustical keyboard absolved of liability under an implied warranty of fitness for purpose where an ordinary consumer bought it in pieces from a street vendor and attempted to reassemble it himself even though the words "Do Not Open or Attempt to Repair This Product" were engraved on the outside?

The inquiry is best placed first because a list of determinative facts makes little sense until the reader knows the inquiry to which those facts are relevant. The following, for example, are not easy to understand:

facts before inquiry:	Where an ordinary consumer bought an acoustical keyboard in pieces from a street vendor and attempted to reassemble it himself even though the words "Do Not Open or Attempt to Repair This Product" were engraved on the outside, is the manufacturer absolved of liability under an implied warranty of fitness for purpose?
facts and inquiry intermingled:	Is the manufacturer of an acoustical keyboard, which was bought from a street vendor by an ordinary consumer who attempted to reassemble it himself even though the words "Do Not Open or Attempt to Repair This Product" were engraved on the outside, absolved of liability under an implied warranty of fitness for purpose?

In some cases, even the most determinative facts are so complex that they cannot be reduced to a short list and a reader would drown in a series of "where" clauses. That tends to happen where a set of determinative facts raises several independent issues, and where the facts themselves are difficult to describe concisely. In such cases, lawyers sometimes use a different format, expressing the determinative facts in an introductory paragraph, and then posing the Question or Questions. (An example is the Question Presented in the brief in Appendix E.)

In a persuasive Question Presented, the least confusing way to refer to the parties is generically: "a malpractice insurer," "a prisoner," "an employee," and so forth. Procedural designations are often confusing. "Appellant" and "appellee" tell the court virtually nothing. The same is true of "plaintiff" and "defendant" unless the issue is really procedural or the Question itself makes clear what kind of plaintiff and what kind of defendant are involved. Although most uses of "plaintiff" and "defendant" are confusing, these are not (for the reasons just stated):

> Has a defendant been properly served where the summons was handed to him in a plain manila envelope?

> Does a complaint state a cause of action for personal injuries if it alleges only that the defendant could have rescued the plaintiff but did not?

And in a criminal case it is never confusing to refer to one party as the defendant. (The other party is always the prosecution.) Although a busy judge can be confused when the parties are referred to by name only, it may be tactically wise to try to personalize a party beset by some institutional opponent, if the context will make clear who is who.[2]

Given the relatively few words involved, a persuasive Question Presented can be one of the most difficult drafting jobs in legal writing. The work is best broken into three stages.

First, write out a narrow statement of the inquiry ("Is a prisoner guilty of escape?") and a separate list of the facts that you believe to be most determinative, omitting facts that are merely explanatory or coincidental.[3] Second, tinker with the list, perhaps while writing and rewriting the other components of the memorandum or brief. Add or subtract facts as you come to understand the issue better, and refine the list's wording as you learn the possibilities and limitations of each fact. Third, work out a concise phrasing of the list and merge it into the inquiry in a single sentence. The Question Presented is often the last part of a document to reach its final form.

§24.2 How to Evaluate Your Questions Presented for Persuasiveness

A picture held us captive.

— *Wittgenstein*

2. See the Question Presented in the brief in Appendix E.
3. See §13.2.

Frank Cooper has suggested six standards[1] for judging the effectiveness of a Question Presented:

1. The issue must be stated in terms of the facts of the case [rather than in terms of assumed conclusions of law or fact].
2. The statement must eliminate all unnecessary detail.
3. It must be readily comprehensible on first reading.
4. It must eschew self-evident conclusions.
5. It should be so stated that the opponent has no choice but to accept it as an accurate statement of the question.
6. It should be subtly persuasive.

We can add one more:

7. It should clearly define the decision the court has been asked to make.

To see these principles at work, consider a case in which a stockbroker gets tired of his work and decides to do something meaningful. He persuades a gourmet bakery to take him on as an apprentice baker. The bakery has perfected a method — which it keeps secret — of adding a citrus taste to croissants. As a precaution, the bakery requires its employees to sign a covenant not to compete with the bakery for three years in either of the two urban counties in an otherwise rural state. After a short time, the stockbroker quits and forms his own company to bake and sell gourmet baked goods. The bakery where he apprenticed sues for an injunction to prohibit that. In the state where this arises, a covenant not to compete is enforceable if the prohibition on competition is "reasonably limited" in duration and geographic area; if it "does not exceed that reasonably necessary for protection of the employer's business"; if it "is not unreasonably restrictive" of the employee's rights; and if it does not violate public policy.[2]

The bakery's attorney might draft this Question Presented:

> Should a successful stockbroker who is entering the baking business be enjoined from violating a three-year covenant not to compete, where he was trained as a baker entirely by the plaintiff, had access to the secret recipe for the plaintiff's biggest-selling product, and has now set himself up in business as the plaintiff's only competitor in a specialized two-county gourmet baked goods market?

From the other side might come a very different Question:

> Is it inequitable to enjoin an apprentice baker from working "in any baking capacity" for three years in an area that includes three-quarters of the state's population, where the plaintiff's only fear of potential in-

---

§24.2   1. Frank E. Cooper, *Writing in Law Practice* 80 (1963).
2. *American Credit Bureau v. Carter,* 462 P.2d 838, 840 (Ariz. Ct. App. 1960).

jury is that, in starting his own business, the apprentice might use a croissant recipe?

Now let us apply the criteria set out above:

1. State the issue in terms of the facts and not in terms of assumed conclusions of law or fact.

Each Question sets out the attorney's theory of the case without arguing it. Even if you do not know much about the legal rules involved in this case, you can predict from the Questions alone a great deal of what will be argued later in the memorandum or brief. The bakery's attorney is certain to argue that the covenant's geographic area is reasonable because of the nature of the market, that its duration is reasonable because of the nature of the product, and that the court should view the apprentice as a stockbroker and financier and not as a person who really makes his living with bread dough in his hands. The apprentice's attorney is equally certain to argue that the covenant is unreasonable in time (three years), substance ("in any baking capacity"), and area (three-quarters of the state's population).

There are three ways to fail this criterion: by omitting some of the core determinative facts; by listing characterizations or factual inferences instead of facts; or by listing conclusions of law instead of facts.

If the baker's attorney had submitted the following Question, the court would have been given an *incomplete set of the most determinative facts:*

> Should an apprentice baker be enjoined from violating a three-year covenant not to compete in the baking business, where the enjoined apprentice was trained as a baker entirely by the plaintiff?

Would this Question persuade you? (Compare it to the bakery's Question on page 318.)

If the baker's attorney had submitted the following Question, some of the "facts" would actually have been *characterizations and factual inferences,* which must be proved later in the document and cannot be assumed here:

> Should an apprentice who deceived the plaintiff into disclosing its hitherto secret recipe, and who has now betrayed his former employer by setting himself up in business, be enjoined from violating a three-year covenant not to compete in the baking business?

Judges ignore Questions that go beyond the solid facts. Here, there is no evidence of deception, and the writer's claim of it is a kind of inference that we call a guess. In the Argument (where it can be proved), the writer might be justified in calling the stockbroker's conduct a betrayal, but in the Question that is just empty rhetoric.

And in the following Question, the "facts" are really *conclusions of law,* which also must be proved later and cannot be assumed here:

> Should the defendant bakery apprentice be enjoined from violating a covenant not to compete where the covenant is reasonably limited in

duration and geographic area, where its prohibitions are reasonably necessary to protect the employer's business, where it does not unreasonably restrict the employee's rights, and where it does not violate public policy?

Judges will ignore this, too. Inferences and conclusions cannot be posited as a factual givens. They must be *argued* in the Argument. Questions that contain them mean nothing.

If you find characterizations and conclusions in a Question you have written, cut them out and *replace them with the facts that would make them true.* Which facts, for example, make this restraint reasonably necessary to protect the bakery's business? Those facts belong in the Question, and the conclusion of law should come out.

2. Eliminate all unnecessary detail.   There are two ways to get this wrong. One is to list facts that are not among the most determinative.

The other is to add unnecessary specifics about facts that are determinative. In an earlier draft of the bakery's Question, the phrase "was trained as a baker *entirely* by the plaintiff" might have been "was trained as a baker by the plaintiff *and has never received any other instruction or experience in the field.*" Do you see how much clout a single, carefully chosen word ("entirely") can carry (replacing all the italicized words in the earlier version)? Finding the right level of abstraction or compression is not easy. An overly specific formulation of a fact is too detailed to imply the fact's relevance and usually so verbose as to confuse the reader. An overly general formulation often oversimplifies and is too rarefied to open up the picture that you want the reader to see — the picture that captures the decision-maker.

3. Write the Question so that it can be understood when read only once.   Consider this:

> Should this court enjoin the violation of a covenant not to compete, which applied only to the baking industry and included a prohibition on competition that lasted three years, where the defendant was a baking apprentice who has made a considerable income as a stockbroker and continues to derive passive income from his partnership in a brokerage house, where he was trained as a baker by the plaintiff and has never received any other instruction or experience in the field, where he had access to the plaintiff's hitherto secret recipe for a unique form of croissant embodying citrus flavors, where he has now set himself up in business as the plaintiff's only competitor in this field, and where the parties compete in a specialized gourmet baked goods market that extends over two adjacent counties, each of which includes a major city?

Can you understand this in one reading? Can you tell immediately what facts are important? Compare it — phrase by phrase — with the bakery's

Question on page 318. There is no difference in meaning. In fact, the only difference is that the Question above is verbose where it should be concise and detailed where it should be abstract and compressed. (Another way to make a Question unreadable is to use an obtuse sentence structure. See the two examples on page 316.)

It takes much writing and rewriting to make the Question understandable in one reading. It is partly a process of finding the most concise phrasing and partly a process of finding the right level of abstraction or compression.

4. *Omit self-evident conclusions.* For example:

> Should violation of a covenant not to compete be enjoined where the covenant's restraints are reasonable, where they are reasonably necessary to protect the employer's business . . . ?

The answer to this will always be yes. It is a question about what the law is and not how the court should rule in *this* case.

5. *State the Question so that your adversary must accept as accurate each fact listed.* A Question Presented persuades only if based on undeniable descriptions of facts. The Questions on page 318 persuade by listing facts the opposing attorney cannot claim to be untrue or missing from the record, and by describing those facts in words the opposing attorney cannot reasonably claim to be inaccurate. The bakery's attorney, for example, would have reached too far if the bakery's Question had posited that "the injunction covers *only* two counties" because those two counties include three-quarters of the state's population and cannot reasonably be dismissed as "only."

Moreover, in the Questions on page 318, neither attorney has pretended that the other side's strongest facts do not exist. The Questions are two intellectual constructs between which the court must choose, and a court is not likely to choose one that ignores a significant and troubling aspect of the controversy. Thus, the apprentice's attorney must concede that his client suddenly created a company to compete, but he does so in words that suggest that the bakery will not suffer much as a result ("the plaintiff's only fear of potential injury is that, in starting his own business, the apprentice might use a croissant recipe"). The bakery's attorney can hardly ignore the fact that the state's population is concentrated in the two counties covered by the covenant, but she mentions that in a phrase showing why the covenant ought to address that area ("a specialized two-county gourmet baked goods market"). As in a Statement of the Case, the key here is juxtaposition.

6. *Make the Question subtly persuasive.* You want a Question that would cause a disinterested but skeptical reader to think, "This lawyer has the winning side." And you want a Question that would make a judge think, "On these facts, I do not want to rule against this lawyer." The Question should overcome a judge's natural tendency to ask "So what?" or "Is this really so bad that I should use the power of the court to interfere?"

Choose your words carefully to create a picture through nuance. Set out your theory clearly and convincingly. And draft the Question in a positive tone to invite the answer you seek. (The reader should want to say "yes" right after the question mark.)

7. Clearly define the decision the court is asked to make.   Do that by asking a Question that alludes to the governing body of law and lists the most determinative facts.

One way of failing this criterion is to ask a Question that *assumes that the reader already knows the case:*

> Should the violation of a covenant not to compete be enjoined, where the defendant is actually a successful stockbroker who was trained entirely by the plaintiff, who had access to the plaintiff's hitherto secret recipe, and who has now set himself up in business as the plaintiff's only competitor?

Did the plaintiff train the defendant to be a stockbroker? Is this a suit to enjoin competition in the stock brokerage industry? What does a recipe have to do with this? Remember that the reader might not yet have read the Statement of the Case and has certainly not yet read the Argument. Many judges use the Question Presented as an introduction to other parts of the memorandum or brief.

Another way of failing this criterion is to *diffuse the reader's attention* through several Questions that really add up to only one (or a very few). The temptation to pose inappropriately multiple Questions is greatest on appeal:

> 1. Did the Superior Court properly enjoin the violation of a covenant not to compete, which was limited to a three-year period in a two-county area?
> 2. Did the Superior Court properly enjoin the violation of a covenant not to compete, where the enjoined former employee had access to the plaintiff's hitherto secret bakery recipe and has now set himself up as the plaintiff's only competitor?
> 3. Did the Superior Court properly enjoin the violation of a covenant not to compete, where the former employee is a successful stockbroker who does not depend on baking for his livelihood?

This is like trying to cut water with a knife.

You should have one Question Presented for each point in your Argument — not more and not less.

Exercise I.   Bank Robbery (Questions Presented)

The following Questions are all from the same case, which involves the federal bank robbery statute.[1] Using the criteria in §24.2, evaluate the effectiveness of

---

1. See page 178.

each Question. (There is a good reason why you are not told which party propounded each Question: if you cannot tell, after reading a Question, which party propounded it, it has no effectiveness at all.)

    1. Should the court grant the defendant's motion for judgment of acquittal on a charge of committing robbery by intimidation in violation of 18 U.S.C. § 2113(a), where the defendant, although he did not show a weapon or threaten violence, gave a bank teller a note that would put a reasonable person in fear, where the teller did not hesitate to comply with his demand, although she courageously struck him after he took the money she surrendered, and where she testified afterward that she was "shaken up" by this stressful situation?

    2. Whether the Government is entitled to put its case to a jury where a bank teller testified that the defendant — who was charged with bank robbery "by intimidation" — handed her a note announcing that he was conducting a "hold-up," where she gave him all the cash at her window, and where she felt "shaken up" after the defendant's capture, in which she assisted.

    3. Whether the defendant should be granted a judgment of acquittal on Count I of an indictment for bank robbery "by intimidation" where there was uncontroverted evidence that the defendant was pleasant and smiled throughout the alleged robbery; that he made no threatening gestures or statements and carried no visible weapon; and that the teller, after giving him cash, reached over the counter, grabbed him by the tie, and punched him twice in the face.

    4. Has the Government failed to make out a prima facie case of bank robbery "by intimidation" where the sole evidence of intimidation is a note, handed to a teller, that read "please give me money — I don't know how to do a hold-up"?

Exercise II.   Drafting Persuasive Questions Presented

    Draft two persuasive Questions Presented — one favoring each party — using the facts and authority either from an exercise of your teacher's choice in Chapter 11 or Chapter 12 or from a writing assignment that you have previously completed in this course.

VII
APPELLATE BRIEFS

25 Appellate Practice

§25.1   Introduction to Appeals

A *judgment* (or, in equity, a decree) is the document a court makes to terminate a lawsuit and to record the court's final determination of the parties' rights. If either party has been awarded relief, the judgment may include an award of money or an injunction or a declaration of the parties rights and so on.

An *order,* on the other hand, is a court's command during the lawsuit that something be done or not be done while the litigation is still in progress. Depending on the complexity of the case and how long it remains in litigation, many orders or only a few might be entered before judgment. Some orders may control the discovery process; others may manage the court's calendar or the trial itself; and still others may award parties provisional relief, such as preliminary injunctions.

The document you have learned to call an opinion or a decision is neither a judgment nor an order. You have by now read hundreds of opinions, most of them in the casebooks you study for other courses, but you might never have seen an order or a judgment. The order or judgment is a court's *action,* and the opinion records the *reasons* for that action.

Within the limitations described in §25.4, a party aggrieved by a trial court's judgment or order can appeal to a higher court, where a group of judges will decide whether the trial court's judgment or order was correct or erroneous. The appellate process performs three functions. The most obvious is the correction of errors made by trial courts. A second is to cause the law to be applied uniformly throughout the jurisdiction, to the extent that is practical. And the most intellectually challenging function is the making and clarification of the law itself through precedents that fill gaps in the common law and in statutory interpretation.

In those jurisdictions with two levels, or tiers, of appellate courts, the intermediate court tends to view its goal largely as error correction, although it must also necessarily cause some uniformity in application of the law and, to a lesser extent, engage in law formation and clarification. A court of last resort, on the other hand, generally believes that its task is primarily to make and clarify law. Such a court might be willing to perform the other two functions only where the intermediate court has not merely failed to do so, but failed badly. In the jurisdictions with only one appellate court, of course, that court is responsible for all three appellate functions equally.

Issues of state law can be appealed only once in a one-tiered state and no more than twice in a two-tiered state. In federal courts, there can be no more than two appeals because the federal courts are organized into a two-tiered appellate system. But where an issue of federal law arises in the courts of a state with two appellate tiers, three appeals are possible because the United States Supreme Court has jurisdiction to decide federal issues even if originally raised in a state court. Thus, if a defendant convicted in a California criminal trial believes that his conviction is defective because the trial court misinterpreted the state statute defining the crime (a state issue) and because the trial court erroneously admitted into evidence items seized in violation of the Fourth Amendment to the United States Constitution (a federal issue), the defendant can appeal both issues to the California Court of Appeal. If that court affirms, the defendant may be able to appeal both issues further to the California Supreme Court. If unsuccessful there, the defendant may be able to appeal to the United States Supreme Court, but only on the federal issue because the United States Supreme Court has no jurisdiction over issues of state law.

With some exceptions (explained in §25.4), the dissatisfied party generally has a right to seek review by the appellate court immediately above the trial court. That one appeal should be enough, in most instances, to perform the error-correcting function of the appellate process. In a state with a one-tiered appellate system, this appeal *as of right* will be to the state's supreme court, but in other states and in the federal system, it will be to an intermediate court of appeals.

An appeal to a still higher court will probably be *discretionary* because it will not happen unless a court permits it. Although every litigant should be entitled to one appeal for error-correction purposes, the other two functions of the appellate process are performed best if the higher appellate courts in two-tiered jurisdictions can concentrate their efforts on those issues where law needs to be made or clarified. Thus, the higher appellate courts in two-tiered systems tend to be invested with *discretionary appellate jurisdiction,* which means that they are empowered to choose the appeals they will hear and to turn others aside. A party unhappy with a judgment made by a United States District Court, for example, has a right to have that judgment reviewed by a United States Court of Appeal, but there can be no further appeal to the United States Supreme Court unless that court gives its permission by granting a would-be appellant[1] a writ of certiorari.

What kinds of issues are important enough to persuade a discretionary appellate court to exercise its jurisdiction? Generally, such a court may be inclined to grant leave to appeal or a writ of certiorari — the terminology differs from jurisdiction to jurisdiction — where the party seeking permission to appeal wants the court to fill a troubling gap in the jurisdiction's law. A gap might be troubling where lower courts have published decisions coming to opposite results on analogous facts or where a significant part of society needs clarification of the law. Some gaps are large, such as where a court is asked to recognize a cause of action that some states have adopted and others have rejected. But even relatively small gaps can be troubling: a court that has recently recognized a particular cause of action, for example, may need to decide several further appeals until all the elements are clearly defined. If, however, local law is settled, clear, and consistently applied, a discretionary appellate court is likely to give permission to appeal only in two instances. The first is where the intermediate appellate court appears to have made an error that would represent an intolerable failure of the intermediate court's error-correction function. And the second is the unusual situation where the discretionary appellate court is receptive to changing the law.

In the Supreme Court of the United States and in the highest court of every state, all the judges meet together to hear and decide appeals. In some intermediate appellate courts, appeals are heard by panels, rather than by the full court. In the United States Courts of Appeals, for example, decisions are made by panels of three judges; only in rare cases can a party who has lost before a panel persuade the full court en banc to review the panel's decision. Ultimately, of course, the losing party can petition — usually unsuccessfully — for review by the United States Supreme Court.

§25.2 What Happens During an Appeal

Although practice varies from court to court, these are the significant events in an appeal:

First, the appellant *serves and files whatever document is required by law to commence the appeal.* If the appeal is as of right, the document is a notice of appeal, an uncomplicated paper that is usually no longer than a page and need not specify grounds for the appeal. If leave to appeal is required, the appellant must petition for it, specifying errors and arguing their

---

§25.1 1. In this text, "appellant" will be used to refer to the party who commences an appeal, and "appellee" to refer to the opposite party. The terms "petitioner" and "respondent" are used in certain types of appeals in some courts. Before writing a brief, check the court's rules for the terms appropriate to your type of appeal. If you cannot find the answer that way, see how the parties are referred to in a reported case in the same court that *procedurally* resembles your own.

importance. The notice of appeal is short and simple because it is a mere declaration that the appellant is doing what he or she has a right to do, but the petition for discretionary review *asks* for something and is therefore far more complex. Because the denial of such a petition forecloses appeal, its contents are crucial and must be drafted persuasively. The notice or petition must be served and filed within the time required by law, and the time limits can vary from jurisdiction to jurisdiction. A notice of appeal is filed with the clerk of the court being appealed *from,* rather than the clerk of the court being appealed to, but the contrary is true of a petition for leave to appeal.

The second step in the appeal is the *transmittal of the record* from the court below to the court above. Although one might imagine this to be an easy matter of the clerk of one court locating a file and sending it to the clerk of another court, it happens that way only in cases where the record is very simple. A record can be simple, for example, where the appeal is from an order dismissing a complaint for failure to state a cause of action. There the record might not include much more than the complaint, the papers submitted by both parties in connection with the defendant's motion to dismiss, and the court's order.

Most appeals, however, arise only later in the litigation, and in those cases the preparation and transmittal of the record can delay matters for months and add thousands of dollars to the cost of the appeal. Wherever the trial court has held a hearing or trial, one or more court reporters will have to type up a transcript from stenographic notes, a time-consuming process that can produce literally volumes of material.

The third step — required in some jurisdictions and optional in others — is the assembling of an abbreviated version of the record called the *joint appendix* or the *record appendix.*[1] At the appealing party's expense, it is printed in sufficient quantity that a copy can be given to each judge who will hear the appeal. The appellate judges need the joint appendix because the full record can be gargantuan, and the appellate court will have only one copy of it. Even if all the judges hearing an appeal were to work in the same building, it would be impractical to ask them to share a single copy, which may be bound into several bulky volumes. Moreover, in many appellate courts the judges do not do all of their work in the same building: they have additional chambers near their homes, which may be scattered about a state, a district, or a circuit, and they gather only when scheduled to hear oral arguments and to deliberate. Whether chambers are scattered or located centrally, the judges can work most efficiently if each has a copy of the most important parts of the record, and if the full record is available in the clerk's office as a reserve.

Although rules vary from jurisdiction to jurisdiction, there are generally two methods of assembling the appendix. The parties can agree on a joint appendix, but that does not happen often. More frequently, the appellant

---

§25.2 1. The joint appendix is not the Statement of the Case. Nor is it the type of appendix that you might add to the brief to set out in full those statutes that a court might be asked to construe. The Statement of the Case and a statutory appendix are each only a few pages long, and both are part of the brief. The joint appendix is often larger than the brief, and it is bound separately.

designates those portions of the record that he or she wants in the appendix; the appellee counter-designates portions to be added; and the portions are combined and printed in the same sequence in which they appear in the full record.

The fourth step is the *drafting of briefs,* which each attorney files with the appellate court and serves on opposing counsel. For many attorneys, this is the most intellectually challenging part of litigation, and it is the subject of Chapters 26-27.

In a court without discretionary jurisdiction, the fifth step — and the first in which the appellate court becomes actively involved — is *screening.* Until relatively recently, most appeals were given a full adjudication that included oral argument and a formal opinion, whether or not published. Because of geometrically increasing appellate caseloads, that time is gone forever. Now, in most appellate courts, the appellant must struggle to get a full adjudication, and a wise appellee fights to prevent it. If the appeal is not given full treatment, it is shunted onto a summary adjudication track, where there may be no oral argument or formal opinion, where the judges might not even meet to discuss the appeal. The result of that is usually affirmance. Courts that do not have discretionary jurisdiction use screening to ensure that their error-correction function is performed economically while they concentrate on the most important appeals, which are still given full adjudicatory treatment. The factors that motivate a court without discretionary jurisdiction to give an appeal full adjudicatory treatment are not very different from the factors that would cause a discretionary court to accept an appeal that it is not obligated to decide. Screening is done by one or more specially assigned judges, who may be assisted by attorneys employed by the court to study the briefs and the record. In some courts, every appeal is screened, while in others screening occurs only when a party — usually the appellee — requests it. Some courts require the attorneys to meet with a judge in a pre-briefing or pre-argument conference, which is used partly for screening, partly to clarify and limit the issues, and partly to encourage negotiation between the parties. A few courts without discretionary jurisdiction — most notably the United States Court of Appeals for the Second Circuit — refuse to screen (except perhaps in pre-argument conferences) and require oral argument in every case on the theory that the screening consumes as much judicial effort as it saves.

In virtually all appeals in a discretionary court and in fully adjudicated appeals in a court without discretionary jurisdiction, the next step is *oral argument.* Each attorney is allotted a predetermined period, such as fifteen minutes, to speak in open court with the judges, who might ask many questions or only a few. Oral argument is particularly satisfying work because it is the attorney's only chance to speak directly with the judges about the problems and issues raised by the appeal. Where the judges and the attorneys are perceptive and well-prepared, oral argument can be the most scholarly type of conversation known to the practice of law,[2] and it is the subject of Chapter 28.

---

2. "I can see the Chief Justice as he looked at that moment. . . . [B]efore counsel began to argue, the Chief Justice would nib his pen; and then, when everything was ready, pulling

After oral argument, the judges confer and discuss the merits of the appeal. In some courts, this conference occurs on the same day as argument; in others, it may happen several days later. One judge is selected to write the court's opinion. In some courts, the assignment is made by chance rotation, but in others it is made by the presiding judge. In the United States Supreme Court, the assignment is made by the most senior judge among the majority. The assigned judge drafts an opinion and circulates it to the other judges, who might suggest changes or might draft and circulate concurring or dissenting opinions of their own. In routine appeals, the draft majority opinion is often quickly approved, and concurrences and dissents may be held to a minimum. But in more complex and troubling cases, views can change, and an opinion originally written as a dissent might be transformed into the court's opinion, while the original majority draft is demoted into a dissent.

If the losing party can appeal further, the whole process may begin again, with a new notice of appeal or petition for some sort of leave to appeal — more likely the latter, as one moves up the appellate ladder.

§25.3   The Roles of the Brief and of Oral Argument

To understand the different roles of the brief and oral argument, you must be able to visualize the effect of increasingly crowded dockets on the work of appellate judges.[1]

Depending on the court, an appellate judge might in a month hear oral arguments and confer with colleagues on several dozen appeals, and in many courts substantially more than a hundred. For each appeal, the judge will have to read at least two briefs[2] and in multiparty cases or public-interest cases[3] a half-dozen briefs or more, together with portions of the record.

---

up the sleeves of his gown, he would nod to the counsel who was to address him, as much as to say 'I am ready; now you may go on.' I think I never experienced more intellectual pleasure than in arguing that novel question to a great man who could appreciate it, and take it in; and he did take it in, as a baby takes in its mother's milk." This is how Daniel Webster recalled his oral argument to the Supreme Court, led by Chief Justice John Marshall, in *Gibbons v. Ogden,* 22 U.S. (9 Wheat.) 1 (1824), one of the leading Constitutional cases of the nineteenth century. (The quote is from 1 Charles Warren, *The Supreme Court in United States History* 603 (1935).) Although pens have not been "nibbed" since they were made from feathers, modern appellate litigators know every other sensation Webster described.

§25.3   1. For example, in 1987 the number of appeals filed in the United States Courts of Appeals was nine times the number filed in 1960, but during the intervening 27 years the number of judges in those courts only doubled. Robert L. Stern, *Remedies for Appellate Overloads: The Ultimate Solution,* 72 Judicature 103, 103 (1988). This is typical of the effect of the litigation explosion on all courts — federal and state, trial and appellate. Obviously, when caseloads increase this fast, judges have less and less time to spend on each case.

2. The appellant files an opening or main brief, and the appellee responds with an answering brief. The appellant may rejoin with a reply brief but is not required to do so.

3. In cases that would affect groups that are not parties, the court may grant permission for nonparties to file briefs as amicus curiae (friends of the court).

The judge will have to write majority opinions in a proportion of the appeals not summarily disposed of; on a five-judge court, for example, each judge is assigned one-fifth of the majority opinions. In addition, the judge may feel obligated to write several concurring or dissenting opinions. The judge will also have to read opinions drafted by other judges and at times will write memoranda to colleagues suggesting changes in those opinions. The judge will spend a fair amount of time reading some of the cases and statutes cited to in all these briefs and draft opinions. And the judge may have screening and other administrative responsibilities. With all this work, the typical appellate judge would find it a luxury to spend as much as an hour reading the average brief, and the time available is often no more than half an hour per brief. That is why briefs, although large, must be carefully crafted to reveal their logic while demanding the least possible time and effort from the reader. Judges spend more time, of course, on briefs where the appeal raises deeply troubling issues than on briefs in more routine cases. And a judge who writes an opinion might read the briefs more thoroughly than one who does not.

In a work environment like this, the brief and oral argument are asked to perform different functions. Each is critical, but in a different way.

The brief can best lay out the theory of the appeal by explaining in persuasive detail the authorities and evidence on which a favorable decision should be based. A successful brief not only persuades the judge that your client should win, but it can also be used as a manual explaining to the judge exactly how to make the decision and how to justify it in an opinion. A judge may use the brief for initial screening, to prepare for oral argument, to prepare for the conference with other judges, and while writing the opinion.

The oral argument, on the other hand, can do two things better than the brief can. First, in oral argument the attorney can more immediately motivate the court by focusing on the most important ideas — the few facts, rules, and policies — that most make the attorney's theory of the appeal compelling. Although the brief should show both the forest and the trees, the oral argument can be a bit more powerful at illuminating the forest. (Conversely it is a horrible medium through which to examine the trees.) Second, in oral argument the attorney can try to discover, through the bench's questions, each judge's doubts, and the attorney can on the spot explain exactly why those doubts should not prevent a ruling in the attorney's favor. Oral argument, in fact, is the attorney's only opportunity to learn directly from the judges the precise problems they have with the attorney's theory. Oral argument's greater efficiency at these two things is not a reason to skimp on trying to accomplish them through the brief as well. Oral argument lasts only a few minutes, and memories of it can fade. The brief, on the other hand, has permanence: it is always among the judge's working materials, and it "speaks from the time it is filed and continues through oral argument, conference, and opinion writing."[4]

Briefs and oral argument have assumed these roles more through evolution than by design, as courts have gradually realized how different kinds of

---

4. Herbert Funk Goodrich, *A Case on Appeal — A Judge's View*, in *A Case on Appeal* 10-1 (ALI-ABA 1967).

information can most efficiently be conveyed. Detail is communicated best in writing, which can be studied. Conversation, on the other hand, both encourages spontaneous dialogue and lends itself to the broad sweep of underlying ideas.

§25.4 *Limitations on Appellate Review*

You have already learned of one limitation on the scope of appeals: many courts have *discretionary appellate jurisdiction* and use it to avoid deciding large numbers of cases.[1]

In addition, appellate courts will disturb an order or judgment only if it is based on *reversible error*. An appellate court will affirm unless the appellant can point to a specific error by the trial court that the law considers ground for reversal. Be careful of two kinds of situations, neither of which will lead to a reversal. In the first, the result below seems unfortunate, but no error by the court below can be identified. In the absence of reversible error, an appellate court will not substitute its preferences for what the trial court did. That is because an appeal is not an open-ended reconsideration of what happened in the trial court. It is only a review for the kind of mistake the law categorizes as error. In the second situation, error can be identified, but it did not cause the order or judgment appealed from. Even if the result below was unfortunate, and even if the court below committed error, an appellate court will reverse only if the result below is traceable to the error. Error that affected the result below is called *material* or *prejudicial*. Error without such an effect is called *harmless*.

To identify error, and to figure out whether it was material or harmless, start with the procedural posture in the trial court. For example, assume that the plaintiff has requested a particular jury instruction; that the trial court denied the request and instead gave another instruction; that the jury returned a verdict for the defendant; and that, on the basis of the verdict, the trial judge entered a judgment for the defendant. The issue on appeal cannot be whether the plaintiff should have won below; rather, it is whether the trial court so erroneously instructed the jury that the entire case should be tried again to a jury properly instructed. If the instruction was error, but if the record shows that the error was not so material as to lead the jury astray, the error was harmless and will not be reversed. The error would be harmless, for example, if the evidence in support of the verdict was so overwhelming that a properly instructed jury would have returned the same verdict.

Appellate review is mostly (but not entirely) limited to *issues of law*. A jury's verdict is a purely factual determination and thus not generally reviewable on appeal.[2] Where a case is tried to a judge without a jury, the

§25.4 1. See §25.2.

2. As you may have realized by now, a dissatisfied party attacks a jury's verdict by challenging judicial conduct that permitted or caused the jury to return the verdict. The dissatisfied party might argue that the judge improperly instructed the jury or that the judge should have granted a motion for a directed verdict, a motion for judgment notwithstanding the verdict, or a motion for a new trial.

judge makes findings of fact that correspond to a jury's verdict. Are judicial findings of fact reviewable on appeal? In some appellate courts, they are not. In the appellate opinions you have read for other courses, you may have noticed the stock phrasing used in such courts to introduce a factual finding over which an appellant is unhappy: "The trial court found as a fact, not reviewable by us on appeal, that . . ." In other appellate courts, judicial fact finding is reversible — but only if it is "clearly erroneous."[3] This standard is harder on appellants than that applied to a trial judge's conclusions of law, which can be reversed if merely "erroneous."

Appellate review is further limited to *issues preserved below*. An issue is preserved below only if the appellant raised it and only if the court below decided it. Because an appeal is a review for error, an appellate court will not concern itself with matters the lower court did not decide. An issue is waived unless the appellant raises the issue below and seeks a decision there. There are two exceptions to the requirement that error be preserved. The more rigid exception concerns subject matter jurisdiction,[4] defects in which can never be waived because a court should on its own motion refuse to adjudicate a case outside its authority. The more flexible exception concerns "plain error," which is error so fundamental to the process of justice that it cries out to be corrected even if the appellant seemed unconcerned about it when it happened. Be careful: "plain error" cannot be invoked whenever an appellant has been careless below. Only in the rarest of circumstances is an appellate court so shocked that it will save an appellant who, in the court below, did not even try to save himself.

What happens where, in the trial court, a party advanced several different grounds, all in support of the same relief, and where the court granted the relief on one ground and ignored the others? The ignored grounds are not waived: it would have been pointless to press for a decision on them. In fact, if an appellate court rejects the ground adopted by the lower court, the appellate court can still affirm, if it chooses to do so, on one of the grounds ignored by the lower court. A correct result is affirmable even if the lower court accomplished it for the wrong reason.

Appellate review is still further limited to issues that are actually *raised on appeal*. An appellate court does not survey the record below looking for error: in the adversary system, that is the job of the appellant's attorney. If the appellate court has discretionary appellate jurisdiction, an issue is waived unless raised in the petition seeking leave to appeal. In any appellate court, an issue is waived unless raised in the brief.[5] Only very rarely does

---

3. *See, e.g.,* Rule 52(a) of the Federal Rules of Civil Procedure. This is explained more fully in §27.3.

4. Subject matter jurisdiction is a court's power to decide various categories of disputes. Personal jurisdiction, on the other hand, is a court's power to adjudicate the rights and liabilities of a particular party. Defects in personal jurisdiction are waivable, but defects in subject matter jurisdiction are not. See Rule 12(h) of the Federal Rules of Civil Procedure.

5. Issues are not waived merely because they are omitted from oral argument. There are two reasons. The first is that one of the goals in oral argument is to focus on the heart of the case, leaving many of the details for the brief. The second is that, even if an attorney wanted to mention in oral argument every ground asserted in the brief, an appellate court's questioning is often so thorough that the attorney would not have an opportunity to do so. However, courts often ask in argument whether an attorney abandons a particular ground raised in the brief, and an affirmative answer is an explicit waiver.

an appellate court overlook this limitation and itself raise an issue not asserted by a party. This happens most strikingly when the appellant's attorney has not realized that some of the judges are interested in changing rules of law that the parties have taken for granted.

Appellate courts will review only *final* orders and judgments. Although finality generally occurs when the court below has nothing left to adjudicate, in many jurisdictions the law hedges the concept often. One reason is that finality itself is not always easy to recognize. Sometimes an order may plainly be one that does not terminate litigation on a particular issue, but it may so alter the positions of the parties that the practical effect would be final if not reviewed. Another reason is that it is hard to accomplish the purpose of the final order rule — economizing everyone's effort and speeding the real end of a lawsuit by reviewing on appeal only the trial court's finished product — without at the same time precluding review of some types of interlocutory orders that ought not be immune from appellate scrutiny. As a result, most jurisdictions have developed, through statutes and case law, a number of exceptions to the final order rule.[6]

With two exceptions, appellate courts will refuse to consider facts that do not appear in the *record below*.[7] One exception involves the doctrine of judicial notice, through which a court — trial or appellate — will, without evidence, accept as proven certain facts that are beyond dispute.[8] Do not make more of this than it really is. The following are examples of the kinds of indisputable facts of which courts will take judicial notice: A meter equals 39.37 inches. Cleveland is in Cuyahoga County, Ohio. March 23, 1994, was a Wednesday.

The other exception is for what are called "legislative facts," which are generalized social, economic, or scientific information that guides a court in the development of law — as opposed to the "case facts" or "adjudicatory facts," which are the specific events that transpired between the parties. Legislative facts can include empirical data on the detrimental effects of

---

6. For example, under 28 U.S.C. §§ 1291 and 1292 (1988 & Supp. IV 1992), federal appellate courts are authorized to review a variety of interlocutory orders, including orders granting or denying preliminary injunctions. And the Supreme Court has developed a collateral order doctrine "whose reach is limited to trial court orders affecting rights that will be irretrievably lost in the absence of an immediate appeal." *Richardson-Merrell, Inc. v. Koller,* 472 U.S. 424, 430-31 (1985). One jurisdiction dispenses with the finality rule for civil cases in its intermediate appellate court, N.Y. Civ. Prac. Law § 5701(a)(1), although not in its highest appellate court, N.Y. Const. art. VI, § 3(1), (2), (4).

7. You can determine whether a fact is truly in the record by focusing on the procedural posture below. If the order appealed from is one dismissing a complaint for failure to state a cause of action, a fact is in the record if it is alleged in the complaint. That is because, for the purpose of deciding a motion to dismiss a complaint, all facts properly pleaded are treated as though they could be proven. (And, of course, on such a motion the only factual record before the trial court is the complaint itself.) But the situation is different where the motion below challenged a party's evidence, rather than allegations (see §§20.2.1 and 20.2.3). For example, assume that the appeal is from a summary judgment. If a fact appears as an allegation in a pleading but does not appear in any evidentiary form, it is not "a fact in the record" because the motion below tested evidence and not allegations.

8. For example: "A judicially noticed fact must be one not subject to reasonable dispute in that it is either (1) generally known within the territorial jurisdiction of the trial court or (2) capable of accurate and ready determination by resort to sources whose accuracy cannot reasonably be questioned." Fed. R. Evid. 201(b).

racial segregation, or on the national deterioration of groundwater quality, or on the ways consumers use videocassette recorders — all useful in determining public policy. Although the adversary system is not very efficient at collecting legislative facts,[9] appellate courts need them when making or changing law. And although legislative facts can be placed in the trial record, an attorney called in to handle an appeal sometimes needs to put before the appellate court legislative facts not developed in the record below. The appellate attorney might include in the brief published empirical research that complements but does not crowd out the legal analysis that is the core of argument.[10] Empirical material added on appeal is not set out in the Statement of the Case, because it is not part of the record below. Rather, it appears, with citations, in the Argument, most often in support of policy contentions.

The law presumes an order or judgment to be correct unless an appellant demonstrates that the appropriate *standard of review* has been violated. The standard of review will vary from one kind of appeal to another. Think of it as a formula of deference. Depending on the type of decision made below, the appellate court may defer — to a specified degree — to the decision of the trial court judge. Some types of decisions, for example, will be reversed if "erroneous"; others only if "clearly erroneous"; and yet others only if "an abuse of discretion." (Standards of review are explained in detail in §27.3.)

Finally, appellate courts are temperamentally "affirmance-prone." Unless deeply troubled by what happened below, an appellate judge will be inclined to affirm for several reasons. The trial judge handled the problem first-hand and might know more than distant appellate judges reading a cold transcript of the testimony. Because many trial decisions must be made instantly "in the heat of battle," it is unrealistic to expect perfection from a trial judge. Every reversal disturbs the status quo, and circumspect people like judges are not comfortable disturbing the status quo unless it is truly necessary. And reversals impose tangible costs, which can be large, such as retrials.

---

9. Legislatures are far more efficient at using the knowledge of experts, collecting and studying empirical research, and weighing conflicting scientific analyses. Courts must rely on individual attorneys, who are rarely able to match the resources of legislative staffs.

10. A brief that uses a fair amount of empirical material is called a "Brandeis brief," after the successful one submitted by Louis D. Brandeis in *Muller v. Oregon,* 208 U.S. 412 (1908).

26

Appellate Briefs

§26.1   Appellate Brief Format

This chapter describes the format of an appellate brief and how judges read appellate briefs. Chapter 25 explains how appeals work. Chapter 27 explains how to develop a theory of the appeal, write the brief, and handle the standard of review. In addition, Chapters 18-20 explain generally how to develop persuasive theories and arguments and how to handle procedural postures. Many of skills used in writing an office memorandum are valuable here as well: organizing proof of a conclusion of law (Chapter 9), selecting authority (Chapter 10), working with precedent and statutes (Chapters 11-12), analyzing facts (Chapter 13), paragraphing (Chapter 14), using an effective style (Chapter 15), and citing and quoting properly (Chapter 16).

Although rules on format differ from court to court, the required structure might commonly include the following:[1]

1. a cover page containing a caption and other information that might be required by local rules;
2. a Table of Contents (sometimes called an Index);
3. a Table of Authorities;
4. where the appeal rests on the interpretation of a constitutional provision, statute, administrative regulation, or court rule, a reprinting of the relevant material;
5. a Preliminary Statement;

---

§26.1   Some courts require additional material, such as a statement specifying how the court acquired jurisdiction over the appeal in question. And some courts restrict the material that may appear in an appendix to a brief.

6. a Question Presented or Questions Presented;
7. a Statement of the Case;
8. a Summary of Argument;
9. an Argument, broken up with point headings;
10. a Conclusion; and
11. an indorsement.

As you read the description below of each of these components, compare the sample briefs in Appendices E and F.

The *cover page* includes the caption, followed by the document's title (such as "BRIEF FOR APPELLANT") and the name, address, and telephone number of the attorney submitting the brief. The caption includes the name of the appellate court, the appellate court's docket number, and the names of the parties and their procedural designations (appellant, appellee, etc.) in the appellate court. Many courts require that the caption also include the parties' procedural designations in the trial court.[2] In federal appellate courts, the appellant is listed first in the caption, but in most state appellate courts the parties appear in the same order in which their names appeared in captions in the trial court. The cover page does not have a page number.

The *Table of Contents* begins on the page after the cover page. It lists all of the components of the brief (except the cover page and the Table of Contents itself); reproduces the point headings and sub-headings from the Argument; and sets out the page on which each component, point, or subpoint begins. Because the point headings and sub-headings are reproduced verbatim in the Table of Contents, a reader can look there for an outline of the argument and for a quick grasp of the attorney's theory of the appeal. When read together in the Table of Contents, the point headings and subheadings should express the theory persuasively and coherently.

The *Table of Authorities* appears on the first page after the Table of Contents. It indexes the cases, statutes, constitutional provisions, court rules, administrative regulations, treatises, and law review articles cited in the argument, together with references to the pages in the brief where each authority is cited. In the Table, every authority is listed in a complete citation conforming to Bluebook rules, and an asterisk is placed to the left of those citations that form the core of the writer's theory. A footnote identifies those citations as "authorities chiefly relied on" or similar words to the same effect.

The Table of Authorities is broken down into three sections headed "Cases," "Statutes," and "Miscellaneous." Cases are listed in alphabetical order. If constitutional provisions, court rules, or administrative regulations are cited, they are listed with statutes, and the heading is enlarged to accommodate them. (In a brief where all of these materials are cited, the head-

---

2. In a criminal case, the prosecution's *trial court* procedural designation is always implied and never expressed. For the accused, the trial court procedural designation is, of course, "defendant" — as in "Merritt Bresnahan, defendant." But it would seem silly to write "People of the State of New York, Prosecution." Phrases like "State v. Bresnahan," "People v. Bresnahan," "Commonwealth v. Bresnahan," and "United States v. Bresnahan" unambiguously communicate that Bresnahan is being prosecuted by whatever government customarily uses the designation that precedes the "v."

ing would read "Constitutional Provisions, Statutes, Court Rules, and Administrative Regulations.") Under the heading, the citations appear in the following order: federal constitutional provisions, state constitutional provisions, federal statutes, state statutes, court rules, federal administrative regulations, state administrative regulations. "Miscellaneous" is reserved for secondary authority, such as restatements, treatises, and law review articles, and they are listed there in that order.

Both the Table of Contents and the Table of Authorities should be set up on the page so that they are easy to use. In the Table of Authorities, for example, the authorities and the brief's page numbers should be separated so that the difference is immediately obvious. Imagine a Table filled with entries like this:

S. Burlington County NAACP v. Township of Mt. Laurel,
67 N.J. 151, 336 A.2d 713, cert. denied, 423 U.S. 808
(1975) 9, 12

Tidewater Oil Co. v. Mayor of Carteret, 44 N.J. 338, 209
A.2d 105 (1965) 10, 15

Village of Euclid v. Ambler Realty Co., 272 U.S. 365
(1926) 8, 14

As a reader, you would probably find the following a bit easier on the eye:

S. Burlington County NAACP v. Township of Mt.
Laurel, 67 N.J. 151, 336 A.2d 713, cert. denied,
423 U.S. 808 (1975) 9, 12

Tidewater Oil Co. v. Mayor of Carteret, 44 N.J.
338, 209 A.2d 105 (1965) 10, 15

Village of Euclid v. Ambler Realty Co., 272 U.S.
365 (1926) 8, 14

For pagination purposes, a brief is broken down into two parts. The two Tables (sometimes called the "front matter") are paginated together in lowercase roman numerals. The rest of the brief (the "body") is paginated separately in arabic numbers, beginning with "1," on the first page after the Tables. Although this may seem odd, it has a very practical purpose. Because the Tables must include page references to the body, the body is typed before the tables are. And because you cannot know how many pages the Tables will occupy until they are typed, the body must begin on page 1. The only efficient solution is to use two separate paginations: lowercase roman for the Tables and arabic for the body.

The *Constitutional Provisions, Statutes, Regulations, and Court Rules Involved* is the easiest part of the brief to draft. It is a place where the court can learn two things. The first is a list of the codified or promulgated law (as opposed to precedent) that is *critical* to the decision the court is asked to make.[3] The second is either the precise wording of those relevant portions or — if the relevant portions are extensive — an indication that they are reproduced in an appendix to the brief. If the material is complicated enough to warrant an appendix, the reference to it could read something like this:

> The following statutes and court rules are set out in the Appendix: Sections 362 and 363 of title I of the Bankruptcy Reform Act of 1978, *as amended,* 11 U.S.C. §§ 362, 363 (1988), together with Bankruptcy Rules 1002 and 1003.

On the other hand, if the provisions are short, this portion of the brief might be written in a manner somewhat like the following:

> The First Amendment to the United States Constitution provides, in pertinent part, as follows:
>
>> Congress shall make no law . . . abridging the freedom of speech or of the press; or the right of the people . . . to petition the Government for a redress of grievances.

(A reasonable editing of the relevant provisions aids the court. Be careful to indicate deletions, as you would with any other quote.)

Phrase the heading of this section of the brief to fit its content. The bankruptcy example above would appear under the heading, "Statutes and Court Rules Involved," while the heading over the First Amendment would read "Constitutional Provisions Involved."

The *Preliminary Statement* briefly sets out the appeal's procedural posture by identifying the parties (if that is necessary), listing the relevant procedural events, and describing the order or judgment appealed from. If it can be done very concisely, the Preliminary Statement might also describe the reasoning of the court below and identify the grounds on which the decision below is challenged on appeal. The point is to tell the court why the matter is before it and to specify the type of decision the court will have to make. That can usually be done in less than a page. This portion of the brief goes by different names in different courts. Where it is not titled "Preliminary Statement," the heading might read "Proceedings Below," "Nature of the Proceedings," or the like.[4]

---

3. A provision is critical to the decision if the parties disagree about its meaning and if the court cannot dispose of the appeal without resolving the disagreement. *A court rule that merely provides for the type of motion made below is not critical to the decision* unless the parties disagree about the rule's meaning and the court has been asked to resolve the disagreement. Although custom requires the use of the misleading word "Involved" in the heading to this portion of the brief, the only provisions printed under the heading are those that are *at the heart* of the issues before the court. They are much more than "Involved."

4. In some courts, the Preliminary Statement is called the "Statement of the Case," and the Statement of the Case — as that term is used in this book — is called a "Statement of Facts."

A persuasive *Question Presented* is explained in Chapter 24.[5]

The *Statement of the Case* is explained in Chapter 23.[6]

A *Summary of the Argument* is what its name implies. The point headings and sub-headings, as they appear in the Table of Contents, outline the argument. But the Summary does more: it condenses the argument into a few paragraphs — usually one paragraph per issue — with more meat in them than can be put into headings. The Summary should not repeat the point headings.

The *Argument* can be divided into points, each of which is a separate and integral theory that, standing alone, would be enough to support a ruling in the client's favor on a question presented. It is unusual in law school briefs for either side to have more than two points, and the appeals assigned often lend themselves to only one point. Points and point headings are explained in Chapter 22.[7]

Although some lawyers use the *Conclusion* to reargue and resummarize the theory of the appeal, the better practice is to limit the conclusion to a one-sentence reiteration of the relief desired, together with an unamplified identification of the ground on which the relief would be based. For example:

> For all the foregoing reasons, the order of the Circuit Court for Albemarle County should be affirmed on the ground that the complaint does not state a cause of action.

A judge who needs to know immediately what you want should be able to find that precisely stated in the Conclusion. This is particularly important where there are cross-appeals:

> For the foregoing reasons, the District Court's order should be affirmed insofar as it enjoins enforcement of Glendale Ordinance 88-162, and in all other respects the District Court's order should be reversed.

---

5. In some cases argued to the Supreme Court of the United States, Questions Presented are not expected to meet criteria 1 and 6 in §24.2. If the controversy is really between two bodies of law (such as "Whether Title IV violates the equal protection clause"), *and* if the events between the parties would not be critical to the Court's decision, the Questions Presented would be framed without lists of determinative facts. (Be careful, though: in some controversies between bodies of law, the facts do matter because they show why a statute either is or is not unconstitutional.)

6. A literal reading of Rule 28(a)(4) of the Federal Rules of Appellate Procedure would seem to suggest that the Preliminary Statement must be merged into the Statement of the Case. But the federal Courts of Appeals do not really require that. As Chapter 23 explains, it is essential to start the Statement of the Case with a paragraph that summarizes your factual theory in a compelling way. If you were to merge the Statements, this compelling paragraph would become hidden behind a paragraph or two of unexciting description of the procedural posture.

7. Point headings in briefs to the United States Supreme Court do not necessarily comply with criteria 6 or 8 in §22.2. In part that is because of the reasons explained in note 5 above. And in part it is because a Supreme Court Justice already knows much of what a case is about even before reading the briefs. The Court considers only a few appeals, which it selects (see §25.1) for the purpose of making law.

or where an appellant seeks alternative relief:

> For the foregoing reasons, Mr. Merkle's conviction should be reversed because the Superior Court admitted into evidence a "confession" coerced in violation of his Fifth Amendment rights, or, in the alternative, this matter should be remanded to the Superior Court for re-sentencing because the original sentence exceeds the statutory maximum.

The *indorsement* is similar to the indorsement in a motion memorandum. (See §21.1.)

Every court has rules governing the contents of briefs and other submitted documents. The rules are designed to make briefs easier for judges to use, and judges understandably become exasperated when the rules are ignored. Egregious violations of court rules can result in the court's striking the brief, in financial penalties imposed on the attorney, and even in dismissal of the appeal.

§26.2   How Judges Read Appellate Briefs

How does a judge read a brief? The answer may vary considerably from judge to judge, but the following is not unusual:

> [B]efore the oral argument I read over the briefs and some material parts of the records, in somewhat cursory fashion, enough to know what the points in the case are and what the positions of the opposing parties are. When the oral argument is over, the answer to the controversy is sometimes indisputably clear. But in most cases it is not and a real study is in order. Usually I first read both parties' statements of the questions presented; then I read the appellant's statement of the general nature of the controversy. Then I look at his outline of argument to see what points he makes. Then I look at the appellee's outline of argument to see what he is going to do in reply. Then I go to the joint appendix to see what the trial court or the administrative agency did. Then I read the appellant's statement of the facts and the appellee's statement. Thereafter I examine the two briefs one point at a time, first the appellant's and then the appellee's, on the first point; then both briefs on the second point, etc. If the point is an obvious one, or if one side or the other seems to be wholly without strength on it, I do not spend too much time on that point in my first study. On the really contested points I study both sides, read the cases, and, if facts are critical, check the record references. The briefs on the critical points are often reread and reread.[1]

---

§26.2   1. E. Barrett Prettyman, *Some Observations Concerning Appellate Advocacy,* 39 Va. L. Rev. 285, 296 (1953).

Other judges might read the parts of a brief in a different sequence — perhaps reading the point headings before anything else — and a given judge might vary the sequence from case to case. But the following observations generally describe the use to which a brief is put:

First, you must write for several different readers. Depending on the court, an appeal might be decided by three to nine judges. And briefs are also read by law clerks or research attorneys who assist judges by studying the briefs and recommending decisions.

Second, briefs — like memos — are not read from beginning to end at a single sitting. They are read in chunks, at different times, depending on the needs of the reader. (You probably read an appliance or automobile owner's manual in pretty much the same way, and — as explained in §19.1 — a brief is a manual for making a decision.)

Third, a brief is read for differing reasons, depending on who is reading and when, and the brief must be constructed to satisfy all of these uses without frustrating the reader. If screening[2] is done after briefs are filed, that is the first purpose to which a brief will be put. The judges will also either scan or study the brief in preparation for oral argument, and afterward they will read it again to decide how to vote. One judge will be assigned to write the court's opinion, and while writing that opinion, he or she will reread various portions of the brief several times, looking for the detail needed to justify and explain the decision. And all along the way, the judges will be assisted by law clerks who check up on the details of the brief while the judges focus on the broader principles. Each segment of the brief must be written to satisfy all of these purposes.

Finally, a brief must include several different places where a judge can "enter" the brief by learning what the appeal is about. A judge will go first to a part of the brief that reveals the fundamental issues in the appeal and your theory on each issue. A judge ought to be able to find that material plainly set out in four different places: the point headings and sub-headings (collected in the Table of Contents); the Questions Presented; the Summary of Argument; and the Statement of the Case (read together with the Preliminary Statement). Each judge has a favorite starting place. Not only do you have no way of knowing when you write the brief where a given judge prefers to begin, but you are writing for several judges and must accommodate them all. Thus, you must draft these four components so that each can separately be a self-sufficient and self-explanatory entry point for any predictable reader.

---

2. See §25.2.

27 Writing the Appellate Brief

§27.1 Developing a Theory of the Appeal

In Chapter 18 (which you might review before continuing here), you learned that a theory is attractive only if it is solidly built on the record and the law, explains away unfavorable facts, is framed in terms of basic fairness to the parties, and appeals to logic and common sense. An effective appellate theory, however, has some additional qualities.

First, a persuasive theory of the appeal is grounded on the procedural posture below and the standard of review in ways described in §27.3. For the attorney urging reversal, the theory is one of *error*, while for the attorney defending the result below, the theory is one of *the absence of error*. And neither error nor its absence can be explained without taking into account the procedural posture below and the standard of review.

Second, a persuasive appellate theory does not ignore any of the limitations on appellate review described in §25.4. An appellate court will reject a theory that would violate restrictions on the court's own power to act.

Third, a persuasive appellate theory goes beyond a technical analysis and addresses the judges' concern about a fair and just result. An appellant must show both error and injustice: "If you can convince the appellate judges that the court below is wrong as an intellectual matter, but leave them with the impression that no worthwhile damage was done, the prior result will be affirmed."[1] Although an appellee might succeed by showing either an absence of error or an absence of harm, the wiser strategy is to try to show both, if that can credibly be argued.

§27.1 1. Edward J. Lampron, *Observations on Appellate Advocacy,* 14 N.H.B.J. (No. 3) at 105, 106 (Winter 1973).

Fourth, a persuasive appellate theory is soundly grounded in public policy. Judges engaged in law formation or clarification are understandably concerned about the wider consequences of what they do. How would the precedent the court will create in your case affect others in the future?

Fifth, a persuasive appellate theory asks the court to make no more law than is necessary to the attorney's goal. Most judges do not believe that their purpose on the bench is to change society in fundamental ways, and you will have a better chance to win if your theory asks only for those changes that are truly necessary to the result you want.

Finally, a persuasive appellant's theory raises no more than two, three, or at the very most four claims of error. A theory is damaged, not strengthened, by adding additional but weaker grounds to the two or three best ones available. The weaker grounds by their mere assertion cheapen the stronger ones and take up room in the brief that is better used to more fully develop the grounds most likely to cause reversal. Good theory development requires the good judgment to choose the strongest grounds, the self-discipline to focus the court's attention on them alone, and the courage to ignore other grounds that may seem tempting but, in the end, are unlikely to persuade.

§27.2   The Process of Writing a Brief

Before you begin to write, digest the record, do a significant amount — but *not all* — of the research, and develop the basic shape of your theory.

Digesting the record is more than merely reading it: study the record to identify potential reversible error[1] by the trial court and to find every fact that could be used either to prove error or to defend what the trial court did. Look for both kinds of facts — regardless of whom you represent. Facts favorable to your position will, of course, become ammunition. But your theory must also show the appellate court why and how the facts that run against you should not become determinative.

Before starting to write, do enough research to have all the ingredients for your theory. That includes all the major authorities on each issue, as well as enough of the lesser authorities for you to have a good handle on relevant policy, on the procedural posture that governed the decision below, and on the standard of review in the appellate court (explained in §27.3). But you do not need to find everything in the library on your issue before you begin to write. In fact, if you try to do that, your brief will probably suffer. Remember the inseparability of writing and thinking: when you begin

---

§27.2 1. Unless error is material to a final order or judgment, is preserved in the trial court, is not already waived on appeal, and can be shown to be reversible from facts already in the record, an appellee will have a good argument for an affirmance. See §25.4.

to write, you will understand more about the kinds of details from authorities that you will need to fill out the Argument (see §10.7).

Just as a judge does not read a brief from beginning to end, neither does a lawyer write it that way. The Table of Contents and Table of Authorities are always done last, after the rest of the brief has already been typed (see §26.1). The order in which the other parts are written differs from lawyer to lawyer and from appeal to appeal because one lawyer's work habits are not necessarily effective for someone else and because an effective lawyer adapts to the individual task at hand. Eventually, you will settle into a range of work habits that are effective for you, and your first brief is an opportunity to begin to define yourself in that way.

To help you start, consider two very different methods of writing a brief.

Order in Which a First Draft Might Be Written	
Model I	*Model II*
1. point headings	1. Questions Presented
2. Argument	2. Statement of the Case
3. Statement of the Case	3. point headings
4. Questions Presented	4. Argument
5. rest of brief	5. rest of brief

A lawyer who uses Model I outlines the Argument by composing the point headings and sub-headings and by listing under each heading the material to be covered there when the Argument is written. The logical next step is drafting the Argument itself. This lawyer might draft the Statement of the Case after the Argument on the ground that the value of specific facts is not fully understood until after the Argument is written. The Questions Presented would be written afterward because the lawyer identifies the most determinative facts — the ones recited in the Questions — while working out the Argument and the Statement of the Case.

Conversely, a lawyer using Model II would begin the first draft by writing the Questions Presented on the theory that the other parts of the brief will be more focused if the issues are first precisely defined. A lawyer who uses this model writes the Statement of the Case next, using it to work out the details of the theory of the appeal (which the Model I lawyer does while writing the Argument). Both lawyers draft the point headings before the Argument because the Argument is easier to write in segments (which the headings create).

A lawyer with flexible work habits might use Model I in an appeal where the authority and issues are difficult and complex and Model II in a more fact-sensitive appeal. Some lawyers write the Question Presented and the Statement of the Case (and sometimes even the Argument) simultaneously, moving back and forth from one pad to another (or from one word process-ing disk file to another).[2]

Before writing each subsequent draft, work on something else for a while or take a break to put the brief out of your thoughts. Come back to it in a frame of mind that enables you to put yourself in the judge's position: If you were a skeptical judge, would you be persuaded? Is the brief clear and easy to read? Does it teach you the appeal and show you how to make the deci-sion? Reverting to your role as writer, have you organized the Argument around some variation of the paradigm explained in Chapter 9 and in §20.3? Or do you begin applying a rule to the facts before you have finished proving it (a sure sign that your organization is out of control)? At the other ex-treme, have you invested so much energy in proving a rule that you have forgotten to show the court how the rule governs the facts of your appeal? (When reviewing the Argument in general, see the lettered checklist on or-ganization in Chapter 9.) If a particular rule is not clearly expressed in the authorities, have you stated it yourself and then proved it with a synthesis? Where a gap in the law must be filled, have you defined the gap and ex-plained the extent of local law before you begin to rely on persuasive au-thority? Have you used argument techniques (§19.2) and fact description tactics (§23.2)? Do your Point Headings and Questions Presented satisfy the criteria in §§22.2 and 24.2? Throughout the brief, ask yourself the ques-tions in the paragraphing, style, and quotation checklists in Chapters 14, 15, and 16.

It is a good idea — even before you begin research — to set up a schedule with a series of deadlines. Start from the date on which the brief is due, and figure out how many days it will take to have the final draft typed, proofread, and photocopied. Then set a deadline on which those tasks will begin and all rewriting must stop. Figure out how long it will take to turn a second or third draft into a final draft and so on, working your way backward in time to deadlines where each draft must be finished and, for the first draft, where each component must be done. Writing a brief is a big job, and writing it in the time available requires self-discipline from you.

§27.3 Handling the Standard of Review and the Procedural Posture Below

(Before reading this section, you might review Chapter 20 on procedural postures.)

On appeal the question is not whether the appellant should have won in

---

2. Some lawyers find it useful to begin work on the oral argument before completing the brief. They find that planning the oral argument sharply focuses their attention on the cen-tral problems in the appeal. And when they make practice oral arguments to colleagues, they find themselves unexpectedly saying things that would work well in the brief. You probably will not be able to do this the first time you write a brief, when you are trying to find your way through unfamiliar tasks in a limited period of time. But it might be worth trying with your second or third appeals.

the trial court, but instead whether the relevant standard of review was violated in the particular ruling appealed from. For that reason, judges become quite annoyed with attorneys who write and speak as though there were no standards of review. In fact, the appellant's goal is to show that the standard of review has been violated, and the appellee's goal is to show that it has not.

How much error does it take to cause reversal? That depends on the jurisdiction, the court, and the procedural posture below. The jurisdiction matters because standards of review differ somewhat from state to state and between the states and federal government.[1] The procedural posture matters because, even within the same jurisdiction, different standards are applied to different rulings by the court below.

Many rulings of law — such as orders dismissing pleadings, summary judgments, directed verdicts, jury instructions, and judgments notwithstanding the verdict — are evaluated on appeal "de novo."[2] For appeals from these rulings, the appellate court does not use a standard that defers in any way to the trial court. Instead, the appellate court measures error simply by asking itself whether it would have done what the trial court did. The appellate court can do that because all of these rulings present pure questions *of law*. They do not require the trial judge to determine facts or exercise discretion.

Most law school appellate advocacy assignments involve de novo standards of review. If that is true of your assignment, you probably will not have much difficulty arguing within the standard properly. A de novo standard is neutral, like a pane of clear glass through which light passes without distortion. As you will see in a moment, the other standards are like filters and lenses that modify the image.

If the jurisdiction permits a judge's findings *of fact* to be challenged on appeal,[3] the appellate court will apply a higher standard, one which grants a certain amount of deference to what the trial court has done. In federal appeals, for example, a judge's fact-finding will be reversed only if it is "clearly erroneous."[4]

And on an issue where the lower court has *discretion,* the result below will be reversed only for an "abuse of discretion," which, again, represents a degree of deference to the trial court. A trial court has a wide range of discretion on issues of equity and on issues concerning management of the progress of the litigation, such as rulings on discovery motions and on the conduct of the trial.

The diagram on the next page illustrates how standards of review work and how they are related to procedural tests in trial courts. (Read the diagram *from the bottom up.*)

---

§27.3   1. In addition, in some states the standards of review in the intermediate appellate court might differ from those in the state's highest court.

2. "De novo" is the term used in federal courts for this type of standard. Many states use other but synonymous phrases, such as "independent and nondeferential review."

3. See §25.4.

4. *See, e.g.,* Rule 52(a) of the Federal Rules of Civil Procedure.

APPELLATE COURT

4.
Because the granting or denial of a preliminary injunction is a discretionary decision in a trial court, the appellate court will reverse only if the trial court abused its discretion. (*This is the standard of review.*)

3.
Plaintiff wins the motion, and defendant appeals.

TRIAL COURT

1.
Plaintiff moves for a preliminary injunction in the trial court. →

2.
The trial court will grant a preliminary injunction only if the plaintiff is threatened with irreparable harm, is likely to succeed on the merits, will suffer more if the injunction is denied than the defendant would if the motion were granted, and seeks relief not adverse to the public interest. (*This is the procedural test in the trial court.*)

The only way to find out which standard controls a given appellate issue is to research local law in the same manner that you would research rules governing the procedural posture in a trial court.[5] Look for authority that tells you not only what the standard is, but also what it means and how it works. Where a court mentions the standard of review in a decision, it usu-

---

5. See §20.4. You can look under "Appeal and Error" in the digests or add the term "standard of review" (or "standard review") to a computer inquiry that you have already used to find substantive cases. But do this only after you have found the substantive cases you need. If you look for substantive cases and standards of review in the same search, the standard of review term in your inquiry might exclude valuable substantive cases.

ally does so immediately after reciting the facts and immediately before beginning the legal analysis. This is an example of the type of language you will find:

> A dismissal for failure to state a claim pursuant to Fed. R. Civ. P. 12 is a ruling on a question of law and as such is reviewed de novo. [Citation omitted.] Review is limited to the contents of the complaint.[6]

Here we learn what the standard is ("de novo"), and we learn a little — but certainly not everything — about how the standard operates ("Review is limited to the contents of the complaint"). Occasionally, a court will tell you much more about how the standard is used:

> "In reviewing the [National Labor Relations] Board's decision, we must scrutinize the entire record, 'including the evidence opposed to the Board's view from which conflicting inferences reasonably could be drawn.'" [Citation omitted.] Nevertheless, this court will defer to the Board's judgment and the Board's factual findings shall be conclusive if supported by substantial evidence on the record considered as a whole. [Citation omitted.] This "court may not substitute its judgment for that of the Board when the choice is 'between two fairly conflicting views, even though the court would justifiably have made a different choice had the matter been before it *de novo*.'" [Citation omitted.] We shall also defer to the Board's inferences in areas where the Board is considered to have "specialized evidence and expertise." [Citation omitted.][7]

And the court might explain at the same time both the standard of review and the rules governing the procedural posture in the trial court:

> The grant or denial of a motion for preliminary injunction is a decision within the discretion of the trial court. [Citation omitted.] Appellate review . . . is very narrow. [Citation omitted.] Accordingly, a district court's decision will be reversed only where there is a clear abuse of discretion. [Citation omitted.] That discretion is guided by four requirements for preliminary injunctive relief: (1) a substantial likelihood that the movants will ultimately prevail on the merits; (2) that they will suffer irreparable injury if the injunction is not issued; (3) that the threatened injury to the movants outweighs the potential harm to the opposing party and (4) that the injunction, if issued, will not be adverse to the public interest. [Citation omitted.][8]

Occasionally, you will come across an issue that is subject to a bifurcated or even (as in the example below) a trifurcated standard of review. Each portion of this test for laches has a different standard of review:

> Our standard of review on the laches issue has various components. We review factual findings such as length of delay and prejudice under the clearly

---

6. *Kruso v. International Tel. & Tel. Corp.*, 872 F.2d 1416, 1421 (9th Cir. 1989).
7. *NLRB v. Emsing's Supermarket, Inc.*, 872 F.2d 1279, 1283-84 (7th Cir. 1989).
8. *Haitian Refugee Center, Inc. v. Nelson*, 872 F.2d 1555, 1561-62 (11th Cir. 1989).

erroneous standard; we review the district court's balancing of the equities for abuse of discretion; and our review of legal precepts applied by the district court in determining that the delay was excusable is plenary. [Citation omitted.][9]

How do you handle the standard of review in a brief? Do three things:

First, set out the relevant standard of review at or near the beginning of the Argument section of the brief (or, if you have more than 1 point, each point's standard of review can be set out shortly after the point heading).[10] While doing so, identify the procedural posture below and invoke the procedural test that governs it. And — if it can be done succinctly — tell the court how the standard was violated (if you are the appellant) or how it was not (if you are the appellee). For example, from an appellant's brief:

> This is an appeal from a summary judgment, which is reviewed de novo in this court. [Citation omitted.] Summary judgment should occur only where there is no genuine issue as to any material fact and the movant is entitled to judgment as a matter of law. [Citation omitted.] In this case, the movant was not entitled to judgment as a matter of law.

This passage tells us that the standard is de novo, and that the appellant's theory of error is that the second element of the test for summary judgment was not satisfied. (The writer does not say that there was a genuine dispute as to a material fact, which means that only one element of the summary judgment test is at issue.)

An appellee might write the paragraph above differently. In the second sentence, an appellee might write "is appropriate where" instead of "should occur only where." (Why?) And in place of the last sentence, an appellee might write "Here, the appellant concedes that there was no issue as to a material fact, and the record below amply demonstrates that the appellee was entitled to judgment as a matter of law."

A good place to put this material is between a point heading and the first sub-heading. Cite to local authority to prove the procedural rule that governed the trial court and the standard of review on appeal. Unless the law is unclear, a conclusory proof is usually sufficient because these rules are the type with which an appellate court would be routinely familiar. (Notice how this is handled in the Appendix E and F briefs.)

Second, argue *through* the standard of review. If, for example, you are appealing from a decision committed to a trial court's discretion, show throughout rule application[11] that the trial court abused its discretion. If

---

9. *Bermuda Express, N.V. v. M/V Litsa*, 872 F.2d 554, 557 (3d Cir. 1989).

10. This is now required in federal appeals. See Rule 28(a)(5) of the Federal Rules of Appellate Procedure. ("The [appellant's] argument must . . . include for each issue a concise statement of the applicable standard of review; this statement may appear in the discussion of each issue or under a separate heading placed before the discussion of the issues.") Rule 28(b) permits the appellee to omit this statement "unless the appellee is dissatisfied with the statement of the appellant."

11. See Chapter 9.

you are the appellee in such a case, show the opposite. It is not enough merely to state the standard of review at the beginning and then ignore it for the rest of the Argument. Instead, use it and corollary rules wherever they are relevant, weaving the substantive and procedural law together to show either error (if you seek reversal) or the absence of it (if you urge affirmance).

But a de novo standard need not be referred to throughout the Argument unless the very neutrality of the de novo standard helps your case. Because the de novo standard grants no deference at all to the trial court, arguments can be based entirely on the substantive law once the court has been told that a de novo standard is in effect.

Third, throughout the brief (and in oral argument), describe the facts just as they were in the procedural posture in the trial court. (That is because the standard of review is geared to the procedural posture below.) If the appeal is from the dismissal of a complaint, for example, describe the facts as allegations ("the complaint alleges that the defendant struck the plaintiff"). Describe them as evidence ("Smith testified that the defendant struck the plaintiff") if the appeal is from a judgment resulting from a motion challenging the quality of evidence (see §20.2.3) or from an order resulting from a case management motion (see §20.2.4). But if the facts are undisputed, describe the facts as truth ("the defendant struck the plaintiff").

If you are unsure of how to do any of these things, take a look at several opinions in which the court for which you are writing has used the same standard of review in appeals from the same procedural posture involved in your case. Chances are that you will see them invoked near the beginning of the opinion and used at logically appropriate spots thereafter. Look for a definition of the standard, and try to learn its relationship to other procedural rules and get a feel for the court's expectations about how the standard should be used.

VIII

INTO THE COURTROOM

28 Oral Argument

§28.1 Your Three Goals at Oral Argument

First, you want to engage the judges' attention by getting them *interested* in your case and *motivated* to rule in your favor. They will hear many other arguments on the same day, and they will read many other briefs in the week they read yours. They will forget your theory of the appeal unless you touch their natural desire to do the right thing.

Second, you want to focus the judges' attention on *the few aspects of your case that are most determinative:* the one or two issues that are fundamental, the facts that are most prominent in your theory, the rule or rules for which a decision in your favor would become precedent, and the policy considerations that most compel the result for which you argue. Judges expect oral argument to help them find the heart of the dispute. That is because — as you have already learned — oral argument works best when it concentrates on the few large ideas that are most relevant, while details are best left to the briefs (see §25.3).

Third, you want *access to the court's thinking.* Ideally, you want to discover each doubt the judges have about your theory and every confusion they entertain about any part of your case — all so you can satisfy doubt and clear up confusion. And you want to learn which issues the judges think are most important: if those are profitable issues for you, you can concentrate on them, and if they are the wrong issues, you can try to persuade the court of that. The only way you can get access to the court's thinking is through the questions you are asked when the judges interrupt you. In fact, you go to court *for the express purpose of being interrupted* because the most effective thing you can do in oral argument is to persuade through your answers to the judges' questions. And when the judges interrupt, they are usually not trying to debate with you. For the most part, they are telling you what troubles them and asking you to help them make the decision.

§28.2 The Structure of an Oral Argument

The appellant typically begins by reminding the court of the nature of the case, the facts most essential to the appellant's theory, the procedural history, and the issue before the court. This is a reasonably effective opening:

Good morning, Your Honors. I am Clyde Farnsworth, representing Merritt Bresnahan, the appellant here and the defendant below. This is an appeal from a criminal conviction.

> An alternative start would be "May it please the court. I am . . ." Usually, it would help to name the crime, but the attorney delays that so he can define his client first.

Ms. Bresnahan suffers from a medical condition known as gender dysphoria syndrome. A person with this condition is psychologically of one gender but was born with the reproductive organs of the other gender. Psychotherapy has been shown to have no effect on this disorder. But the suffering it causes is so profound that clinics at leading hospitals must resort to sex reassignment surgery to alleviate the condition. And wise medical practice requires that before so radical a step, the patient must dress and live as a person of the psychological gender for a long period.

> This recitation is pared to the bone, but it brings out all the facts that are most determinative for a decision in the attorney's favor. The attorney has a duty to point out the most adverse facts as well. That can be done through juxtaposition, as in a written fact statement. Here it is done through implication: has the surgery yet been performed? What does that mean about the defendant's physical state?

On her doctor's orders, Ms. Bresnahan was so dressed when she was arrested for violating section 240.35 of the Penal Law, which punishes anyone who — in the words of the statute — is "in any way disguised by unusual or unnatural attire" and "loiters, remains, or congregates in a public place" with others similarly attired. When arrested, Ms. Bresnahan was walking to

> This is one of the few situations where words should be quoted in an oral argument: they are the very words the court must interpret.

lunch in the financial district of Manhattan with two other people who suffer from the same disease.

By appropriate motions in the trial court, Ms. Bresnahan sought dismissal of the charge on the grounds that her conduct could not violate the statute, and that, if it did, the statute would invade, among other things, her constitutional right to privacy. Review in this court is de novo. Even though the People concede that Ms. Bresnahan was following her doctor's orders according to accepted medical treatment, the trial court denied the motions and convicted her.

This is the procedural posture below. The appellate court needs to know it because it determines the standard of review.

The questions before this court are whether the legislature really meant to punish people like Ms. Bresnahan, and, if the legislature did, whether her constitutional right to privacy nevertheless protects her freedom to choose her own clothing.

Notice how the facts are used once again to set up the theory.

The legislature did not intend . . .

The statement of the issues leads into the argument that follows.

The sequence need not be as it is here. For example, it might be more effective in another case to state the procedural history or the issue, or both, before the facts. But the facts are what make this opening compelling, and they usually provide the energy in a compelling start. One of the leading appellate advocates of this century said that "in an appellate court the statement of the facts is not merely a part of the argument, it is more often than not the argument itself. A case well stated is a case far more than half argued."[1]

If you represent the appellee, your opening should be designed to show the court vividly how your theory differs from the appellant's:

> If the court please, I am Allan Kuusinen, for the People.
>
> The defendant concedes that he is and was anatomically male but had dressed up as a woman to disguise that fact. When arrested, he was walking down the street with two other men who were similarly disguised. They could have committed any of a number of crimes and left their victims utterly unable to identify them.

---

§28.2   1. John W. Davis, *The Argument of an Appeal*, 26 A.B.A. J. 895, 896 (1940). Some courts study the briefs so carefully before argument that they consider a fact recitation to be a waste of time, and in those courts attorneys are discouraged — either informally or through the courts' rules — from opening with the facts.

That is exactly the danger the legislature meant to prevent. And because the legislature's goal is reasonable, section 240.35 does not violate the defendant's constitutional right to privacy.

Usually, the body of the argument begins most effectively with a statement of the rule or rules on which your conclusion rests. If two or more separate conclusions are being urged, the transition from one to another should be clear to the listener:

> . . . Thus, section 240.35 was never intended to punish a patient for complying with an accepted medical treatment.
>
> The second question before the Court is whether section 240.35, if it has the meaning urged by the People, violates Ms. Bresnahan's constitutional right to privacy. . . .

Except in the opening, an appellee's argument does not differ much structurally from an appellant's. Although some of what an appellee says grows out of notes taken while the appellant argues, most of an appellee's argument can be planned in advance. From the appellant's brief, the appellee knows before argument the theory the appellant will advance.

Unless the bench is "cold,"[2] the judges' questions may so occupy you that you are surprised to find that your time is about to or already has run out. (Your time is finished when the chief or presiding judge, in a firm tone, says "Thank you.") When your time has expired, conclude with a brief sentence in which you specify the relief you seek ("Therefore, the judgment below should be affirmed because . . ."). If you are in the midst of answering a question when your time runs out, ask for permission to finish the answer and, if permitted, finish quickly and concisely. If, on the other hand, the judges continue to ask you questions after your time expires, answer them fully: the court has impliedly enlarged your time. If you complete your argument before your time expires, conclude anyway, pause to see whether you will be asked further questions, and, if not, sit down. Whatever the situation, you can signal your intent to finish by using an introductory phrase such as "In conclusion, . . ."

If the appellant has reserved one or two minutes for rebuttal,[3] the appellant can use that time, after the appellee's argument, in order to reply. A court considers its time wasted if an appellant uses rebuttal to reiterate arguments already made or to raise new arguments for the first time. Rebuttal should be used instead to correct significantly inaccurate or misleadingly incomplete statements made by the appellee, and preferably not more than one or two of those. If the appellee's misstatements are trivial, an appellant looks petty correcting them. If it turns out that there is no need for rebuttal, an appellant makes a confident impression by waiving it. A rebuttal ends with a sentence reminding the court of the relief sought.

---

2. A "hot" bench is one that erupts with questions. A "cold" bench is one that listens impassively.

3. The time reserved is subtracted from the time allowed for the appellant's main argument. You can reserve time by telling the court after you introduce yourself in the opening to your main argument.

§28.3   *Questions from the Bench*

Some questions are neutral requests for information about the record, the law, the procedural posture, or the theory of the appeal. Some are challenges, asking you how you would overcome an adverse policy or equity argument or a contrary interpretation of authority or the record. Some are expressed as concerns: the judge asks how a particular problem in the case can be resolved. Some questions are openly friendly, usually asking the attorney to focus on an aspect of the case that the judge believes to be particularly persuasive. And some questions are neutral prompts, suggesting that whatever the attorney is discussing at the time can be dispensed with in favor of more relevant material. Some questions are asked because the answer is crucial to the judge's thinking. Others grow out of the spontaneity of the moment, and the answer may have little or no impact on the decision.

When you hear a question, listen to it carefully, and do not be afraid to pause for a moment to think before answering. (Never interrupt a question.) Try to figure out the question's purpose and exactly what is troubling the judge. Then craft your answer to satisfy the skepticism or curiosity implied by the question. In the answer, do not give too little or too much. It is a mistake to give a one-sentence reply to a question that a judge plainly considers to be the crux of the case, but it is also a mistake to spend three minutes resolving a straightforward request for simple information.

Do not leap to large assumptions about a judge's predispositions from the questions the judge asks. A neutral judge might ask challenging questions just to see whether your theory will hold up. A friendly judge might ask challenging questions to cause you to argue matters that the judge believes might persuade others on the bench. And an adverse judge might ask friendly or neutral questions out of politeness and a sense of fairness.

In any event, answer the question on the spot. Do not promise to get back to it later at a place in your outline where you had already planned to discuss the subject: other questions may prevent you from getting that far, and the answer will be most persuasive immediately after the question is asked. Even if a question asks you to discuss an entire issue earlier than you had planned, do it and rearrange the order of your presentation to accommodate the judge's needs. Later, when you reach the spot where you had intended to discuss the issue, simply skip what you have already covered.[1]

In answering, state your conclusion first and your reasoning second. As you have seen in so many ways, the law-trained mind most easily understands discourse that lays out a conclusion before proving it. If you get wrapped up in a lot of preliminary material before producing a conclusion,

---

§28.3   1. In some schools, students are assigned to coauthor briefs, usually in teams of two, and to split the oral argument. If your school follows this practice, you may be asked questions about material that your colleague intends to argue. Do not respond by saying that your colleague will answer the question. Judges resent that, and you should know enough of the other student's material to be able to give at least a summary answer. If you are arguing first, your colleague can, during his or her allotted time, elaborate on your summary. Courts, by the way, discourage lawyers from splitting arguments, in part because of this problem.

the conclusion can be obscured or even lost, and you will create the appearance of being unhelpful or even evasive.

Answer the question you are asked, not one you would rather have been asked. The only way you can persuade is by facing directly the problems raised by the question and by showing the judge why those problems should not prevent a decision in your favor. *In every fully litigated case, each side has points of weakness.* If your side of your case did not have them, your adversary would have given up long ago. Where a judge has truly identified a point of weakness, face it and give a realistic counter-argument. Here are three different samples:

> I agree, Your Honor, that in that hypothetical the police would have had probable cause, but the facts of the hypothetical are not the facts of this case. . . .

> Yes, *Soares* did so hold, but later rulings of this court have impliedly undermined *Soares*. . . .

> Certainly, the record does reflect two isolated events that might be construed as evidence of good faith by the defendant, but the record also includes many, many events, stretching over several years, that show exactly the opposite. . . .

Hedging and lack of candor are ways of avoiding what you must do, and they harm your credibility with the court. (If you can surround yourself with an aura of honesty and forthrightness, your arguments will be all the more persuasive.)

During the answer, build a bridge to the rest of your argument. If the question causes you to make part of your planned argument out of order, you can return to your argument at a point that is logically related to the answer. If the answer covers material that you had not planned to speak about, use the answer to lead back to your planned argument. If this is done smoothly, it may be hard for a listener to tell where the answer has ended and the planned presentation has picked up again. Bridge-building helps you redirect the argument back to your theory of the appeal so you can show the court how your theory, as a coherent whole, satisfies each concern raised from the bench. It is, after all, the theory that you are selling.

You will be better able to manage questions if you develop what one judge calls "controlled flexibility": "a relaxed resilience allowing one to respond to a judge's question, coupled with an internal gyro compass enabling one to return gracefully to a charted course."[2]

If you are asked a question to which you do not know the answer, the best thing to say is exactly that. Judges are skilled interrogators, and you will quickly be found out if you try to fake your way through an answer. If you once knew the answer, you might feel a little better saying something like "I'm sorry, Your Honor, but I don't recall." Judges know that you are

---

2. Frank Morey Coffin, *The Ways of a Judge* 131 (1980).

human, and, unless the point you do not know is a big one, you gain credibility by admitting that you cannot answer.[3]

If you think you understand the question but are not certain, signal that in your answer so that the judge can help you out in case you have missed the gist of the question:

> If Your Honor is asking about the possibility that the issue has not been preserved for review — and please correct me if I've misunderstood — trial counsel made a timely objection and moved for . . .

If you plainly do not understand the question, ask for clarification:

> I'm sorry, Your Honor; are you asking about whether the order appealed from is final?

This is one of the very few kinds of questions that *you* might ask during an oral argument.

If a judge asks about a case or a statute about which you have forgotten something, it is appropriate to ask for help:

> I'm sorry, Your Honor, but did *Mansfield* precede the holding in *Soares*?

§28.4   Delivery, Affect, and Style

The most effective way to present arguments is in a tone of what has been called "respectful intellectual equality":[1]

> [I]f the lawyer approaches a court with an appreciation so great that it amounts to awe, perhaps verging on fear, he will not be able effectively to stand up to the court's questioning. . . . It is just as important, however, not to talk down to a court, no matter how much the individual advocate may be more generously endowed with quick perception. . . . The only proper attitude is that of a respectful intellectual equality. The "respectful" part approximates the quantum and type of respect that a younger [person] should show when speaking to an older one. . . . It is not inconsistent with this element of respect, however, for the advocate to argue an appeal on the basis that it is a discussion among equals. . . . Counsel must stand up to the judges quite as he would stand up to the senior members of his own firm. If he permits himself to be overawed . . . , then he — and his case — are well on their way to being lost.[2]

---

3. In practice, a lawyer might offer to file a supplemental brief or memorandum if he or she is afraid that the unanswered question might be crucial to the decision. These offers are usually refused, which is a signal that the point is not critical after all.

§28.4   1. Frederick Bernays Wiener, *Oral Advocacy*, 62 Harv. L. Rev. 56, 72-74 (1948).
2. *Id.*

Although the judges' power is their authority to decide your case, it is their *need* to decide the case that — paradoxically — causes them to look to you for intellectual leadership.

What works best in this situation is not a speech, but a *conversation* in which you take the initiative, talking *with* the judges — not at them. It is a peculiar species of conversation, limited by the formalities of the occasion and by a focus on the decision the bench must make, but it is a conversation nonetheless. If you do the following, you can create for yourself a persuasive presence that helps you to reach and engage the bench:

Look straight at the judges — preferably making eye contact — throughout the argument. Look at your notes only to remind yourself of the next subject for discussion, and even then get your eyes off your notes and back to the bench as quickly as possible. Whenever you look away from the judges, their attention can wander to other thoughts, partially tuning you out. And judges become annoyed with lawyers who read their arguments to the court.[3]

Stand up straight and do not distract the court with restless or anxious movement. Do not play with a pen, shuffle your papers around frequently, put your hands in your pockets, or sway forward and back. Limit your gestures to those that naturally punctuate your argument. A visually busy lawyer radiates nervousness, rather than the confidence needed to establish psychological leadership. Every lawyer — even the most experienced — is nervous before making an oral argument, but that anxiety tends to disappear once the attorney becomes engaged in the conversation. (For beginners, the moment of engagement — when you are so caught up in the work that you forget to be nervous — might not come for several minutes into the argument. But with each succeeding performance that moment will move closer and closer toward the opening, until eventually it coincides with the words "May it please the court" or "Good morning, Your Honors.")

Speak loudly enough that the judges do not have to strain to hear you. If you are soft-spoken by nature, breathe in deeply before you begin and exhale while speaking your first words. Do this again whenever your voice falters. Make your lungs do the work, not your throat muscles. You will be surprised at how well your voice can carry. (If you already have a powerful voice, do not get carried away: nobody likes to listen to shouting.)

Use the tone and volume of your voice to emphasize the more important things you say. A monotone becomes monotonous. Pause before or after your most important remarks.

Communicate tenacity and what one judge has called "disciplined earnestness": "a communicated sense of conviction that pushes a case to the limits of its strength but not beyond. One somehow brings together one's words and body language, facial expression and eye contact, to radiate a sense of conviction without making every point a life-and-death issue."[4]

Unless asked, avoid multitudes of detail in discussing authority. Be-

---

3. See U.S. Sup. Ct. R. 28.1 ("The court looks with disfavor on any oral argument read from a prepared text") and Fed. R. App. P. 34(c) ("Counsel will not be permitted to read at length from briefs, records, or authorities").

4. Frank Morey Coffin, *The Ways of a Judge* 132 (1980).

cause oral argument works best when focused on the big ideas in the appeal, you are better off concentrating instead on rules of law, policy arguments, and broad descriptions of authority. Citations and the minutiae of authority are very hard to follow when delivered orally, and they ought to be in your brief anyway. If your case is built on a synthesis of authority, describe it generally ("the majority of jurisdictions," "the recent trend of cases in other states," "seven of the federal circuits," "this court has previously held"). But if there is controlling authority, that itself is a big idea and deserves attention, especially where you are asking a court to construe an unsettled statute or to overrule precedent. But even then, do not give the full citation: the name and sometimes the year of a case are enough. And if you must quote — as you might with a crucial statute or holding — limit yourself to the half-dozen or so essential words that the court must interpret.

Know your record thoroughly, use it to its full advantage, and do not discuss "facts" outside the record. And — as with authority — do not supply unnecessary detail unless asked for it. Concentrate on the few facts that are most determinative, and mention along the way one or two facts that most bring the story to life. Some facts do not logically have legal significance, but they help the judges "see" the story and put the case into a realistic perspective. For example, in the appellant's opening in §28.2, it is certainly not legally determinative that, when arrested, the defendant "was walking to lunch in the financial district of Manhattan with two other people who suffer from the same disease," but it helps the court visualize the defendant's theory that the conviction appealed from represents a preposterous application of a statute.

§28.5 Formalities and Customs of the Courtroom

Dress not merely for business, but in conservative clothing that conveys the impression that you are a careful and reliable professional.

Stand at the lectern throughout your argument. Do not stroll out from behind it unless you must go to your materials in order to answer a question.

In court, lawyers do not speak to each other. They speak only to the bench and — when the bench gives permission — to witnesses and juries. But because there are no witnesses or juries in appellate courts, you will speak only to the judges.

The dignity of the occasion will be demeaned if you speak in slang, in emotional rhetoric, or in terms that unnecessarily personalize the attorneys or judges. Even when discussing your adversary's arguments, refer to them as the party's, rather than as the lawyer's. There is a world of tonal difference between "The plaintiff mistakenly relies . . ." and "Mr. Maggione has mistakenly told you . . ." Similarly, do not speak to the bench in flattering language. Judges are satisfied with respect; they are offended by obsequiousness.

While your adversary argues, listen attentively and without facial expressions that could convey your opinion of what is transpiring. Make whatever notes you will need to help you respond in your own argument (if you are the appellee) or in rebuttal (if you are the appellant). Do not interrupt your adversary's argument.

§28.6   Preparation for Oral Argument

Prepare two versions of the same presentation. One version should include the material that you *must* argue — in other words, the core of your case — and, when delivered without interruption, it should fill no more than 30 or 35 percent of the time you are allowed. The other version is an expanded development of the first. It includes the first version, as well as supplemental material that makes the core of your case more persuasive, and, without interruption, it should fill about 80 or 90 percent of the available time. You will know within the first three or four minutes of the argument whether the bench is hot or cold. If it is hot, you can deliver the core presentation and work the supplemental material into your answers. If the bench is cold, you can deliver the expanded argument.

There are many ways to prepare notes to use at the lectern. After you have argued several times, you will figure out which type and style of notes work best for you. But the consensus of experienced advocates is that you are better off with the fewest notes because you will need them only to remind you of the subjects you intend to cover and of a few key phrases that you intend to use.[1] In fact, if you are well prepared, you will know your case so well that a single page on a legal-size pad will often be sufficient.

You can outline both versions of your argument on a single page divided by a vertical line. For example, the lawyer who wrote the appellant's brief in Appendix E might be able to make an oral argument from a very condensed page of notes like the one on the next page.

Some advocates take to the lectern notecards with synopses of the record and of the major relevant cases. You might or might not find such synopses helpful. If you already know your case thoroughly, the cards may only get in your way.

Take the record and each brief to the podium as well, in case you are asked about their contents. Especially with the record, use tabs to mark for quick reference passages that the judges might want explained.

Plan your argument by weaving together policy, the facts, and the controlling rules of law into the seamless theory enunciated in your brief. Show how policy and the facts compel your conclusion, while the technical law can be used to justify it. If the standard of review and the procedural posture below place burdens on you, be sure to show the court how you have carried those burdens. If the burdens rest on your adversary, show instead how he

---

§28.6   1. If, in preparing the argument, you come up with an excellent phrasing for a difficult concept, you might write down those few words to remind yourself to use them. Otherwise, your notes should be only a list of subjects to cover.

core	_suppl_

facts
  disease
  treatment (no psythrpy)
  how arrested
  motions below	

issues
  1. "wh'r leg're really meant to
      punish people like B"
  2. if yes, rt to priv	

statutory issue
  1. not disguised "med prof'n
     considers her clothing to
     be an accurate communi-
     cation of the state of her
     gender"
	how gender determined
	"no magic moment" when be-
	  comes fem

2. modern med treatment	hosps & clinics accepted trtmt kind of pain
3. history	farm revolt sim statutes gap in auth
rt to priv issue 1. scope of rt	clothing cases
2. no comp'g st int	fund rt st's crime cont theory
3. even if comp'g, ovrbrd	lesser restrict
4. not "rat'l basis" summary	no cause/effect

or she has failed to carry them. Remember that you cannot cover all the arguments you made in the brief: focus on the most important material.

Make a ruthless list of every weakness in your case and every question that you would be tempted to ask if you were a judge — and prepare an answer to each of those questions. Remember that you are not just trying to win a case; you are helping the judges make law. What rule will a decision in your favor stand for? (It would become precedent.) The judges will care deeply about policy concerns. If they do as you ask, how will the law in future treat facts that are similar to — but not exactly the same as — yours? What would be the practical effects in the courts, in the economy, and in society as a whole? Why is the rule you advocate better than the one your adversary urges? (If you are having a hard time imagining hard questions that you might be asked, study your adversary's brief and the precedents that are contrary to your position.)

Try also to predict which concessions you will be asked to make. Figure out which concessions you cannot afford to make and which you will have to in order to protect the reasonability of the rest of your case. If you think about this for the first time when you are actually asked to make the concession, a very large part of your case could easily disappear in a snap misjudgment.

Practice making your argument to a person who will ask you tough questions but who knows little about your theory of the appeal. If the person mooting you knows too much about your theory, the experience will be unrealistic.

Finally, go to the library the day before you argue. The time between submission of the brief and oral argument might equal up to a month in law school courses and perhaps several months in the practice of law. Check the *Shepard's* supplements to see whether controlling statutes have been amended or repealed, whether one of the key cases has been overruled, and whether any of the recent precedents has been reversed or affirmed. You need not check every citation in your brief, but you do not want to discover in the courtroom that some important texture of the law has changed.

§28.7   State v. Dobbs and Zachrisson: *An Oral Argument Dissected*

To help you understand how oral argument influences judicial decision-making, this chapter concludes with a dissection of the arguments in a real appeal,[1] comparing them to the decision subsequently made by the court to whom the arguments were addressed.

In the city where this case arose, Dobbs operated an illegal book-making business in one neighborhood, and Zachrisson ran a similar enterprise in another area. Dobbs and Zachrisson were each indicted on 16 counts of bribery and one count of conspiracy to bribe. (They were not indicted for illegal gambling, perhaps because the police lacked the evidence required by the gambling statute.) At trial, a police officer named Porfier testified that Zachrisson had given her money for not enforcing the law against him and Dobbs and arresting their competitors instead. The prosecution also introduced tape recordings of conversations between Porfier and the defendants. Dobbs and Zachrisson testified in their own defense, but a jury convicted on all 34 counts.

---

§28.7   1. The names of the parties, judges, and attorneys and the citations to local authority have all been changed. The wording of the local statutes has been altered slightly for clarity. To make the story easier to follow, many of the facts have been simplified, but not in ways that are relevant to the court's analysis. Some of the people described here are composites from a larger cast of characters in the original appeal.

At trial, Zachrisson and Dobbs each asserted the defenses of entrapment and coercion, which are separately defined in the state's Criminal Code:

§ 32.   Defense of Entrapment

In a prosecution for any crime, it is an affirmative defense that the defendant engaged in the prohibited conduct because he was induced or encouraged to do so by a public servant, or by a person acting under a public servant's direction, where the public servant or the person acting under his direction acted for the purpose of obtaining evidence against the defendant for the purpose of a criminal prosecution, and where the methods used to obtain that evidence created a substantial risk that the crime would be committed by a person not otherwise disposed to commit it. Conduct that merely provides a defendant with an opportunity to commit a crime is not entrapment.

§ 963.   Bribery; Defense of Coercion

(a) In a prosecution for bribery, it is a defense that the defendant conferred a prohibited benefit on a public servant as a result of that public servant's coercion of the defendant.

(b) For the purposes of this section, a public servant coerces a defendant when he or she instills in the defendant a fear that, if the defendant does not comply with the public servant's wishes, the public servant will cause physical injury to the defendant or another, cause damage to property of the defendant or another, cause criminal charges to be brought against the defendant or another, or otherwise abuse the public servant's power as an official of the government.

Porfier testified that initially she approached Zachrisson in an attempt to recruit him and perhaps other bookies as informants. She suggested that Zachrisson set up a meeting with any other bookies that Zachrisson thought might be interested. Zachrisson suggested Dobbs. A meeting of the three of them was arranged, but Dobbs did not show up. At this and other meetings, Porfier wore a "body wire" (a hidden microphone that transmits to a nearby tape recorder). Zachrisson told Porfier that he needed police protection from aggressive bookies with mob connections who were moving into his territory. The jury heard a tape recording of Zachrisson telling Porfier that if she made it easier for him to make a profit, he could "send some money your way." Porfier told him that she would have to think it over, and that he should find out whether Dobbs wanted to make the same arrangement.

A week or so later, Zachrisson and Porfier met again. Porfier told Zachrisson that she would accept money from Zachrisson and Dobbs, that she would not arrest them or their employees, and that she would arrest their competitors. Zachrisson told her that Dobbs was "interested." Zachrisson began making periodic payments to Porfier of $100 to $200 (all of which Porfier turned over to the police department). Zachrisson and Dobbs continued their operations without police interference, and some of their competitors were arrested.

A few months after this arrangement began, Zachrisson told Porfier that he and Dobbs — whom Porfier had still not yet met — wanted to expand their gambling enterprises and were willing to bring in Porfier as a silent partner. Zachrisson told Porfier that she would receive a percentage of the profits in exchange for police protection for Zachrisson and Dobbs. Porfier and Zachrisson met one more time, and that was the only meeting attended by Dobbs. Dobbs stated that he agreed with Zachrisson's goals, but Porfier did not start receiving a share of the profits until a few weeks later.

Zachrisson testified that he paid Porfier because he was afraid that he would be arrested if he did not, and he presented evidence that during the time these payments were being made he had complained to others that Porfier was "shaking me down." Dobbs testified that Porfier had threatened to put him out of business if he did not agree to pay her off.

Both defendants moved for directed verdicts of acquittal on the grounds that the evidence of coercion and entrapment was so clear that those issues had ceased to be questions of fact for the jury. (If this confuses you, see §20.2.3.) The trial court denied the motions. On appeal to the state's supreme court, both defendants argued in their briefs that their convictions should be reversed because the motions should have been granted.

Dobbs asserted two additional grounds for reversal. First, he argued that the trial court committed reversible error in instructing the jury that if they convicted him of conspiracy, they could also convict him of bribery because of the acts of a co-conspirator (Zachrisson). There was no evidence that Dobbs gave any money to Porfier directly, but the trial court instructed the jury that Dobbs could be found guilty of bribery for the payments made by Zachrisson if the jury concluded beyond a reasonable doubt that Dobbs and Zachrisson had conspired to bribe Porfier.

Second, Dobbs argued that his rights to a speedy trial had been violated because the trial did not occur until 18 months after indictment. There are two separate rights to a speedy trial. One is provided by the Sixth Amendment to the United States Constitution ("an accused shall enjoy the right to a speedy and public trial"), which applies to state prosecutions as a result of the due process clause of the Fourteenth Amendment. The other right is provided by section 27 of the state's Criminal Procedure Code, which provides that an indictment must be dismissed if the prosecution is not ready for trial within six months after the indictment. (The constitutional test lacks such a clear deadline and in general is much more elastic.) Delay in coming to trial might arise from prosecutorial tardiness, from tardiness on the defense side of the case, from court congestion, or from some combination of these sources. When a defendant moves to dismiss an indictment for lack of a speedy trial, the trial court tries to determine the sources of delay. Delay due to defense tardiness is ignored as "excludable time." (Otherwise, defendants would profit from procrastination by their own attorneys.) Delay caused by prosecutorial tardiness is "chargeable time" because prosecutors are expected to take the initiative in moving cases to trial. You will see in a few moments whether this state treats court congestion delay as excludable or chargeable time. An appellate court will not automatically reverse a conviction where the trial court erroneously denied a speedy trial motion. As you learned in §25.4, reversals occur only for trial court errors that are material or prejudicial.

Reproduced below is a condensation of the transcript of the oral arguments in the state supreme court.[2] Immediately after the transcript is a synopsis of the court's opinion. When you compare the oral arguments to the court's decision, try to understand the cause-and-effect relationship: how do the arguments seem to have influenced what the court did? Without actually interviewing the judges themselves and without reading the court's internal memoranda and the briefs submitted by the parties, we cannot reconstruct with certainty the process through which the court reached its decision, but some tentative conclusions are possible.

THE CHIEF JUDGE: Mr. Womack?

WOMACK [for Zachrisson]: May it please the court. I will argue the issues of coercion and entrapment. My brief sets out the statutory definition of coercion in a bribery case. The evidence at trial was that Zachrisson, after he had made one or two payments, went to a friend of his and reported, in the friend's words, that he was being "shaken down." The friend then went to a judge in a neighboring county and reported that Zachrisson was being shaken down by the police, that over a period of months the police had been intimidating Zachrisson and asking him for money in exchange for favors. You can't read the summary of the meetings here and not be convinced that the police were the principal participants, instigators and initiators of all the activity that lead up to the money changing hands. I think there is a question of law as to whether this was voluntary.

JUDGE BECENTI: The police denied it, didn't they?

WOMACK: Yes.

JUDGE BECENTI: Doesn't that make it a question of fact, to be resolved by a jury?

What do you think of this opening? Does it suggest immediately that what happened in the trial court should make us uncomfortable? How would you have improved it?

2. Those portions of the oral arguments that are most closely related to the state supreme court's decision are reproduced here, and the rest omitted. For the most part, the words in the transcript are the words actually spoken by the attorneys and the judges, but some phrasing has been altered slightly to help you understand what happened and to smooth over transitions from one part of the argument to another.

WOMACK: No, I think entrapment can be decided on the undisputed, undeniable facts here.

JUDGE BECENTI: As a matter of law?

WOMACK: As a matter of law. Porfier has known the defendants for approximately six years, knew that they were small-time gamblers, knew that they were involved with after-hours bars, having dealings with them over a year and a half period. Those are misdemeanors, but bribery is a felony. The testimony was that everybody knew the defendants were gamblers. Yet the police spent all that time, seeing them on a regular basis and never arrested them for any gambling offenses.

JUDGE BECENTI: They investigated organized crime and gambling, didn't they —an ongoing thing?

WOMACK: If they were investigating organized crime, what came of it? Why did it take them almost two years to get the defendants for bribery?

JUDGE STEIN: Doesn't that argument cut both ways because if it took that long the coercion wasn't very effective?

WOMACK: I disagree. Porfier exacted promises of a hundred dollars a week from these defendants. Porfier manufactured a crime. She got very little money from Zachrisson and then pressured him to introduce her to Dobbs. And that in itself was improper conduct.

JUDGE BECENTI: You'd have to argue that that's entrapment as a matter of law, wouldn't you? The facts were decided against you in the trial court, and we're bound by that.

WOMACK: Yes, I would argue that it was entrapment as a matter of law and that coercion was proved. Porfier engaged in improper conduct because she decided that she wanted to get the defendants for a higher crime than gambling. And in this way Zachrisson's reluctance to commit the crime was overcome by persistence. I believe in this case that's obvious. Zachrisson resisted making payments, and the pay-

---

The state supreme court can reach the questions of coercion and entrapment only if there are issues of law and not of fact (see §20.4). In a trial court, what might seem to be a fact issue can at times be converted into a law issue through one of the motions described in §20.2.3. That is what these defendants tried to do through their motions for directed verdicts. Trial and appellate judges are inclined to let juries decide matters like these as fact issues unless there is a good reason not to. Here, is the court being given a good reason?

Generally, rhetorical questions do not persuade. It is more effective to lay out each step of the argument.

Is this the most compelling way to describe what happened? Can you think of something better?

Do you find this theory persuasive? If you do not, is that because the theory is faulty or because it is not being adequately supported by the facts and law at the attorney's disposal?

ments did not begin until long after the demands had started. Porfier just kept going because she wasn't satisfied with arresting the defendants on petty gambling charges.

JUDGE STEIN: Is there anything wrong about that, as long as it doesn't amount to entrapment? If something is going on, is there any reason why police can't wait before arresting until they accumulate more evidence?

WOMACK: No, Your Honor, if it's indeed going on, but in this case it wasn't going on when Porfier first got involved. I see my time is up. Thank you.

THE CHIEF JUDGE: Ms. Underwood?

UNDERWOOD [for Dobbs] Your Honors, Johnny Dobbs met with this police officer only once, and that was after the officer demanded that Dobbs be there. He came only after she made five separate demands that he meet with her. Dobbs met with the officer on one occasion and never saw her again. There was no evidence in this trial that he had anything else to do with Officer Porfier. And at that one meeting, he said only one thing of any substance. When the officer suggested that she should arrest some competing gamblers to shake them down, Dobbs said, "Do we really have to arrest people? I don't want that to happen." He disagreed with the plan proposed. And when somebody said, "Johnny, you're not saying much," he replied, "You don't learn anything by talking." These are not words of joining a conspiracy. These are not words of attempting to bribe anyone. And if this is the only evidence in the case, he cannot be considered to have joined a conspiracy. He certainly didn't do it through his own words. The law is clear and settled that the words of somebody else cannot bind a defendant to a conspiracy. There was no evidence that he ever committed any other act in this whole scheme. On this kind of record, the jury should not have been instructed that they could convict Dobbs of bribery.

In fact, Porfier tried five times to get

Notice how this attorney starts off with her best facts to undermine the bench's confidence that whatever happened in the trial court was probably not unjust. (Remember that appellants have the burden of demonstrating error and that appellate courts are affirmance-prone). This presentation paints a vivid picture with a few, very carefully selected facts. As you read the synopsis of the state supreme court's decision, try to figure out what effect that picture had on the bench.

Dobbs to meet with her. And when he finally did meet with her — and this leads into the issues of coercion and entrapment — the first thing she said was "I can put you out of business; I can go into your neighborhood tomorrow and arrest your people and close you down." These words are coercive as a matter of law. And it is also entrapment as a matter of law because the police officer forced the meeting where she made these coercive statements. Here, the police officer created the crime of bribery . . .

JUDGE ORTIZ [interrupting]: You haven't mentioned your speedy trial issue, which you argue in your brief. You still press it?

UNDERWOOD: Yes, absolutely, every point in the brief. In the trial court we tried to demonstrate — and the court wouldn't permit us — that other cases that had been indicted after Dobbs were tried before him, even though those other defendants were not in jail.

JUDGE ORTIZ: You consistently answered ready?

UNDERWOOD: Every time.

JUDGE ORTIZ: There was an 18-month delay?

UNDERWOOD: Yes, Your Honor.

JUDGE ORTIZ: The only excuse given in the trial court was calendar congestion?

UNDERWOOD: Yes.

JUDGE ORTIZ: And you sought no continuances or adjournments during this period?

UNDERWOOD: Not one.

JUDGE ORTIZ: When you made your motion for speedy trial relief, you claimed both a constitutional violation and a violation of our speedy trial statute?

UNDERWOOD: Yes, both issues raised below . . .

JUDGE BECENTI [interrupting]: Were there extensive plea bargaining negotiations?

UNDERWOOD: Not one minute of it, Your Honor.

JUDGE STEIN: Has there been any showing of prejudice?

This transition is smooth but also clearly announced so that the bench can follow the attorney's organization.

Notice how the attorney picks up the questions and uses it as a springboard for argument.

Are Judge Ortiz's questions hostile? Or does he seem to be helping the attorney make clear that the delay was not caused by the defense and that the question has been properly preserved for appellate review?

This exchange seems to have sparked the interest of Judges Becenti and Stein. What do you think Judge Ortiz was trying to accomplish?

This is the tough question. And in answering, the attorney tries to put the best appearance on a fact that she must admit.

UNDERWOOD: Yes, in the human sense, but not in the sense that we couldn't find any evidence.

JUDGE BECENTI: Any lost witnesses, anything like that?

UNDERWOOD: No.

JUDGE STEIN: Were the defendants in jail during this time or were they out on bail?

UNDERWOOD: No, Dobbs was not in jail.

JUDGE STEIN: Have you read our opinion in *Weatherby*?

UNDERWOOD: Yes, Your Honor, I know . . .

JUDGE STEIN [interrupting]: That must not have disappointed you.

UNDERWOOD: Well, . . .

JUDGE ORTIZ [interrupting]: You say this was 18 months?

UNDERWOOD: Yes.

JUDGE ORTIZ: *Weatherby* was 18 and a half months.

UNDERWOOD: Yes, I know, Your Honor.

JUDGE ORTIZ: And Weatherby is now at home.

UNDERWOOD: If the court please, I chose to concentrate today on the other grounds for reversal because I know Your Honors were aware of that, and I feel that that was an argument I didn't need to press any further. I think I've taken all my time. Thank you very much.

THE CHIEF JUDGE: Mr. Lysander?

LYSANDER [for the State]: May it please the cou . . .

JUDGE STEIN [interrupting]: What about *Weatherby*, Mr. Lysander, isn't that dispositive of the speedy trial issue?

LYSANDER: Your Honor, in this case, the speedy trial motion was made orally and not in writing. It was made on the eve of trial and without any prior notice to the prosecution. *Weatherby* is distinguishable because there the issue was raised in the trial court in a way that permitted the prosecution to find out the reason for every delay and to put that reason in the trial court record. That didn't happen here.

JUDGE STEIN: In this appeal, did the prosecution oppose the motion in the trial court on the ground that it needed an op-

Any equivocation by the attorney on these matters would be quickly discovered and cause the court to lose confidence in the attorney's candor. These are not facts that are open to reasonable interpretations. Either Dobbs was in jail, for example, or he was not.

Weatherby seems at least superficially to favor Dobbs. If Judges Stein and Ortiz had to make a decision on this issue right now, how do you think they would rule? Why do you think so? As you read the argument for the State and the synopsis of the court's decision, remember the prediction you made here.

As you read the synopsis of the state supreme court's decision, ask yourself whether this might be a diplomatic way of explaining a strategy decision. If so, why would the explanation need to be diplomatic?

Judge Stein has gotten *very* interested in the speedy trial aspect of the case.

Do you think this attorney was prepared to answer questions on the speedy trial issue?

portunity to prove that each delay was justified?

LYSANDER: I'm not sure, Your Honor.

JUDGE STEIN: Perhaps the motion should have been made in writing and with prior notice to the prosecution, but if it were not and if the prosecution didn't object to that, I would think that your procedural objection would have been waived.

LYSANDER: Your Honor, this was a pre-*Bachman* case. Before your holding in *State v. Bachman*, both the prosecution and defense were presenting their arguments in trial courts under somewhat lax procedural standards. However, . . .

JUDGE STEIN [interrupting]: But the defendant shouldn't be prejudiced then by that fact, if there were relaxed standards.

LYSANDER: That's correct, Your Honor, but I'm simply saying that the prosecution would be prejudiced in that we were never given the opportunity to have a hearing to develop a complete factual record for the reasons for each delay.

JUDGE STEIN: But wasn't the only excuse advanced trial court congestion?

LYSANDER: The prosecution answered ready for trial for the first time only three months after the indictment, and there was difficulty getting a free courtroom on that date.

JUDGE STEIN: And we held in *Weatherby* that courtroom congestion is no excuse.

LYSANDER: But you also held in *Greenfield* that the trial court's inability to schedule a trial was an excuse. And there has never been an allegation of prejudice to Dobbs because of the delay, and Dobbs was the only defendant to raise this issue in the trial court.

JUDGE ORTIZ: But the question is now before us, and it was raised below — although you say it was raised orally instead of on papers —

LYSANDER: That's correct.

JUDGE ORTIZ: The only excuse the prosecution offered is calendar congestion, is that correct?

LYSANDER: That is the only excuse I am

Read coldly in a transcript, this answer might seem flippant. But if it is spoken in the proper tone of voice it becomes exactly the "respectful intellectual quality" that persuades. We can never know how much the court was influenced by this answer (or by the prosecution's brief), but compare the answer to the court's decision on this issue.

Has this attorney had any effect at all on Judges Ortiz and Stein? When you read the synopsis of the court's decision, notice how they vote.

aware of, but we never had an opportunity for a hearing, so I do not know what would have developed had there been a hearing.

JUDGE ORTIZ: At the time the motion was made, there was no excuse given other than that?

LYSANDER: No, but as a practical matter, when a motion like that is made on the eve of trial all of a sudden — just before a three-and-a-half-week trial that everybody has been preparing for — on the eve of trial when the defendant suddenly claims his speedy trial rights have been violated, the prosecutor would have to do an investigation in order to be able to account for each and every continuance that happened in the past.

JUDGE STEIN: Was there any request by the prosecutor for additional time to answer the motion — so the prosecutor could develop the record that you're now suggesting could have been developed?

LYSANDER: I don't believe that there was, Your Honor, but if there had been, that would have defeated the ends of getting the trial completed as soon as possible. [pauses] Concerning the question of whether the defendants were entrapped by the police. . . .

(The remainder of the State's argument is omitted.)

STATE v. DOBBS AND ZACHRISSON

BECENTI, J. Dobbs's bribery convictions are reversed, his conspiracy conviction is affirmed, and all of Zachrisson's convictions are affirmed.

Dobbs's bribery convictions are reversed because the trial court erroneously instructed the jury that they could convict him of bribery for the payments made by Zachrisson. There was no evidence that Dobbs actually made any bribe payments. Guilt of a substantive offense like bribery may not be predicated solely on a defendant's participation in an underlying conspiracy.

A conspirator is not necessarily an accessory to a crime committed in furtherance of the conspiracy. Under section 129 of the Criminal Code a person is criminally responsible, as an accessory, for the act of another if he or she "solicits, requests, commands, importunes, or intentionally aids" the other person to engage in that offense. Conspicuously absent from the statute is any reference to one who conspires to commit an offense. That omission cannot be supplied by construction. It may be true that in some instances a conspirator's conduct will suffice to establish liability as an accessory, but the concepts are different. To permit mere guilt of conspiracy to establish the defendant's guilt of the substantive crime without any evidence of further action on the part of the defendant would be to expand the basis of accessory liability beyond the legislative design. In interpreting our own state's Criminal Code, we decline to follow the rule followed in federal prosecutions.

But we reject Dobbs's further claim that his statutory and constitutional rights to a speedy trial were violated by the delay between his indictment and his trial. Dobbs does not claim to have been prejudiced by the delay in coming to trial. He was not incarcerated, and he does not assert that any of his witnesses disappeared or suffered a fading of memory. *State v. Weatherby* is therefore distinguishable from this appeal. Moreover, when Dobbs moved in the trial court to dismiss for lack of a speedy trial, court congestion was assigned as the reason for the delay, and the prosecution was ready for trial within three months of the indictment. Thus, Dobbs is not entitled to dismissal pursuant to our speedy trial statute, which requires that the prosecution be ready on time but places no corresponding obligation on the trial court. See *State v. Greenfield*.

Finally, defendants urge that the prosecution failed to disprove the bribery defense of coercion beyond a reasonable doubt and that the evidence establishes the affirmative defense of entrapment as a matter of law. The record does not support these contentions. The defendants' motions were correctly denied, and the issues were properly submitted to the jury.

The record before us presents a conflict between the prosecution's version of events and that of the defendants. The defendants asserted that the police officers induced their participation in the bribery scheme and employed coercive tactics to ensure compliance. Although the record does reveal some evidence of conduct that might be construed as harassment, there is also evidence of mutual cooperation. Hence, resolution of the issues was a purely factual matter within the province of the jury.

[There were no dissents.]

APPENDICES

Appendix A
Basic Legal Usage

Beginners sometimes have trouble with the following words and phrases:

AFFIRM: Precedent can be followed or overruled, but lawyers do not usually say that a precedent has been "affirmed." An appellate court "affirms" when it refuses to reverse the ruling of a lower court *in the same litigation*. See *OVERRULE*.

AND/OR is both ambiguous and awkward. Instead, when writing about a situation where either *and* or *or* might be accurate, use *or* and add to your list an extra item that conveys the meaning of *and*:

> **wrong:** Under Rule 11 of the Federal Rules of Civil Procedure, sanctions can be imposed on the attorney and/or on the client.

> **right:** Under Rule 11 of the Federal Rules of Civil Procedure, sanctions can be imposed on the attorney, on the client, or on both.

APPEAL: The past tense is spelled *appealed*.

ARGUE: Lawyers argue, but courts do not. Argument is intended to persuade others. One argues when one lacks the power to decide, and one argues to those who have that power. A court therefore "decides," "holds," "finds," "rules," "concludes," and so on. Individual judges might "argue," but only in dissent.

COUNSEL: Other forms are spelled *counselor*, *counseling*, and *counseled*.

COURT refers to an institution and not a group of people. The word is therefore used with singular verbs and pronouns.

wrong:	The court have held . . .
	They reversed . . .
right:	The court has held . . .
	It reversed . . .

DICTUM is the singular, and **DICTA** the plural. Do not use a singular verb with *dicta* or a plural verb with *dictum*.

FIND and **FOUND:** When a court "holds," it settles a question of law, but when a court "finds," it decides from the evidence what the facts are. Conclusions of law are not "found."

GUILTY: A guilty defendant has been convicted, in a criminal prosecution, of committing a crime. Cases that end this way are captioned "State v. Smith," "People v. Smith," "Commonwealth v. Smith," or "United States v. Smith." If, in a civil case, Smith loses to a private plaintiff who wants money damages or an injunction or some other type of civil relief, Smith is *liable*. In a civil case, there is no such thing as guilt.

HOLD: See *FIND* and *SAY.*

I: Pronouns identifying the writer are frowned on, except for the use of *we* in judicial opinions. Your goal is to emphasize the ideas under discussion, rather than your own role. "I believe," "we submit," "in our case," and the like are distracting clutter.

INNOCENT: Despite what you hear on the evening news, defendants do not plead "innocent," and juries do not find them "innocent." In a criminal trial, the question is whether the prosecution has proved guilt beyond a reasonable doubt. If it has, the defendant is "guilty." If it has not, the defendant is "not guilty." The jury takes no position on whether the defendant is innocent. "Innocence" has little meaning in criminal law, which cares about whether guilt can be proved and not about whether defendants are guilty or innocent. When a defendant pleads "not guilty," the defendant does not claim to be innocent: instead, the plea is simply a demand that the government prove guilt beyond a reasonable doubt.

IT, when used as a referent, can cause vagueness. See *THIS.*

JUDGMENT: in legal writing, *judgment* is *always* spelled with only one *e*. In a general-purpose, Webster's-type dictionary, you can find "judgement" listed as an acceptable alternative spelling. But the type of judgment described in the first paragraph of page 327 is *always* spelled with only one "e" in the United States (see any *law* dictionary). And out of force of habit, American lawyers customarily use the one-"e" spelling for other meanings of the word.[1]

MOTION, in the procedural sense, is a noun, not a verb. A motion is a request for a court order or a judgment. To get an order or judgment, a lawyer "moves" or "makes a motion." A lawyer does not "motion for an order." (Like everybody else, a lawyer "motions" by making a physical gestures, such as when hailing a taxi.) And a lawyer does not "move *the court* for an order." In that phrase and others like it, "the court" is understood (and need not be stated) because only courts and administrative tribunals can grant orders. And to many readers, adding "the court" looks silly because it evokes other meanings. (For example: The judge wiped away a tear, and it was clear that the witness's story had moved the court. Or: "To what new location are we moving this court?" asked Hercules as he lifted the big granite building with the pillars in front.)

OUR: See *I*.

OVERRULE and **REVERSE** mean different things. On appeal, the judgment or order of the court below in the same case can be *reversed*, but a court *overrules* precedent created in a prior case. In addition, for reasons explained in §10.2, a court cannot overrule the precedent of a higher court, a court of equal rank, or a court in another jurisdiction. (In another context, *overrule* has an entirely different meaning: when a trial judge rejects an attorney's objection to something the opposing attorney has done, the objection is "overruled.")

REVERSE: See *AFFIRM* and *OVERRULE*.

SAY: Statutes do not *say* things, and courts *say* only in dicta. When a court "holds," it is doing and not merely talking, just as a legislature does when it en*acts* a statute. (In statutes, legislatures "provide," "create," "abolish," "prohibit," "penalize," "define," and so forth.) The verb "to hold" has synonyms — "to conclude," "to determine," "to decide," "to reason," "to define," etc. — but "to say" is not one of them. On the other hand, a judge writing a concurrence or dissent does not act for the court, and therefore can accurately be considered to *say* things.

STIPULATE is a term of art and means a formal agreement (or part of one) between the parties to a lawsuit. Judicial opinions cannot "stipulate" (although they might refer to stipulations made by the parties). Nor can statutes or lawyers' briefs "stipulate."

---

1. In Britain, the two-"e" spelling is more common.

THAT, when used as a referent, can cause vagueness. See *THIS*.

THE is sometimes omitted by lawyers, but only before the following party designations: *plaintiff*, *defendant*, *appellant*, *appellee*, *petitioner*, and *respondent*. Other omissions of "the" make the writer sound semiliterate. And much of the time you will appear more literate if you retain "the" even before party designations. It is fine to title a document "Memorandum of Law in Support of Defendant's Motion for Summary Judgment," but inside the memorandum you are better off writing "The defendant is entitled to summary judgment because the plaintiff has adduced no evidence that could show . . ."

THE COURT: In some students' writing, "the court ruled in *Johanneson* . . ." will be followed by "the court ruled in *Di Prete* . . .," even if *Johanneson* was decided by the United States Supreme Court and *Di Prete* by a county trial court. Because opinions are printed in law school casebooks and discussed in law school classrooms without any differentiation within the hierarchy of authority (see §10.2), students are sometimes led into the sloppy habit of writing as though there were only one court in the entire common law world.

THIS and other referents (*IT*, *THAT*, *WHICH*) are vague unless the objects or ideas they refer to are immediately clear to the reader. For example:

> On September 9, the supplier threatened to withhold deliveries to the manufacturer, which, due to desperate need, purchased elsewhere at higher cost. The supplier then notified the manufacturer's own customers of the situation. *This* caused the damages for which the manufacturer now seeks recovery.

To what does "this" refer? The communication to the customers? The threat? The timing of the threat? The entire pattern of behavior? How could the meaning be made more clear?

VERBAL is not a synonym for "oral." "Verbal" means "having to do with words" — both spoken and written. A "verbal communication" is one that was made in words and not through shrieks and gestures. An "oral communication" is a spoken one, rather than one made in writing. In popular usage, *verbal* has so often been used as a synonym for "oral" that general-purpose dictionaries have come to accept that usage as an alternative (but not favored) meaning. But law needs clear ways of differentiating between the written and the spoken word and between communication through words and communication through other means. If you have learned about the parol evidence rule and the Statute of Frauds, you have begun to appreciate how critical the differences between written and oral communication can be and how often lawyers must talk about them. Because of the importance those differences are accorded in law, legal usage of *verbal* has not evolved in the same way that popular usage has. (Although "the misuse of *verbal* for *oral* is common, . . . we should not let the distinction between these words be blurred in legal prose."[2]) A lawyer who tells a judge that the parties made a "verbal" contract is apt to be interrupted with a question like "Counselor, do you mean they made an oral contract? Or do you mean that this is a contract expressed in words and not an implied contract inferable from the parties' conduct?"

WE: See *I.*

WHEN and **WHERE** are not used to set out definitions.

wrong:	Burglary is *where* [or *when*] the defendant breaks and enters the dwelling of another, in the night-time, to commit a felony therein.
right:	Burglary is the breaking and entering of the dwelling of another, in the nighttime, with intent to commit a felony therein.

WHICH, when used as a referent, can cause vagueness. See *THIS.*

2. Bryan Garner, *A Dictionary of Modern Legal Usage* 563 (1987).

Appendix B
24 Rules of Punctuation

Punctuation is not decoration. Proper punctuation shows the reader how your sentences are structured, and that makes your writing more clear and the reader's job easier.

Your teacher may mark your work in part by referring to some of the paragraphs in this appendix.

Commas

Never place a comma between a subject and its verb or between a verb and its object. | **B-1**

> **wrong:** The argument that the defendant committed arson by holding a lighted cigarette to a wall of the Astrodome, is not supported by the case law.

Here the writer seems to have added a comma because the reader will be out of breath after reading the gargantuan subject of this sentence. The solution is to eliminate the offending comma and recast the whole sentence:

> **right:** The case law does not support the argument that the defendant committed arson by holding a lighted cigarette to a wall of the Astrodome.

Generally, do not use a comma as a substitute for an omitted word. | **B-2** Commas are most often asked to substitute for the word *that.* In nearly every instance, *that* belongs in the sentence and the comma does not:

wrong:	The court held, Antwerp Forwarders are liable for loss of the piano.
right:	The court held that Antwerp Forwarders are liable for the loss of the piano.

B-3 **Do not place a comma between the parts of a double subject. And — with two exceptions — do not place a comma between the parts of a double predicate or a double object.** A comma does not belong inside this double subject:

wrong:	*The Supreme Court of Pennsylvania, and the Supreme Judicial Court of Massachusetts* have adopted the same rule.
right:	The Supreme Court of Pennsylvania and the Supreme Judicial Court of Massachusetts have adopted the same rule.

Nor does it belong inside this double predicate:

wrong:	The plaintiff *served a request for admissions, and awaited the result.*
right:	The plaintiff served a request for admissions and awaited the result.

or this double object:

wrong:	The jury convicted *Malone, and the Grutz brothers.*
right:	The jury convicted Malone and the Grutz brothers.

Essentially, each of these examples is a list of two items, and generally the items in a list of two are separated only by a conjunction. There are two exceptions. The first is where the second item in the list is to be emphasized:

right:	The plaintiff's motion is supported by sixteen exhibits, but not one affidavit from a person with firsthand knowledge.

The other exception is where the list is so complicated that a comma is needed to help the reader know where the first item ends:

right: The plaintiff argues that Gripstra defrauded him of his life savings, and that the bank did nothing to stop it.

Use a comma to separate two or more adjectives modifying, in series, the same noun: ▢ **B-4**

right: The plaintiff's attorney made a long, impassioned summation.

But delete the comma if the adjectives are separated by a conjunction.

right: The plaintiff's attorney made a long and impassioned summation.

also right: The plaintiff's attorney made a long but ineffectual summation.

Use commas to set off nonrestrictive words, phrases, and clauses, but not to set off restrictive words, phrases, and clauses. ▢ **B-5** A restrictive word, phrase, or clause is one that cannot be deleted from the sentence without destroying the basic sense of the sentence. The phrase in the middle of this sentence should be surrounded by commas because it is *not* restrictive:

wrong: The Court of Special Appeals the second highest court in the state was created only a few decades ago.

right: The Court of Special Appeals, the second highest court in the state, was created only a few decades ago.

If "the second highest court in the state" were deleted, some meaning would be lost, but the basic sense of the sentence would be intact. ("The Court of Special Appeals was created only a few decades ago.") But if the phrase is left in, the sentence is unreadable without the commas (as you can see from the "wrong" example above).

Readers depend on your use of commas to tell them whether a word, phrase, or clause is restrictive. Sometimes, the presence or absence of commas determines what the sentence actually communicates. In the two examples below, the words are identical, but the difference in punctuation changes the meaning of the sentence.

nonrestrictive clause:	The defendant, who has expressed remorse before being sentenced to prison, is well on the way to rehabilitation.

This is a sentence about a particular defendant whom we might as well call Smith. Smith stood before a judge and said he was sorry, and the judge then sentenced Smith to prison. The sentence records the writer's optimism that Smith will become a right-thinking and law-abiding member of society. The subject of the sentence is "The defendant." The clause that comes afterward ("who has expressed remorse before being sentenced to prison") is nonrestrictive because it *describes* Smith but does not *define* him. (It would define him if it showed how he is different from *all* other defendants.) Compare the example below with the one above:

restrictive clause:	The defendant who has expressed remorse before being sentenced to prison is well on the way to rehabilitation.

This is a sentence about *all* defendants who have stood before judges and said they were sorry. The writer is not speaking about any particular defendant and might never have heard of Smith. The sentence records the writer's optimism that all defendants who apologize will become right-thinking and law-abiding members of society. The subject of the sentence is "The defendant who has expressed remorse before being sentenced to prison." The clause that is part of that subject ("who has expressed remorse before being sentenced to prison") is restrictive because it *defines* the category of defendants about whom the writer has something to say.

The writers of these two examples might have similar views of human nature, but — because of the way they have punctuated their sentences — they have said two entirely different things.

B-6 Use a comma to set off an independent clause from a preceding dependent clause.

right:	After the plaintiff's microwave oven blew up, she sued the manufacturer.
also right:	The plaintiff sued the manufacturer after her microwave oven blew up.
wrong:	The plaintiff sued the manufacturer, after her microwave oven blew up.

B-7 Similarly, use a comma to set off all but the shortest prefatory phrase from the rest of the sentence.

wrong:	Because of the appeal execution of the judgment has been stayed.

| right: | Because of the appeal, execution of the judgment has been stayed. |

| right: | At trial, the disputed evidence was admitted. |

| also right: | At trial the disputed evidence was admitted. |

Use commas to set off a word, phrase, or clause that has been inserted into a sentence as an appositive or an aside. **B-8**

| right: | Wiley, the plaintiff, appealed. |

| right: | The motion will, on those grounds, be denied. |

If an aside is less closely related to the structure of the rest of the sentence, use parentheses or dashes instead:

| right: | The complaint was served on December 11 (nine days after the stipulation). |

| right: | The legislature decided — regardless of the effect on court backlogs — not to increase the number of judges in the state. |

If a transitional word precedes a clause, set it off with a comma. If it occurs in the middle of a clause, set it off with commas if it **B-9** **amounts to an aside.**   Some of the most commonly used transitional words are *accordingly, consequently, furthermore, hence, however, moreover, similarly, therefore,* and *thus.*

| right: | Furthermore, this appeal is frivolous. |

| also right: | This appeal is frivolous; however, sanctions should be imposed on the attorney alone. |

| also right: | We therefore impose on the attorney a fine of five hundred dollars. |

| also right: | We are not unmindful, however, of the appellant's responsibility here. |

Use commas appropriately when referring to places and dates. **B-10** When specifying both a locality (city or county) and the larger geographic entity within which it is found (county, state, or nation), set off the latter with commas.

| wrong: | The novel is set in Klamath County, Oregon even though she was living in Paris, Texas when she wrote it. |

| right: | The novel is set in Klamath County, Oregon, even though she was living in Paris, Texas, when she wrote it. |

Similarly, when expressing a precise date (month, day, year), set off the year with commas.

| wrong: | The court relied on the June 16, 1904 manuscript. |

| right: | The court relied on the June 16, 1904, manuscript. |

But in dates made up only of the month and year, place no comma between the month and year.

| wrong: | The month was October, 1983. |

| right: | The month was October 1983. |

B-11   **When a word, phrase, or clause should be "set off" by commas, that means one comma preceding and a second comma following.**   If you carelessly omit one of the commas, the reader must struggle to figure out what you are trying to say.

| wrong: | The Court of Special Appeals, the second highest court in the state was created only a few decades ago. |

| right: | The Court of Special Appeals, the second highest court in the state, was created only a few decades ago. |

| wrong: | Joe who has been granted parole, will be released. |

| right: | Joe, who has been granted parole, will be released. |

(Of course, one of the commas is omitted if the set-off word, phrase, or clause begins or ends the sentence.)

Commas and Semicolons

B-12   **In a list of three or more, separate the listed items with commas unless they are so complicated that semicolons would do a better job.**

| right: | The plaintiff sued, went to trial, and lost. |

right: The court ordered the corporation dissolved; placed the property under the control of a receiver; and enjoined the defendants from conducting business by interstate telephone, wire, or delivery service.

If two independent clauses are joined by a conjunction in the same sentence, place a comma before the conjunction. $\boxed{\textbf{B-13}}$

wrong: The wholesaler contracted to buy pipe but the manufacturer breached.

right: The wholesaler contracted to buy pipe, but the manufacturer breached.

If two independent clauses are joined in the same sentence but are not separated by a conjunction (such as *and* or *but*), separate them with a semicolon. $\boxed{\textbf{B-14}}$

wrong: The wholesaler contracted to buy pipe, however, the manufacturer breached.

The word *however* is *not* a conjunction.

right: The wholesaler contracted to buy pipe; however, the manufacturer breached.

A *comma splice* is the incorrect use of a comma to separate independent clauses not joined by a conjunction.

Law students seem particularly tempted to use a comma instead of a semicolon where the second clause begins with a conjunctive adverb such as *however, moreover, accordingly, hence, consequently, nevertheless, otherwise, thus,* or *therefore.* There are three ways of curing a comma splice. The first is to convert the comma into a semicolon. The second is to keep the comma but add a conjunction. (But this does not work if the second clause begins with an adverb: in the incorrect example above, try inserting *and* or *but* before *however.*) The third is to convert the comma into a period and to turn the second clause into a separate sentence. (But where the clauses are short and are surrounded by other short sentences, this may produce sing-song sentences.) The cure you select should depend on the context and your goals in the passage where the comma splice occurs.

Hyphens

If two or more words are combined into a single adjective, hyphenate them. $\boxed{\textbf{B-15}}$

wrong:	a forty page brief
right:	a forty-page brief
wrong:	an off the record conference at the bench
right:	an off-the-record conference at the bench

But an adverb and adjective are not hyphenated.

wrong:	legally-sufficient grounds
right:	legally sufficient grounds

B-16 **When hyphenating a word between lines, break up the word only between syllables.** A syllable of only one or two letters is not broken off at all.

wrong:	A large proportion of the sanct- ions ordered under Rule 11 have occurred in the Southern District of New York and the Eastern District of Illinois.
right:	A large proportion of the sanc- tions ordered under Rule 11 have occurred in . . .

If you are not absolutely certain of a word's syllable breaks, consult a dictionary. To an experienced reader, hyphenation in the middle of a syllable looks semiliterate.

Dashes

B-17 Use a dash only to set off an aside that either deserves emphasis or is not closely related to the structure of the rest of the sentence. The dash is not an all-purpose piece of punctuation.

wrong:	The Supreme Court affirmed — it held that Congress had intended to create an immunity in cases like these.
right:	We reverse, and — because this is not the first time we have so held — we point out to the District Courts that the wisest practice is to use the exact wording of the pattern jury instructions.

right: The legislature decided — regardless of the effect
on court backlogs — not to increase the number of
judges in the state.

On a typewriter or computer, construct a dash by joining two | **B-18**
hyphens, and insert a space before the dash and another space
after it.

wrong: The legislature decided - regardless of the effect on
court backlogs--not to increase the number of
judges in the state.

right: The legislature decided -- regardless of the effect on
court backlogs -- not to increase the number of
judges in the state.

Colons

Use a colon to introduce material that satisfies an expectation | **B-19**
raised by the words preceding the colon.   Typical uses of a
colon are to introduce a list or an explanation that clarifies the first part of
the sentence.

right: The Supreme Court has restated this principle numerous times: in *Griswold*, in *Stanley*, in *Eisenstadt,* and in other cases.

Do not use a colon in any of the following situations: | **B-20**

a. **between a preposition and its object:**

wrong: The corporation does business in: Sri Lanka, Tan-
zania, Nigeria, and Malta.

right: The corporation does business in Sri Lanka, Tan-
zania, Nigeria, and Malta.

b. **between a verb and its object:**

wrong: The area codes he calls most often are: 202, 212,
213, 215, 312, 415, and 913.

right: The area codes he calls most often are 202, 212,
213, 215, 312, 415, and 913.

c. after the following words and phrases:

such as
for instance/for example
that is
namely

Parentheses and Brackets

| **B-21** | Use brackets — not parentheses — to enclose alterations in quotations. |

| wrong: | The court reasoned that "(t)he policy of protecting individual liberties would be eroded if . . ." |
| right: | the court reasoned that "[t]he policy . . ." |

If your typewriter does not make brackets, add them in ink. Brackets and parentheses convey entirely different messages to the reader.

| **B-22** | Where numbers are used in text to denote items in a list, enclose each number completely in parentheses. |

| wrong: | At common law, a person was guilty of burglary if he or she 1) broke and 2) entered . . . |
| right: | At common law, a person was guilty of burglary if he or she (1) broke and (2) entered . . . |

Quotation Marks with Other Punctuation

| **B-23** | Be careful about punctuation at the end of a quotation.   Where you add quoted words to a sentence you wrote yourself, placement of punctuation might get tricky at the end of the quotation. These are the rules: *A comma or a period goes INSIDE the quotation marks,* even if it is your comma or period and did not appear in the original quotation. *But a colon, semicolon, or dash goes OUTSIDE the quotation marks.* |

↝ QUESTION MARK ALSO

| right: | The defendant may have called the plaintiff "the worst Elvis impersonator in the state," but that is hardly defamatory. |
| also right: | In fact, it would be futile to try to find defamatory meaning in "the worst Elvis impersonator in the |

state": our state is so richly endowed with excellent Elvis impersonators that our least talented practitioner might be considered brilliant elsewhere.

Apostrophes

Use apostrophes properly. A judge or supervising attorney will view an inability to use apostrophes properly as a sign of semi- literacy on your part. If you do not know how to use apostrophes, you will mix up plurals (more than one) with possessives (which show ownership), or you will mix up either plurals or possessives with contractions. (In your legal writing, contractions should appear only when you are quoting someone else. See 16-P.)

B-24

Compare the following:

> *It's* means "it is." (This is a contraction.)
> *Its* means that *it* owns whatever follows. (This is a possessive.)
>
> *Who's* means "who is" or "who has."
> *Whose* is the possessive of *who.*
>
> *You're* means "you are."
> *Your* is the possessive of *you.*
>
> *Parties* means more than one *party.*
> *Party's* is the possessive of *party.*
> *Parties'* is the plural possessive of *party.*

What is wrong with each of the sentences below? Each of them will strike the reader as a verbal atrocity.

> These meetings were always conducted at the *informers* whim.
>
> The courts have limited this precedent to *it's* facts.
>
> Both the legislature and the *court's* have refused to modify the rule.

The rules on apostrophes are not hard to learn:

a. To make a noun plural, in most cases add an *s* without an apostrophe. Of course, some nouns take special forms. Where the noun ends in *y,* the *y* is usually converted to *ie.* There are other exceptions—with words like *sheep* and *dictum*—but you already know them.

b. To make most nouns possessive, add an apostrophe and an *s*. Again, there are exceptions. For example, if the noun already has an *s* because it is plural, place the apostrophe after the existing *s* and do not add another one (*parties'*).

c. Pronouns have their own possessive and plural forms. There are only a few pronouns, and you learned their possessive and plural forms long ago. If you have forgotten, the examples here should jog your memory.

d. Words often contracted cause trouble.   The ones you should watch out for are *who, you,* and — most especially — *it*. Since the contraction is formed with an apostrophe, the word's possessive cannot be. Accordingly, words that are often contracted form the possessive by adding an *s* without an apostrophe:

contraction:	*it's* ("it is")
possessive:	*its*
contraction:	*you're* ("you are")
possessive:	*your*
contraction:	*who's* ("who is")
possessive:	*whose*

Appendix C
Sample Office Memorandum

This appendix contains an office memorandum of the type described in Chapter 7.

(Appendix D is a motion memorandum as described in Chapter 21. The Appendix D memorandum was written later in the same case to persuade a court to rule in the client's favor.)

[handwritten margin note: GERLACH LIKED THINGS A LITTLE DIFF. THAT WHATS HERE IN NEUMANN]

[handwritten note above box: PUT OFFICE MEM. AT TOP]

TO: Clyde Farnsworth

FROM: Christine Chopin

DATE: March 1, 1994

RE: Eli Goslin; constructive trust

ISSUE

Will a constructive trust in favor of Eli Goslin be imposed on the title to his home and only asset, which he
deeded over to his nephew after the latter promised to
make the remaining three years of payments to prevent
foreclosure, where Goslin made no statement at the time
that would reveal his reasons for giving the deed, and
where the nephew has since then threatened to throw
Goslin out of the home?

[handwritten margin note: WILL A COURT IMPOSE A CONSTRUCTIVE TRUST... WOULD BE BETTER HERE]

[handwritten margin note: COURT IS DOING THE THING]

BRIEF ANSWER

A court is likely to impose a constructive trust in
Goslin's favor on the nephew's title to the house. Goslin
is able to prove each of the four elements of the New York
test for a constructive trust: (1) a confidential or fiduciary relationship between Goslin and his nephew;
(2) a promise, implied by the nephew's actions, to hold
title while allowing and helping Goslin to live in the
house; (3) Goslin's transfer of title to the nephew in
reliance on that promise; and (4) unjust enrichment by
the nephew if the promise is broken. New York courts have
uniformly held these elements to be satisfied where -- as
happened here -- a person in a vulnerable situation deeds
the bulk of his or her assets to someone like a trusted
relative who pays either nothing or a fraction of the
property's fair value.
(This memorandum does not consider an action to set
aside the deed on the grounds of fraud, undue influence,
or impaired capacity -- all of which have already been
researched and rejected.)

[handwritten margin note: BASICALLY INVOLVES SATISF. OR YES NO]

FACTS

Eli Goslin, the client, is a 74-year-old arthritic
widower who has been retired for nine years. He has been
married twice, and both wives are deceased. His son is
dead, and his daughter lives in Singapore. His only income is from social security.

Until last year, he also had income from an investment, but when that business went bankrupt, he became
unable to meet the mortgage payments on his house. The
house was Goslin's only asset. He has lived there for 24

-1-

years, and when these events occurred, the mortgage had
only three more years to run. He has no other place to
live.

After Goslin found that he could no longer pay the
mortgage, Herbert Skeffington, a nephew, offered to
make the remaining $11,500 in payments as they became
due. Within a few days afterward, Goslin, without stating his purpose to anyone, gave a deed to the property to
Skeffington and got the bank to agree to transfer the
mortgage to him. At the time, the house was worth approximately $95,000 and was unencumbered except for the
mortgage that Skeffington had offered to pay. Aside from
the promise to make mortgage payments, Skeffington gave
no value connected to the deed.

Goslin has told us that he made the deed for the following reason: ''At the time, it seemed like the right
thing to do. He was going to pay the mortgage, and after a
certain point —— maybe after I'm gone —— the place would
become his. I didn't think it would end up like this.''
Skeffington had not asked for a deed, and Goslin arranged
for the deed before telling the nephew about it. Goslin
knew at the time that Skeffington would not need a deed to
make the mortgage payments: the bank would have been
willing to accept Skeffington's check if it were accompanied by Goslin's payment stub, or, alternatively,
Skeffington could simply have given the money to Goslin,
who could in turn have paid the bank.

As far as Goslin knows, Skeffington has made the payments as they have become due.

At the time of the deed, neither party said anything
about changing the living arrangements in the house.
Goslin continued to live alone there until a few weeks
ago, when Skeffington's rental apartment was burned out
and he moved, along with his wife and two children, into
the house. Goslin neither agreed to nor protested this. A
few days later, Skeffington ordered Goslin to move out,
which Goslin has refused to do. Since then Skeffington
has, at the top of his voice, frequently repeated the demand. While yelling at Goslin, Skeffington has twice,
with the heels of his palms, suddenly shoved Goslin in
the chest and sent him staggering. Skeffington has
threatened to strike Goslin again and to pack up Goslin's
belongings and leave them and Goslin on the sidewalk.
Skeffington takes the position that his family has no
other place to go, and that the house is the only thing he
owns.

Skeffington is 36 years old, and throughout Skeffington's life he and Goslin have seen each other at least
monthly at family get-togethers, including each other's
weddings. Seventeen years ago, Goslin contributed
$3,200 to Skeffington's college tuition. The two of them
have never discussed whether this was to be treated as a
gift or a loan, and Goslin does not recall which he in-

The conclusion
was stated in the
first sentence of
the Brief Answer.

-2-

403

The conclusion was stated in the first sentence of the Brief Answer. The first sentence in the Discussion states the rule, which is proved conclusorily (§9.3.2) and will lead to an umbrella-paradigmed explanation (§9.3.3). Headings show where each element is discussed. Under the first heading, the first sentence states the first element's sub-conclusion (§9.3.3), and the second sentence states its supporting rule.

tended or even whether he had an intent at the time. He says that he considered both the tuition money and his nephew's offer to pay the mortgage to be ''the sort of thing people in a family do for each other.'' In any event, except for the mortgage payments, the nephew has never given Goslin money directly or indirectly, and he has not announced an intention to compensate Goslin for the tuition money.

RESTATE CONCLUSION HERE

DISCUSSION

A constructive trust will be imposed where the record shows ''(1) a confidential or fiduciary relation, (2) a promise, (3) a transfer in reliance thereon, and (4) unjust enrichment.'' McGrath v. Hilding, 363 N.E.2d 328, 330 (N.Y. 1977) (citations omitted).

SUBHEADING ¶

Confidential or Fiduciary Relationship

Goslin's relationship with his nephew satisfies the first element.

A substantiating proof of the rule (§9.3.2), synthesizing two holdings (§11.5). *Tebin* and *Sharp* are such obvious analogies that rule application is partly implied.

A confidential or fiduciary relationship exists where one person is willing to entrust important matters to a second person. A relationship between an aunt and a niece has been held to be a confidential one for the purpose of a constructive trust where the aunt turned over a substantial amount of her finances to the niece and relied on the niece's care while ill. Tebin v. Moldock, 241 N.Y.S.2d 629, 637–39 (1st Dep't 1963), modified on other grounds, 200 N.E.2d 216 (N.Y. 1964). A confidential relationship can exist even between an unsuccessful suitor and the woman who has refused to marry him where she accepts from him a deed to his farm and home. Sharp v. Kosmalski, 351 N.E.2d 721, 723 (N.Y. 1976).

A counter-analysis (§9.1), smoothly introduced. It would have been more awkward to begin "Skeffington's lawyer might argue . . ."

Although a confidential relationship might not exist between an uncle and a nephew if contact has been rare and if both viewed the relationship as merely technical, that is not true here. Goslin and his nephew have seen each other at least monthly since the nephew was a boy; they attended each other's weddings, frequent family social activities, and other events; and Goslin contributed to the nephew's college tuition.

Implied Promise by the Transferee

The sub-conclusion for the second element.

The courts are also likely to find here a promise — even if not stated in words — by the nephew to hold title in name only for Goslin's benefit while doing nothing that might prevent Goslin from continuing to live in his home.

–3–

All that is required is a promise. It need not be written, and the Statute of Frauds will not prevent a constructive trust. Sharp, 351 N.E.2d at 723–24; Pattison v. Pattison, 92 N.E.2d 890 (N.Y. 1950); Foreman v. Foreman, 167 N.E. 428 (N.Y. 1929). (''Equity in this area has always reached beyond the facade of formal documents, absolute transfers, and even limiting statutes on the law side.'' Tebin, 241 N.Y.S.2d at 638.)

The promise need not even be expressly stated where it ''may be implied or inferred from the very transaction itself.'' Sharp, 351 N.E.2d at 723. In Sharp, a 56-year-old farmer conveyed his farm to a 40-year-old woman who had declined his offer of marriage. After the transfer, the woman ordered the farmer off the property. Although the record contained no evidence of a promise in words, the Court of Appeals held that an understood promise was inherent in the actions of both parties because

> it is inconceivable that plaintiff would convey all of his interest in property which was not only his abode but the very means of his livelihood without at least tacit consent upon the part of the defendant that she would permit him to continue to live on and operate the farm.

Id. at 724.

In family relationships, New York courts have been extremely reluctant to accept a transferee's claim, under suspect circumstances, that a transfer was an absolute gift. For example, in Sinclair v. Purdy, 139 N.E. 255 (N.Y. 1923), a brother, who was employed as a court clerk and was continually being asked to pledge his property for other people's bail, deeded it over to his sister, receiving nothing in return. The Court of Appeals held that the circumstances implied a promise, and Judge Cardozo wrote for the court that

> [h]ere was a man transferring to his sister the only property he had in the world. . . . Even if we were to accept her statement that there was no distinct promise to hold it for his benefit, the exaction of such a promise, in view of the relation, might well have seemed to be superfluous.

Id. at 258.

The courts are likely to consider Goslin's circumstances to be at least comparable to those of the farmer in Sharp and the brother in Sinclair. Goslin owned nothing of substance other than his home. At the time of the transfer, he had been retired for nine years, and his only income was from social security. His income had just been reduced because of the bankruptcy of a small business in which he had had an interest. The house itself was

The supporting rule, synthesized from several cases. Because it is at least a little surprising, it needs an extended explanation and proof. Some corollary rules explain the meaning of "All that is required is a promise." (The first corollary rule tells you that the promise need not be written.)

Rule application begins (§9.1). This element is the heart of Goslin's controversy, and the reader needs an extended explanation of why the

–4–

405

worth approximately $95,000 at the time of the transfer, and the three years of mortgage payments remaining totalled $11,500. Even Skeffington's promise to make the mortgage payments cannot be considered a payment to Goslin because, if Skeffington really took clear title, the mortgage payments would benefit him and not Goslin. In addition, seventeen years ago, the nephew had received $3,200 from Goslin for college tuition, and he had not returned any of it. Although the parties have never talked with each other about whether the tuition money was a gift or a loan, the courts are likely to consider the label unimportant and instead focus on mutual family responsibilities. Accordingly, the courts are not likely to conclude that Goslin intended to make an absolute gift of his house. Instead, they will more probably hold that Goslin and his nephew had an unstated understanding that the nephew's mortgage payments were to reciprocate Goslin's contributions to the nephew's college tuition.

The courts will probably so hold even though the nephew could have made the mortgage payments without having received a deed. Of all the facts here, the most troubling is the lack of any need to deed the house over to the nephew. For example, the bank would have accepted the nephew's check, as long as it was accompanied by a stub from Goslin's payment book, and the stub could have been filled out by Goslin or his nephew. Or the nephew could have simply given Goslin the money and let him make the payments.

But under the case law, the lack of a need for a transfer is irrelevant. The farmer in <u>Sharp</u>, for example, seems to have given a deed for purely sentimental reasons, but the Court of Appeals considered it to be subject to a constructive trust anyway. <u>Sharp</u> can most reasonably be interpreted to stand for the proposition that, no matter how quixotic a transferor's purpose may have been, a promise of some kind will be implied where the parties have a family or other emotionally charged relationship and where the property transferred is the bulk of the transferor's assets. Although Goslin did not have the same practical need to make a transfer that the court clerk had in <u>Sinclair</u>, the Court of Appeals did not treat the court clerk's need as essential in that decision.

Transfer in Reliance on the Promise

The transfer itself is not in dispute here, and, for the reasons described above, Goslin should be able to prove that he granted the deed in reliance on his nephew's promise.

—5—

Margin notes

rule will be applied this way. The rule application centers on analogies to *Sharp* and *Sinclair* (§11.3).

A counter-analysis. Again, notice how it is introduced.

The counter-analysis weaves *Sharp* and *Sinclair* together to show you what they have in common. This is a form of synthesis (§11.5).

The nephew must concede part of this element, and the rest is proved through the explanations of the first two elements.

Unjust Enrichment

Goslin should also be able to establish the fourth element, which has been described variously as ''unjust enrichment under cover of the relation of confidence,'' Sinclair, 139 N.E. at 258; as a situation where ''property has been acquired in such circumstances that the holder of the legal title may not in good conscience retain the beneficial interest,'' Sharp, 351 N.E.2d at 723; and as circumstances where ''discernible promises, made in a confidential relationship, have been broken or repudiated, and the trusted one will be unjustly enriched by reason of the breaches,'' Tebin, 241 N.Y.S.2d at 634.

In Sharp and in Tebin, the courts held that a plaintiff need not prove that the party who accepted the transfer did so with a fraudulent intent. ''A constructive trust may be imposed even though the transferee fully intended to perform his promise at the time of the conveyance.'' Ferrano v. Stephanelli, 183 N.Y.S.2d 707, 711 (1st Dep't 1959). It is enough to show that the entrusted party has breached the promise on which the grantor relied.

Here, the nephew took a deed upon promising to make three years of mortgage payments and without paying anything for Goslin's sizeable equity. On these facts, the courts are likely to decide that the nephew has tried to pervert into a windfall his assumption of a family responsibility. (The nephew's offer to pay the remaining mortgage could have been seen by both parties as reciprocation for Goslin's help in putting the nephew through college, although that is not necessary to a ruling in Goslin's favor.)

CONCLUSION

Goslin can demonstrate all the elements of a constructive trust. He had a relationship of confidence with Skeffington because they are uncle and nephew and have acted that way for years. The most reasonable interpretation of the facts is that both parties understood an implied agreement that Skeffington would take title in name only and for the purpose of protecting the house for Goslin's use. The deed was a transfer of Goslin's home and only asset and could have been made only in reliance on that promise. And without a constructive trust, Skeffington would be unjustly enriched because he would have clear title to a $95,000 asset in exchange for $11,500 in mortgage payments.

The sub-conclusion for the final element. The rule, which defines unjust enrichment, is proved through a conclusory synthesis of three holdings. It can be conclusory because the definition is one that a reader can easily accept. But a surprise is in a corollary rule, which dispenses with any need to prove fraudulent intent. That gets more explanation through *Sharp*, *Tebin*, and *Ferrano* in the second paragraph.

Rule application.

Not Necessary in our memo

—6—

All of the elements of a constructive trust are therefore established, and a court is likely to impose one.

Respectfully Submitted,

Christine Chopin

Christine Chopin

−7−

Appendix **D**
Sample Motion
Memorandum

This appendix contains a motion memorandum of the type described in Chapter 21. The memorandum was written to persuade a court to grant a client's motion for a preliminary injunction.

(Appendix C is an office memorandum as described in Chapter 7. The Appendix C memorandum was written earlier in the same case to record an objective prediction of the court's eventual decision.)

SUPREME COURT OF THE STATE OF
NEW YORK, IROQUOIS COUNTY

ELI GOSLIN,

                    Plaintiff

       –against–   No. 2109/94

HERBERT SKEFFINGTON,

                    Defendant

MEMORANDUM IN SUPPORT OF
PLAINTIFF'S MOTION FOR A
PRELIMINARY INJUNCTION

Petra Diaz, Esq.
Attorney for Plaintiff
32 Fontanka Street
Bedford Falls, NY 14218
(914) 555–1111

TABLE OF CONTENTS

TABLE OF AUTHORITIES

CASES

PRELIMINARY STATEMENT

Eli Goslin, the plaintiff, is a widower living on social security. His only asset is his home, and he has no
other place to live. The defendant, Herbert Skeffington, is Mr. Goslin's nephew. Without stating an intention to make an absolute gift, Mr. Goslin gave this
nephew a deed. Since then, the nephew has assaulted
Mr. Goslin and ordered him to move out.

Mr. Goslin brought this action to impose a constructive trust on the nephew's deed, and he has simultaneously moved for an order that would preliminarily enjoin
the nephew from assaulting him, endangering his health,
conveying any interest in the property, or in any way
impeding Mr. Goslin's use of his home. This memorandum is
submitted in support of that motion.

QUESTION PRESENTED

In an action to impose a constructive trust, should a
nephew be preliminarily enjoined from assaulting his
elderly uncle and from interfering with the uncle's use
of his home and only asset, where the uncle gave the nephew a deed but never expressed an intention to make an absolute gift, and where the nephew has physically
attacked the uncle and threatened to remove him bodily
from the house?

The issue here is not exactly the same one posed in the office memo in App. C. Now a motion has been made, and the case is in a procedural posture (§§20.1, 20.3). (On Questions Presented, see Chap. 24.)

STATEMENT OF THE CASE

A 74-year-old retired man living on social security
found himself unable to make payments on a home mortgage
that otherwise would have been paid off within three
years. He has no other place to live and has resided for
24 years in this home, which is his only asset. A nephew
offered to make the remaining payments. The uncle gave
the nephew a deed without stating an intention to make an
absolute gift. After receiving the deed, the nephew ordered his uncle to move out. After the uncle refused, the
nephew has punched and threatened him.

The uncle is the plaintiff, Eli Goslin.

The nephew is the defendant, Herbert Skeffington.

The opening fact paragraph that summarizes the theory (see p. 307). Record cites are not needed in this paragraph except for facts that are not explained more fully later in the Statement of the Case (see p. 310, §23.4 fn. 1).

The Family Involved

Mr. Goslin is arthritic and 74 years old, and the nephew is 36. (Goslin Aff. ¶¶ 1-2.) Mr. Goslin's wife and son
are both dead, and his daughter lives in Asia. (Id.)
Mr. Goslin and the nephew have seen each other at least
monthly at family get-togethers throughout the nephew's

The reader should be able to see a picture of a man who is elderly, alone, and vulnerable.

-1-

life and had attended each other's weddings. (Id. at
¶ 15.) Seventeen years ago, Mr. Goslin had helped to pay
the college expenses of the defendant, and prior to the
events here at issue, the nephew never returned this
money or reciprocated in any other way. (Id. at ¶ 11.)

The Mortgage

Because of a business reversal last year, Mr. Goslin
lost all his income other than social security and became
unable to pay his mortgage. The mortgage would have been
amortized in three additional years. (Id. ¶ 2.) To prevent foreclosure, the nephew finally offered to make the
remainder of Mr. Goslin's mortgage payments as they became due. (Id. at ¶ 2–3; Skeffington Aff. ¶ 11.)

The payments the nephew offered to make would have to-
talled $11,500. (Skeffington Aff. ¶ 12.) At the time, the
house was worth approximately $95,000, and Mr. Goslin's
equity was worth approximately $83,500. (Mendez Aff. ¶¶
3–4.) Although the amount Mr. Goslin had contributed to
the nephew's college tuition was $3,200, that money
would have grown substantially over the intervening
seventeen years if Mr. Goslin had invested it instead.
Even if put into a conservative investment like United
States savings bonds, it would be worth at least $8,500
today. (Id. at ¶ 9.)

The Deed

Except for this house, Mr. Goslin has no place in which
to live. (Goslin Aff. at ¶ 2.) He made out a deed to his
nephew as part of what he believed to be a mutual effort
in which he thought that his nephew ''was trying to help
me keep — rather than lose — my home.'' (Id. at ¶ 3.) At
the time of the deed, Mr. Goslin expressed no intention
to make, through this deed, an absolute gift of his home
and only asset, and he says now that he had no such intention. (Id. at ¶ 4.) The nephew has submitted no evidence
to the contrary.

Although, when he made the deed, Mr. Goslin understood
that the nephew would have been able to tender the mortgage payments to the bank without having title to the
house, Mr. Goslin thought a deed appropriate because he
expected that ''after a certain point — maybe after I'm
gone — the place would become'' the nephew's. (Id. at
¶ 9.) Mr. Goslin believed that the nephew's offer to make
the mortgage payments to be ''the sort of thing people in
a family do for each other'' — and in no way different
from Mr. Goslin's payment of some of the nephew's college
expenses (Id. at ¶¶ 9–10, 14.) And Mr. Goslin says that he
offered the deed in the same spirit. (Id. at ¶ 9.)

–2–

An argument im-
plied through the
facts. After reading
the math, you
think that the
nephew will get
this house for al-
most nothing un-
less a court
intervenes. But the
writer did not say
that. The writer in-
stead gave you the
raw data in a way
that makes you
draw that infer-
ence on your own.
Goslin gave the
nephew something
that would now be
worth at least
$8,500. The neph-
ew gives Goslin
$11,500. Then,
when the dust set-
tles, the nephew
claims something
else worth
$83,500. Your in-
stinctive reaction
is to say, "Wait a
minute!"

The Nephew's Attempts to Remove Mr. Goslin

Eight months after receiving the deed, the nephew moved his family into Mr. Goslin's home without Mr. Goslin's permission, and he ordered his uncle to move out. (<u>Id.</u> at ¶¶ 1–3.) The nephew does not deny that at least twice in the last few weeks he has struck his uncle, and that he has continued to order his uncle to leave, often yelling at the top of his voice. (<u>See id.</u> at ¶¶ 1, 3, 5–6.) Nor does the nephew deny that he has threatened to strike Mr. Goslin again and to pack up Mr. Goslin's belongings and leave them and Mr. Goslin on the sidewalk. (<u>See id.</u>)

Motivating arguments are implied here. The goal is to induce the judge to feel both alarm and anger. (Did you feel those emotions?)

ARGUMENT

THE DEFENDANT SHOULD BE PRELIMINARILY ENJOINED FROM ASSAULTING MR. GOSLIN, ENDANGERING HIS HEALTH, CONVEYING TITLE TO MR. GOSLIN'S HOME, OR IN ANY OTHER WAY IMPEDING MR. GOSLIN'S USE OF HIS HOME.

The ultimate conclusion (§9.3.3).

A party should be granted a preliminary injunction if he can demonstrate (1) that he is likely to succeed on the merits; (2) that, absent a preliminary injunction, he is likely to suffer irreparable harm concerning the subject of the action; and (3) that a balancing of the equities favors a preliminary injunction. <u>Town of Porter v. Chem—Trol Pollution Services, Inc.</u>, 60 A.D.2d 987, 988, 401 N.Y.S.2d 646, 647 (4th Dep't 1978). The record before the court on this motion contains ample evidence of all of these elements.

The governing procedural test. It will lead to an umbrella-para-digmed explanation (§20.3). For this procedural test, a conclusory proof is sufficient (see pp. 279-81).

A. Mr. Goslin is likely to succeed on the merits in the underlying action to impress a constructive trust on the title to his home, which is held by the defendant.

The facts here fit the classic pattern of abuse of family trust and confidence in which New York courts have traditionally impressed a constructive trust. Mr. Goslin — an elderly man in such financial difficulty that he might lose his home, his only asset — deeded it over to a trusted nephew, the defendant, whom Mr. Goslin once helped put through college. (Goslin Aff. ¶¶ 2–3, 11.) Mr. Goslin made out the deed only after the nephew offered to prevent foreclosure by paying the $11,500 remaining due on the mortgage. (<u>Id.</u> at ¶¶ 2–3.) The nephew paid nothing for Mr. Goslin's equity, which was approximately $83,500 at the time of the deed. (<u>Id.</u> at ¶¶ 7–8.) Since

The sub-conclusion for the first element of the test for a preliminary injunction. See p. 280.

This paragraph summarizes the motivating arguments. It is inserted before the justifying arguments begin (see p. 258).

obtaining the deed, the nephew has assaulted and ha-
rassed Mr. Goslin, trying to intimidate him into leaving
the home that the nephew promised to save and in which Mr.
Goslin has lived for 24 years. (<u>Id.</u> at ¶¶ 1, 3, 5–6.) In
these circumstances, the nephew's claim of an absolute
gift is inherently incredible.

The rule that re-
solves the first ele-
ment of the test for
a preliminary in-
junction. See the
diagram on p. 280.
Tucker proves a
rule of preliminary
injunction law that
lessens Goslin's
burden of persua-
sion.

A constructive trust should be imposed where the
record shows ''(1) a confidential or fiduciary relation, (2) a promise, (3) a transfer in reliance thereon,
and (4) unjust enrichment.'' <u>McGrath v. Hilding</u>, 41
N.Y.2d 625, 629, 363 N.E.2d 328, 330, 394 N.Y.S.2d 603,
606 (1977) (citations omitted). On a motion for a preliminary injunction, the movant is required to make only
a prima facie showing and need not provide the full quantum of evidence that would be needed to prove the underlying cause of action at trial. <u>Tucker v. Toia</u>, 54 A.D.2d
322, 326, 388 N.Y.S.2d 475, 478 (4th Dep't 1976).

The sub-sub-con-
clusion for the first
element of the test
for a constructive
trust (p. 280).

    1.   <u>The defendant is Mr. Goslin's nephew, and
         the relationship between them is by
         definition confidential.</u>

The rule support-
ing that sub-sub-
conclusion.

A confidential relationship exists where one person
is willing to entrust important matters to another person. The relationship between an aunt and a niece is a
confidential one for the purposes of a constructive
trust action where the aunt turned over a substantial
amount of her finances to the niece and relied on the
niece's care while ill. <u>Tebin v. Moldock</u>, 19 A.D.2d 275,
284–85, 241 N.Y.S.2d 629, 637–39 (1963), <u>modified on
other grounds</u>, 14 N.Y.2d 807, 200 N.E.2d 216, 251
N.Y.S.2d 36 (1964). A confidential relationship can exist even between an unsuccessful suitor and the woman who
has refused to marry him where she accepted from him a
deed to his farm and home. <u>Sharp v. Kosmalski</u>, 40 N.Y.2d
119, 121–22, 351 N.E.2d 721, 723, 386 N.Y.S.2d 72, 75
(1976).

Rule proof begins.

Rule application
begins. This was
handled almost by
implication in the
office memo in
App. C. In persua-
sive writing, it has
to be argued more
overtly, as here.

Here, Mr. Goslin and his nephew had, at the time of the
deed, a trusting family relationship on which a person in
Mr. Goslin's position could naturally hope to rely. Seventeen years ago, Mr. Goslin had given the nephew $3,200
for college tuition, and the nephew had not yet reciprocated. (Goslin Aff. ¶ 11.) The two had seen each other at
least monthly since the nephew was a boy and had attended
each others' weddings and a number of other family functions. (<u>Id.</u> at ¶ 15.)

–4–

<u>2</u>. <u>The record shows an unstated promise by the defendant nephew to hold title in name only and for Mr. Goslin's benefit and to do nothing that might prevent Mr. Goslin from living in his own home.</u>

A promise implied through conduct alone will support a constructive trust. A written instrument is not needed. <u>Sharp</u>, 40 N.Y.2d at 122, 351 N.E.2d at 723–24, 386 N.Y.S.2d at 75; <u>Pattison v. Pattison</u>, 301 N.Y. 65, 92 N.E.2d 890 (1950); <u>Foreman v. Foreman</u>, 251 N.Y. 237, 167 N.E. 428 (1929). ''Equity in this area has always reached beyond the facade of formal documents, absolute transfers, and even limiting statutes on the law side.'' <u>Tebin</u>, 19 A.D.2d at 284–85, 241 N.Y.S.2d at 638.

Not only is a written promise unnecessary to a constructive trust, but the Court of Appeals has held that the promise need not even be orally stated where it ''may be implied or inferred from the very transaction itself.'' <u>Sharp</u>, 40 N.Y.2d at 122, 351 N.E.2d at 723, 386 N.Y.S.2d at 75. In <u>Sharp</u>, a 56–year–old farmer conveyed his farm to a 40–year–old woman who had declined his offer of marriage. After the transfer, the woman ordered the farmer off the property. Although the record contained no evidence of a promise in words, the Court of Appeals held that an understood promise was inherent in the actions of both parties because

> it is inconceivable that plaintiff would convey all of his interest in property which was not only his abode but the very means of his livelihood without at least tacit consent upon the part of the defendant that she would permit him to continue to live on and operate the farm.

<u>Id.</u> at 122, 351 N.E.2d at 724, 386 N.Y.S.2d at 75.

In family relationships, New York courts have been extremely reluctant to accept, under suspect circumstances, a transferee's claim that a transfer was an absolute gift. For example, in <u>Sinclair v. Purdy</u>, 235 N.Y. 245, 139 N.E. 255 (1923), a brother, who was employed as a court clerk and was continually asked to pledge his property for other people's bail, deeded it over to his sister, receiving nothing in return. The Court of Appeals held that the circumstances implied a promise, and Judge Cardozo wrote for the court that

> [h]ere was a man transferring to his sister the only property he had in the world. . . . Even if we were to accept her statement that there was no distinct promise to hold it for his benefit, the exaction of such a promise, in view of the relation, might well have seemed superfluous.

–5–

The sub-sub-conclusion for the first element of the test for a constructive trust (p. 280).

The rule supporting that sub-sub-conclusion, followed by proof of that rule.

Rule application
begins.

Here, justifying ar-
guments and moti-
vating arguments
are made at the
same time. The
justifying argu-
ment is that the
second element of
the test for a con-
structive trust is
satisfied. The mo-
tivating argument
is that the nephew
is victimizing a
vulnerable person
and should be
stopped.

A counter-argu-
ment (§19.4).

Part of this ele-
ment is not in dis-
pute at all, and the
rest is proved
above.

<u>Id.</u> at 254, 139 N.E. at 258.

Mr. Goslin was just as unlikely to have given away his home. He owned nothing else of substance. (Goslin Aff. ¶ 4.) At the time of the deed, he had been retired for nine years, and his only income was from social security. (<u>Id.</u> at ¶ 2.) His income had just been reduced because of the bankruptcy of a small business in which he had had an interest. (<u>Id.</u>) The house itself was worth approximately $95,000 at the time, and the three years of mortgage payments remaining totalled $11,500. (<u>Id.</u> at ¶¶ 7–8.) (Even the nephew's promise to make the mortgage payments cannot be considered a payment to Goslin because, if the nephew really took clear title, the mortgage payments would benefit him and not Goslin.) Seventeen years ago, the nephew had received $3,200 for college tuition and had not yet reciprocated. (<u>Id.</u> at ¶ 11.) At the time of the deed, Mr. Goslin was 74 years old, arthritic, and without any other place to live. (<u>Id.</u> at ¶¶ 1–2.) On these facts, it can hardly be believed that Mr. Goslin would have made an unconditional gift of all the equity in his home. The more plausible explanation is that he and his nephew had an unexpressed understanding that the nephew's mortgage payments were to reciprocate Mr. Goslin's assistance with the nephew's college education.

That is so even though the nephew did not need a deed in order to make Mr. Goslin's mortgage payments. Under the case law, the absence of a need for a deed is irrelevant. The farmer in <u>Sharp</u>, for example, seems to have given a deed for purely sentimental reasons, but the Court of Appeals considered it to be subject to a constructive trust anyway. <u>Sharp</u> can reasonably be interpreted to stand for the proposition that –– no matter how quixotic a transferor's purpose may have been –– a promise of some kind will be implied where the parties have a family or other emotionally charged relationship and where the property transferred is the bulk of the transferor's assets. Although Goslin did not have the same practical need to make a transfer that the court clerk had in <u>Sinclair</u>, the Court of Appeals did not treat the court clerk's need as essential to its decision.

<u>3</u>.   <u>The nephew himself contends that the deed</u>
       <u>was a transfer.</u>

As to the third element of the test for a constructive trust –– a transfer in reliance on the promise –– the nephew himself contends that the deed was a transfer. For the reasons set out above, the record shows that Mr. Goslin granted the deed in reliance on the nephew's promise.

–6–

418

4. Without a constructive trust, the nephew will be unjustly enriched.

The final element of the test for a constructive trust has been described variously as ''unjust enrichment under cover of the relation of confidence,'' Sinclair, 235 N.Y. at 253, 139 N.E. at 258; as a situation where ''property has been acquired in such circumstances that the holder of the legal title may not in good conscience retain the beneficial interest,'' Sharp, 40 N.Y.2d at 121, 351 N.E.2d at 723, 386 N.Y.S.2d at 74; and as circumstances where ''discernible promises, made in a confidential relationship, have been broken or repudiated, and the trusted one will be unjustly enriched by reason of the breaches,'' Tebin, 19 A.D.2d at 280, 241 N.Y.S.2d at 634. The courts held in Sharp and in Tebin that a plaintiff need not prove that the party who accepted the transfer did so with a fraudulent intent. ''A constructive trust may be imposed even though the transferee fully intended to perform his promise at the time of the conveyance.'' Ferrano v. Stephanelli, 7 A.D.2d 420, 424, 183 N.Y.S.2d 707, 711 (1st Dep't 1959). It is enough to show that the entrusted party has breached the promise on which the grantor relied.

Here, the nephew took a deed upon promising to make three years of mortgage payments and without paying anything for Mr. Goslin's equity of approximately $83,500. (Goslin Aff. ¶¶ 2–3, 7–8.) The nephew took the deed from an elderly man who desperately needed to stay in his own home because he had no other place to go — and continues now to have no other place to go. (Id. at ¶¶ 1–2.) The nephew took the deed at a time when Mr. Goslin had made mortgage payments for 24 years and needed to do so for only three more years to be able to live there for the rest of his life without making any mortgage payments at all. (Id. at ¶ 1.) And the nephew's offer to make mortgage payments is most reasonably seen as reciprocation for Mr. Goslin's help in putting the nephew through college. Here, the nephew has tried to pervert into a windfall his assumption of a family obligation.

B. Without an injunction, Mr. Goslin is threatened with irreparable harm in the form of assault and the loss of his own home.

A movant is threatened with irreparable harm when the opposing party creates a risk of injury that a final judgment could not sufficiently remedy. Schlosser v. United Presbyterian Home, 56 A.D.2d 615, 615, 391 N.Y.S.2d 880, 881 (2d Dep't 1977). By definition, that is true where a defendant's conduct would leave a plaintiff

—7—

Margin annotations:

The sub-sub-conclusion for the final element of the constructive trust test (p. 280).

The rule and proof of it.

Rule application begins.

This completes proof that the record satisfies the first element of the test for a preliminary injunction. (See p. 280.)

The sub-conclusion for the second element of the preliminary injunction test (p. 280).

The governing rule, followed by rule proof.

Rule application
begins.

with ''no alternative residence . . . during the pen-
dency of the action.'' <u>Id.</u> at 615, 391 N.Y.S.2d at 881. In
<u>Schlosser</u>, a defendant landlord was preliminarily en-
joined from imposing disputed rent increases that the
plaintiff senior citizens would have been unable to afford.

In the matter now before this court, the defendant
nephew has assaulted Mr. Goslin, who is 74 years old and
arthritic. (Goslin Aff. ¶¶ 1–3, 5–6.) He has also threatened to assault him again and to pack up his belongings
and leave them and him on the street, even though he has
no other place to go. (<u>Id.</u>) Although a preliminary injunction is discretionary, <u>City of Buffalo v. Mangan</u>, 49
A.D.2d 697, 697, 370 N.Y.S.2d 771, 772 (4th Dep't 1975),
and ''a drastic remedy to be sparingly used,'' <u>Town of
Porter v. Chem–Trol</u>, 60 A.D.2d at 988, 401 N.Y.S.2d at
647, an injunction should be granted where necessary to
preserve a deteriorating status quo until the court can
make a judgment on the merits, <u>Tucker</u>, 54 A.D.2d at 325,
388 N.Y.S.2d at 478. This court should exercise its discretion and provide even a drastic remedy where an elderly person in frail health is threatened with assault
and the loss of his only asset and only available place to
live.

The sub-conclu-
sion for the third
and final element
of the preliminary
injunction test.

   <u>C</u>. <u>This injunction would not burden any
       legitimate conduct by the nephew,
       and the equities are therefore favorably
       balanced.</u>

The rule, followed
by proof of it.

A balance of the equities favors a preliminary injunction where the threatened irreparable injury would be
''more burdensome'' to the movant than any harm the opposing party might experience because of an injunction.
<u>Metropolitan Package Store Ass'n, Inc. v. Koch</u>, 80
A.D.2d 940, 941, 437 N.Y.S.2d 760, 761 (3d Dep't 1981).
Even where the facts are in dispute, a preliminary injunction should be granted where necessary to preserve
the status quo and where the injunction will not cause
the enjoined party ''great hardship.'' <u>City Store Gates
Mfg. v. United Steel Products</u>, 79 A.D.2d 671, 671, 433
N.Y.S.2d 876, 877 (2d Dep't 1980).

Rule application.

Here, Mr. Goslin would suffer far more hardship if he
were locked out or assaulted, or if his health were otherwise endangered, than the defendant would suffer if
none of these things were to happen.

–8–

CONCLUSION

Therefore, this court should grant an order preliminarily enjoining the defendant nephew from assaulting Mr. Goslin, endangering his health, conveying any interest in the property, or in any way impeding Mr. Goslin's use of his home. Mr. Goslin is likely to succeed on the merits of the underlying action for a constructive trust. He is threatened with irreparable harm in the form of violence and the loss of his only available place to live. And the defendant would suffer no harm if enjoined.

Respectfully Submitted,

Petra Diaz, Esq.
Attorney for Plaintiff
32 Fontanka Street
Bedford Falls, NY 14218
(914) 555-1111

Appendix **E**
Sample Appellant's
Brief

This Appendix contains the appellant's brief from a hypothetical appeal. (Appendix F contains the appellee's brief from the same appeal.) To economize your reading, each brief has been limited to only two of the issues that could have been raised on these facts.[1] The material that remains is substantial enough to give you realistic examples of how various tasks might be handled in a brief you would be assigned to write.

These briefs come with two caveats.

First, do not imitate something in these briefs without understanding why it was done here and without determining whether it would be effective in an appeal for which you are writing a brief. If, for example, you find that you like the style of the Questions Presented in one of these briefs, consider the possibility that that style might not work as well with your theory and with the facts and law of your appeal. One of your most important goals is to learn how to make your own writing decisions so that you can begin to develop a professional self-sufficiency. That goal is defeated if you imitate unquestioningly the appearance of a sample brief.

The second caveat concerns differences in brief format from jurisdiction to jurisdiction. This brief and the brief in Appendix F follow a format that homogenizes the rules of many jurisdictions. Every jurisdiction's rules have at least a few local idiosyncrasies that would seem quirky elsewhere. Although these briefs were written for a hypothetical appeal set in New York, the idiosyncrasies of New York format have been eliminated from what you

---

1. In addition to the grounds asserted here, a defendant in a similar case might also argue that the statute involved is unconstitutionally vague, that it violates First Amendment rights to freedom of expression and to freedom of assembly and association, and that it violates the Fourteenth Amendment right to equal protection.

will read here.[2] That is because sample briefs ought to illustrate those brief-writing practices that are most common nationally. If, however, you are asked to follow local format rules with which these briefs would be inconsistent — and your teacher will tell you if that is so — be careful to observe those rules in spite of what you see here.

---

2. For example, in New York, the non-appealing party is called the "respondent," even though the appealing party is the "appellant." (See N.Y. Civ. Prac. L. § 5511.) The common practice elsewhere, however, is that the non-appealing party is a "respondent" only when the appealing party is a "petitioner," and an "appellant" is always opposed by an "appellee." The briefs in these appendices follow national (and not New York) practice in this and in several other respects.

COURT OF APPEALS OF THE STATE OF NEW YORK

THE PEOPLE OF THE STATE OF NEW YORK,
                    Appellee

–against–

MERRITT BRESNAHAN,
                              Defendant–Appellant

No. 94–341

BRIEF FOR DEFENDANT–APPELLANT

Clyde Farnsworth, Esq.
Attorney for Defendant–Appellant
32 Fontanka Street
Bedford Falls, N.Y. 14218
(914) 555–1111

TABLE OF CONTENTS

TABLE OF AUTHORITIES

CASES

*Authorities chiefly relied on are marked with an
asterisk.

MISCELLANEOUS

STATUTE INVOLVED

Section 240.35(4) of the New York Penal Law provides as follows:

A person is guilty of loitering when he . . .
   4. Being masked or in any manner disguised by unusual or unnatural attire or facial alteration, loiters, remains or congregates in a public place with other persons so masked or disguised, or knowingly permits or aids persons so masked or disguised to congregate in a public place; except that such conduct is not unlawful when it occurs in connection with a masquerade party or like entertainment if, when such entertainment is held in a city which has promulgated regulations in connection with such affairs, permission is first obtained from the police or other appropriate authorities. . . .
   Loitering is a violation.

PRELIMINARY STATEMENT

Merritt Bresnahan appeals from a conviction for loitering under section 240.35(4) of the Penal law. Before trial, she moved to dismiss on the ground that section 240.35(4) violates her right to privacy under the United States Constitution. The Criminal Court of New York City and County reserved decision until the end of trial. After the close of the evidence at trial, Ms. Bresnahan additionally moved for a trial order of dismissal on the ground that the People had not introduced legally sufficient evidence that she had been — as a conviction under section 240.35(4) would require — ''masked or in any manner disguised by unusual or unnatural attire or facial alteration.'' The Criminal Court, Judge Celeste Remay, denied both motions, convicted Ms. Bresnahan of violating section 240.35(4), and sentenced her to a fine of two hundred dollars. Ms. Bresnahan appealed the denial of the two motions; Appellate Term affirmed; and this appeal followed.

QUESTIONS PRESENTED

Merritt Bresnahan suffers from gender dysphoria syndrome, a chronic and potentially disabling disorder in which the patient experiences unremitting anguish from a belief that his or her reproductive organs are not those of the patient's true gender. Psychotherapy has no effect on this disorder, and the only medically accepted treatment is sex reassignment surgery, preceded by a long period of hormonal injections. Responsible medical

This is an alternative format for a Question Presented (see pp. 316-17).

–1–

432

practice includes requiring such a patient to dress, during the hormonal, pre-operative phase of treatment, in the clothing of the gender that matches the patient's belief. Ms. Bresnahan was so dressed, as prescribed by her doctors, at the time she was arrested for loitering under Penal Law § 240.35(4). She was charged with no other offense. The questions presented on appeal are the following:

1. Whether the trial court should have granted Ms. Bresnahan's motion for a trial order of dismissal, where the sole evidence that she was ''masked or . . . disguised'' showed only that she was dressed exactly as her doctors had prescribed.

2. Whether the trial court should have granted Ms. Bresnahan's motion to dismiss the information on the ground that section 240.35(4) violates her right to privacy under the United States Constitution.

STATEMENT OF THE CASE

At trial, Ms. Bresnahan's doctors testified without contradiction that she suffers from gender dysphoria syndrome; that she has been compelled to enter a long-term treatment program at the Gender Identity Clinic at Murray Hill Hospital; and that her prescribed medical treatment requires her to wear female clothing. (R. at 81–96, 388–406, 409–44.) She was arrested for doing exactly that.

The opening paragraph that summarizes the theory (see p. 307 and p. 310, §23.4 fn. 1).

At Murray Hill Hospital, Ms. Bresnahan has been under the treatment of a physician and a psychotherapist. Both specialize in treating this disorder, and both testified at trial. They supplied all of the medical evidence before the trial court. The People called no expert witnesses.

Gender Dysphoria Syndrome

Gender dysphoria syndrome, also known as transsexualism, is a chronic disorder in which the patient suffers from ''an unrelenting and uncontrollable feeling that he or she is not the gender that matched the reproductive organs assigned at birth'' (R. at 389). Transsexuals find their reproductive organs to be ''repugnant'' (R. at 391); often are unable to maintain normal social relationships (R. at 390); suffer from ''drastic depressions precipitated by loathing their own bodies'' (R. at 392); and, in some cases, become at risk to suicide or mutilation of their own bodies (id.). The cause of the disorder is unknown (R. at 398), and psychotherapy cannot provide effective treatment (R. at 396). A transsexual is not a homosexual or a transvestite (R. at 400). The

–2–

433

syndrome becomes apparent in early childhood, often at
about four years of age, and the child's gestures and
play habits are uniformly of the opposite gender (R. at
401–02). As a result, the child ''suffers merciless
teasing and rejection, which continues in more sophisticated form throughout adulthood'' (R. at 402). Because a transsexual ''despises his or her own body and is
in turn found disgusting by others, such a person is
among the most unhappy patients a psychotherapist can
treat'' (R. at 403).

Treatment for Gender Dysphoria Syndrome

The trial court heard descriptions of the treatment
programs at nine gender identity clinics in North
America and Europe. Each such clinic prescribes treatment along the following pattern:

The patient is first given ''an exhaustive psychological workup to confirm the diagnosis'' (R. at 419). Then,
over a period of six months to two years, the patient is
given hormonal injections which alter the body's appearance (id.). During this period, a clinic typically
requires the patient to ''live and dress as the gender
the patient believes him– or herself to be,'' and, if the
patient does not satisfy this requirement, treatment is
stopped ''because sex reassignment surgery would not
then be indicated as a permanent change in the patient's
life'' (R. at 419–20).

At an appropriate point, the patient is provided with
sex reassignment surgery, in which the original sexual
organs are replaced with those that are consistent with
the patient's ''psychological gender'' (R. at 422). After such surgery, a transsexual who was, for example,
born with male reproductive organs would have ''an internal sexual structure like that of a woman who has
undergone a total hysterectomy and ovariectomy, which
is not unusual in naturally born women after a certain
age'' (R. at 423–24). Medically, such a transsexual
would at this point be considered a female (R. at 423),
although there may be later procedures and continued
hormonal treatment (R. at 425–26).

Sex reassignment surgery is only one of ''several
stages in a sex role assimilation, and it must be
preceded by a complete psychological and social assimilation'' (R. at 427). The surgery is thus ''not viewed
medically as a sex change operation'' because a substantial amount of gender has already been transformed before the surgery takes place (R. at 426).

After completion of treatment the typical patient
''lives a far happier life'' as a result of the elimina-
tion of the patient's inner conflict and of the elimina-

—3—

All this medical de-
tail is intended to
help the court vis-
ualize the case as a
medical problem.
The theory thus
implied is that
medicine is doing
what we would
want it to do, and
that the criminal
law should find
other problems to
worry about.

tion of conflict between the patient and others unable to
tolerate the disorder (R. at 406).

It is ''irresponsible'' medical practice to provide
physical treatment without at the same time requiring
''cross-dressing'' because of the need to ensure that
the patient is able to live the life to which surgery will
irreversibly commit her (R. at 326, 399). There are two
additional benefits: to prepare the patient for surgery
(R. at 341-43, 432-36) and to relieve some of the patient's suffering until hormonal therapy has made surgery possible (R. at 347-49, 401-04).

Both doctors testified that medicine considered Ms.
Bresnahan, at the time of her arrest, to be dressed in
clothing appropriate to her state of gender because gender is determined by hormonal composition and psychological condition, as well as by reproductive organs and
chromosomes (R. at 344, 405-06, 443). They had informed
Ms. Bresnahan of this fact and prescribed cross-dressing for her (R. at 349, 405-06, 440-42).

Ms. Bresnahan testified that she had been so informed
and was cross-dressing ''under doctor's orders'' (R. at
176-80). She had dressed exclusively in female clothing
and lived as a woman since the age of 16 because of a belief, held since her earliest childhood memories, that
she was born female (R. at 173, 178-79). She testified in
detail about her childhood play with dolls and several
years of conflict with parents, other children, and
school authorities ''because of my femininity'' (R. at
182-96). Her office colleagues accepted her as a woman
(R. at 199) and at the time she was arrested, she was on
her way to lunch, accompanied by two other transsexuals
who also work in the financial district of Manhattan (R.
at 203).

The Arrest

At the time of the arrest, Ms. Bresnahan was employed
as a financial analyst for a stock brokerage firm (R. at
170). She was arrested on the street one block from her
office, was strip-searched at a police station, and was
later compelled to explain to her supervisor the reason
why she had not returned from lunch on the afternoon she
was arrested (R. at 202-07). Her psychotherapist confirmed that Ms. Bresnahan had experienced a ''profound'' depression after the arrest, and that her
treatment plan had to be extended approximately six
months as a result (R. at 407-09). Ms. Bresnahan testified that for several days after the arrest she felt unable to return to her office (R. at 208) and that she no
longer felt safe in public (R. at 210-11).

The reader should
be able to see a
picture of a useful
member of society
who has been vic-
timized by the ma-
chinery of justice
for no rational rea-
son.

-4-

435

The absence of a particular kind of evidence can itself be a fact.

Use of Gender Disguises in Crime

The People submitted no evidence of any pattern of robbery, theft, or other crimes committed by groups of people disguising their gender.

The Decisions Below

At the close of the evidence, the trial judge ruled from the bench on Ms. Bresnahan's motion to dismiss on the ground that a conviction would violate her right to privacy, as well as her motion for a trial order of dismissal on the ground that her conduct was not within the intent of the statute. The trial judge denied the first motion, holding that section 240.35(4) can constitutionally penalize cross-dressing by a transsexual. (R. at 468.) And the trial judge denied the second motion, holding that a person is ''masked or . . . disguised'' within the meaning of section 240.35(4) when that person ''is wearing the clothing of one gender but has the reproductive organs of the other.'' (R. at 470.)

The Appellate Term affirmed without opinion (R. at 481).

SUMMARY OF ARGUMENT

The People did not produce evidence legally sufficient to demonstrate a violation of Penal Law § 240.35(4), and the Criminal Court therefore erred in denying Ms. Bresnahan's motion for a trial order of dismissal. The Criminal Court heard extensive and uncontradicted expert testimony that Ms. Bresnahan suffers from a disease that requires her to dress as she did when arrested. An examination of the statute's history and that of similar statutes elsewhere shows that the Legislature's real purpose was to deter political violence by groups of masked or disguised individuals. Moreover, a cross-dressing transsexual is not disguised at all because the weight of scientific opinion, recognized in the case law, is that cross-dressing accurately informs the bystander of the patient's state of gender. No reported decision anywhere in the United States has held that a statute like section 240.35(4) can be enforced against a cross-dressing transsexual. Whenever courts in other jurisdictions have been asked to use similar statutes to punish persons with gender dysphoria syndrome, the courts have either declared the statutes unconstitutional or have held that they do not apply to transsexuals.

In addition, the Criminal Court should have granted Ms. Bresnahan's motion to dismiss the information on the

-5-

ground that section 240.35(4) violates her constitutional right to privacy. The right to privacy can be invaded only (1) where the People can demonstrate a
compelling state interest and (2) where the invasion is
no larger than necessary to accomplish that interest.
Here, the only interests advanced by the People are a desire to prevent the use of disguises in crimes committed
by gangs and an interest in preventing groups of disguised males from gaining access to women's washrooms.
These interests are not compelling, and even if they
were, they support no intrusion greater than a statute
that limits its punishment to persons who appear
together in public disguised _for a criminal purpose_.
Section 240.35(4) instead punishes all persons who appear together in public with their identities obscured,
no matter how innocent the purpose.

Even if a compelling state interest were not required,
section 240.35(4) cannot be sustained under the lesser
''rational basis'' test. The People have not introduced
any evidence that section 240.35(4) is connected to any
verifiable danger to the public. Although section
240.35(4) is claimed to be justifiable as a crime control
measure, even under the rational basis standard there is
no basis for an assumption that people who cross-dress
for medical reasons will also do so to commit crimes.

In the only case on point with this appeal, the
Illinois Supreme Court has ruled that an ordinance similar to section 240.35(4) cannot constitutionally be enforced against transsexuals. The only cases that have
permitted governmental regulation of an adult's appearance have involved prison inmates, nude bathing, massage parlor employees, and public employees.

ARGUMENT

I.   THE CRIMINAL COURT SHOULD HAVE GRANTED MS.
     BRESNAHAN'S MOTION FOR A TRIAL ORDER OF
     DISMISSAL BECAUSE THE PEOPLE FAILED TO
     INTRODUCE LEGALLY SUFFICIENT EVIDENCE THAT
     SHE HAD BEEN ''MASKED OR . . . DISGUISED''
     IN THE SENSE REQUIRED BY PENAL LAW
     § 240.35(4).

> The conclusion for Point I. Only one element of the offense is in dispute.

The trial court heard uncontroverted evidence that
Ms. Bresnahan suffers from gender dysphoria syndrome
and that she was arrested while dressed exactly as her
doctors had prescribed for her (R. at 368). Their treatment plan followed accepted medical practice, and she
was compelled to enter treatment because of a medical
condition that caused her profound suffering. The People prosecuted her because they consider her conduct to
be a threat to society. But the history of section

> A summary of the motivating arguments, inserted before the justifying arguments begin (see p. 258).

–6–

437

The rule.

240.35(4) and of like statutes in other states demonstrates that the Legislature did not intend that people wearing clothing medically appropriate for them would be punished for being ''masked or . . . disguised.''

At the close of the evidence, Ms. Bresnahan moved for a trial order of dismissal on the ground that the People had not introduced legally sufficient evidence that she had been —— as a conviction under section 240.35(4) would require —— ''masked or in any manner disguised by unusual or unnatural attire or facial alteration.'' The trial court denied the motion, ruling that section 240.35(4) is satisfied by evidence establishing, among other things, that ''a defendant is wearing the clothing of one gender but has the reproductive organs of the other'' (R. at 470). A determination that the evidence was legally

The standard of review (§27.3).

sufficient will be affirmed on appeal if, after resolving factual inferences in favor of the People, a rational trier of fact could have found all the elements of the offense proved beyond a reasonable doubt. People v. Acosta, 80 N.Y.2d 665, 672, 609 N.E.2d 518, 522, 593 N.Y.S.2d 978, 982 (1993). But even when viewing the record in the light most favorable to the People, the evidence here is legally insufficient because the Legislature did not intend section 240.35(4) to punish the conduct proved in the trial court.

Everything under sub-heading A is rule proof.

A. Section 240.35(4) is derived from legislation designed to protect the public from violent criminals in disguise.

Compare the image of these murders with the image of Bresnahan's arrest, in business clothing, in the financial district of Manhattan. What effect do you think this will have on the judicial reader (§18.7)?

Section 240.35(4) is descended from a statute enacted in 1845 after an insurrection that had broken out among male Hudson Valley tenant farmers who were unable to pay their rents and had begun to disguise themselves as Indians and women for the purpose of murdering officials serving them with writs. See People v. Simmons, 79 Misc. 2d 249, 253, 357 N.Y.S.2d 362, 366 (Crim. Ct., Kings County 1974) (dicta). The original legislation was entitled ''An Act to Prevent Persons Appearing Disguised and Armed'' (emphasis added), and, among other things, it provided that

> Every person who, having his face painted, discolored or concealed or being otherwise disguised in a manner calculated to prevent him from being identified, shall appear in any road or public highway, or in any field, lot, wood or enclosure, may be pursued and arrested. . . .

–7–

438

1845 N.Y. Laws, ch. 3 § 1.

In 1881, this provision was codified in the former Code of Criminal Procedure, which defined a vagrant as ''[a] person who, having his face painted, discolored, covered or concealed, or being otherwise disguised, in a manner calculated to prevent his being identified, appears in a road or public highway, or in a field, lot, wood, or enclosure.'' N.Y. Code Crim. Proc. § 887(7) (McKinney 1958). A parallel provision, more closely resembling the section at issue in this appeal, appeared later in the former Penal Law. See N.Y. Penal Law §§ 710, 711 (McKinney 1944). Section 240.35(4) appeared in its present form when the current Penal Law was enacted. 1965 N.Y. Laws, ch. 1030. Section 887(7) of the prior Code of Criminal Procedure was deleted shortly thereafter. 1967 N.Y. Laws, ch. 681.

No reported opinion interprets section 240.35(4), and only three reported cases interpret any of the predecessor statutes. In the earliest, a trial court concluded that section 887(7) of the former Code of Criminal Procedure was not violated by a man who stood in front of a theater, advertising the entertainment within while wearing a dress, wig, slippers, and makeup. People v. Luechini, 75 Misc. 614, 136 N.Y.S. 319 (Erie County Ct. 1912). The court noted that, if this behavior were considered criminal,

> there is no reason why the disguised circus ''barker,'' the midway ''ballyhoo,'' or even the masquerader at the ball could not be convicted of vagrancy under this statute, . . . and such a conviction, although perhaps it might be deemed righteous by many, would be going far beyond anything conceived by the legislature.

Id. at 616, 136 N.Y.S. at 320–21.

Both of the other two cases are distinguishable from this appeal. In People v. Gillespi, 15 N.Y.2d 529, 202 N.E.2d 565, 254 N.Y.S.2d 121, amended, 15 N.Y.2d 675, 204 N.E.2d 211, 255 N.Y.S.2d 884 (1964), and People v. Archibald, 27 N.Y.2d 504, 260 N.E.2d 871, 312 N.Y.S.2d 678 (1970), this Court, without opinion, affirmed convictions, under section 887(7) of the former Code of Criminal Procedure, of defendants who appeared in public in female clothing where there was no evidence that they were anything other than unequivocally male. There was certainly no evidence in either case that the defendant was, at the time of the offense, wearing clothing considered by the weight of scientific opinion to be appropriate to that defendant's gender. Instead, the evidence in both cases established that the defendants had concealed their true identities by disguising their

The history of the statute is one of the tools for determining the intent of the legislature (§12.1).

Defining a gap in local law that will be filled through a comparison with parallel statutes in other jurisdictions (§12.1). On the process of gap-filling, see §10.5.

Distinguishing adverse authority (§19.4). If this writer had said nothing about Gillespi and Archibald, the court could have decided that it was bound by these two cases. (Compare the way the prosecution argues them in App. F. See pp. 464–65, 472.)

–8–

By this point, the reader should be satisfied that there is a gap in local law. The foundation is now complete (§10.5.1), and the writer can begin to compare section 240.35(4) with parallel statutes elsewhere (§10.5.2).

true genders. In contrast, Ms. Bresnahan provided the trial court with abundant and uncontroverted evidence that she has for some years worn female clothing at all times, that the weight of scientific opinion considers female clothing to be appropriate to the medically determined state of her gender at the time of her arrest, that she had been informed of that fact by both a physician and a psychotherapist, and that both doctors had prescribed the wearing of female clothing at all times as part of a pre-operative treatment plan (R. at 318–52, 395–406, 418–44).

A few other states have at times maintained statutes similar to section 240.35(4). Although no reported decision determines whether any of these statutes can be violated by a transsexual's wearing of medically prescribed clothing, the context in which all of them were enacted plainly shows that they were meant to punish people who used disguises to facilitate political violence. In that way, they are remarkably similar to the antecedents of Penal Law § 240.35(4).

For example, the former Texas Penal Code provided that ''[i]f any person shall go into or near any public place masked or disguised in such manner as to hide his identity or render same difficult to determine, he or she shall be guilty of a misdemeanor, . . . provided this article shall not apply to private or public functions, festivals or events not fostered or presented by any secret society or organization.'' Tex. Penal Code § 454a, repealed by 1973 Tex. Gen. Laws, ch. 399 (emphasis added). This section was enacted in 1925, at a peak of Ku Klux Klan violence, together with other sections entitled ''Masked individuals parading on public highway'' (section 454f), ''Masked person entering church'' (section 454d), ''Masked person entering house'' (section 454c), and ''Masked persons assaulting . . .'' (section 454e). 1925 Tex. Gen. Laws, ch. 63.

The Georgia Anti-Mask Act provides that ''[a] person is guilty of a misdemeanor when he wears a mask, hood, or device under which a portion of the face is so hidden, concealed, or covered as to conceal the identity of the wearer'' when that person is in a public place or on another's property without written permission. Ga. Code Ann. § 16–11–38(a) (1992). The statute provides exemptions for circumstances like Halloween, theater performances, and Mardi Gras. Id. § 16–11–38(b). Noting that the statute was aimed at ''mask-wearing Klansmen and other 'hate' organizations,'' the Georgia courts have held that the statute is violated only where the mask-wearer intends to conceal his or her identity and ''knows or reasonably should know that the conduct provokes a reasonable apprehension of intimidation, threats or violence.'' State v. Miller, 398 S.E.2d 547, 550, 552 (Ga. 1990).

These statutory comparisons strongly suggest

–9–

A similar statute in Oklahoma criminalizes the act of wearing ''a mask, hood or covering, which conceals the identity of the wearer.'' Okla. Stat. Ann. tit. 21, § 1301 (1983). This section was enacted just before — and apparently for the same reason as — former section 454a of the Texas Penal Code. 1923–24 Okla. Sess. Laws, ch. 2. When enacting section 1301, the Oklahoma legislature also made it criminal for a masked or disguised person to demand entry to a house, Okla. Stat. Ann. tit. 21, § 1302 (1983), and made it an aggravated offense to commit assault while masked or disguised, § 1303.

A California statute punishes persons who ''wear any mask, false whiskers, or any personal disguise (whether complete or partial) for the purpose of . . . [e]vading or escaping discovery, recognition, or identification in the commission of any public offense [or c]onceal-ment, flight, or escape, when charged with, arrested for, or convicted of, any public offense. . . .'' Cal. Penal Code § 185 (West 1988). This statute was enacted during another period of widespread Ku Klux Klan violence. 1873–74 Cal. Stat., ch. 614.

A few municipalities have enacted ordinances prohibiting persons from appearing in public in clothing customarily worn by the other gender. Only four reported cases have construed ordinances of this type on facts comparable to this appeal. In one of them, the Illinois Supreme Court ruled — for reasons set out in Point II of this brief — that an ordinance penalizing ''[a]ny person who shall appear in a public place . . . in a dress not belonging to his or her sex, with intent to conceal his or her sex'' could not constitutionally be enforced against transsexuals. City of Chicago v. Wilson, 389 N.E.2d 522, 523 (Ill. 1978) (quoting Chi. Mun. Code § 192–8). Enforcement of a similar Houston ordinance was enjoined on the same grounds. Doe v. McConn, 489 F. Supp. 76 (S.D. Tex. 1980). A comparable Cincinnati ordinance was declared unconstitutional for violating First Amendment rights. City of Cincinnati v. Adams, 330 N.E.2d 463 (Ohio Mun. Ct. 1974). In the remaining decision, the trial court declined to hold the ordinance unconstitutional but instead decided that a transsexual lacks the capacity to develop the mens rea required for a violation. City of Columbus v. Zanders, 266 N.E.2d 602 (Ohio Mun. Ct. 1970).

> B. A necessary and lawful medical treatment would become impossible in this State if a transsexual, dressing as medically prescribed, can be held to have violated section 240.35(4).

In this state and in others the law has recognized and endorsed sex reassignment surgery. A health insurer in

–10–

that the policy behind section 240.35(4) would not be furthered by convicting Bresnahan.

The material under sub-heading B continues rule proof through even more explicit policy arguments. Much of the policy relates to Bresnahan's own medical condition. The reader is thus sensitized to the rule application that begins under sub-heading C (which is one of the reasons why this material was organized in this way).

In a jurisdiction's highest court, motivating arguments and policy arguments often coincide because that kind of court's main business is the making and refining of law (in which policy is perhaps the strongest motivating factor). See pp. 256-57 and 328.

this state cannot escape liability for the costs of sex reassignment surgery on the ground that it is merely ''cosmetic'' and not a needed medical procedure. Davidson v. Aetna Life & Casualty Ins. Co., 101 Misc. 2d 1, 420 N.Y.S.2d 450 (Sup. Ct., N.Y. County 1979). A professional sports organization that discriminates against a transsexual athlete can be held liable under the New York Human Rights Law, N.Y. Exec. Law §§ 290–301 (McKinney 1993). Richards v. United States Tennis Ass'n, 93 Misc. 2d 713, 400 N.Y.S.2d 267 (Sup. Ct., N.Y. County 1977). Under section 207 of the New York City Health Code, a birth certificate can be amended reflecting a court-ordered change of name following ''convertive surgery.'' See Anonymous v. Mellon, 91 Misc. 2d 375, 398 N.Y.S.2d 99 (Sup. Ct., N.Y. County 1977). A number of other states have similarly provided for the amendment of a birth certificate after sex reassignment surgery. See, for example, Ariz. Rev. Stat. Ann. § 36–326(A)(4) (1986); Cal. Health & Safety Code §§ 10475–79 (West 1991); Haw. Rev. Stat. § 338–17.7(a)(4)(B) (1985); Ill. Comp. Stat. Ann. ch. 410, § 535/17(1)(d) (West 1993); La. Rev. Stat. Ann. § 40.62 (West 1992); Mass. Gen. Laws Ann. ch. 46, § 13 (West Supp. 1993); N.J. Rev. Stat. § 26:8–40.12 (West 1987); N.M. Stat. Ann. § 24–14–25(D) (Michie 1978).

The Criminal Court heard extensive and uncontradicted expert testimony to the effect that sex reassignment surgery is the only successful treatment for gender dysphoria syndrome, but that such surgery must be preceded by an extended period in which the patient dresses according to her psychological sex (R. at 318–52, 395–406, 418–44). The same view is also reflected in the case law and in the medical literature. See, for example, Doe v. McConn, 489 F. Supp. 76, 77–80 (S.D. Tex. 1980); City of Chicago v. Wilson, 389 N.E.2d 522, 524–25 (Ill. 1978); City of Columbus v. Zanders, 266 N.E.2d 602, 604–06 (Ohio Mun. Ct. 1970); Sharon B. Satterfield, Transsexualism, 7 J. Soc. Work & Hum. Sexuality 77, 80–86 (1988); Jerold Taitz, Judicial Determination of the Sexual Identity of Post–Operative Transsexuals: A New Form of Sex Discrimination, 13 Am. J.L. & Med. 53, 55–56 (1987). In Davidson v. Aetna Life & Casualty, the court noted that

> The overall process of sex–reassignment surgery is both long and arduous. . . . Among the requirements [for treatment at the Johns Hopkins Hospital Gender Identity] Clinic is that the patient has lived in the female role for a minimum of one year, proving to her own satisfaction and to others her ability to be rehabilitated gainfully in society as a female and to function satisfactorily emotionally, vocationally and socially as a female without a vagina although possibly hormonally estrogenized. . . . The

-11-

Clinic further states that the operation cannot be
looked upon as a sex change operation; rather it is
simply the final anatomical step in a gender role
assimilation of which the psychological and social
steps have already been carried out.

101 Misc. 2d at 4, 420 N.Y.S.2d at 452. As the Criminal
Court was informed through expert medical testimony,
the practice of pre-operative ''cross-dressing'' is
necessary for three reasons. The first is to test the patient's determination and ability to live fully as her
psychological gender before surgery irreversibly commits her to it (R. at 326, 399). The second is to prepare
her for the drastic and final step of surgery (R. at 341-
43, 423-26). And the third is simply to relieve some of
the patient's suffering until hormone therapy has made
surgery possible (R. at 347-49, 401-04).

Where a statute's meaning is in doubt ''and a choice
between two constructions is afforded, the consequences
that may result from the different interpretations
should be considered,'' Braschi v. Stahl Assocs. Co., 74   Some canons of
N.Y.2d 201, 208, 543 N.E.2d 49, 52, 544 N.Y.S.2d 784, 787   construction
(1989). ''It is the duty of the courts to construe stat-   (§12.1).
utes reasonably and so as not to deprive citizens of important rights,'' Pansa v. Damiano, 14 N.Y.2d 356, 360,
200 N.E.2d 563, 565, 251 N.Y.S.2d 665, 668 (1964). The
interpretation of section 240.35(4) urged by the People
is unreasonable because it would deprive citizens of a
right to needed medical treatment.

  C. Because Ms. Bresnahan wore clothing that   Rule application
      was medically appropriate for her and did   begins.
      so under medical advice, she was not
      ''masked or . . . disguised.''

A cross-dressing transsexual is not disguised. This
is not a defendant who lives daily life as a man but had at
the time of arrest concealed his identity by dressing as
a woman. Ms. Bresnahan's identity is that of a woman. Her
friends, neighbors, and colleagues know her as a woman.
Medicine considers her primarily to be a woman. And at
the time of arrest she was dressed as a woman.

As explained above, the weight of scientific opinion
is that cross-dressing accurately informs the bystander
of a transsexual's gender. That is recognized in the case
law, and there was abundant evidence of it at trial. The
People introduced no expert evidence to the contrary.
Thus, the trier of fact in the trial court was not permitted to draw a factual inference that Ms. Bresnahan was or
is male. And without such an inference the evidence was   The writer argues
legally insufficient to support the verdict, even under   that the prosecu-
the deferential standard of review used on appeal.   tion's case flunks

-12-

the standard of re-
view. Rule applica-
tion is the place to
do this.

No reported decision anywhere in the United States has
held that a statute like section 240.35(4) can be enforced against a cross-dressing transsexual. And the
law has established a policy — through the amendment of
birth certificates and through interpretation of health
insurance contracts — of assisting persons afflicted
with gender dysphoria syndrome to obtain treatment
through sex reassignment surgery. That policy would be
subverted if section 240.35(4) were interpreted to prohibit the necessary and inoffensive pre-operative procedure of cross-dressing.

More canons of
construction.

This Court has more than once noted that it ''will not
blindly apply the words of a statute to arrive at an unreasonable or absurd result. If the statute is so broadly
drawn as to include the case before the court, yet reason
and statutory purpose show it was obviously not intended
to include that case, the court is justified in making an
exception through implication.'' Williams v. Williams,
23 N.Y.2d 592, 599, 246 N.E.2d 333, 337, 298 N.Y.S.2d
473, 479 (1969) (citations omitted). ''It is, moreover,
always presumed that no unjust or unreasonable result
was intended and the statute must be construed consonant
with that presumption.'' Zappone v. Home Ins. Co., 55
N.Y.2d 131, 137, 432 N.E.2d 783, 786, 447 N.Y.S.2d 911,
914 (1982).

Summing up to
complete Point I.

Thus, even viewing the evidence in the light most favorable to the prosecution, the People failed to make out
a prima facie case that Ms. Bresnahan was ''masked or in
any manner disguised,'' and the Criminal Court therefore committed reversible error in denying her motion
for a trial order of dismissal.

The conclusion for
Point II.

II.   THE CRIMINAL COURT SHOULD HAVE GRANTED MS.
      BRESNAHAN'S MOTION TO DISMISS THE
      INFORMATION BECAUSE PENAL LAW § 240.35(4)
      VIOLATES HER RIGHT TO PRIVACY UNDER THE
      UNITED STATES CONSTITUTION.

The standard of
review (§27.3).

This court reviews determinations on the constitutionality of statutes de novo, with no deference to the
decisions appealed from. See People v. Uplinger, 58
N.Y.2d 936, 447 N.E.2d 62, 460 N.Y.S.2d 514 (1983), cert.
dismissed, 467 U.S. 246 (1984); People v. Onofre, 51
N.Y.2d 476, 485–86, 415 N.E.2d 936, 939, 434 N.Y.S.2d
947, 949–50 (1980), cert. denied, 451 U.S. 987 (1981).

The organization
of this point is
more complicated
than that of Point I
because the law
involved is more
complex. The writ-
er must prove two
different rules. The

-13-

A. The constitutional right to privacy includes the right to choose one's own clothing.

This Court has observed that the right to privacy

> is not, as a literal reading of the phrase might suggest, the right to maintain secrecy with respect to one's affairs or personal behavior; rather, it is a right of independence in making certain kinds of important decisions . . . undeterred by governmental restraint — what we referred to in People v. Rice (41 N.Y.2d 1018, 1019) as ''freedom of conduct.'' . . . [T]he Supreme Court took pains in Carey v. Population Services Int'l (431 U.S. 678, 684–85) to observe that ''the outer limits'' of the decision-making aspect of the right to privacy ''have not been marked by the Court.'' . . .

Onofre, 51 N.Y.2d at 485–86, 415 N.E.2d at 939, 434 N.Y.S.2d at 949–50. The right to privacy grows out of the First Amendment guarantees of freedom of speech and association, the Fourth Amendment right to freedom from unreasonable governmental searches and seizures, the Ninth Amendment's reservation to the people of powers not expressly granted to government, the Fourteenth Amendment's equal protection clause, the concept of liberty inherent in the Fourteenth Amendment due process clause, and the penumbras of history and logic surrounding the Bill of Rights as a whole. Onofre, 51 N.Y.2d at 485–86, 415 N.E.2d at 939, 434 N.Y.S.2d at 949.

Pointing to Stanley v. Georgia, 394 U.S. 557 (1969), and Eisenstadt v. Baird, 405 U.S. 438 (1972), this Court has further concluded that the United States Supreme Court has not limited the right to privacy to situations of ''marital intimacy'' or ''procreative choice.'' Onofre, 51 N.Y.2d at 487, 415 N.E.2d at 939–40, 434 N.Y.S.2d at 950. In Stanley, the Supreme Court held that the right to privacy is violated by a statute that criminalizes the possession of obscene materials in one's own home. In both Stanley, 394 U.S. at 564, and Eisenstadt, 405 U.S. at 453–54 n.10, the Court quoted with approval Justice Brandeis's dissent in Olmstead v. United States, 277 U.S. 438 (1928), where he noted that ''[t]he makers of our Constitution . . . conferred, as against the Government, the right to be let alone — the most comprehensive of rights and the right most valued by civilized man'' (emphasis added).

This Court held in Uplinger that the right to privacy was violated by section 240.35(3) of the Penal Law, another subdivision of the same loitering statute at issue in the present appeal. Section 240.35(3) had penalized

-14-

first is stated in sub-heading A and proved through the material under that sub-heading. The other is stated in sub-heading B and proved there. The sub-heading A rule allows Bresnahan to invoke the sub-heading B rule. The paragraph between the Point II heading and sub-heading A sets out.

The sub-heading A rule is proved through a synthesis of *Onofre, Stanley, Eisenstadt, Uplinger,* and other cases (§ 11.5).

loitering ''in a public place for the purpose of engaging, or soliciting another person to engage, in deviate
sexual intercourse or other sexual behavior of a deviate
nature,'' and this Court ruled that the state cannot
constitutionally punish loitering which neither is done
for a criminal purpose nor is ''offensive or annoying to
others.'' Id., 58 N.Y.2d at 938, 447 N.E.2d at 63, 460
N.Y.S.2d at 515.

The United States Supreme Court has assumed that the
constitutional right to privacy includes ''matters of
personal appearance.'' Kelley v. Johnson, 425 U.S. 238,
244 (1976). The issue in Kelley was whether a police department could establish hair-grooming regulations for
its officers. In holding that the department had demonstrated a sufficiently strong governmental interest to
overcome the officers' assumed privacy rights, the
Court noted that it perceived a ''highly significant''
distinction between the privacy rights of police officers to an appearance of their own choosing, on one hand,
and, on the other, privacy rights of persons not employed
by a uniformed police department. Id. at 245. Relying on
Kelley, the Illinois Supreme Court has ruled that an ordinance punishing any person appearing in public ''in a
dress not belonging to his or her sex, with intent to conceal his or her sex'' cannot constitutionally be enforced against transsexuals. City of Chicago v. Wilson,
389 N.E.2d 522, 523 (Ill. 1978) (quoting Chi. Mun. Code
§ 192-8). The defendants in Wilson were -- like Ms. Bresnahan -- transsexuals, and (as explained more fully below) the issues presented to the Illinois Supreme Court
were the same right-to-privacy issues raised in this
appeal.

As long ago as 1958, the United States Supreme Court
noted in passing the existence of a constitutional right
to wear clothing of one's own, rather than of the government's, selection. In Kent v. Dulles, 357 U.S. 116, the
court concluded that a citizen cannot constitutionally
be deprived of the right to travel abroad on the ground
that the choice of where to journey ''may be as close to
the heart of the individual as the choice of what he eats,
or wears, or reads.'' Id. at 126 (emphasis added). The
right to autonomy in one's personal appearance is connected to what the Supreme Court has called the histori-
cally recognized right of ''every individual to the
possession and control of his own person,'' Union
Pacific Ry. Co. v. Botsford, 141 U.S. 250, 251 (1891).
Through the Fourteenth Amendment, the right to privacy
is protected from state, as well as federal, interference. Roe v. Wade, 410 U.S. 113 (1973).

A counter-argu-
ment (§19.4).

None of this is altered by the Supreme Court's decision in Bowers v. Hardwick, 478 U.S. 186 (1986). There,
the Court decided that the Constitution has not granted a
fundamental right to engage in sex with a person of one's

own gender. The Court held that an activity that has been criminalized in most states throughout the nation's history cannot be considered to be ''implicit in the concept of ordered liberty.'' <u>Id.</u> at 191–94 (quoting <u>Palko v. Connecticut</u>, 302 U.S. 319, 325 (1937)). In contrast, as explained throughout this brief, the law in many states has for several years taken steps to protect the medical treatment of transsexuals; no reported decision anywhere in the United States has ever held that a statute like section 240.35(4) can be enforced against transsexuals; and the Supreme Court itself observed in <u>Kent</u> that the liberty to wear what one pleases is one of those liberties natural to a free society.

    B.   <u>The right to privacy is a fundamental right and can be invaded only where the People can demonstrate a compelling state interest and only where the invasion is no larger than necessary to accomplish that interest.</u>

See note in the margin on pp. 444-45.

    It is settled law that the right to privacy is a fundamental right. <u>Carey v. Population Services Int'l</u>, 431 U.S. 678, 684–86 (1977); <u>Roe</u>, 410 U.S. at 147–64; <u>Griswold v. Connecticut</u>, 381 U.S. 479, 485 (1965). The Supreme Court has repeatedly held that a state can invade the right to privacy, or any other fundamental right, only where it can demonstrate a compelling state interest requiring such an invasion. <u>Carey</u>, 431 U.S. at 685–86; <u>Roe</u>, 410 U.S. at 147–65; <u>Griswold</u>, 381 U.S. at 485. Even where a state can show a compelling interest that could justify some limitation on the right to privacy or another fundamental right, any such limitation must ''be narrowly drawn to express only those interests.'' <u>Carey</u>, 431 U.S. at 686.

Another proof through a synthesis — this time of *Carey, Roe,* and *Griswold.*

    In <u>Carey</u>, for example, the Supreme Court struck down section 6811(8) of the New York Education Law, which made it criminal, among other things, to advertise the sale of contraceptives and to distribute even nonprescription contraceptives without first obtaining a pharmacist's license. The state argued that the prohibition on advertising was justified because contraceptive advertisements would offend and embarrass large portions of the public and would encourage sexual activity among young people, but the Court held instead that neither of these considerations could be considered compelling in the face of First Amendment rights and the right to privacy. <u>Id.</u> at 700–02. The state argued further that the prohibition on distribution of contraceptives by non-pharmacists was justified by the state's interests in promoting quality control, protecting the health of the user, and preventing minors from selling contraceptives, but the Court held these concerns were neither compelling nor (excepting the last) even likely to be achieved by the state's invasion of contraceptive users' right to privacy. Id. at 686–91.

A counter-argument (§19.4).

All of this has been left in place by Planned Parenthood v. Casey, 112 S. Ct. 2791 (1992). That decision ''reaffirm[ed]'' Roe. Planned Parenthood at 2804, 2812–16. And it cited with approval Carey, Eisenstadt, and Griswold. Planned Parenthood at 2805–11. Although the Planned Parenthood court adopted an undue burden test, rather than the compelling state interest test, in abandoning the trimester framework set out in Roe, it did so only in an attempt to balance what Roe itself called ''the State's 'important and legitimate interest in protecting the potentiality of human life.''' Planned Parenthood at 2817 (quoting Roe). There is no equivalent competing interest in a case, like the present one, where a person is prosecuted merely for wearing clothing prescribed by doctors. The Planned Parenthood opinion spoke at length of the Court's awareness that its own ''legitimacy'' could be damaged if ''frequent overruling'' were to ''overtax the country's belief in the Court's good faith.'' Id. at 2814–15. For those reasons, the compelling state interest test still governs privacy law outside the context of abortion, and it is likely to continue doing so.

    C.   Section 240.35(4) is not supported by a compelling state interest.

Rule application begins here and continues under sub-heading D. (Remember that the rules in Point II measure whether a statute is constitutional. They are applied to the statute as though the statute were a fact.)

Here, the only compelling interests claimed by the People are, first, a desire to prevent the use of gender and other disguises in crimes committed by groups of people and, second, an interest in preventing groups of disguised males from gaining access to women's washrooms and other areas where women may be vulnerable. There is no evidence anywhere in the record to suggest that at any time in this century police anywhere in New York State have encountered difficulties apprehending groups of criminals who have disguised themselves in clothing of the opposite gender. Nor is there any evidence in the record of even a single crime in this state committed by a group of men who got into a women's washroom or the like disguised as women.

Again, motivating arguments and policy arguments are often merged when a court is asked to make law.

These same interests were cited by the city of Chicago in an unsuccessful attempt to justify an ordinance similar to section 240.35(4), but the Illinois Supreme Court held them to be so insubstantial that they could not even meet the lesser standard of providing a rational basis for the city's invasion of constitutional privacy rights. City of Chicago v. Wilson, 389 N.E.2d at 523–25. In Wilson, transsexuals had been arrested, even though their pre-operative treatment called for them to cross-dress. The court found the record there as barren as the record here of evidence that could substantiate even a rational basis, much less a compelling state interest, and —— in the only reported decision on the privacy issue posed by the present appeal —— the Illinois Supreme Court held that, ''as applied to the defendants here,'' the Chicago ordinance created an ''unconstitutional infringement of their liberty interest,'' id. at 525.

> D. Even if one of the interests advanced by the People were deemed compelling, section 240.35(4) nevertheless invades privacy rights more than would be necessary to satisfy such an interest.

Even if a government's interest is compelling, it must choose the least restrictive means to accomplish it. In deciding right-to-privacy cases, the courts have often looked for guidance to decisions applying First Amendment and other fundamental rights. For instance, in Griswold, 381 U.S. at 485, where it determined that Connecticut's complete prohibition on the use of contraceptives violated the right to privacy because it could not be supported by a compelling state interest, the Supreme Court quoted with approval NAACP v. Alabama, 377 U.S. 288, 307 (1964), a First Amendment freedom of association case, for the principle that a ''governmental purpose to control or prevent activities constitutionally subject to state regulation may not be achieved by means which sweep unnecessarily broadly and thereby invade the area of protected freedoms.'' In United Mine Workers v. Illinois State Bar Ass'n, 389 U.S. 217, 222 (1967), another freedom of association case, the Court noted that it has ''repeatedly held that laws which actually affect the exercise of these vital rights cannot be sustained merely because they were enacted for the purpose of dealing with some evil within the State's legislative competence, or even because the laws do in fact provide a helpful means of dealing with such an evil'' (emphasis added).

Section 240.35(4) is not the least restrictive alternative to achieve either of the purposes advanced by the People, and the statute is therefore defectively overbroad. Even if this Court were to conclude that the state has a compelling interest in preventing the use of gender disguises in crimes committed by groups of people, that conclusion could sustain only a statute that limits its punishment to persons who appear together in public disguised for a criminal purpose, and section 240.35(4) is not so limited. Instead, it punishes all persons who appear in public with their identities obscured, no matter how innocent the purpose. Here, there was ample and un-

An argument in the alternative: just in case the court disagrees with sub-heading C, the writer argues that Bresnahan should win anyway on another ground (§19.4).

-18-

contradicted evidence that Ms. Bresnahan dressed as she
did as a result of the requirements of a widely recognized medical treatment program. As set out more fully in
Point I of this brief, the law in New York and elsewhere
has made adjustments to further the objectives of this
kind of treatment by amending birth certificates and requiring reimbursement under properly drawn health insurance contracts where persons suffering from gender
dysphoria syndrome are forced to go through the same type
of medical treatment that led to Ms. Bresnahan's arrest.
No valid governmental purpose is advanced by restrict-
ing a transsexual's choice of attire, and the statute
could have been drafted to avoid such an imposition on
her liberty.

> E.   Even if a compelling state interest were
>   not required, section 240.35(4) cannot
>   survive scrutiny under the lesser
>   ''rational basis'' test.

As explained more fully above, the Illinois Supreme
Court has ruled that an ordinance similar to the statute
here at issue cannot constitutionally be enforced
against transsexuals. In City of Chicago v. Wilson, 389
N.E.2d 522 (Ill. 1978), the city claimed both of the purposes asserted by the People in the present appeal, together with two others: ''to protect citizens from being
misled or defrauded'' and ''to prevent inherently antisocial conduct which is contrary to the accepted
norms.'' Id. at 524. The Illinois court determined that
none of these rationales could meet even the lesser rational basis test applicable where a constitutionally
protected right is not deemed fundamental or, in equal
protection cases, where discrimination is not based on a
suspect classification.

A governmental purpose satisfies the rational basis
or rational connection test where ''there is an evil at
hand for correction, and . . . it might be thought that
the particular legislative measure was a rational way to
correct it.'' Williamson v. Lee Optical Co., 348 U.S.
483, 488 (1955). But here the People have not introduced
any evidence that section 240.35(4) is connected to any
verifiable danger to the public. Although section
240.35(4) is claimed to be justifiable as a crime control
measure, the Illinois Supreme Court concluded that even
under the rational basis standard ''we cannot assume
that individuals who cross-dress for purposes of therapy are prone to commit crimes.'' City of Chicago v.
Wilson, 389 N.E.2d at 525.

Nor can section 240.35(4) be justified by a desire to
promote a particular standard of sexual morality. Not
only was such a purpose unpersuasive in City of Chicago

Margin notes:

Another argument on the alternative: just in case the court rejects the rule in sub-heading B, the writer argues that Bresnahan should win under the alternative and less favorable test.

A counterargument.

Another counterargument.

–19–

450

v. Wilson, but it would be inconsistent with the law's policy, described in Point I of this brief, of encouraging treatment of gender dysphoria syndrome through sex reassignment therapy. And this Court expressly rejected just such a purpose in People v. Onofre, 51 N.Y.2d at 489, 415 N.E.2d at 942, 434 N.Y.S.2d at 952.

Finally, in Kelley v. Johnson, 425 U.S. 238, 245 (1976), the Supreme Court permitted a police department to regulate the appearance of its officers but noted that there is a ''highly significant'' difference between the broad rights of ''the citizenry in general'' and the narrower rights of public employees. Since Kelley, the only cases that have permitted governmental regulation of an adult's appearance have involved prison inmates, e.g., Hill v. Estelle, 537 F.2d 214 (5th Cir. 1976); nude bathing, e.g., Williams v. Kleppe, 539 F.2d 803 (1st Cir. 1976); massage parlor employees, e.g., Harper v. Lindsay, 616 F.2d 849 (5th Cir. 1980); public employees, e.g., Ball v. Board of Trustees of the Kerrville, Ind., School Dist., 584 F.2d 684 (5th Cir. 1978), cert. denied, 440 U.S. 972 (1979); and prohibitions on nudity and semi-nudity, e.g., South Florida Free Beaches, Inc. v. City of Miami, 734 F.2d 608 (11th Cir. 1984). (Goldman v. Weinberger, 475 U.S. 503 (1986), was not a right–to–privacy case; it held instead that armed services personnel do not have a free–exercise–of–religion right under the First Amendment to wear yarmulkes indoors while on duty.)

F.   Section 240.35(4) violates Ms. Bresnahan's constitutional right to privacy.

For the reasons set out above, the purposes advanced by the People do not arise to a compelling state interest. Even if they did, under the cases described above, section 240.35(4) nevertheless cannot be enforced against transsexuals because it does not accomplish those purposes in the least restrictive manner. The required ''[p]recision of regulation,'' NAACP v. Button, 371 U.S. 415, 438 (1963), could be achieved only by a statute that would punish appearing in public in prohibited attire for a criminal purpose. Moreover, enforcement of section 240.35(4) against transsexuals cannot survive scrutiny even under the lesser rational basis test.

For three reasons, the right–to–privacy question in this appeal is not governed by this Court's decisions in People v. Gillespi, 15 N.Y.2d 529, 202 N.E.2d 565, 254 N.Y.S.2d 121, amended, 15 N.Y.2d 675, 204 N.E.2d 211, 255 N.Y.S.2d 884 (1964), and People v. Archibald, 27 N.Y.2d 504, 260 N.E.2d 871, 312 N.Y.S.2d 678 (1970), where constitutional challenges to a predecessor statute of sec-

-20-

Because Point II is complex, this summing up is complicated enough to deserve its own sub-heading.

A counter-argument. These cases were discussed in Point I to show that they do not preclude an interpretation of the statute that favors

451

Bresnahan. Here, they are discussed again to show that they do not preclude a favorable constitutional ruling. That happens here because it would appear defensive to do it earlier in Point II. Notice how *Archibald* and *Gillespi* are distinguished.

tion 240.35(4) were turned aside. First, in neither case did a defendant challenge the statute for violating the constitutional right to privacy. In <u>Gillespi</u>, this court was asked to decide only whether the statute was unconstitutionally vague and an unreasonable and arbitrary exercise of police power. In <u>Archibald</u>, the appeal was based only on due process and First Amendment grounds. Second, even if those defendants had raised some type of privacy issue, they could not have raised the question presently before the court. In neither case was there any evidence that a defendant suffered from gender dysphoria syndrome or any other medical condition that would have required attire that might be deemed to violate the statute. Third, even if <u>Archibald</u> and <u>Gillespi</u> had determined precisely the privacy issues presently before the court, those cases would have been impliedly overruled by this Court's later decisions in <u>People v. Onofre</u>, setting out this Court's perception of the right to privacy, and <u>People v. Uplinger</u>, striking down, on the basis of that perception, another subdivision of the same loitering statute at issue in this appeal.

Thus, the Criminal Court should have granted Ms. Bresnahan's motion to dismiss the information on the ground that section 240.35(4) violates her constitutional right to privacy.

CONCLUSION

For all the foregoing reasons, Ms. Bresnahan's conviction should be reversed, and the information dismissed.

Clyde Farnsworth, Esq.
Attorney for Defendant—Appellant
32 Fontanka Street
Bedford Falls, N.Y. 14218
(914) 555—1111

-21-

452

Appendix F
Sample Appellee's Brief

This brief responds to the appellant's brief that appears in Appendix E. (See the introductory note at the beginning of Appendix E.)

COURT OF APPEALS OF THE STATE OF NEW YORK

THE PEOPLE OF THE STATE OF NEW YORK,

Appellee

–against–

MERRITT BRESNAHAN,

Defendant–Appellant

No. 94–341

BRIEF FOR APPELLEE

Hon. Martha Bosley
District Attorney
New York County
BY: Allan Kuusinen, Esq.
Asst. District Attorney
1 Hogan Place
New York, N.Y. 10013
(212) 555–1111

TABLE OF CONTENTS

TABLE OF AUTHORITIES

CASES

*Authorities chiefly relied on are marked with an
asterisk.

-iii-

---

*Authorities chiefly relied on are marked with an
asterisk.

STATUTE INVOLVED

Section 240.35(4) of the New York Penal Law provides as follows:

A person is guilty of loitering when he . . .
    4. Being masked or in any manner disguised by un-
usual or unnatural attire or facial alteration,
loiters, remains or congregates in a public place
with other persons so masked or disguised, or knowingly permits or aids persons so masked or disguised
to congregate in a public place; except that such
conduct is not unlawful when it occurs in connection
with a masquerade party or like entertainment if,
when such entertainment is held in a city which has
promulgated regulations in connection with such affairs, permission is first obtained from the police
or other appropriate authorities. . . .
    Loitering is a violation.

PRELIMINARY STATEMENT

The defendant was convicted in New York City Criminal
Court, New York County, Judge Celeste Remay, of loitering in violation of Penal Law § 240.35(4). Before trial,
the defendant moved, pursuant to Criminal Procedure Law
§§ 170.30(1)(a) and 170.35(1)(c), for an order dismissing the information on the ground that Penal Law
§ 240.35(4) violates his right to privacy under the
United States Constitution, and the Criminal Court reserved decision on this motion until the end of trial.
After the close of evidence at trial, the defendant moved
for a trial order of dismissal, pursuant to Criminal
Procedure Law §§ 290.10 and 320.20, alleging an absence
of legally sufficient evidence that he had been ''masked
or in any manner disguised by unusual or unnatural attire'' in the sense prohibited by section 240.35(4).
Ruling from the bench, the Criminal Court denied both
motions, convicted the defendant, and sentenced him to a
fine of two hundred dollars. The Appellate Term affirmed
without opinion, and this appeal followed.

QUESTIONS PRESENTED

Is a person ''masked or in any manner disguised by unusual or unnatural attire,'' within the meaning of Penal
Law § 240.35(4), when his sexual organs are all male but
he assumes a female voice and gestures and wears a skirt,
blouse, high-heeled shoes, and stockings -- all for the
admitted purpose of causing others to believe he is a
woman?

-1-

Does the constitutional right to privacy permit a
state to penalize congregating in public by three or more
men dressing as and imitating women where men so disguised could gain entrance to women's washrooms and similar places, and where a victim of a crime committed by
such men could mistakenly identify them to the police as
women?

STATEMENT OF THE CASE

The Defendant's Disguise

When arrested the defendant was wearing a blouse, a
skirt, high-heeled shoes, stockings, and women's undergarments. (R. at 109, 187.) He was standing on a street
corner in the company of two other men similarly dressed
(R. at 108–10, 114, 193–94). When arrested and at trial,
the defendant had a penis, testicles, and a scrotum (R.
at 110, 189, 373, 449). That was also true of his two companions, who pleaded guilty at arraignment and are not
parties to this appeal. (R. at 3–5, 114–15.)

The arresting officer at first believed the defendant
and his companions to be women (R. at 101), and the defendant admitted that his purpose in dressing as he did was
to create exactly this impression (R. at 213). The arresting officer testified that the defendant and his
companions convincingly affected feminine voices, in-
flections, gestures, and walks (R. at 98–101) and
''would have succeeded in fooling me'' if the officer had
not overheard one of them make a remark the substance of
which was not testified to because of a defense objection
(R. at 98, 103). When arrested, the defendant was not
travelling to or from a masquerade party (R. at 209).

The Medical Evidence

The defendant's own witnesses admitted that he had
never had a vagina, uterus, or ovaries (R. at 373, 449).
They also admitted that regardless of any medical treatment that may be performed on him in the future, he would
never have ovaries or a uterus, but that he would have
male sex chromosomes for the rest of his life (R. at 374–
75, 448).

The defendant claimed that he planned to undergo surgery to remove his penis, testicles, and scrotum and replace them with an artificially constructed vagina (R.
at 197), but he and his doctors all admitted that such an
operation had not yet occurred (R. at 189, 197, 373,
449). Although both doctors testified that they had advised the defendant to wear female clothing before surgery (R. at 349, 405–06, 440–42), they and the defendant

–2–

These two para-
graphs summarize
the prosecution's
theory (see p.
307). The record
cites are included
here (despite §23.4
fn. 1 on p. 310) be-
cause the prosecu-
tion states these
facts completely
here and will not
describe them
more fully later in
the Statement of
the Case.

From out of the
mass of medical
details, the prose-
cution pulls facts
that create a differ-
ent picture from
the one painted in
the defendant's
brief.

Notice how this
sentence juxtapos-
es two related facts
to neutralize the

one that would
otherwise harm
the prosecution
(see p. 309).

all admitted that the three of them had known all along
that such conduct could lead to legal difficulties (R.
179-80, 406, 442). The doctors also admitted that their
pre-operative treatment plan would not be ''significantly'' disturbed if a patient like the defendant were
to refrain, before surgery, from appearing in public
with two or more other men in female dress (R. at 408,
449).

The Decisions Below

The Criminal Court found as a fact that the defendant
was ''anatomically a man'' both at the time of arrest and
at the time of trial (R. at 467). The court denied the defendant's motion for a trial order of dismissal, holding
that a defendant is ''masked or in any manner disguised
by unusual or unnatural attire'' within the meaning of
section 240.35(4) when that defendant ''is wearing
clothing of one gender but has the reproductive organs of
the other'' (R. at 470). Discovering no constitutional
infirmity in the statute, the court also denied the defendant's motion to dismiss the information (R. at 468).
The defendant was convicted (R. at 471-72), and the
Appellate Term affirmed (R. at 478).

SUMMARY OF ARGUMENT

The Criminal Court properly denied the defendant's
motion for a trial order of dismissal. The only element
in dispute involved the question of whether the defendant was ''in any manner disguised by unusual or unnatural attire.'' Here, the defendant and his co-defendants
dressed as women, and the arresting officer testified
that he at first believed them to be women. The defendant's own experts testified that his reproductive organs were male. Nothing in the statute requires the
People to prove that a defendant had disguised himself in
order to commit some unlawful or antisocial act. In fact,
this Court has twice held that section 240.35(4)'s predecessor statutes did not require the People to prove a
malicious intent, and that even the most innocent of
reasons will not excuse going out in public disguised in
unnatural attire among a group similarly disguised.
Section 240.35(4) does not interfere with the defendant's medical treatment because it does not prohibit an
individual male from appearing in public dressed in female clothing. The statute instead prohibits three or
more persons from appearing in public disguised and in
concert, and it does so because in a crime-ridden society
groups of disguised people can be dangerous. A disguise
such as the one used by the defendant can be so convincing

-3-

462

that a victim may firmly believe that he or she has been
robbed by women even though the criminals were in fact
men. Not only does the disguise prevent identification
of criminals, but a group disguised in the way these defendants were can gain admission to confined areas, such
as washrooms, where women are particularly vulnerable
to attack.

Section 240.35(4) does not violate the defendant's
constitutional right to privacy, and the Criminal Court
properly denied his motion to dismiss the information.
The United States Supreme Court has held that a state can
regulate attire without offending the constitutional
right to privacy unless the party challenging the regulation can show that there is no rational connection between that regulation and some form of public good. Only
in matters of marriage, procreation, contraception,
abortion, child rearing, education, and family relationships must a state demonstrate a compelling state
interest, and none of those categories include any sort
of right for a group of men to disguise themselves as
women.

The defendant has not shown that section 240.35(4)
lacks a rational relationship to a public need. Under the
rational connection or rational basis test, a statute is
constitutional even if not perfectly consistent with
the Legislature's goals. This Court has affirmed convictions under section 240.35(4)'s predecessor statute, and those convictions were attacked on the same
constitutional grounds asserted by the defendant here.
Even if the men in this appeal were not disguised in order
to commit crimes, the Legislature is entitled under the
Constitution to regulate together both the truly dangerous and the apparently dangerous, particularly where
even the apparently dangerous strikes the public as
immoral.

<u>ARGUMENT</u>

I.   THE CRIMINAL COURT PROPERLY DENIED THE
     DEFENDANT'S MOTION FOR A TRIAL ORDER OF
     DISMISSAL BECAUSE THERE WAS LEGALLY
     SUFFICIENT EVIDENCE SUBSTANTIATING EACH
     ELEMENT OF LOITERING, AS DEFINED BY PENAL
     LAW § 240.35(4).

The defendant's expert medical witnesses conceded
that, both at the time of trial and of the offense, he had
a penis, testicles, and a scrotum and did not have a vagina or ovaries. After denying the defendant's motion
for a trial order of dismissal, the trial judge found as a
fact that the defendant was, at the time of the offense, a
male. When arrested he was wearing a blouse, a skirt,

The conclusion for Point I.

Summing up the theory while em-phasizing motivat-ing arguments (see p. 258).

–4–

463

high-heeled shoes, stockings, and women's undergarments. When a determination that the evidence was legally sufficient is challenged on appeal, the People are entitled to all favorable and permitted factual inferences. People v. Acosta, 80 N.Y. 665, 672, 609 N.E.2d 518, 522, 593 N.Y.S.2d 978, 982 (1993). And it was both permissible and reasonable for the trial judge to infer that the defendant had disguised himself by dressing in female clothing. When the sufficiency of the evidence is challenged, the conviction must be affirmed — as this one should be — if a rational trier of fact could have found all the elements of the offense proved beyond a reasonable doubt. Id.

> *The standard of review (§27.3).*

A. The only element in dispute raised the question of whether the defendant was ''in any manner disguised by unusual or unnatural attire.''

> *The prosecution's theory depends on a narrow definition of the issue.*

Under section 240.35(4), a defendant is guilty of loitering if he (1) is ''in any manner disguised by unusual or unnatural attire,'' (2) ''loiters, remains or congregates in a public place,'' and (3) does so ''with other persons so . . . disguised.'' Nothing in the statute requires the People to prove that a defendant disguised himself for the purpose of committing some unlawful or antisocial act. As explained more fully below, this Court has twice held that under section 240.35(4)'s predecessor statutes the People need not prove a malicious intent. People v. Archibald, 27 N.Y.2d 504, 260 N.E.2d 871, 312 N.Y.S.2d 678 (1970); People v. Gillespi, 15 N.Y.2d 529, 202 N.E.2d 565, 254 N.Y.S.2d 121, amended, 15 N.Y.2d 675, 204 N.E.2d 211, 255 N.Y.S.2d 884 (1964). Section 240.35(4) provides an exception where permission has been obtained from ''the police or other appropriate authorities'' for a ''masquerade party or other like entertainment.''

> *This is the overall rule, but it is not the one at the core of the prosecution's theory in Point I (see the note in the margin on p. 465).*

The defendant concedes every element of the offense but one. He admits that when arrested he was wearing female clothing and was standing on a street corner, and that the two persons with him when he was arrested have the same kinds of sexual organs he does and were wearing clothing similar to his. He does not maintain that he was so dressed in connection with an officially sanctioned masquerade party ''or like entertainment.'' Instead, he claims that he was not ''disguised by unusual or unnatural attire'' because at the time of his arrest he had plans to have a sex change operation and become a woman at some date in the future.

B. Under this Court's precedents, a defendant
is ''disguised by unusual or unnatural
attire'' when wearing clothing that
misleads the public about the defendant's
true gender.

This Court held in Archibald and in Gillespi that even
the most innocent of reasons will not excuse disguising
one's self with attire normally used by the opposite
gender and going about in public with others similarly
clothed. The defendant in Archibald was arrested on a
subway platform while returning home from a masquerade
party and wearing a dress, a wig, high-heeled shoes,
makeup, and women's undergarments. He was convicted under section 887(7) of the prior Code of Criminal Procedure (repealed by 1967 N.Y. Laws, ch. 681), which made no
exception for masquerade parties and which provided
that a person could be sentenced as a vagrant if he appeared in public ''disguised, in a manner calculated to
prevent his being identified,'' N.Y. Code Crim. Proc.
§ 887(7) (McKinney 1958). Relying on the straightforward wording of the statute, the Appellate Term rejected
the defendant's contention that ''the People must prove
a specific intention of employing the disguise to commit
some illegal act.'' People v. Archibald, 58 Misc. 2d 862,
863, 296 N.Y.S. 2d 834, 836 (1968). This Court affirmed
without opinion but citing to Gillespi.
The defendants in Gillespi were also convicted under
former Code of Criminal Procedure § 887(7) for dressing
like the defendant in this case. They argued on appeal
that the statute was unconstitutional, that evidence
that a man wore a woman's clothing is not sufficient
proof that he was ''disguised,'' and that such a conviction could not be sustained without evidence of intent to
mislead for a criminal purpose. This court nevertheless
affirmed.
The only other reported New York case on this question
is a trial court decision from 1912, People v. Luechini,
75 Misc. 614, 136 N.Y.S. 319 (Erie County Ct.), which
held for the defendant but which has been impliedly
overruled in substance by this Court's later decisions
in Archibald and Gillespi. Only one other court in the
United States, a municipal court in Ohio, has issued a
reported decision adopting a position similar to the one
urged by the defendant on this question, and that decision -- City of Columbus v. Zanders, 266 N.E. 2d 602 (Ohio
Mun. Ct. 1970) -- was based on a theory of diminished mental capacity that is not recognized in New York law. See
N.Y. Penal Law §§ 15.00-15.25 (McKinney 1987).
Moreover, the Legislature could have placed words in
section 240.35(4) requiring proof of a criminal purpose
or creating an exception for disguises used by transsexuals, but it did neither of those things. ''[W]here as

This resolves the
only element in
dispute and is
therefore the gov-
erning rule.

Rule proof begins.

-6-

465

A canon of con-
struction (§12.1).

here the statute describes the particular situation in
which it is to apply, 'an irrefutable inference must be
drawn that what is omitted or not included was intended
to be omitted or excluded.''' <u>Patrolmen's Benevolent</u>
<u>Ass'n v. City of New York</u>, 41 N.Y.2d 205, 208–09, 359
N.E.2d 1338, 1341, 391 N.Y.S.2d 544, 546 (1976) (quoting
Consol. Laws of N.Y., Book 1, Statutes, § 240 (McKinney
1971)).

Section 240.35(4) unambiguously penalizes the act of
appearing in public ''disguised by . . . unnatural attire'' with others ''so . . . disguised.'' ''[W]here

Another canon.

the statutory language is clear and unambiguous, the
court should construe it so as to give effect to the plain
meaning of the words used.'' <u>Patrolmen's Benevolent</u>
<u>Ass'n</u>, 41 N.Y.2d at 208, 359 N.E.2d at 1340, 391 N.Y.S.2d
at 546. Although the consequences of a particular interpretation may be important where a statute lends itself
to two different meanings, ''[i]f the construction to be

And another.

accorded a statute is clearly indicated, it is to be
adopted by the courts regardless of consequences.''
<u>Town of Smithtown v. Moore</u>, 11 N.Y.2d 238, 244, 183
N.E.2d 66, 69, 228 N.Y.S.2d 657, 661 (1962). The plain
meaning of section 240.35(4) is ''clearly indicated''
by the words the Legislature did use, and, although no
legislative committee reports or similar documents explain the purpose of section 240.35(4), there are good
reasons for drafting the statute as the Legislature did.

Section 240.35(4) is a necessary and reasonable regulation of public behavior. It does not prohibit an individual male from dressing up in female clothing and then

Policy is now used
to complete proof
of the rule. Be-
cause the court
has been asked to
make law here,
policy arguments
and motivating ar-
guments tend to
merge (see pp.
256-57 and 328).

appearing in public — as shocking as that behavior might
be to a very large proportion of the population. It does
not even forbid several males from doing that at the same
time, as long as the clothing does not create an illusion
so complete as to obscure their true identities. The
statute instead prohibits three or more persons from appearing in public disguised and in concert, and it does
so because of the serious danger such behavior poses for
others.

The difficulties of law enforcement would be magni-
fied if a crime-ridden society were to permit the appearance in public of groups of people who cannot readily
be identified, and for that reason legislatures in other
states have enacted statutes similar to section
240.35(4). <u>See</u>, for example, Cal. Penal Code § 185 (West
1988); Ga. Code Ann. § 16–11–38(a) (1992); Okla. Stat.
Ann. tit. 21, § 1301 (West 1983). In this state and elsewhere, the law of conspiracy is based on the concept that
a greater public danger is created when criminals act
together than where they act individually. The danger is
multiplied where a disguise not only prevents identification of criminals after a robbery or other crime, but
where the illusion created by the disguise is so con-

–7–

vincing that a victim may firmly believe that he or she
has been robbed by women although in fact the criminals
were men. Moreover, where the disguise misleads the observer as to the true gender of a group of males, that
group can gain admission to confined areas, such as
washrooms, where women are particularly vulnerable to
attack. If the defendant's interpretation of section
240.35(4) were to prevail in this Court, any three people
who can demonstrate an interest in a sex change operation
would be licensed to disguise their true identities and
put the public at risk.

   C.   The People presented legally sufficient
        evidence that this defendant was
        ''disguised by unusual or unnatural
        attire.''

     Rule application begins.

   In reviewing trial evidence for legal sufficiency,
the evidence must be viewed in the light most favorable
to the People. People v. Malizia, 62 N.Y.2d 755, 465
N.E.2d 364, 476 N.Y.S.2d 825, cert. denied, 469 U.S. 932
(1984). Here, the defendant was disguised. He and his co-
defendants dressed as women, and the arresting officer
testified that he at first believed them to be women (R.
at 101). The defendant's own experts testified that his
reproductive organs were male (R. at 373, 449). Although
the defendant's doctors testified that medical science
sympathizes with his psychological confusion, the New
Jersey Superior Court, Appellate Division, has noted
that ''most experts would be satisfied'' that a pre-
operative transsexual, such as the defendant, ''should
be classified according to the biological criteria,''
M.T. v. J.T., 355 A.2d 204, 209 (N.J. Super. Ct. 1976)
(dicta) (emphasis added). In M.T., a post-operative
transsexual had married and subsequently sued for support and maintenance. The husband argued that the marriage was void because the transsexual had always been
male. In a thorough opinion, the New Jersey Appellate
Division carefully considered the medical literature
and legal authority and concluded that, although a sex
change operation could render one female, a pre-operative transsexual is male.

     The standard of review is used to tilt rule application favorably to the prosecution.

   Even as to post-operative transsexuals, New York authority is not very confident that a man can ever become a
woman. One trial court has held that a health insurer can
be made to pay for a sex change operation if it is not explicitly excluded in the insurance policy, Davidson v.
Aetna Life & Casualty Ins. Co., 101 Misc. 2d 1, 420
N.Y.S.2d 450 (Sup. Ct., N.Y. County 1979), but that court
held only that the operation could alleviate psychological suffering, not that it could produce a woman. Another trial court did hold that for practical purposes a

     A counter-argument (§19.4).

-8-

467

post—operative transsexual could be considered the equivalent of a woman, <u>Richards v. United States Tennis Ass'n</u>, 93 Misc. 2d 713, 400 N.Y.S.2d 267 (Sup. Ct., N.Y. County 1977), but that decision remains the opinion of a single trial court unreviewed on appeal and joined only by dicta in two isolated change—of—name cases, <u>In re Anonymous</u>, 57 Misc. 2d 813, 293 N.Y.S.2d 834 (Sup. Ct., N.Y. County 1968); <u>In re Anonymous</u>, 155 Misc. 2d 241, 587 N.Y.S.2d 548 (N.Y.C. Civ. Ct. 1992). Another change—of—name decision specifically refused to consider the question of whether a post—operative transsexual had acquired the opposite gender. <u>In re Anonymous</u>, 64 Misc. 2d 309, 314 N.Y.S.2d 668 (Sup. Ct., N.Y. County 1970).

Even <u>Richards</u>, a trial court decision, does not accurately represent the law generally. All of the reported cases that have considered that matter have held that pre—surgery transsexuals are not considered women under the various federal and state statutes that prohibit sex discrimination in employment. <u>See</u>, for example, <u>Sommers v. Budget Marketing, Inc.</u>, 667 F.2d 748 (8th Cir. 1982); <u>Kirkpatrick v. Seligman & Latz, Inc.</u>, 636 F.2d 1047 (5th Cir. 1981); <u>Holloway v. Arthur Andersen & Co.</u>, 566 F.2d 659 (9th Cir. 1977); <u>Sommers v. Iowa Civil Rights Comm'n</u>, 337 N.W.2d 470 (Iowa 1983). In each of these decisions, a pre—surgery transsexual's cross—dressing disguise caused so much difficulty with restrooms and other aspects of the workplace that the courts held it justifiable to fire the transsexual. Even post—surgery transsexuals have not been protected by the same statutes. <u>Ulane v. Eastern Airlines, Inc.</u>, 742 F.2d 1081 (7th Cir. 1984), <u>cert. denied</u>, 471 U.S. 1017 (1985); <u>In re Grossman</u>, 316 A.2d 39 (N.J. Super. Ct. 1974).

Moreover, although the New York City Board of Health will issue an amended birth certificate to a post—operative transsexual, deleting any reference to gender and incorporating a court—ordered change of name, courts have repeatedly refused to compel the Board to issue birth certificates that call transsexuals women, even after surgery. <u>Anonymous v. Mellon</u>, 91 Misc. 2d 375, 398 N.Y.S.2d 99 (Sup. Ct., N.Y. County 1977); <u>Hartin v. Director of Bureau of Records & Statistics</u>, 75 Misc. 2d 229, 347 N.Y.S.2d 515 (Sup. Ct., N.Y. County 1973); <u>Anonymous v. Weiner</u>, 50 Misc. 2d 380, 270 N.Y.S.2d 319 (Sup. Ct., N.Y. County 1966). These courts have acquiesced in the Board of Health's adoption of a report by the New York Academy of Science, which found that, even after surgery, ''male—to—female transsexuals are still chromosomally males while ostensibly females,'' and which warned that a post—operative transsexual's desire for ''concealment of a change of sex . . . is outweighed by the public interest for protection against fraud.'' <u>Weiner</u>, 50 Misc. 2d at 382–83, 270 N.Y.S.2d at 322 (quoting the Academy report). For these and other reasons, New

York has moved with caution where the aspirations of transsexuals have led them to seek special benefits. For example, this Court has affirmed the denial by the Commissioner of Social Services of financial assistance to pay for a sex change operation desired by an indigent transsexual. <u>Denise R. v. Lavine</u>, 39 N.Y.2d 279, 347 N.E.2d 893, 383 N.Y.S.2d 568 (1976).

Thus, there was legally sufficient evidence before that court substantiating every element of the offense defined by section 240.35(4), and the Criminal Court therefore properly denied the defendant's motion for a trial order of dismissal.

II. THE CRIMINAL COURT PROPERLY DENIED THE DEFENDANT'S MOTION TO DISMISS THE INFORMATION BECAUSE PENAL LAW § 240.35(4) DOES NOT VIOLATE THE UNITED STATES CONSTITUTIONAL RIGHT TO PRIVACY.

> The conclusion for Point II.

Review is de novo where the constitutionality of a statute is at issue. <u>See People v. Uplinger</u>, 58 N.Y.2d 936, 447 N.E.2d 62, 460 N.Y.S.2d 514 (1983), <u>cert. dismissed</u>, 467 U.S. 246 (1984).

> The standard of review.

A. <u>Section 240.35(4) would violate the constitutional right to privacy only if the defendant could demonstrate that it is not rationally connected to any need for public protection.</u>

> The rule.

The United States Supreme Court has held that a state can regulate attire without offending the constitutional right to privacy so long as there is a rational connection between that regulation and some form of protection provided to the public. In the leading decision on the question, the Court distinguished an interest in controlling one's own appearance from the more well-established right to control one's body, and it concluded that the Constitution allows a government more freedom to regulate appearance than ''certain basic matters of procreation, marriage, and family life.'' <u>Kelley v. Johnson</u>, 425 U.S. 238, 244 (1976). There, the Court ruled that a state has the power to regulate an individual's appearance unless that individual can demonstrate that the state's regulation ''is so irrational that it may be branded 'arbitrary' and therefore a deprivation of [the individual's] 'liberty' interest in freedom to choose his own'' appearance. <u>Id.</u> at 248.

> Rule proof begins.

A compelling state interest is not required here because the right to dress as one pleases — if it is a right at all — is not one of the fundamental rights at the core

> The beginning of many counter-arguments needed to

dispose of the
competing test.
Much synthesis
goes on here.

of freedoms protected through a constitutional right to
privacy. Under <u>Griswold v. Connecticut</u>, 381 U.S. 479
(1965), <u>Roe v. Wade</u>, 410 U.S. 113 (1973), and their progeny, a state was able to regulate an individual's decisions concerning procreation and allied questions only
if the state could demonstrate that it has a compelling
interest in doing so and that its means of regulation are
the least restrictive manner of satisfying that interest. But in <u>Bowers v. Hardwick</u>, 478 U.S. 186, 190 (1986),
which determined that a homosexual's right to privacy
was not violated by a state sodomy statute, the Court interpreted its right–to–privacy precedents to require a
compelling state interest only in matters of marriage,
procreation, contraception, abortion, child rearing,
education, and family relationships. And although the
Supreme Court might have ''reaffirm[ed]'' that line of
cases in <u>Planned Parenthood v. Casey</u>, 112 S. Ct. 2791,
2804 (1992), it also refused to enforce a compelling
state interest test in abortion cases -- thus impliedly
questioning the use of that test in any right–to–privacy
case. Moreover, in the only reported decision to consider whether a statute like section 240.35(4) violates the
constitutional right to privacy, the Illinois Supreme
Court did not require a compelling state interest and
instead applied the rational connection test. <u>City of
Chicago v. Wilson</u>, 389 N.E.2d 522 (Ill. 1978).

Even if <u>Griswold</u> and its progeny had not been weakened
by <u>Planned Parenthood</u>, they never required a compelling
state interest outside the context of reproduction. In
<u>Bowers</u>, the Supreme Court held that ''[n]o connection
between family, marriage, or procreation on the one hand
and homosexual activity on the other has been demonstrated.'' <u>Id.</u> at 191. Nor is there any connection between family, marriage, or procreation on one hand and
men disguising themselves as women on the other. In <u>Kel-
ley</u>, the Court even declined to determine whether the
Fourteenth Amendment -- and presumably the right to privacy inherent therein -- actually provides a right to
wear whatever one wants. <u>Id.</u> at 244. Instead, the Court
merely assumed the existence of such a right because the
regulation there at issue was so plainly supported by a
rational connection to the public interest that the more
difficult question of whether such a right exists at all
could be deferred to another day. <u>Id.</u>

Where a fundamental right has been found in a case involving personal appearance, the matter of appearance
has been merely incidental to a First Amendment issue of
freedom of speech, not a right to privacy. <u>See Cohen v.
California</u>, 403 U.S. 15 (1971) (antiwar slogan on jack-
et); <u>Tinker v. Des Moines Indep. Community School Dist.</u>,
393 U.S. 503 (1969) (antiwar armbands). Since <u>Kelley</u>,
abundant precedent has permitted governmental regula-

-11-

470

tion of appearance because individuals challenging the regulation of appearance were unable to demonstrate that it lacked a rational connection with a need to protect the public in some way. See, for example, South Florida Free Beaches, Inc. v. City of Miami, 734 F.2d 608 (11th Cir. 1984) (ordinance prohibiting shirtless jogging); Harper v. Lindsay, 616 F.2d 849 (5th Cir. 1980) (ordinance regulating attire of massage parlor employees); Williams v. Kleppe, 539 F.2d 803 (1st Cir. 1976) (prohibition on nude bathing).

The defendant mistakenly relies on People v. Onofre, 51 N.Y.2d 476, 415 N.E.2d 936, 434 N.Y.S.2d 947 (1980), cert. denied, 451 U.S. 987 (1981). Onofre was impliedly overruled by the Supreme Court in Bowers because the New York sodomy statute struck down in Onofre was in every substantive way identical to the Georgia sodomy statute upheld by the Supreme Court in Bowers. Moreover, Onofre was not premised on any provision of the New York State Constitution, and the ever-expanding federal right-to-privacy theory enunciated in Onofre is condemned in Bowers, 478 U.S. at 194–95.

B. The defendant has not shown that section 240.35(4) lacks a rational connection to some need for public protection.

Rule application begins.

Under the rational connection or rational basis test, a ''law need not be in every respect logically consistent with its aims to be constitutional. It is enough that there is an evil at hand for correction, and that it might be thought that the particular legislative measure was a rational way to correct it.'' Williamson v. Lee Optical, Inc., 348 U.S. 483, 487–88 (1955). In Williamson, the Court held that an Oklahoma statute was constitutional because none of the rights asserted against it were fundamental and because it had a rational connection to an identifiable risk to the public. Among other things, the statute prohibited opticians (who grind lenses and fit frames) from selling eyeglasses except on a prescription written by an optometrist or an ophthalmologist, both of whom have at least diagnostic training and the latter medical training as well. Although the Court recognized that the Oklahoma statute ''may exact a needless, wasteful requirement in many cases,'' it found a rational connection, sufficient to justify the statute, because ''in some cases the directions contained in the prescription are essential'' and the ''legislature might have concluded'' that wastefulness on many occasions is balanced by what is essential on others. Id. at 487 (emphasis added). Thus, the essence of the test is deference to the legislature, as ''it is for the legis-

-12-

lature, not the courts, to balance the advantages and disadvantages'' of a statute that need be supported only by a rational connection to a public need.

So, too, in Kelley, the Court upheld a police department's regulation of its officers' hair grooming. The Court pointed to the public's interest in being served by police officers neatly and uniformly attired and groomed, and it concluded that governmental decisions of this kind are ''entitled to the same sort of presumption of legislative validity as are state choices designed to promote other aims'' within the state's general authority. Id. at 247. The Court held it to be reversible error to evaluate such a challenge on the basis of ''whether the State can 'establish' a 'genuine public need' for the specific regulation'' because the true test is whether the party challenging the regulation ''can demonstrate that there is no rational connection between the regulation . . . and the promotion of safety of persons and property.'' Id. In Bowers, the Supreme Court went even further and held that a legislature can have a rational basis to proscribe conduct simply because the public perceives it to be ''immoral and unacceptable.''

The defendant has not carried such a burden in this appeal. This Court has affirmed convictions under section 240.35(4)'s predecessor statute, People v. Archibald, 27 N.Y.2d 504, 260 N.E.2d 871, 312 N.Y.S.2d 678 (1970); People v. Gillespi, 15 N.Y.2d 529, 202 N.E.2d 565, 254 N.Y.S.2d 121, amended, 15 N.Y.2d 675, 204 N.E.2d 211, 255 N.Y.S.2d 884 (1964), and other states have similar enactments, Cal. Penal Code § 185 (West 1988); Okla. Stat. Ann. tit. 21, § 1301 (West 1983) — all because of the danger that would be created if groups of people were permitted to disguise their identities in public without any supervision by the police and because of the deeply held public belief that it is immoral for a person to disguise his or her true gender. Even Professor Tribe notes that governments throughout the world have traditionally felt it within their competence to regulate attire for the public good. Laurence H. Tribe, American Constitutional Law 960–61 (1978). In a modern society that is more mobile and anonymous than ever before, it would be cause for insecurity among public and police if potential crime victims could not be confident that groups of strangers met on the street and elsewhere are in fact who and what they appear to be.

Policy and motivating arguments combine.

The type of disguise chosen by the defendant in this appeal is a particular cause for governmental concern. It is immediately clear that people who disguise themselves with ski masks or the like are involved in something suspicious, even if those people are not identifiable. Here, however, the defendant and his companions so convincingly dressed themselves up as women

-13-

that the arresting officer did not at first recognize them to be men (R. at 101). They could have gained entrance to a women's washroom, to the dressing rooms in apparel stores, and to other areas where women would be vulnerable to harassment or attack. They could also have committed a crime while deceiving the victim into believing that the perpetrators were women and not men. Even if these particular men were not disguised in order to commit crimes, the Legislature is entitled — under the rule articulated in Williamson and like cases — to ''balance the advantages and disadvantages'' and to regulate together both the truly dangerous and the apparently dangerous where the Legislature deems that necessary to protect the public and particularly where even the apparently dangerous strikes the public as immoral.

For even lesser reasons, regulation of the attire of massage parlor employees has been permitted, even though many employees might inadvertently violate the regulations for perfectly innocent reasons. See, for example, Harper v. Lindsay, 616 F.2d 849 (5th Cir. 1980). Prohibitions on nude bathing, Williams v. Kleppe, 539 F.2d 803 (1st Cir. 1976), and even shirtless jogging, South Florida Free Beaches, Inc. v. City of Miami, 734 F.2d 608 (11th Cir. 1984), have been upheld, although the public interest they protect is only aesthetic.

Although the Illinois Supreme Court, in City of Chicago v. Wilson, 389 N.E.2d 522 (Ill. 1978), held that an ordinance similar to section 240.35(4) could not be enforced against transsexuals, there are two reasons why that holding should not be persuasive in the instant appeal. The first is that, although the City of Chicago court applied a rational connection test to the challenged statute, it incorrectly placed the burden of proof on the government, rather than on the party challenging the ordinance. The court reasoned that ''the State is not relieved from showing some justification for its intrusion,'' id. at 524, and it concluded that ''[i]nasmuch as the city has offered no evidence to substantiate its reasons for infringing on the defendants' choice of dress . . . we do find that section 192–8 as applied to the defendants is an unconstitutional infringement of their liberty interest,'' id. at 525. In Kelley, the Supreme Court held this approach to be error, and it there reversed a lower court that had done the same thing. The second reason is that the statute at issue in City of Chicago was a far more drastic one than section 240.35(4). Section 192–8 of the Chicago Municipal Code punished any person who appeared in public ''in a dress not belonging to his or her sex,'' even when that person was alone. Section 240.35(4) does not do that: its scope is limited to the more dangerous situation in which people appear in public both disguised and in groups.

A counter-argument.

–14–

Not only is section 240.35(4) narrowly drawn, but a conviction under it does not create a criminal record because the offense it defines is a violation and not a crime. N.Y. Penal Law §§ 10.00(1), (3), (6) (McKinney 1987); N.Y. Crim. Proc. Law § 160.60 (McKinney 1992) Moreover, the impact of section 240.35(4) on the defendant in this appeal is not very substantial. The statute does not prohibit him from dressing as a woman before he has a sex change operation. It punishes him only for so dressing in public with two or more other men who are doing the same thing. Both the defendant's physician and the defendant's psychiatrist testified that if he were to refrain before his surgery from going out in public with other men dressed as women, there would be no ''significant'' detrimental effect on his pre-operative therapy (R. at 408, 449).

Thus, section 240.35(4) does not violate the defendant's right to privacy under the United States Constitution, and the Criminal Court properly denied his motion to dismiss the information.

<u>CONCLUSION</u>

For all the foregoing reasons, the defendant's conviction should be affirmed.

Hon. Martha Bosley
District Attorney
New York County

BY: Allan Kuusinen, Esq.
Asst. District Attorney
1 Hogan Place
New York, N.Y. 10013
(212) 555-1111

-15-

Index

Index

Hierarchy of authority, 10.2
Hyphen, use of, App. B (B-15, B-16)

I, usually inappropriate in legal writing,
    App. A
Imagery and story-telling, 18.7
Indicate as an imprecise verb, 15.5 (15-B)
Indorsement
    in an appellate brief, 26.1
    in a motion memorandum, 21.1
Innocent, distinguished from *not guilty,*
    App. A
Involve as an imprecise verb, 15.5 (15-B)
Issues
    of fact, 1.3.2
    of law, 1.3.2
        interdependence with facts and
        rules, 3.2
        judicial opinions, issues in, 3.1-3.2
It as a vague referent, App. A

Judgment
    correct spelling, App. A
    defined, 25.1
Judgment notwithstanding the
    verdict, 1.3.4, 20.2.3
Jump citations. *See* Pinpoint citations
Justifying arguments, distinguished from
    motivating arguments, 19.2

Law review articles, status of in hierarchy
    of authority, 10.2
Lawyer noises, imitation of, 15.5 (15-O)
Legalese (legal argot), 5.1, 15.1, 15.5
    (15-M, 15-N, 15-O)
Legislative history, use of in statutory
    interpretation, 12.1
Library, how to work effectively in, 10.7
Long windups, 15.5 (15-G)

Memoranda,
    motion, 21.1-21.2, App. D
    office, 7.1-7.2, App. C
Modifiers, confusing placement of, 15.5
    (15-K)
Motion (in the procedural sense), noun and
    not a verb, App. A
Motions
    case management motions, 20.2.4
    motion for directed verdict, 1.3.3,
        20.2.3
    motion for judgment as a matter of
        law, 20.2.3
    motion for judgment notwithstanding the
        verdict, 1.3.4, 20.2.3
    motion for summary judgment, 1.3.2,
        20.2.3
    motion to dismiss, 1.3.1, 20.2.1
    post-trial motions, 1.3.4

Motivating arguments
    justifying arguments, distinguished
        from, 19.2
    statements of the case, implying
        motivating arguments in, 23.1

Nominalizations, 15.5 (15-A)
Nouns, building sentences around
    concrete, 15.5 (15-A)

Objective writing. *See* Predictive writing
Only, confusing placement of, 15.5 (4-K)
Opinions (judicial). *See also* Precedent
    anatomy of, 3.1
    briefing (for class), 4.1-4.2
    interdependence of facts, issues, and
        rules, 3.2
    judgments, distinguished from, 25.1
    orders, distinguished from, 25.1
Oral argument
    delivery, affect, and style, 28.4
    example of, dissected, 28.7
    formalities and customs, 28.5
    goals of, 28.1
    preparation for, 28.6
    questions from the bench, 28.3
    role of, 25.3, 28.1
    structure of, 28.2
Order, defined, 25.1
Organization. *See also* Paradigm for
        structuring proof
    argumentation, organization in, 19.2
    paragraphing and organization, 14.1,
        14.3
    testing writing for effective
        organization, 9.5
Our, usually inappropriate in legal writing,
    App. A
Outlining, fluid, 6.3, 9.4
Overrule, distinguished from *reverse,*
    App. A

Paradigm for structuring proof, 9.1-9.5,
    20.3
    combinations of separately structured
        explanations, 9.3.3, 20.3
    comprehensive explanations, 9.3.2
    conclusory explanations, 9.3.2
    cryptic explanations, 9.3.2
    examinations, use IRAC instead, 17.2
    procedural posture, and, 20.3
    reader's need for, 9.2
    substantiating explanations, 9.3.2
    testing writing for effective
        organization, 9.5
    variations in depth, 9.3.2
    variations in sequence, 9.3.1
Paragraphs
    descriptive writing, 14.2
    organization, and, 14.1
    paragraph coherence, 14.1, 14.5 (14-D)

Index

broad and narrow rule formulations, 3.2,
4.2, 11.2
causes of action, 2.4
criteria, using (instead of elements), 2.1
elements, 2.1
interdependence with issues and
facts, 3.2
judicial opinions, rules in, 3.1-3.2, 4.2
organizing the application of, 2.2
structure of, 2.1

Say as an inappropriate verb for statutes
and precedent, App. A
Section symbol, how to make on a
typewriter or computer, 16.2.2
Semicolons, use of, App. B (B-12, B-13,
B-14)
Sentences
concrete nouns and verbs, built
around, 15.5 (15-A)
front-loaded, 15.5 (15-C)
sing-song, 15.5 (15-I)
thesis, 14.3-14.4, 14.5 (14-A)
topic, 14.3-14.4, 14.5 (14-A)
transition, 14.3-14.4, 14.5 (14-G)
unnecessarily long, 15.5 (15-H)
Service of process, 1.3.1
Sexist wording, 15.5 (15-S)
Standards of review, 27.3. *See also*
Procedural postures
Statement of Facts (in an office
memoranda), 7.1
Statement of the Case
in an appellate brief, 23.1-23.4, 26.1
in a motion memorandum, 21.1, 23.1-
23.4
Statutory interpretation
how to present, 12.2
ten tools of, 12.1
Stipulate as a verb of contract only, App. A
Strategy, 18.2, 19.2
Style
clarity, 15.1, 15.5
conciseness, 15.2, 15.5
forcefulness, 15.3, 15.5
legalese (legal argot), 5.1, 15.1, 15.5
(15-M, 15-N, 15-O)
older judicial opinions mislead students
about appropriate legal writing
style, 6.6
testing writing for effective style, 15.5
vividness, 15.1, 15.5
Substantiating explanation (variation of
paradigm for structuring
proof), 9.3.2
Summary judgment, 20.2.3
Summary of Argument (in an appellate
brief), 26.1
Synthesis (of precedent), 11.5

Table of Authorities
in an appellate brief, 26.1
in a motion memorandum, 21.1
Table of Contents
in an appellate brief, 26.1
in a motion memorandum, 21.1
Terms of art, 15.5 (15-M, 15-N)
That as a vague referent, App. A
The, inappropriate to omit, App. A
The court, overuse of, App. A
Theory of the case, motion, or
appeal, 18.1-18.7, 19.2, 27.1
There is and *it is* as grammatical
expletives, App. A
Thesis sentences, 14.3-14.4, 14.5 (14-A)
This as a vague referent, App. A
Throat-clearing
introductory sentences, 14.5 (14-B)
phrases, 15.5 (15-G)
Topic sentences, 14.3-14.4, 14.5 (14-A)
Transition sentences, 14.3-14.4, 14.5
(14-G)
Transitional words and phrases, 15.3, 15.5
(15-E)
Treatises, status in the hierarchy of
authority, 10.2

Verbal, not a synonym for *oral,* App. A
Verbs
bringing the reader to the verb
quickly, 15.5 (15-C)
building sentences around verbs that
let the reader see the action, 15.5
(15-A)
placement in relation to subject and
object, 15.5 (15-D)
relationships, verbs that communicate
precise, 15.5 (15-B)
to be, avoid, 15.5 (15-A)
Vividness, 15.1

We, usually inappropriate in legal writing,
App. A
When and *where,* not words of definition,
App. A
Which as a vague referent, App. A
Writing, process of, 6.1-6.6
appellate briefs, 27.2
creativity, theory development, and
imagery, 18.3, 18.6, 18.7, 27.1
first draft, least important part of
writing, 6.4
fluid outlining, 6.3, 9.4
four stages of writing, 6.1
motion memoranda, 21.2
office memoranda, 7.2
outlining, fluid, 6.3, 9.4
paradigm, 9.4
rewriting, 6.5